Folly and Fortune in Early British History

Folly and Fortune in Early British History

From Caesar to the Normans

Kenneth Henshall

First published 2008 by
PALGRAVE MACMILLAN

Palgrave Macmillan in the UK is an imprint of Macmillan Publishers Limited, registered in England, company number 785998, of Houndmills, Basingstoke, Hampshire RG21 6XS.

Palgrave Macmillan in the US is a division of St Martin's Press LLC, 175 Fifth Avenue, New York, NY 10010.

Palgrave Macmillan is the global academic imprint of the above companies and has companies and representatives throughout the world.

Palgrave® and Macmillan® are registered trademarks in the United States, the United Kingdom, Europe and other countries.

ISBN 978-1-349-36407-7   ISBN 978-0-230-58379-5 (eBook)
DOI 10.1057/9780230583795

This book is printed on paper suitable for recycling and made from fully managed and sustained forest sources. Logging, pulping and manufacturing processes are expected to conform to the environmental regulations of the country of origin.

A catalogue record for this book is available from the British Library.

Library of Congress Cataloging-in-Publication Data

Henshall, Kenneth G.
  Folly and fortune in early British history : from Caesar to the
  Normans / Kenneth Henshall.
     p. cm.
  Includes bibliographical references and index.

  1. Great Britain—History—To 1066.   2. Great Britain—History—Invasions.
     3. Great Britain—Politics and government—To 1485.   4. Great Britain—
     History, Military—55 B.C.–449 A.D.   5. Great Britain—History, Military—
     449–1066.   6. Great Britain—Foreign relations.   I. Title.

  DA135.H38 2008
     942.01—dc22   2008024820

10   9   8   7   6   5   4   3   2   1
17   16   15   14   13   12   11   10   09   08

Transferred to Digital Printing in 2014

Contents

Figures

Tables

Colour Plates

Thomas Thornycroft's statue of Boadicea (Boudica),
near Westminster Station.

A reconstructed Iron Age farm, at the Archaeolink Prehistory Park
near Inverurie. Bennachie, the assumed site of the Battle of Mons
Graupius in AD 83–4, is in the background to the right.

The entrance gate to Lunt Roman Fort, at Baginton near Coventry,
from the inside. Lunt was a 'bridgehead fort' (wooden and usually a
temporary base in enemy territory), built around AD 60 and almost
certainly in response to Boudica's uprising.

Viroconium (Wroxeter), near Shrewsbury, was a major Roman centre
subsequently occupied for some time by Britons. It is believed by some
to have been a main base for King Arthur.

The helmet believed to have belonged to the early seventh century
king Raedwald, reconstructed from remaining fragments at Sutton Hoo.
Replica at Sutton Hoo Centre.

External view of buildings at the West Stow Anglo-Saxon Village
in Suffolk. The house with the eaves down to the ground was
experimental and showed that such sunken buildings were unlikely.
The three buildings at the back are, from the left, hall, living house
(for up to ten people), and workshop. Anglo-Saxon buildings tended
to be rectangular, as opposed to Celtic round huts.

King Alfred's best-known statue, in Winchester.

The Middleton Viking Cross in St Andrew's Church, near Pickering
in North Yorkshire. The cross clearly shows a Viking with pointed helmet,
shield (top right, not to scale), spear, sword, knife (at belt), and axe.

Preface

As will be explained in some detail in the Introduction, this book attempts to re-emphasise the human factor in human history. In particular, it seeks to examine the role of the 'all too human' trait of folly in the unfolding of history, especially history's pivotal moments. My attention was drawn to the significance of folly through research carried out with a military historian for a book on the Pacific War, a horrific conflict in which numerous tragic examples of folly stood out quite starkly. Warfare by its nature reveals particularly dramatic illustrations of folly, but it is not an exclusive domain in that regard.

Mine is not the first book to address folly. One earlier classic is Barbara Tuchman's highly regarded work of 1984, *The March of Folly: From Troy to Vietnam*. Tuchman's work focuses on the collective folly of governments in a selection of examples from world history, culminating in America's involvement in Vietnam – understandably still very meaningful reading for critics of American policy in Iraq. It is an essentially political book and she explicitly avoids individual folly and military (battlefield) folly. My book, by contrast, does focus on the folly of individuals, moreover often in a military context, and is narrower in its time and place, namely, early Britain – especially the territory now called England – from 55 BC (Caesar) to AD 1066 (the Norman Conquest). I will refer to other differences in the Introduction, where I discuss folly, but I should emphasise here that our works come together in the broad sense of highlighting the idea of folly as a potential and often actual historical determinant.

Another writer on this theme, for a more popular readership, is the veteran war correspondent Erik Durschmied. His best-known work is probably *The Hinge Factor: How Chance and Stupidity Have Changed History* (1999). Like Tuchman he covers events across a vast amount of time and space in world history. However, unlike Tuchman, in his treatment he prioritises number (16 events) over depth. Understandably, he focuses very much on military engagements, often seeks folly at individual level, and also recognises links with chance. In these three latter regards my own book is closer to Durschmied than to Tuchman, but in contrast, I limit time and place to early Britain and try to give fuller coverage of events. As opposed to discussing selected and contextually unrelated events, I try to provide context and flow, with the aim of showing how the course of British history has been shaped by these factors of foolishness and chance. As will become clear in the Introduction, I also have a somewhat different view of chance from Durschmied.

There are difficulties in trying to assess historical folly, and some historians would suggest that we do not know enough about historical context to be able to make such judgements, but I disagree. Such judgements have in fact already been made, in popular terms at least, moreover sometimes by contemporaries or near-contemporaries, as seen for example in the case of Aethelred the 'Unready'. One of my aims is to examine the appropriateness of the popular judgement on Aethelred, and similarly the popular judgements on other figures associated with folly. I also question the actions of some historical figures who are not necessarily widely thought of as foolish, particularly King Harold of Hastings fame.

There are frequent links between folly and fortune, which again are discussed in some detail in the Introduction. For example, one person's folly can be their adversary's good fortune. Similarly, an act that seems *prima facie* to be folly can on examination turn out to be the result of misfortune, such as for example in the intervention of unforeseeable external circumstances. By the same token, a foolish act can be masked and even nullified by sheer good fortune. Thus I have made fortune another, if secondary, theme.

As indicated above, the book covers approximately the first millennium of recorded British history, from Caesar to the Normans. It is divided into three main parts, each concerned with the arrival in Britain of a new group (or groups) with aggressive – or at least intrusive – intent. Part 1 examines the coming of the Romans, Part 2 the coming of both the Anglo-Saxons and later the Vikings, and Part 3 the coming of the Normans. Each of these had a number of pivotal consequences. For example, roughly speaking, one can say that during the first half-millennium, under Roman influence, Britain was looking southward. For the second half-millennium, with the arrival of Germanic and Scandinavian peoples, it turned northwards. The arrival of the Normans in 1066, despite their northern origins, effectively signalled a turn to the south again for almost another half-millennium, under Norman and then French (Angevin) kings – though this particular book ends with the Norman Conquest, and coverage of subsequent Norman/French rule will be the subject of a later book.

One early-twelfth century historian, Henry of Huntingdon, reflecting the contemporary idea that invasions were acts of punishment by God, referred to 'five plagues' being visited upon Britain: the first the Romans, the second the Scots/Picts, the third the English (i.e. Anglo-Saxons), the fourth the Danes (i.e. the Vikings), and the fifth the Normans. In this book I cover the visitations of four of these 'pestilential' groups in detail, and give some but limited coverage of the Scots and Picts.

Each of the three parts starts with an introduction, then proceeds to a chronological account, then, prior to a final summary, provides a substantial section on why things turned out the way they did, in which I try to examine the issue of folly in particular by showing the various options that seem to have been available. I use questions in this section as a means of probing choice of options, but for those who don't like questions, don't worry – I provide my own answers. As an educator I do greatly value the Socratic use of thought-provoking questions, and I would encourage interested readers to try to provide their own responses and not just follow mine (for I may not be right). In many cases I try to encourage readers to put themselves in the role of the historical figure(s) in question and think what they would do, bearing in mind the limitations of the age. And for really enthusiastic readers, I would encourage them to make up – and answer – their own questions, on a whole range of issues. (I'm sure that just as I don't have all the answers, neither do I have all the questions.)

After the main parts I have added an overall conclusion and then three appendices. The first is a short appendix on the legendary – or possibly entirely mythical – King Arthur, who looms so large in legend that one cannot ignore him, but who is the subject of such a vast literature it would seriously divert the chronological flow of Part 2 if discussion of him were included in it. The second gives a timeline from the first century BC to the eleventh century AD, and the third a list of kings of England from the Anglo-Saxons to the Normans, both of which, I hope, will be useful ready-references.

However, the chronological flow of the main parts of the book is not necessarily constant in coverage, for, in line with thematic considerations, I dwell more on certain figures and points in time than others. When covering the latter stages of the Roman occupation, for example, I do not name every military governor or similar specifics. However, the reader will still find a chronological continuity, for I do not like gaps, and do like to provide context. Put in pictorial terms, I see the flow of this book as a river, narrower and faster in some places, wider and slower in others, with a number of bends at these slower places. It is these bends, these 'turning points', which I find the most interesting and on which I focus most. And upon examination, the cause of these turning points often seems to involve human error and/or fortune.

My sources are a mixture of primary and secondary, in the ratio of about 1:2. Primary sources are closer to the events described, often actually contemporary or close to it, and they are one tool with which scholars make their assessment of events, but they are very prone to subjectivity and distortion – again, please refer to the Introduction for further details on this difficulty. Secondary sources are valuable in providing the insights of other more recent writers, and especially those of specialists on particular figures or events or time-periods who can provide finer detail than is usually available in a general history, though my secondary sources do include some of these latter general works since they provide useful overviews and broader context. A full bibliography of both primary and secondary sources used is given (in separate lists) at the end of the book.

I should add that I frequently use direct quotations from primary sources, to give a certain immediacy. Obviously these are in translation from the Latin or Greek or Old English as the case may be, and where possible I use translations from a 'bygone era' to convey an air of antiquity. This may be seen with some justification as a stylistic whim on my part, and as a translator myself I appreciate that in general older translations may not be as reliable as more recent ones, but I have checked the older versions quoted here against more recent ones for accuracy.

The reader will find that I frequently use words such as 'seemingly', 'possibly', and 'perhaps', etc. This may be irritating to some extent, but I am afraid it is often the only honest way to write history. We can know some facts for sure, such as that William won at Hastings in 1066, but there is much we cannot be certain about. There is nothing more dangerous than a writer who treats mere assumptions as facts. I thus try hard to indicate clearly what is fact, what the sources report as fact, and what is assumption or speculation either on my part or that of the sources.

This book is intended for the general reader, but I hope it may find some use also as a supplementary text for the undergraduate student of British history or possibly Military Studies. I include a considerable number of annotations, both to indicate sources and to provide further detail, for another of my hopes is that readers will follow up sources and develop an interest in the topics covered.

Finally, a typographical note. Even the briefest scan of relevant books indicates that there is considerable variety in the spelling of Celtic, Anglo-Saxon, and Scandinavian names. I have tried my best to be consistent, such as, for Anglo-Saxon names, following the spelling in an authoritative version of the *Anglo-Saxon Chronicle* (Swanton 1996). However, when quoting names given by other authors in titles or comments, I keep their own spelling. I also give any significant variants in brackets at the first mention of a name. Having said all that, I am human (for better or for worse) and am quite capable of inconsistency. If Shakespeare can get away with spelling his own name four different ways, I trust I will be forgiven for the occasional lapse, for which I apologise in advance.

Acknowledgements

In addition to Michael Strang and Ruth Ireland at Palgrave Macmillan, who have provided invaluable help and advice, there are numerous people I would like to acknowledge as having contributed in one way or another to this book, and to whom I express my sincere thanks. These include (in no particular order): Rob Moseley at Lunt Roman Fort, David Sharp at Fishbourne Palace, and Alan Baxter at the West Stow Anglo-Saxon Village, for taking the time to chat with me and from whom I learnt much about latest developments; Mark Keighley of the Archaeolink Prehistory Park for his kind provision of several of his own photographs; Marion Dines at Maldon for an interesting discussion and a much-appreciated guiding hand to access the site there; Tony Blows at Ewyas Harold for little-known information about Harold Godwineson; Colleen Borrie at the University of Canterbury for technical photographic advice; Ken Strongman and Susan Bouterey at the University of Canterbury for supporting my research; Chris Connolly, Margaret Burrell, Graham Zanker and others at the University of Canterbury for commenting on parts of my manuscript; Eric Mouhica at the University of Canterbury for helping me with correspondence in French; Margaret and Seamus Hilley of Dromore, County Tyrone, for ferrying me around to various often obscure sites; Heather and John Pickering of Horsforth, Leeds, for providing a home-base for my research in Britain; Kay and Barry Vincent of Yoxford, Suffolk, for their guidance at local sites; Vivien and Douglas Bridges for stimulating discussion; and my son Simon for technical assistance with computer-generated diagrams.

Though almost all the photographs in this book were taken by me (unless indicated otherwise), I gratefully acknowledge permissions granted where the object itself was copyright. My thanks go to Marie Espahn and the Bayeux Tapestry Museum, Theresa Calver and Colchester Museum(s), Lynette Titford and the National Trust regarding Sutton Hoo, Barbara Birley and the Vindolanda Trust regarding the Roman Army Museum, Rob Moseley and the Coventry City Council regarding Lunt Roman Fort, Christine White and the St Edmundsbury Council/ West Stow Anglo-Saxon Village Trust, and Ann Hartas, churchwarden at St Andrew's Church in Middleton. Special thanks in this section are due to the aforementioned Mark Keighley for providing me with several of his own photographs of the Iron Age Farm at the Archaeolink Prehistory Park – my own having been taken in dreadful weather but anyway of decidedly lesser photographic merit.

I am also grateful to Sally Byers at Wiley-Blackwell Publishing for confirming clearance of the extracts I have quoted from Donald Scragg's translation of the poem of the Battle of Maldon – and of course to Donald Scragg himself.

Every attempt has been made to obtain all permissions believed necessary. If anything in this regard has been overlooked, the publishers would be happy to be contacted by the relevant parties.

My final and biggest 'thank you' is to my wife, Carole, for her support and encouragement through the many long hours of research for this book, and for her welcome company as we trudged through muddy fields in search of yet another ancient site.

Introduction

Humans, History, Folly, and Fortune

At the risk of stating the obvious, I believe in the centrality of human beings in human history. It is human beings who create systems and institutions, be they economic or political or legal or social or whatever, though of course these are often shaped in response to circumstances created by Nature or some other non-human agency. Sometimes these human creations seem to take on a life of their own and the human factor ends up pushed into the background. What I would like to do in this book is to restore pride of place to that human factor and draw attention to how human behaviour – with all its erraticisms – has helped shape history.

As a commentary on human nature history can be somewhat misleading, though that should not prevent us from learning from it. In early history in particular, we know relatively little of the ordinary man, woman, and child. With the exception of certain archaeological finds, our perceptions of life in those scantily and unreliably documented days are principally formed around recorded power-holders, and it can be argued that to achieve and/or hold onto power, more often than not an individual had to be exceptionally strong and even ruthless and that therefore they are not necessarily representative of people in general. But we have to work with what we have available to us.

Our humanness causes all sorts of problems for historians. One of these – as suggested above – is the unreliability of written sources, though this can be offset in some cases by the availability of non-literary sources such as archaeological finds. For much of recorded history many if not most of those doing the recording have made little or no attempt to avoid subjectivity, or even blatant bias. This is seen, for example, in the panegyrists of successful figures such as William the Conqueror. It is to a large extent understandable, for it could be very risky to criticise a powerful victor, and by the same token politically helpful to the writer to praise the victor and blacken their defeated enemies. It is almost inevitably the victor's view of history that prevails, but even records written by the defeated side can resort to scapegoating and other distortions

1

and cannot be guaranteed to be any more reliable, though they do provide a different perspective.

As literary theory in particular has shown, it is also important to note that we can be subjective even when we are trying hard not to be. Try as we might to be objective and clinical and precisely balanced, and to carefully avoid value judgements and so on, we can still end up giving a subjective account of things in the mere selection of which elements we include when discussing an event or period or topic. The same can apply to the sequencing and prioritising of selected elements. I will not dwell on this, but readers interested in further illustration of textual problems might wish to refer to the start of section 3.5, where after further discussion I list the remarkably varied range of literature-based interpretations that can be made of the Battle of Hastings. I also touch upon literary deconstruction again briefly in Appendix 1, on Arthur. (And yes, this book too can be said to be subjectively skewed in seeking out folly and fortune, but I hope I'm at least considered honest in being 'up front' with that.)

Another problem our humanness presents is the interpretation of human behaviour, behaviour which can so often be irrational – at least to the observer, for it may not seem irrational to the person who is doing the behaving. Such interpretation is difficult enough for modern psychologists and is even more so when we consider humans from a different historical (and cultural) context. This is evident, for example, in the matter of morality, which in turn is often linked with religion. Did a 'pagan' find it easier to kill an enemy or rival than a Christian did? Were Christians somehow more 'civilised'? What of values? How acceptable was it to punish a miscreant's family as well as the miscreant, and how acceptable was maiming or blinding as a punishment? And what of the concept of human rights? Few people nowadays would endorse slavery, yet it was commonplace – even a norm and a measure of status – in earlier times. Was life so much cheaper? And, as Hobbes would have it, was life really so 'nasty, brutish, and short'?

These are very difficult issues and I do not pretend to have the answers. One key thing, however, is to avoid the pitfall of what is often termed in literary and cultural studies 're-accentuation', namely simplistically interpreting aspects of life in a different time and/or place in terms of the values of one's own time and place. But, notwithstanding these difficulties, unlike some historians I do not believe we should simply suspend our critical judgement and avoid any interpretation of historical human behaviour, for how else can we learn from history if we do not think about our behaviour in the past? To back away from any evaluative judgement of people in a different context, simply because they are indeed in a different context, seems to me an excessive case of what anthropologists term 'cultural relativism', in which behaviours are related to their own particular cultural context – which of course is eminently sensible – but unfortunately in practice often end up somehow immune from a broader critical evaluation. Of course, in making our judgements, it is important to contextualise as much as possible, just as it is important to indicate clearly where we have ventured into our own personal view. But we do also need to recognise basic commonalities in human behaviour. Though the particulars will differ, selfishness is selfishness, rashness is rashness – and folly is folly.

Another pitfall is that of thinking in terms of fixed concepts of races and nations, which was a not uncommon approach among earlier historians. Of course, it is probably true to say that the great majority of us have a sense of nationhood, and likewise national pride (or shame), as is evident for example in international sport. Indeed, many lives have been lost for the sake of one's nation. Though a 'nation' in the normal sense is largely a construct, that does not deprive it of value, for it still helps our sense of belonging and identity. But it is nonetheless more realistic to think in fluid terms than in rigidly nationalistic terms, as anyone who has traced their ancestry and discovered 'foreign' elements will appreciate. To historians nowadays England/Britain is thought of not as some rigidly fixed historical entity that has been home to some specific biologically distinct race(s), but as a place in which boundaries have shifted and in which over many centuries various Celtic, Germanic, Scandinavian, Mediterranean, and other peoples and cultures have come together – sometimes pacifically, sometimes belligerently – and produced a very rich mix. And that mix is by no means an end product, for the process of increasing diversity is ongoing and the last century in particular has seen arrivals from well beyond Europe.

In my quest to re-emphasise the human factor, I shall make a modest start in this book by focusing in particular on one of the very things that makes us 'human, all too human', and that is the matter of human folly. I personally see this as a significant but under-appreciated driver of history. Despite the hurdles of behavioural differences across time and place, I do believe that folly is reasonably identifiable. Of course we do not have knowledge of all the particulars that may have entered into an individual's decision-making, but in a lot of cases I believe we can understand sufficiently to make such a judgement, such as by considering the options available to them – perhaps not all the nuances of those options, but enough to give us a reasonable idea. We can also judiciously bear in mind any judgement by contemporaries, though of course mindful of their own motives.

I should add a reminder that historians themselves are human. I have been told by some that I myself am guilty of folly in thinking it possible to judge historical folly, yet (as will become clear in the text) not a few eminent historians do exactly that, some even making strong and unqualified statements about 'spectacularly foolish acts' by various historical individuals. At least, by examining supposed acts of folly in some detail, as well as other questionable acts seemingly overlooked, I hope my conclusions will not be seen as simplistic.

Regarding a definition of 'folly', as mentioned in the Preface, I differ from Barbara Tuchman. In her book *The March of Folly*[1] she specifies three main criteria, in line with her focus on folly at the level of governmental policy: that a policy or decision is perceived as counter-productive and foolish by contemporaries rather than through hindsight; that a feasible alternative course of action is available; and that it is a group decision/policy of enduring consequence – for she explicitly states that she is keen to remove individual personality from consideration and to avoid judgement of acts by any one individual. It is also apparent that she sees folly as persistent pursuit of something demonstrably foolish, rather than a one-off act. Moreover, she also deliberately avoids military folly.

By contrast, my own definition of folly is less constrained, partly because my focus is not confined to government. I do consider very much military folly and individual folly. In some cases individuals with great power could be deemed to be 'one-man governments' anyway. I do not confine myself to contemporary or near-contemporary judgement, for in some cases this is not necessarily any more reliable than judgement through hindsight. Indeed, in many cases it is surely less so. For example, few contemporaries criticised Caesar or William the Conqueror for foolishness, though it can be argued that both were guilty of folly but were lucky enough to get away with it. Criticising a power-holder is surely risky and not necessarily conducive to a long and happy life. Other historical figures were not necessarily foolish, but were scapegoated as such by contemporaries or near-contemporaries, such as the fifth century British overlord Vortigern. Moreover, I do not insist that folly should involve stubbornly repeated counter-productive acts, for there are many cases of single-act folly with serious consequences – it only takes one faulty link in a chain to cause serious failure.

Within the range of this book, which covers approximately the first millennium of recorded British history, there are a number of acts/persons still popularly considered foolish. The action of the above-mentioned Vortigern, in inviting into the country the Anglo-Saxons who were subsequently to take it over, is one. Another is the behaviour of Aethelred the 'Unready', at the turn of the millennium, in paying out massive sums to the Vikings to no ultimate avail. I look at these and other supposed acts of folly in some detail – being particularly concerned with any 'epochal' consequences – and the reader may be surprised at some of my conclusions. The reader may similarly be surprised at my comments and conclusions regarding certain figures who are supposed to be heroes.

It might be felt that personality is a factor in foolishness, and this is very probably true. However, it is even more difficult to judge personality than specific behaviours and it is dangerous territory for historians. Some do, nevertheless, make judgements on personality and perhaps we could say that specialists on a particular historical figure do have an acceptably reliable understanding of their subject. Though I comment evaluatively on specific behaviours I generally steer clear of commenting on personality, but I do venture some occasional comments, particularly in Part 3 with regard to Harold Godwineson and Duke William, drawing in large part on their principal present-day biographers.

A secondary theme in this book is that of fortune. This quite often seems to be linked to folly. For example, when two adversaries meet, the folly of one can often prove to be the good fortune of the other. Or perhaps we should say in not a few cases, especially with complex battles, 'the greater folly': as Erik Durschmied has remarked, many a battle ends up in the records showing the victor as brilliant and the loser as less so, when in actuality the outcome may well have depended on who committed the bigger blunder.[2] And as another link, supposed folly can sometimes be shown to be the result of misfortune, such as when external circumstances intervene or in the broader sense that a particular outcome of a given act could not reasonably be predicted and the act is therefore not able to be deemed foolish – though popular perceptions do not necessarily reflect such in-depth analysis. Moreover, by the same token, an act of folly can sometimes be masked by the intervention of good fortune. As we shall see, all these various types of fortune are on display in the period covered by this book. And there is nothing new in all this: the early twelfth century historian, William of Malmesbury, observed that 'Fortune can make a mockery of human affairs'.[3]

As suggested above, I treat '(mis/)fortune' here as an outcome that cannot be reasonably predicted. History is a classic area for the application of Chaos Theory, particularly the Butterfly Effect, whereby a series of seemingly 'inconsequential' acts combine with circumstances to produce a massive and to all intents and purposes unpredictable outcome. In strict theory there is actually very little sheer luck in life. The outcome of a throw of the dice is technically not luck but a function of which faces were upwards when the dice left the hand, the angle and speed of the roll, the friction of the surface, etc., and it is predictable in theory. However, putting such theory into practice would surely be next to impossible – certainly for us humans.

I mentioned in the Preface that Erik Durschmied also sees a link between folly and chance. However, our views are not necessarily the same. Durschmied tends to focus upon one specific incident as a determinant of outcome, whereas, while I do recognise the apparent primacy of a given event, I myself try to place it in the context of a series of events. In my opinion there are usually too many variables to try to attribute an outcome to just one. For example, a case can be made that William the Conqueror was, in terms of mathematical probability, foolish in attempting to invade England and that he was saved from being recorded in history as a deluded fool thanks to the still greater folly of his adversary Harold. Harold's folly was William's fortune, but that was not all that helped William, for one can also consider the favourableness of the winds, Harald Hardraada's attack less than three weeks before Hastings, and so on. This is one reason why I generally use the term 'fortune' rather than 'chance', for it has a more human connotation to it. 'Chance' is happenstance and does not necessarily involve outcomes relevant to humans, but 'fortune' relates more obviously to a human path through life – some might say 'destiny', but that would tend to suggest something pre-ordained and would take us into the realm of providential history.

Another perhaps surprising link between folly and fortune takes us to ancient Rome. Given the reputation of the Roman army for clinical efficiency, one might expect their generals to have been the epitome of rationality and experts in the evaluation of relative probabilities of success for a range of military tactical options, of which they invariably chose the most appropriate. However, this was not always the case. While a good sound general was respected, a lucky general was respected even more, because he was felt to have the backing of the gods. And a lucky general, by definition, would typically be one who took risks and did not always adopt the optimal tactic, either by failure to realise it – for generals after all are human – or as a deliberate high risk gamble in the hope of quick and profitable returns. But of course, if the gods chose to look the other way and let the opponent make a wiser choice of tactic, moreover unimpeded by ill fortune, then the outcome for our Roman general could be defeat and accusations of folly. This would not, perhaps, seem the ideal way to conduct a military campaign, but 'lucky' Julius Caesar got away with it, as we shall see.

There is indeed a fine and by no means fixed line between risk – even 'calculated' risk – and folly. Some might consider betting on odds of say 1 in 3 is foolish, others might think it quite reasonable. Here again we are in muddy waters, for we have to factor in other circumstances, such as what is at stake, and of course, personality. Are you by nature cautious, or are you adventurous? And if you think being cautious prevents any accusation of folly, can you not still be guilty of foolishness by being 'over-cautious' and missing out on a 'golden opportunity'? Such arguments could go on endlessly.

In any event, I hope that by the end of this book we will have seen quite a bit of folly and fortune, insofar as we can identify them, and come to a fuller appreciation of their role in human history, particularly with regard to pivotal moments.

1
The Roman Eagle Lands

1.1 Introduction

After its conquest by Rome, Britain – or much of it – became an outermost part of the Roman Empire. It would seem not to have been a particularly happy place for many of the Romans there, who saw it as being at the edge of the world (or even beyond it), with cold, wet weather, and hostile locals constantly harassing the borders. Nonetheless it was to experience Roman occupation for almost four centuries, and Roman influence over a still greater period.

Though there is evidence of trade links going back some centuries earlier, the first visitation by Rome as a threat was a brief incursion in 55 BC by Julius Caesar. This was a reconnaissance trip with limited forces, and he returned the following year with more serious intent. However, the second incursion too was short-lived, and after gaining submissions from some tribal leaders he withdrew to the continent after a few months – though claiming great success in order to boost his own military and political status. In theory it is from this point that it can be claimed that Britain had partly joined the empire, through certain regional client kings acknowledging Rome's overlordship and paying tribute to it.

A far more substantial Roman advent was to take place almost a century later, in AD 43, at the command of Emperor Claudius – again for largely political motives. The invaders encountered varying degrees of resistance among the tribes, who were by no means united, ranging from no opposition to grudging submission to determined and total opposition.

For example, from the outset of the Claudian campaign, significant opposition came from Caratacus of the Catuvellauni (later leading the Silures and Ordovices), till his betrayal by the Roman sympathiser Queen Cartimandua of the Brigantes – though her former husband, Venutius, became a determined opponent of the Romans.

Most significant of all was the major revolt led by Queen Boudica of the Iceni in AD 60, which could – and in my view should – have sent the Romans

7

packing. Instead, through what seem to have been foolish tactics by the Britons and a consequent disastrous defeat, Rome's dominant presence was confirmed. This presence was, with varying ups and downs of fortune such as ongoing encounters with the northern Picts, to remain till the early years of the fifth century, when Rome itself was sacked by the Goths and the Romans finally withdrew or, depending on one's interpretation, were finally expelled.

As we shall see, folly and fortune certainly played their part in events on both sides. Roman history is indeed a rich source of such factors. At the mention of 'folly', for example, one easily calls to mind the behaviour of some of Rome's emperors, notably Caligula ('Little Boot', the nickname of Gaius Caesar, r. 37–41) and Nero (r. 54–68), both of whom feature indirectly in Part 1. And Claudius (r. 41–54), despite his victory in Britain and despite being considered generally competent by present-day historians, was thought of at the time as an imbecile by many in Rome – his own mother described him as 'a monster of a man, not finished but merely begun by Dame Nature'[1] – and most definitely had his moments of serious erraticism.

The contemporary or near-contemporary written sources for the Roman presence in Britain are, understandably, overwhelmingly Roman. Julius Caesar himself wrote in considerable, if somewhat biased, detail about many of his military campaigns, and both his British ventures are described in his *Gallic War* (*De Bello Gallico*, 51 BC). The historian Tacitus, whose father-in-law, Julius Agricola, served in Britain both as soldier and eventually as governor (77–84), provides an 'almost eye-witness' account of Britain in the late first century AD in his writings *Agricola* (*De Vita et Moribus Iulii Agricolae*, 98), *Annals* (*Annales*, c. 117), and *Histories* (*Historiae*, c. 109). The Greco-Roman Cassius Dio, writing his massive history of Rome in the early third century (80 books, various titles generically known as *Histories*), makes significant comment on Britain, basing some of his writing on Tacitus but also adding material of his own that is now lost. Greek writers such as Strabo and Diodorus provide occasional further relevant comment pertaining to the early years. The latter stages of Roman rule are less well recorded, though some commentary is provided by Ammianus Marcellinus and the Byzantian Zosimus. Throughout the period other Roman historians add occasional detail, such as Suetonius in his *Lives of the Twelve Caesars* (*De Vita Caesarum*, 121), but do not focus systematically on Britain.

Part 1 of this book focuses on the early years of Roman presence and/or influence, from 55 BC to AD 60, and thus is reasonably well served by literary sources, albeit from the Roman perspective.

Ancient British sources are few and somewhat removed chronologically, making only a very limited contribution. The two earliest are Gildas's *Concerning the Ruin and Conquest of Britain* (*De Excidio et Conquestu Britanniae*, c. 545) and Bede's *Ecclesiastical History of the English People* (*Historia Ecclesiastica Gentis Anglorum*, 731), though Bede often draws on Gildas and in some cases Roman sources such as Orosius.

To compensate for a paucity of literary sources for some periods, there is a good supply of material sources, especially through archaeological excavations. These include numerous coins (including pre-Roman), utensils, weapons, everyday letters on wooden tablets (notably the 'Vindolanda Tablets' of Romans stationed in the north of England near Hadrian's Wall),[2] other inscriptions, including graffiti – and in the case of Boudica's campaign, red burnt layers as evidence of destruction. And of course, there are still many Roman edifices left standing, and many Roman roads and defence works are still evident. It seems most likely that it will be archaeologists – or possibly amateur metal detectorists – who may make any further breakthrough in knowledge of this period, rather than some chance find of a long-lost manuscript (as happened, for example, some centuries ago with the finding of lost writings by Tacitus). In particular, one hopes to see before too long the firm identification of the site of Boudica's disastrous last battle, which still remains a major mystery.

1.2   Caesar's first foray, 55 BC: Foolish but fortunate?

According to tradition, Rome was founded in 753 BC under Romulus. Initially governed by kings, from 509 BC it became a republic, headed by magistrates known as consuls, who were advised by the powerful Senate, composed of dignitaries and increasing numbers of former consuls. Serving consuls typically were restricted in their power by short terms of office and the fact that they generally served in pairs, with each consul having the right to veto acts by the other. Julius Caesar (100–44 BC), from a powerful family, rose through various offices and, with the help of judicious use of his wealth, became one such consul in 59 BC. His consular power was shared with another consul (Bibulus), whom he largely ignored, but his real power was as one of the 'triumvirate' with Pompey and Crassus – a group of three men, in theory appointed for special administrative duties, but in practice the leading power-holders. Anxious to enhance his reputation, Caesar secured for five years (later extended) the essentially military governorships of Cisalpine Gaul (Italy north of the Apennines to the Alps), Transalpine Gaul (extending west to the Atlantic coast and north to present-day Belgium), and Illyricum (present-day Albania, Croatia, Slovenia), together comprising a massive spread of territory.

His incursion into Britain was, in effect, an extension of his Gallic campaign, primarily driven by joint political and military ambition. It would be greatly impressive to conquer both the 'Ocean' (the open ocean outside the Mediterranean), which the Romans had long held in dread, and the hostile tribes living in this remote and mysterious island.[3] Rome had expanded its territory significantly during the third and second centuries BC, evolving from an

Italian city-state to a major Mediterranean-based empire, and the addition of Britain would symbolise a further significant expansion. In more material terms, the island was noted through traders for its natural resources such as gold, silver, lead, and tin and its rich harvests of grain thanks to its fertile soil and relatively advanced agriculture. Suetonius also refers to rumours about excellent British pearls and gives this as one reason for Caesar's interest.[4]

Caesar's own justification, as recorded in his detailed account of the Gallic War (*De Bello Gallico*, 51 BC, in which he writes of himself in the third person), was that by 55 BC he was aware that some of the Britons were aiding the Gauls in their resistance to Rome.[5] That is, he implies that his expedition into Britain was punitive, to pacify hostile elements. This may have been a subtle, politically defensive tactic by Caesar, for technically he would have needed authorisation from the Senate to undertake a formal conquest.

But at the same time, his observation about British support for the Gauls was undoubtedly true. Among other things, as he himself remarks, some of the British tribes, notably on the coast, had only arrived relatively recently from the continent,[6] which would mean they would, in many cases, have retained strong links with their continental relatives. The Atrebates, for example, held territory on both sides of the Channel, and so did the Parisi. And from the Britons' perspective, it would not take much imagination to suspect that Rome's expansionist activities on the continent may well extend sooner or later to Britain, so it made sense to keep the Romans busy in Gaul and hope that they were defeated there.

In fact, Caesar made constructive use of one such link by appointing Commius, a continental Atrebatian whom he saw as an ally, as king of his defeated tribe in 57 BC, and then in 55 BC sending him to Britain, where Caesar believed him to be held in considerable respect, to 'smooth the way' by visiting the various tribes and encouraging them to pledge loyalty to Rome prior to his (Caesar's) arrival.[7] By this stage traders had alerted the Britons of Caesar's plans and a deputation of worried British envoys had arrived in Gaul and promised their allegiance to Caesar. They were sent back to Britain with Commius in the summer of 55 BC, with promises in return from Caesar that they would suffer no harm if they honoured their word. Furthermore, Caesar sent a scouting vessel under the tribune Gaius Volusenus to reconnoitre the situation in Britain, especially the Britons' military capability, and the coastline with regard to landing and harbouring a fleet.

By now Caesar had moved his forces to a departure point close to Britain, near modern-day Boulogne, and was assembling a fleet. Owing to the unstable situation in Gaul he did not want to spare too many men, and decided to take just two legions, the Seventh and the Tenth, totalling some 8000–10,000 men. They occupied around 80 transport vessels, and there were also a few (number unspecified) more agile warcraft. In addition, he arranged for a further 18 transports to set sail from a neighbouring port, carrying cavalry.

Despite this apparent planning, things did not necessarily go Caesar's way. Volusenus had come back after a mere five days, during which time he does not appear to have set foot on British soil. His report about the coastline and suitable landing sites was also seemingly less than helpful. It was getting late in the season, and not wishing to tarry any longer Caesar set off with his fleet on the night of 24 August, but his separate fleet of 18 cavalry transports was delayed, apparently in getting the cavalry on board, and was given orders to follow as soon as possible.

Caesar's main fleet arrived off the British coastline, probably near Dover, around nine o'clock the following morning, but Caesar and his men

> saw the forces of the enemy drawn up in arms on all the hills. The nature of the place was this: the sea was confined by mountains so close to it that a dart [spear] could be thrown from their summit upon the shore. Considering this by no means a fit place for disembarking, he remained at anchor till the ninth hour [2 p.m.], for the other ships to arrive there.[8]

However, the second fleet, with the cavalry, did not appear, and in the afternoon Caesar moved some seven miles northwards along the coast, to a more suitable but still less-than-ideal landing site, believed to be the beach at Walmer near Deal in Kent.[9] But the Britons had simply followed them along the coast and were waiting for them. The Romans were now facing a number of difficulties and started to lose a little heart. Caesar outlines the situation regarding landing:

> This was the greatest difficulty for the following reasons, namely, because our ships, on account of their great size, could be stationed only in deep water; and our soldiers, in places unknown to them, with their hands embarrassed, oppressed with a large and heavy weight of armour, had at the same time to leap from the ships, stand amidst the waves, and encounter the enemy; whereas they [the enemy], either on dry ground, or advancing a little way into the water, free in all their limbs, in places thoroughly known to them, could confidently throw their weapons and spur on their horses, which were accustomed to this kind of service. Dismayed by these circumstances and altogether untrained in this mode of battle, our men did not all exert the same vigour and eagerness which they had been wont to exert in engagements on dry ground.[10]

It was true that the Romans were relatively inexperienced in naval matters, with their real military strength being their land forces, especially their infantry. Among other things, they had not brought assault boats, which could have assisted with the disembarkation from the transports.[11] Moreover, Caesar

Figure 1.1 Shingly Walmer Beach in Kent, almost certainly the site of Caesar's landings and unsafe anchorage in 55 and 54 BC, looking south to the cliffs. (Pevensey Beach in Sussex, where William the Conqueror landed over a thousand years later, is similar shingle but slightly steeper.)

had not helped matters by trying to disembark at low tide.[12] However, the Roman war-galleys were very fast and manoeuvrable, with three rows of oars, and Caesar – generally (but not always) noted for his ability to make sound judgements under pressure – used these vessels very effectively to distract the waiting Britons by ordering them to sheer off, head along the enemy's flanks, and discharge ranged weapons (projectile weapons such as slings and arrows and javelins launched through *catapultae*[13]) at those on the shore. The Britons were indeed rather taken aback, and this gave a particularly heroic soldier on one of the transports, the standard-bearer of the Tenth, an opportunity to urge his men to follow him as he prepared to leap down into the chest-high water, with the words:

> 'Leap, fellow soldiers, unless you want to betray your eagle to the enemy. I, for my part, will perform my duty to the commonwealth and my general.' When he had said this with a loud voice, he leaped from the ship and proceeded to bear the eagle toward the enemy.[14]

His stirring words and actions, resounding with loyalty, duty, and patriotism, had the desired effect. It helped that Caesar was well respected and liked by his men, who considered him a firm but fair fellow soldier who in turn respected them and did his best for them – their loyalty to Caesar had indeed been a major factor in his men's ability to overcome their fear of the Ocean and make the crossing in the first place.[15] The others followed the eagle-bearer, and battle was joined in the shallows.

It was a confused affair by Roman standards, with groups frequently being isolated and surrounded by Britons both on foot and horseback, sometimes being rescued by support from the war-galleys (under Caesar's watchful eye and directions), and sometimes being cut down. But eventually, once they managed to gain a firmer footing, the Romans prevailed, though it was a hard-fought encounter. The Britons retreated, and Caesar lamented the non-arrival of his cavalry transports, which denied him the opportunity to pursue the Britons.

Though the Romans had what seems to have been a very vulnerable beachhead, the Britons – perhaps intimidated by the numbers and weapons and clinical efficiency of the Romans, or perhaps playing for time – decided to sue for peace. The next morning they sent a peace commission to Caesar and submitted to him. They also returned Commius, whom they had taken captive as soon as he had set foot in Britain. Commius's capture went some way to explain why there was a hostile reception for the Romans, as opposed to a brokered peace, but Caesar was still annoyed at the failure of the British leaders to keep their word as sworn to him in Gaul. They in turn argued that it was all the fault of ignorant hotheads and asked forgiveness. Caesar grudgingly pardoned them but asked for hostages. Some were given at once but the Britons said they would have to send back for others from some considerable distance. In the meantime they ordered their people back to the fields, while other kings and chieftains also came along to submit.

But Caesar's troubles were not over yet. Four days after the landing of the main fleet, the second fleet of 18 ships, bearing the cavalry, appeared on the horizon. However, by ill fortune, just as the vessels

> were approaching Britain and were seen from the camp, so great a storm suddenly arose that none of them could maintain their course at sea; and some were taken back to the same port from which they had started; others, to their great danger, were driven to the lower part of the island, nearer to the west; which, however, after having cast anchor, as they were getting filled with water, put out to sea through necessity in a stormy night, and made for the continent.[16]

And that was not all. The same storm, compounded by a full moon and accompanying high tide (which for some reason Caesar seemed unprepared for),[17] caused serious damage that night to Caesar's main fleet too, both those ships at anchor and those beached. Once again Caesar and his men were in a difficult situation:

> A great many ships having been wrecked, inasmuch as the rest, having lost their cables, anchors, and other tackling, were unfit for sailing, a great confusion, as would necessarily happen, arose throughout the army; for there were no other ships in which they could be conveyed back, and all things which are of service in repairing vessels were wanting, and, corn for the winter had not been provided in those places, because it was understood by all that they would certainly winter in Gaul.[18]

Even allowing for Caesar's intentions to stay but briefly in Britain and to winter in Gaul, it is still remarkable that he had not brought with him sufficient provisions to cope with an emergency, and that he seemed to have been relying on acquiring provisions from Britain itself for the duration of his stay there.[19] This was very risky. Not unnaturally, the Britons quickly realised the predicament of the invaders. Knowing the Romans would need grain, they created a trap, leaving an area of grain unharvested in the nearby fields to which they hoped the Romans would be drawn.

Sure enough, while the Tenth legion was put in charge of repairs to the ships, men of the Seventh (numbers unclear) were sent out to fetch grain, and headed straight for the unharvested area. Presently guards at the gates of Caesar's temporary camp reported a large amount of dust in the direction where the men of the Seventh had headed. Caesar realised at this point that it was a trap and immediately set out with two cohorts (around 800 men), ordering the rest to follow. He soon came across the beleaguered men, surrounded by mounted Britons and chariots – the latter being made of light wicker-work and used to speedily deliver or rescue warriors around the battlefield, thereby combining, in Caesar's words, 'the speed of the horse with the firmness of infantry'.[20]

The Britons backed off when they saw Caesar's reinforcements, though one does wonder why. Caesar was reluctant to follow them and led his men back to camp. Roman casualties are unclear: Caesar refers to the Britons merely 'killing a small number' of his men, though Cassius Dio, writing more than two centuries later, states that the Britons 'destroyed them all, save a few, to whose rescue Caesar came in haste'.[21] T. Rice Holmes is critical of Caesar, observing that he 'had exposed the Seventh legion to the risk of a defeat which would have been calamitous'.[22]

According to Caesar, bad weather during the next few days prevented any further conflict[23] – again surprising, but possibly because the chariots were not at their best in wet conditions. More likely, the hiatus was because the Britons were waiting for substantial reinforcements. Certainly the word had spread that the Romans were now very vulnerable. Presently the reinforcements seem to have arrived, for Caesar tells us that soon 'a large force of infantry and of cavalry came up to the camp'.[24]

Caesar formed his legions in front of the camp and, though he does not go into detail about how exactly the battle was fought, the Romans emerged victorious and were even able to pursue the fleeing Britons to some limited extent by means of 30 or so horsemen brought to him by Commius.[25] In addition, everything in the surrounding area was burnt by Caesar's men.

That same day another British commission came to Caesar to sue for peace, and this time Caesar doubled the number of hostages he wanted. However, he asked for them to be delivered to him on the continent, for he was not planning to stay any longer. It was just prior to the equinox, and he wanted to be back across the Channel before the winter. In fact, he and his men left that very same night, for he had now repaired all but 12 of his fleet, and all his men were able to embark. All made it safely back to the continent, though two transports drifted south of the main fleet and the 300 men on board were attacked by local Gauls after disembarking and had to be rescued by the cavalry – which finally thereby got to play a very indirect role in the incursion into Britain, without ever actually setting foot or hoof in it.

Caesar's brief visit of a few weeks to a British beach, with the customary dreadful weather and troublesome locals, was not exactly glorious. Despite the various unconvincing pledges of submission and peace from sundry Britons, his departure may be seen almost as a hurried and relieved escape rather than the dignified exit of a would-be conqueror.

Indeed, many modern commentators are critical of Caesar and his leadership in the expedition. Graham Webster, for example, refers to the expedition as a 'failure of dire proportions'.[26] Sheppard Frere feels that more determined leadership by the Britons could have put Caesar and his men at considerable risk.[27] T. Rice Holmes too feels that the Britons, if better led, could have been much more effective in their attacks on Caesar and his men:

> If they [the Britons] had been commanded by one skilful leader, and had adhered to the simple plan of harassing the Romans when they were endeavouring to embark, they might have achieved something. But they were a mere aggregate of tribal levies under tribal chiefs; and greed and impatience worked their ruin.[28]

Despite being generally favourable towards Caesar, Rice Holmes also refers to his lack of preparation in this expedition of 55 BC.[29] Peter Ellis feels that Caesar's political ambition may have caused him to rush into an ill-prepared and ill-timed expedition, overriding his usual caution.[30] Similarly John Peddie acknowledges Julius Caesar's normal good generalship and leadership, but believes that in the case of 55 BC there was hasty and inadequate preparation, perhaps due to overconfidence, and wonders why he undertook such a risk, moreover so late in the season.[31] Cassius Dio made a similarly negative appraisal:

> From Britain he had won nothing for himself or for the state except the glory of having conducted an expedition against its inhabitants; but on this he prided himself greatly and the Romans at home likewise magnified it to a remarkable degree. For seeing that the formerly unknown had become certain and the previously unheard-of accessible, they regarded the hope for the future inspired by these facts as already actually realized, and exulted over their expected acquisitions as if they were already within their grasp; hence they voted to celebrate a thanksgiving for twenty days.[32]

Nevertheless, Caesar had profited politically by that glory and fame – though had the expedition backfired, it could have been disastrous for his political ambitions. He also now knew, from Rome's reaction, that he would have good support for further action in Britain. Moreover, as Suetonius remarks, it was in his military nature to make reconnaissance,[33] and to a significant extent he could be said to have achieved this too. He had learnt something, for example, about the Britons' use of chariots and their general style of fighting. Such information was indeed useful to him, for he had resolved to return the following year.

Given the less-than-optimal expedition of 55 BC, Julius Caesar was fortunate to have come away relatively unscathed and be in a position to return. Better-organised opposition could have produced a very different outcome and could even have resulted in Caesar's death. For all his lauded generalship, Caesar seems to have made silly and potentially disastrous mistakes.

Ideally, a really good general should leave nothing to chance, but in the Roman world, while it is true that military caution and strategic ability were respected, good fortune (*felicitas*) was in a sense even more highly esteemed, for it was seen as symbolising support from the gods for the favoured recipient.[34] Julius Caesar had the reputation of being one such lucky commander, as he himself acknowledged in referring (in his customary third person voice) to 'Caesar's traditional good fortune in war'.[35]

1.3   Caesar tries his luck again, 54 BC

Caesar was not only lucky, as mentioned earlier, he was also seen as generally astute in military matters – despite the obvious occasional lapse. Learning from the 55 BC expedition, he ordered his men to build as many vessels as they could, but lower in the water and broader than the transports of the previous year, to allow for easier disembarkation and the transporting of more freight and pack animals. He also ordered them all to be fitted for oars, being helped in this by the lower freeboard of the new vessels. The fleet was to assemble at Boulogne.

By July 54 BC, after his return from business elsewhere in the vast territories he governed, he was delighted to find that his men had constructed no fewer than 600 such vessels, as well as 28 warships. He was therefore able to embark five legions – some 20,000–25,000 men – and approximately 2000 cavalry.[36] A further 200 ships, mostly private, also joined the fleet. They departed for Britain on the evening of the sixth of that month, Caesar leaving his deputy Titus Labienus to look after affairs on the continent with similarly 2000 cavalry but just three legions. Clearly, this time Caesar was serious about Britain, though it is not clear whether he intended to establish an ongoing occupation there.

According to Cassius Dio, his claimed justification this time was again punitive, for only two of the tribes that had promised to send hostages had actually done so, though Dio dismisses this as a mere pretext:

> He crossed over again to Britain, giving as his excuse that the people of that country, thinking that he would never make trial of them again because he had once retired empty-handed, had not sent all the hostages they had promised; but the truth of the matter was that he mightily coveted the island, so that he would certainly have found some other pretext, if this had not offered itself.[37]

After a somewhat erratic crossing, the fleet of 54 BC landed the next day in the same location as the previous year's fleet, surprisingly by choice despite his earlier misadventures there.[38] There was no enemy in sight, and Caesar was able to land at around noon and to have his men disembarked by the evening. However, in what seems to have been one of his occasional lapses in caution, despite the serious storm damage caused the previous year, he failed to make proper provision for the safety of his fleet against the southerly winds that were already blowing ominously.

Instead, he demonstrated what was seen as one of his typical strengths – speed of movement and attack to catch the enemy unawares. Immediately upon landing he had sent out advance parties, who had captured some locals. Learning from these locals the whereabouts of the British forces – which apparently had earlier assembled on the coast but had withdrawn once they sighted the size of Caesar's fleet – Caesar set off, with the great majority of his forces, to attack them. This was in the 'third watch', which was between midnight and 2 a.m. He left behind ten cohorts (approximately 5000 men, drawn from various legions) and 300 cavalry to guard the fleet, which he placed under the command of Quintus Atrius.

One wonders how Caesar's men reacted to the command to undertake a night march through unknown enemy territory, especially given that they would have had precious little sleep the previous night during the Channel crossing. Caesar was moreover appearing to base his actions on the words of captured Britons. This was at best risky and once again might suggest a certain rashness and over-confidence on his part.

However, though Caesar refers only to the captives as his source of informa-tion,[39] he may actually have been aided by a young British prince called Mandubratius (also known as Mandubracius and Avarwy), who was seeking Roman support for his claim to the leadership of the Trinovantes and was opposed to Cassivellaunus (Caswallon),[40] who was king of the Catuvellauni and seems to have been widely acknowledged as an over-king of the southern tribes. Mandubratius was seen as a traitor by many of the Britons for having made approaches to Caesar the previous year – in fact, though Caesar may not have realised it, his Roman name was based on the Brythonic (Celtic) term *mandubrad*, meaning 'black traitor',[41] a nickname by which he was known among some Britons. Mandubratius had travelled to Gaul – possibly forced into exile by the Catuvellauni – and had now sailed back to Britain with Caesar's invasion fleet, and under the circumstances Mandubratius would have been more reliable than captives, certainly when it came to guiding. In his *Gallic War* Caesar may have deliberately omitted to mention him as an informant in order to minimise any later hostility towards him.

In any event, it appears Caesar's men had faith in their leader (though how much choice they had is another matter) and that it was justified, for after a 12-mile march they duly came across the enemy at dawn. The enemy, presum-ably having been informed that Caesar was marching towards them, had taken up a defensive position just across the Great Stour River, probably at a site near Thanington, just west of present-day Canterbury. If they had been able to defend the ford there, things might have been different, but they were not, and after failed attempts with their mounted troops and chariots to repel the Romans, the Britons ended up fleeing from the Roman cavalry into the woods and retreating to an established stronghold there, believed to be Bigbury. The fact that this had been very recently reinforced suggests the Britons were expecting they might have to use it.

British fortresses were rarely to pose a problem to the clinically efficient Romans, and Bigbury, the chief fortification of the Cantii (Cantiaci) tribal group of Kent, was no exception, despite its 20-feet high palisade. As Caesar writes:

The soldiers of the Seventh legion formed a testudo [a protective wall of shields likened to the shell of a tortoise] and threw up a rampart [ramp] against the fortification, took the place and drove them out of the woods, receiving only a few wounds.[42]

Caesar did not try immediately to follow up this time, despite having cavalry at his disposal, for the day was drawing to a close and he knew his men needed rest.

The next morning, just after he had sent three detachments of cavalry and infantry to pursue the Britons, he himself was visited by horsemen. They came from Quintus Atrius, and bore bad news:

> The preceding night [8/9 July] a very great storm having arisen, almost all the ships were dashed to pieces and cast upon the shore, because neither the anchors and cables could resist, nor could the sailors and pilots sustain the violence of the storm; and thus great damage was received by that collision of the ships.[43]

Caesar promptly recalled the three detachments and ordered them to wait at Bigbury. He himself, with some cavalry, rode back immediately to inspect the damage. He found that the report had not been exaggerated: some 40 vessels had foundered and were beyond salvage, and most of the others needed serious repair. T. Rice Holmes is very critical of Caesar at this point:

> This second shipwreck was a calamity of which the loss in ships formed the smallest part. It changed the course of the campaign. Why had not Caesar restrained his eagerness to close with the enemy, and employed every available man in beaching the vessels which he had constructed with that very aim? Granted that it might not have been possible to complete even the mere work of dragging them all out of reach of the waves before the storm began, he would still have done right in not presuming upon the favour of fortune.[44]

Caesar ordered his men at Bigbury to return to base-camp at Walmer, with particular urgency for any carpenters among them, and also sent a galley off to Labienus in Gaul to ask him, with similar urgency, to send extra carpenters and also to build and send as many ships as he could. He further ordered all vessels to be beached for repair, and for a huge fortification to be constructed to protect the beached vessels, a job that took 'about ten days, the labour of the soldiers being unremitting even during the hours of night'.[45]

By around 20 July, Caesar was once again able to march the bulk of his forces into the interior, but the delay had allowed the Britons valuable organisational time and now he was facing larger forces, moreover under the command of over-king Cassivellaunus rather than that of local Cantii sub-kings:

> The chief command and management of the war had been entrusted to Cassivellaunus, whose territories a river, which is called the Thames, separates

from the maritime states at about eighty miles from the sea. At an earlier period perpetual wars had taken place between him and the other states; but, greatly alarmed by our arrival, the Britons had placed him over the whole war and the conduct of it.[46]

Caesar headed for Cassivellaunus's home territory, but as he marched he was constantly attacked by mounted British raiders, with considerable success on one particular occasion. At an early point in the Romans' march, as they were making camp, the Britons suddenly attacked, catching them unawares, and killing the tribune, Quintus Laberius Durus, before being repulsed. Caesar would seem to have been embarrassed, remarking that

> the engagement took place under the eyes of all and before the camp, [and] it was perceived that our men . . . were little suited to this kind of enemy.[47]

It was clear to him that, as a general tactic, Cassivellaunus was trying to break Roman formations and draw cavalry and infantry away from the main body of troops to attack them in isolation, using chariots to deliver men. Any attempts at pursuit by the Roman infantry were particularly hampered by heavy armour limiting their mobility. Caesar seemed not only embarrassed but also exasperated and remarked that

> they never fought in close order, but in small parties and at great distances, and had detachments placed in different parts, and then the one relieved the other, and the vigorous and fresh succeeded the wearied.[48]

The nature of these attacks also limited the ability of the Romans to forage, a matter made even more difficult by Cassivellaunus's policy of 'scorched earth' in the Romans' path.

The day after the embarrassing attack, however, the Romans managed a major counter-attack that caused many British casualties and seemed to dishearten them. In particular, the Britons were weakened by deserters:

> Immediately after this retreat, their auxiliaries who had assembled from all sides, departed; nor after that time did the enemy ever engage with us in very large numbers.[49]

Caesar succeeded in marching his forces to the banks of the Thames, probably either near Brentford or Tilbury. And contrary to his comment about the Britons never fighting in a mass, he found that Cassivellaunus's men were indeed massed on the other side – 'numerous forces of the enemy were marshalled on the other bank'.[50] Any bridges had been destroyed, and both the far bank and the river itself had been fortified by sharp stakes at the only fordable point; the stakes were under the surface of the water and not clearly visible. Caesar was aware of this from information gained from prisoners and deserters. Yet as with the Stour earlier, crossing the river presented no particular problem to either the infantry (many of whom were trained to swim in full armour) or the cavalry (who apparently could also swim), and the Romans crossed with considerable speed. The Britons fled and thereafter resorted to their earlier tactics of guerilla-style attacks in the woods.[51]

The failure of a large number of Britons to defend a river that was of significant size and had to be crossed by swimming or by using the only one fordable point in that area – moreover (according to Caesar) fordable only with difficulty at the best of times and now fortified as well – is rather remarkable, and certainly raises questions about the tactics and/or morale of the Britons, just as much as it says something about the efficiency of the Roman forces. One wonders, for example, whether the Romans were able to facilitate their crossing by first pushing the Britons back from the bank by a barrage of ranged weapons (as had been partly successful the previous year in the Walmer landing)[52] and/or whether they were able to swim enough men and horses across the river to push the Britons back from the ford and thereby allow the others to cross, and/or whether there were significant last-minute defections among the Britons. However, Caesar makes no mention of such matters. He does refer immediately afterwards in his account to Cassivellaunus 'giving up hope of open battle and dismissing the larger number of his forces, but retaining about 4,000 chariots',[53] but this is seemingly in the context of Cassivellaunus's subsequent reversion to guerilla tactics, not of the battle itself.

My own view is that it was probably a case of superior Roman ranged weapons pushing the Britons back sufficiently for an advance force of swimmers to seize the far bank[54] in order to facilitate the careful crossing of the others via the ford. It is, however, possible that late defections from the battle-site could also have affected the outcome and that Caesar, if he was aware of any such last-minute defections, may have refrained from mentioning the matter as it may have detracted from the Roman victory – though it is true that Caesar had earlier acknowledged the role of defections in general. Certainly, as we shall see, Cassivellaunus was soon to refer with sadness to defections among his allies, and equally certainly the Trinovantes immediately approached Caesar and sued for peace, accepting Mandubratius as their leader and asking for protection against Cassivellaunus.[55] Other tribes – including even some Catuvellauni – followed their lead and came to submit to Caesar, promptly supplying the many hostages that Caesar demanded. From these Britons Caesar learnt the whereabouts of Cassivellaunus's headquarters, very probably at Wheathampstead, and headed there directly.

The stronghold was very similar to that at Bigbury, and the Romans took it with similar tactics and similar ease, the main difference being that they constructed two ramps, one on either side, as opposed to just one ramp on one side. Again the surviving enemy fled and the Romans were able to avail themselves of the provisions and livestock they left behind.[56] Cassivellaunus himself does not appear to have been at his stronghold at that point – or if he was, then he escaped unharmed.

But Cassivellaunus was not finished yet, and still wielded considerable power. He instructed four Cantii sub-kings to make a combined attack on Caesar's ships at Walmer, which they did, around 5 August.[57] However, despite only having a fifth or so of their forces guarding the ships, the Romans under Quintus Atrius were easily able to repel the attack – so easily, it would seem, that they were able to 'make a sally, slaying many of their men, and also capturing a distinguished leader named Lugotrix, and bring back their own men in safety'.[58] This was to be the final blow for Cassivellaunus, as Caesar records:

> Cassivellaunus, when this battle was reported to him as so many losses had been sustained, and his territories laid waste, being alarmed most of all by the desertion of the states, sent ambassadors to Caesar about a surrender through the mediation of Commius the Atrebatian.[59]

However, the use of Commius – who was hardly a popular figure among those Britons opposed to Rome – suggests it may possibly have been Caesar, rather than Cassivellaunus, who took the initiative in instigating negotiations.

Caesar now ordered Cassivellaunus to do no harm to the Trinovantes or to Mandubratius personally and ordered all the Britons to pay annual tribute to Rome and to supply further hostages. Caesar appears to have been based at or around Wheathampstead at this time, not at his base-camp at Walmer,[60] and to have waited a considerable time, for he did not return to the base-camp till the end of August.[61] He may have been particularly keen to ensure that this time he did actually receive the promised extra hostages, for we have already seen that after the 55 BC campaign only two of the tribes had honoured their promise to send hostages to him in Gaul (the defaulters probably doubting that Caesar would return).

So numerous were his hostages, especially given the irreparable damage to some of his ships and the fact that very few of the extra ships sent by Labienus had actually arrived, that he decided to send the hostages and his men back to Gaul in two voyages – for he had already decided to return to Gaul for the winter, fearing an uprising there.[62] The idea was that the first group of ships would discharge those on board on the continent and then return, but as it happened very few of the ships due to come back to Britain actually did so, and so Caesar, after a frustrating and fruitless wait for more ships, 'lest he should be debarred from a voyage by the season of the year, inasmuch as the equinox was at hand, he of necessity stowed his soldiers the more closely'.[63] They set sail at night, and all arrived safely in Gaul the following morning.

Caesar may have had in mind a third expedition to England, to entrench Roman dominance, but on his return to Gaul he did indeed find it in turmoil. The recent Roman killing of a popular chieftain, Dumnorix, which Caesar himself had ordered, was having serious repercussions. The embittered Gauls presently revolted, led by the renowned young chieftain Vercingetorix, and savage warfare was to continue for the next three years. Any plans for a return to Britain were shelved, and political events in Rome and elsewhere meant that Caesar was unable to implement any such plans even after the Gallic War ended. In one sense Britain was fortunate that Caesar had so much of his time and energy and resources taken up with Gaul and other matters and that he does not seem to have displayed in Britain the same occasional brutality that he did in Gaul.[64]

Suetonius remarked of Caesar that 'he invaded the Britons, a people unknown before, vanquished them, and exacted moneys and hostages'.[65] The term 'vanquished' might be felt to indicate somewhat exaggerated praise by Suetonius of Caesar's achievements in Britain.[66] Indeed, Webster argues that Caesar's impact on Britain was slight and that the Britons may well have come to feel that they were the victors.[67] He also observes that from a military point of view both of Caesar's raids were 'rash in conception, hasty and ill-advised in execution, and almost a total disaster'.[68]

Tacitus, in contrast to Suetonius, felt Caesar could really only be said to have put Britain on the Roman map rather than firmly establishing it as a Roman possession:

> It was Julius of happy memory who first of all Romans entered Britain with an army: he overawed the natives by a successful battle and made himself master of the coast; but it may be supposed that he rather discovered the island for his descendants than bequeathed it to them.[69]

Certainly, in terms of Caesar's stated aim, British involvement in his Gallic campaign was curtailed.[70] Some tribute and pledges had been won, and some client kingdoms (such as of the Trinovantes and the Atrebates) established, whose kings might be expected to support Rome's cause in return for Rome's support of theirs. However, without an occupying force it would be difficult for the Romans to exercise real control in Britain. That was to be achieved almost exactly a century later.

Before discussing that later invasion, let us first consider who the Britons were and what happened in the intervening century.

1.4   Who were the Britons?

What sort of people were the Britons of these times? Tacitus, writing at the end of the first century AD, made the observation that they lacked unity, which was to their great disadvantage:

> Originally the people were subject to kings, now they are distracted by parties [factions] ... through the influence of chieftains. Nor indeed have we [Romans] any weapon against the stronger races more effective than this, that they have no common purpose; rarely will two or three states confer to repulse a common danger: accordingly they fight individually and are collectively conquered.[71]

This would also seem largely the case at the time of Caesar's invasions. Though there was a belated attempt among the southeastern tribes to unify under Cassivellaunus, it is clear that there was serious discord between some of the tribes and that loyalties were fragile. As in many areas around the world at that time, there was no real sense of cohesive nationhood in Britain, leaving the land open to invasion by more unified or otherwise stronger peoples. Nationhood was to take a thousand years more to achieve, following the eventual establishment of widespread dominance by later arrivals in the form of the Anglo-Saxons – ironically a rather mixed grouping themselves.

Tribes had their own bases and their own kings – or chieftains, depending on one's choice of terminology and/or the size of the tribes (Caesar uses *reges* – 'kings' – of them). Leadership criteria were generally based on popular acclaim, typically of a powerful warrior from among a group of appropriate candidates, but in some tribes there was a nascent idea of succession through primogeniture (though still subject to acclaim). In reality, each tribe did what was best for itself (and no doubt within each tribe there were individuals with their own agendas too), and hence some chose to throw in their lot with the Romans, and some to oppose them.

It is important not to think of the Britons as all being in a negative relationship with Rome, for although it could at times be domineering, it could also give power and authority to a ruler, with positive outcomes for both sides.[72] Logically, one might suppose that the weaker tribes would be the readier to submit – in some cases even actually initiating an approach to the Romans – thereby gaining the protection of the powerful invaders and sundry benefits. The Trinovantes are a clear illustration of this, for in return for their support Caesar protected them from oppression by the more powerful Catuvellauni (though how effective his protection was after his departure is another question). A further example is Commius's Atrebates, who were exempted from taxation.[73] Having local tribal support was of course useful to the Romans, for it

Figure 1.2 British tribes in the second century.

enabled the 'divide and conquer' approach and meant that any future Roman military presence could be reduced accordingly.

As Caesar himself had noted, the tribes were a mix of long-established 'indigenous' people and relative newcomers from the continent. Some of the latter might have arrived as recently as a generation or two before Caesar's visits, or even later, while the former were by no means one homogeneous people.

The Britons of this period as a whole have generally been referred to in modern times as 'Celts', a somewhat arbitrary term seemingly following Caesar's reference to the name being used by a Gallic people (discussed presently). However, no classical writer – at least, none whose works survive – ever specifically used such a designation of the Britons.[74] It has always been a rather broad and vague term, and has become even more so after being popularised and indeed romanticised over the last few centuries. In fact, some scholars feel the term has come to include so many broad and diverse elements that it has effectively become meaningless.[75] However, since there is no simple substitute term, I will continue to use it here, if guardedly.

The 'Celts' were first recorded by the Greeks in the sixth century BC as 'Keltoi' (meaning 'strangers'), a people living north of the Alps. It has long been believed that they branched out across much of western Europe, probably in waves that may have started as early as 1500–1000 BC, with another expansionist movement around the sixth century BC and again in the fourth century BC – even capturing Rome in 387–386 BC and dominating it for some years (and similarly Greece a century or so later, Thrace being a 'Celtic' kingdom till 193 BC). They were also believed to have reached Britain by around 1000 BC, and/or by 300 BC, possibly in the form of invasion. However, amidst considerable debate and disagreement, over recent years there has been increasing scepticism about such Celtic expansionism, and about mass migrations and/or invasions into Britain from central Europe in the traditionally assumed time frame. Very recent genetic research suggests that the first arrival of so-called 'Celtic' people probably occurred some six thousand years ago, in the form of a stream of arrivals over some time rather than all at once, and principally from a people that had settled in Iberia and then moved northwards along the Atlantic coast before crossing to Britain (and who remain especially prominent in Ireland). These arrivals mingled with the relatively limited number of Mesolithic Europeans already present in Britain. There is no genetic evidence of a mass arrival from central Europe around two or three thousand years ago.[76]

However, how exactly these Iberian people interacted with earlier Mesolithic peoples, in Britain – which had been inhabited for many thousands of years – and elsewhere, is unclear. No evidence of conflict has yet been discovered. It is, however, certain that the Celts were presently to comprise the great majority of the inhabitants of Britain. The Picts of northern Britain, for so long considered a mysterious people perhaps pre-dating the Celts, are now seen genetically to be of the same ancient Celtic stock.[77]

Caesar, in the opening sentence of his *Gallic War*, states that Gaul is divided into three parts; one being inhabited by the Belgae, the second by the Aquitani, and the third by a people known as 'Celts' in their own language but as 'Gauls' to the Romans. The Garonne river separates the Gauls from the Aquitani, while the Marne and Seine separate the Gauls from the Belgae.[78]

Even given a broad genetic link between British 'Celtic' tribes – a 'kinship' of which the tribes themselves would have been unaware except perhaps through origin myths – as well as a broad linguistic link, and a widespread religious link through Druidism (discussed below), it certainly did not guarantee inter-tribal bonding of a familial nature, or the exact same culture throughout the Celtic world. It is probably best to think of the Britons of those days as a reasonably diverse grouping of predominantly 'Celtic' peoples,[79] with some widespread cultural commonalities – commonalities often shared by the Celts in continental Europe.

Celtic commonalities were indeed generalised by early writers, such as Plato (fourth century BC) and Strabo (a first century BC Greek geographer) and Diodorus Siculus (also a first century BC Greek writer, born in Sicily), though their comments are with reference to continental Celts, for as mentioned above, no classical writer ever specifically referred to the Britons as Celts. Two prominent commonalities would appear to be the Celts' readiness to fight and readiness to get drunk.[80] However, their image is not all bad. Strabo, for example, mentions daring and openness and basic decency:

> The whole race … is war-mad, and both high-spirited and quick for battle, although otherwise simple and not ill-mannered. And therefore, if roused, they come together all at once for the struggle, both openly and without circumspection, so that for those who wish to defeat them by stratagem they become easy to deal with (in fact, irritate them when, where, or by what chance pretext you please, and you have them ready to risk their lives, with nothing to help them in the struggle but might and daring).[81]

Tacitus has already mentioned a lack of unity for the common good, which Strabo may seem to contradict somewhat here in referring to their coming together, but 'all at once' suggests a temporary unity driven by spontaneous emotion rather than reasoned policy. Certainly in this regard Strabo identifies another Celtic weakness, and that is their emotional reactiveness to provocation, which again points to a lack of clinical thinking on their part and hence, a distinct vulnerability. Moreover, 'high-spirited' and 'quick for battle' are not necessarily helpful traits in actually winning battles. In fact, Strabo goes on to identify, as further traits, 'witlessness' and 'levity of character'.[82] Polybius, a second century BC Greek historian, in similar vein refers to the Celts being 'notoriously fickle'.[83]

In another context Diodorus Siculus makes comments specifically on the Britons, referring for example to simple habits, simple thinking, and a lack of vice,[84] showing a similarity with his generalisations about the Celts.

It may be useful here to consider the term 'Britain' (and derivatives). One of the earliest known references is by the afore-mentioned Diodorus, who actually calls the land 'Pretannia', with the name of the inhabitants being 'Pretani'. 'Pretani' is believed to have meant 'the painted ones' (see Caesar's description below) and may therefore be a common noun rather than a proper noun designating a specific tribe. 'Britain' is thus a Celtic term, or more exactly Brythonic, a British branch of Celtic from which Welsh, Cornish, and Breton derive (the Welsh term for 'Britain' being 'Prydain').[85]

Whatever their ethnicity and origins and kinship, the Britons were numerous, as Caesar also observed.[86] In fact, some estimates suggest a population of as many as 5 million, while others suggest just 1 million, and most scholars accept something between 1.5 and 2.5 million.[87] It is also now clear that, contrary to long-held assumptions, the land was not particularly heavily forested, but heavily settled and farmed – certainly in the south, though some of the inland and northern tribes may have been semi-nomadic pastoralists following their sheep and cattle.[88] Arable farming was usually on a communal tribal basis, in which specific land could be allotted to individuals for working (and dwelling) but usually not ownership thereof, for absolute land ownership by individuals was not the norm.[89] Particularly in the south, it was fields and farmhouses that made up the typical scenery – houses (in Britain at least) usually but not always being round, with roofs of thatch or turf. Settlements consisted either of individual houses (capable of accommodating an extended family) or clusters, which could be quite significant in size but still not 'urban' in the modern sense of the word.[90]

So efficient was farming that, despite the large population, there was a surplus of grain that in fact formed a significant export, along with cattle and hides. Other exports, as mentioned earlier, were various metals, including finely wrought gold jewellery (the distinctive curves of Celtic art being well known). Hunting dogs can also be added to the list, along with woollen cloaks. Imports included oils, glass, and sundry luxury goods for the wealthy – including, it would seem from recent excavations of graves of this period, scented hair gels from southwestern France for noble young men.[91] And domestic trade was not necessarily always by barter, for coinage had appeared by the second century BC.

Some Britons ended up as slaves when captured by enemies, and slaves may well have featured on the export list, but slavery was not necessarily endorsed throughout Celtic British society, though it did happen.[92] Criminals, deserters, hostages, and the like were not necessarily imprisoned, but often simply had their civil rights restricted.[93] At the other end of the social hierarchy, a chief/king did not normally have absolute power, and could be given orders by a tribal assembly.

We can also note the following rather jumbled description from Caesar:

> The most civilized ... are those who inhabit Kent, which is entirely a maritime district, nor do they differ much from the Gallic customs. Most of the inland inhabitants do not sow corn, but live on milk and flesh, and are clad with skins. All the Britons dye themselves with woad, which occasions a bluish colour, and thereby have a more terrible appearance in battle. They wear their hair long, and have every part of their body shaved except their head and upper lip. Ten and even twelve [men] have wives common to them, and particularly brothers among brothers, and parents among their children; but if there be any issue by these wives, they are reputed to be the children of those by whom respectively each was first espoused when a virgin.[94]

Some of these comments may be genuine reflections of Caesar's beliefs, or they may have been deliberately intended to portray the Britons in general as a Barbaric Other, to whom the Romans would bring civilisation – a common justification for conquest in world history. It may be, for argument's sake, that some remote tribes wore skins, but this would not be representative of Britons as a whole, for weaving and textiles were quite advanced. In fact, the woollen cloaks worn by both male and female Britons became well known desirable objects in the Roman world and were exported to Rome itself.[95]

Regarding the idea of shared wives – a passage omitted from some older Latin primers, presumably for its content[96] – it is true that the typical family was an extended one with joint responsibilities for children's upbringing and so on, and there was a certain polygamy permitted. However, a key point is that women (apart from slaves) were not the property of men, contrary to what Caesar might be felt to suggest, but in most matters had equal rights (including with regard to polygamy), and retained ownership of any goods they brought into a marriage.[97] Indeed, women enjoyed a good position in Celtic society – better than that of Roman and Greek women – and were also able to become tribal leaders.

Strabo makes the interesting observation that the Celts discouraged growing 'fat' or pot-bellied, and applied a standard girdle measure to young men, those exceeding the standard being punished.[98] This was unlikely to be mere aesthetics, but it is not clear whether it was an injunction against gluttony, or whether being overweight might be a symbol of insufficient hard work, or, most likely, of being less than fighting fit.

The typical Celtic warrior was a farmer who fought as a member of his tribal levy when the occasion demanded it, but there were some permanent elite warriors amongst the aristocracy. There were also some women warriors.[99] Warriors typically carried a sword and a spear.[100] The sword was of heavy iron and good for cutting but not thrusting. It also bent rather easily. Spears were of two types, throwing and thrusting. Points were often serrated to maximise damage. Bows and arrows were used but rarely, and Barry Cunliffe observes that archery never seemed very popular in the Celtic world.[101] Slings were used quite significantly, not so much in open battle but for defending hill-forts. Protection was principally in the form of a shield, typically made of wood or leather or a combination thereof. Helmets were also used, usually of bronze and often with horns, and in rare cases (almost certainly among elites only) tunics of ring mail. However, though there is occasional evidence of use of chain mail, many Celts fought wearing just loose trousers, or even naked – fully so, not just in the sense of not wearing armour.[102] Cunliffe points out that fighting naked was not at all uncommon among the Celts, and is of the view that nakedness may well have had ritual significance,[103] though it may also have been to prevent an enemy getting a handhold.[104] The naked warrior still wore a torc, which was seen as a symbol of protection by the gods. Whatever the justification, my personal view is that fighting without armour does not seem a particularly helpful tactic for minimising casualties and achieving a victory.

In battle, as we have seen in Caesar's account, the Britons – or again more probably the elite permanent warriors amongst them – used chariots. These are also found in numerous excavations on the continent, but their use there seems to have been abandoned by Caesar's time. (Nor do they feature in Ireland.) The reasons for this are not clear. Another battle characteristic is that an elite Celtic warrior was often accompanied by two shield-bearers, who were in some cases also skilled charioteers. Prior to the battle, attempted intimidation of the enemy by insults and boasting of one's own prowess was common, and so too were battle-dances and battle-chants, building up to a 'dreadful din'. Noise and emotions rose to a crescendo, typically fuelled by alcohol, and in turn fuelling ferocity for the first onslaught, which was of great significance. However, there was a danger in this, for if the first onslaught failed, the focused emotion of bravado could soon dissipate and indeed shift polarity to despair. Moreover, emotion is by its nature not conducive to rational thinking or behaviour, either for a main battle plan or for a reserve plan should things go wrong.[105] Once again, we see serious problems regarding the Celts' ability to take on a disciplined, organised, well armed force such as that of the Romans.

The Romans, from their perspective, would appear to have been rather exasperated by the fighting tactics of the Britons, who so often – wisely – avoided pitched battle and employed guerilla tactics, usually utilising large numbers of horses (though not necessarily in an optimal fashion). A tablet from the Vindolanda fort near Hadrian's Wall, probably dating from around the early second century AD, and perhaps advice passed on from one (possibly frustrated) commander to his replacement, confirms that the 'wretched Britons' (*Brittunculi*) did not use armour but did use a lot of horses.[106]

In the matter of beliefs, the Celts were a superstitious people.[107] Their religion was Druidism,[108] a nature-centred belief system that at core related to the agricultural seasons. In line with animistic beliefs, natural objects were seen as having spiritual significance,[109] especially in matters such as fertility. The Druids were also noted for their calendrical and astronomical knowledge, and their magical rites, divinations, propitiations, and sacrifices. Sacrifices appear to have involved humans on occasion[110] – though this would be nothing exceptional by the standards of the ancient world – through a variety of means including the notorious 'wicker man' (a huge hollow standing figure, up to 30 feet tall, made of wicker). Caesar writes:

> Because they think that unless the life of a man be offered for the life of a man, the mind of the immortal gods cannot be rendered propitious, they have sacrifices of that kind.... Some have figures of vast size, the limbs of which, formed with osiers [supple branches], they fill with living men, which being set on fire, the men perish enveloped in the flames.[111]

Caesar may have been intending here once again to depict the Druids/Celts as barbaric and in need of civilising through conquest, but given the Roman propensity for bloodshed, moreover in a variety of gruesome ways, this would be somewhat hypocritical on his part, and so it is likely to be a true account. The particularity of the wicker man also suggests it is not a product of his or any other observer's imagination. Indeed, Strabo too writes of Celts constructing a colossus of straw and wood, filling it with humans and animals and then making a burnt-offering of it.[112]

The Druids, along with their 'life for life' philosophy, preached reincarnation – which Caesar treats as a cynical means on their part of encouraging fearlessness of death among warriors[113] – and hence useful objects such as weapons and food were buried with the dead. It is also worth noting that Druids believed the soul to reside in the head[114] – which may have significant bearing on the Celtic preoccupation with heads, especially those of captives. Strabo, following an eye-witness account by Poseidonius (second century BC), writes:

> When they depart from battle they hang the heads of their enemies from the necks of their horses, and when they have brought them home, nail the spectacle to their houses.... The heads of enemies of high repute, however, they would embalm in cedar oil and exhibit to strangers.[115]

Druids, who comprised both men and women, were held in great esteem, and seemed to have considerable authority and power – including also in matters political – among communities, indicating that they were more than simply priests. Caesar writes of them:

> [They] are engaged in things sacred, conduct the public and the private sac-rifices, and interpret all matters of religion. To these a large number of the young men resort for the purpose of instruction, and they [the Druids] are [held] in great honour among them. For they determine respecting almost all controversies, public and private; and if any crime has been perpetrated, if murder has been committed, if there be any dispute about an inheritance, if any about boundaries, these same persons decide it; they decree rewards and punishments.[116]

Caesar also believed that Britain was the origin and centre of Druidism:

> This institution [Druidism] is supposed to have been devised in Britain, and to have been brought over from it into Gaul; and now those who desire to gain a more accurate knowledge of that system generally proceed thither [to Britain] for the purpose of studying it.[117]

This was not necessarily totally accurate, but we might note that – albeit after Caesar's death – Druidism was presently outlawed in Gaul (by Augustus) and as a result many Druids fled to Britain, where there was a particularly strong base on the Isle of Mona (Anglesey).

Druidism transcended mere tribal affinities, among other things with Druids having regular meetings at a national and indeed international level, as Caesar noted.[118] As a consequence, they may have played an important role in assem-bling 'British' forces against Caesar and later Claudius, as opposed to simply tribal.[119] Clearly, religion had the potential to unify – though of course the opposite is all too often the case.

1.5   The hundred years' respite

After Caesar left Britain in 54 BC, little thought seems to have been given to it by Rome for the next 20 or so years,[120] partly because of turmoil in Rome itself. Caesar was assassinated in 44 BC, and was eventually succeeded by his desig-nated heir (and relative) Octavian, who after a number of political and military struggles managed to entrench his position by about 31 BC, from which point he is often seen as having effectively become Rome's first emperor – though some scholars prefer 30 BC, and others 27 BC or 23 BC, on which last date he was given the *imperium*. In 27 BC he nominally ceded power to the senate, in a system known as the Principate, and in return was given their authority to rule, as well as the designation 'Augustus'. Keen to emulate Julius, whom he much admired and whose name 'Caesar' he had adopted soon after Julius's death, he considered an expedition to Britain that year, perhaps officially to collect unpaid tribute,[121] but cancelled it because of unrest in Gaul and an apparent proposal by the Britons to sign a treaty. By the next year it was clear the Britons would do no such thing, and again he planned an expedition, but again cancelled it, this time because of trouble in the Alps and Pyrenees. Thereafter he appears to have abandoned the idea, possibly because the Britons were posing no threat in Gaul (unlike the case in 55 BC), and/or because it would be too costly to maintain an armed occupation in Britain.[122]

Among other things it is not clear which exactly of the conquered British tribes did duly pay their tribute to Rome. The Catuvellauni may not have done[123] (and they may therefore have been the object of Augustus's intent), but presumably, in their own interests, the client kingdoms did.[124] It is also apparent that sons of at least some client kings spent some time in Rome as part of their 'Romanising' education – which may have been voluntary, but was probably a requirement imposed from Rome.[125] Certainly, some 30 years or so after Caesar left, there is increased evidence of Roman items in the south, suggesting stronger links. At the same time, some of this would reflect increased trade between Britain and Rome, and Rome certainly profited from this, including through commercial taxes. Augustus seems to have been content with this. So too was his stepson and successor Tiberius (r. AD 14–37).

In Britain, during this time, it may be that in some cases tribal identities – and territories – firmed up somewhat, reflecting the range of attitudes towards Rome. And, as settlement intensified, a certain degree of nucleation was evident, leading to the emergence of proto-towns. The inevitable shifts in power-centres and power-holders, as well as inter-relations, can be gauged to some degree from changes in the increasing supply of coinage. Not surprisingly, in view of its position and recent history, the southeast seems to have become particularly prominent, and to have had the closest contact with Rome and the continent. Among other things it appears to have had a more advanced monetary economy than other areas, judging from the fact that it alone minted low denomination coins as well as high, suggesting the use of money in everyday-level transactions.[126] By contrast, in pre-Caesar Britain the far southwest had been a significant point of contact with the continent, but it now seems to have become less obviously so, though the links themselves were maintained.

Commius of the Atrebates had been rewarded by Caesar for his role in 54 BC by being made overlord of the Morini, a coastal Gallic people, seemingly in addition to his position with the Atrebates. Then in 52 BC he fell out with his erstwhile friend Caesar, just two years after Caesar's return to Gaul, and even led a major Morini force to support Vercingetorix in opposition to him.[127] At some point (not in battle) he narrowly survived a Roman assassination attempt.[128] After the defeat of Vercingetorix he presently escaped back to Britain, where – judging from coins with his name, issued from Calleva Atrebatum (Silchester) – he seems to have been (re-?)accepted as king of the British Atrebates. He ruled till around 20 BC and was then succeeded by his son (possibly adopted) Tincommius (Tincommarius), who – perhaps in conjunction with a brother Epillus – ruled for at least another 20 years or so.

Cassivellaunus unfortunately disappears from history. The next known leader of his tribe, the Catuvellauni, is Tasciovanus, who minted coins at Verulamium (St Albans), a major Catuvellaunian centre, around 20 BC. It is possible, though not definite, that Tasciovanus was Cassivellaunus's son. The fact that some five years later he was also minting coins at Camulodunum ('Fortress of the God of War', now Colchester), in the heart of the territory of their rival tribe the Trinovantes, suggests that the Catuvellauni had prevailed in some conflict or merger – though he soon reverted to minting exclusively at Verulamium, perhaps suggesting a reversal. By this stage Mandubratius had been replaced as king of the Trinovantes by Addedomarus, whose rule had started around 20 BC. (The fact that three rulers appear to have started their reign around 20 BC suggests the possibility of some particularly intense activity at this point, though the nature of this is unclear, and it may just be coincidence.) Coins from a Kentish ruler, Dubnovellaunus, also appear in Colchester around this time, though their appearance too is brief, ceasing by around AD 7. Dubnovellaunus appears in Roman records at around this point as one of two British kings who came to Augustus as suppliants, but their reasons are not clear, nor the outcomes. The other supplicant was almost certainly Tincommius, who may have been driven out from the Atrebates at or around the same time.

And the one who drove him/them out may well have been Tasciovanus's son Cunobelinus (better known as Shakespeare's Cymbeline), whose coins appeared from Camulodunum from that same time of around AD 7. Shortly afterwards Cunobelinus also started issuing coins from Verulamium, showing once again that one ruler prevailed over the territories of both the Catuvellauni and the Trinovantes. Presently they also appear in Kent and in the northern part of the Atrebates' territory. Interestingly, while Cunobelinus appears to have held sway over a large area – to such an extent that Suetonius refers to him as 'rex Britannorum', translatable as 'king of the Britons'[129] – his main base seems to have been Camulodunum. This may be felt to suggest the possibility he was an adopted son of the Catuvellaunian Tasciovanus, and was actually a Trinovantian by birth. Whatever his origins, he ruled for over 30 years.

Cunobelinus had three sons: Adminius, Togodumnus, and Caratacus (Caractacus). For unclear reasons, around AD 39, Adminius was banished by his father,[130] and then sought refuge with – and assistance from – the notoriously unstable emperor Caligula (Gaius Caesar), who had succeeded Tiberius in AD 37 at the age of 24.

At this point Caligula was in a Roman camp at the Rhine, which is where Adminius visited him. In September 39 he had suddenly departed from Rome for the camps on the Gaul side of the Rhine, hoping thence to vanquish the Germans on the other side. This was something his father Germanicus had failed to achieve some 20 years before – in turn an attempt to redeem the disaster of AD 9, when the Germans had annihilated three legions under Varus in the Teutoberg Forest in one of Rome's worst ever defeats.

Caligula believed that Adminius's humble stance somehow represented a victory for him (Caligula) over the Britons, and decided to send an expedition to Britain to enforce its subjugation. But neither the German nor the British expeditions came to anything. Caligula spent the winter doing nothing in the camps, and then his 'invasion' of Britain in the spring of AD 40 ended on the sea-shore of Gaul, where, having assembled his troops as if ready to cross the Channel, he apparently told them to gather sea shells, which were then sent to Rome as the spoils of war and/or the Ocean. Suetonius writes:

> Finally, as if resolved to make war in earnest, he drew up a line of battle on the shore of the ocean, placed his ballistas and other artillery, and no-one knowing or able to imagine what he was going to do, all of a sudden commanded they gather sea shells, and fill their helmets and pockets with them, calling them 'the spoils of the ocean due to the Capitol and the Palatine'. As a monument of this victory he erected a lofty tower, from which lights were to shine at night to guide the course of ships, as from the Pharos [the lighthouse at Alexandria].[131]

Some scholars feel this is a tall story, and that Caligula's real reason for the sudden abandoning of the 'invasion' and his abrupt return to Rome was a dangerous escalation of tensions with the Senate.[132] Others suggest it was the fault of the troops, and their fear of crossing the terrifying Ocean, that forced Caligula to abort the invasion.[133] In any event, there was no invasion of Britain by Caligula.

Unsurprisingly, the sadistic and tyrannical Caligula was soon assassinated, in AD 41, by men of the Praetorian Guard, who also proceeded to murder his wife and young daughter (brutally dashing the latter's head against a wall). His uncle Claudius (brother of Germanicus), who had just been with Caligula, hid himself, terrified, in the palace. Standing behind a curtain with his feet sticking out, he was discovered by a guard. Claudius was club-footed, spoke with a stutter, had a constantly shaking head, and was widely ridiculed as dim-witted,[134] and so it may perhaps have been half as a joke (or even a complete joke) that the guard – and presently his fellow soldiers – hailed the bewildered

Claudius as the new emperor. One certainly senses something of the absurd about the business, for Cassius Dio writes:

> The more he [Claudius] attempted to avoid the honour and resist, the more strongly did the soldiers in their turn insist upon not accepting an emperor appointed by others but upon giving one themselves to the whole world.[135]

Before long the Senate endorsed this, possibly out of a reluctance to upset the insistent guards and/or a belief that Claudius would, unlike Caligula, present little trouble and be more amenable to advice from the Senators.

Claudius was fortunate to be emperor – Suetonius refers to it as 'a remarkable freak of fortune'.[136] And it might be that he was fortunate even to be alive, for in the brutal mood of the moment he could easily have been murdered by the unnamed soldier who discovered him hiding. It can certainly be argued that it was an absurdist sense of black humour on the part of the soldier and his colleagues, in wanting to see a 'king of fools' as their own chosen emperor, that saved Claudius and thereby played a major role in the determination of Roman history. And within a year or two it was also to have a major impact on the history of Britain.

Trouble had been brewing there. Cunobelinus had died around AD 41, leading to some instability, but his son, Caratacus, had finally completed a long drawn-out expansion into the Atrebates' territory. A third son of Commius, Verica, had become king of the Atrebates around AD 15, following his brothers Tincommius and Epillus, but was forced out by Caratacus. Just as his brother Tincommius had sought succour from Rome, so too did Verica now.[137] His request for help was something that the new emperor, Claudius, could use to his own advantage, to establish his authority and a reputation as a conquering hero. The early fifth century historian Paulus Orosius, for example, wrote that Claudius wanted to demonstrate his worthiness as a leader and sought everywhere for a war in which he might achieve victory, deciding on Britain because it was in a state of near-rebellion which needed his intervention, and was moreover a land which no one else had dared approach since the mighty Caesar.[138] He was indeed to make it an occupied Roman province almost exactly a hundred years after Caesar had left its shores. The long respite from Roman presence was to end.

1.6   The Claudian invasion, AD 43: Of emperors and elephants

The Roman military were not exactly joyful at the prospect of an invasion of Britain. Despite Julius Caesar having put it on the Roman map, it was still not really part of the empire, and Dio tells us that initially the proposed men, who were to be drawn mainly from those stationed at the Rhine, were reluctant to go even further into barbarian territory: 'The soldiers were indignant at the thought of carrying on a campaign outside the limits of the known world'.[139] Peter Salway is of the view that there could well have been fewer Romans prepared to cross the Ocean to Britain than Britons prepared to welcome the Romans.[140] However, following persuasion from Narcissus, a former slave sent to them by Claudius, the men eventually agreed to follow Aulus Plautius, the commander of the expedition.

The force was composed of four 'citizen legions' – Second, Ninth, Fourteenth, and Twentieth – comprising some 20,000 men, and in addition probably around as many 'auxiliaries' (of non-citizen status, although presently citizenship was to be conferred on auxiliaries after appropriate service). No doubt learning from Caesar's expeditions, Plautius made the Channel crossing in three divisions. Dio writes simply: 'They were sent over in three divisions, in order that they should not be hindered in landing, as might happen to a single force'.[141] This could refer to three phased landings at the same site, or three landings at separate sites, and scholars have argued both ways.[142] Both camps have largely – or at least traditionally – agreed on Richborough being a/the site, but those who favour 'three sites' do not seem to have reached consensus about the other sites, though Fishbourne would be a strong contender, followed by Dover. However, while in any case the landings were unopposed, we should note that in recent years the assumed major site of Richborough is being increasingly questioned, and a view is emerging that the main (or sole) site may have been at or near Fishbourne in Sussex,[143] famed for its palace (believed to date from around AD 60) and its Atrebatian pro-Roman traditions. And we should not forget that an appeal from the Atrebatian Verica was supposedly the trigger for Claudius's invasion. If the Romans did indeed land here, then that would explain the lack of opposition.

The force seems to have assembled at Boulogne, and to have set out 'late in the season',[144] which would suggest midsummer at the earliest. In the traditional view the main force – or the full force, depending on one's interpretation – landed at Richborough, in good shelter just north of the open beach near Deal that Caesar had used, and this was to remain an invasion base for some time. (At the time Richborough was either an island or, more likely, a promontory.)

The main source for details of the campaign is Dio,[145] who states that the Britons did not oppose the landings and adds an explanation (which I quote for precision) that

> the Britons as a result of their inquiries had not expected that they [the Romans] would come, and had therefore not assembled beforehand.[146]

If correct, this can seemingly only relate to the soldiers' reluctance to fight in Britain (as discussed above) lulling the Britons into a false sense of security. And yet, if the Britons were being kept informed, as would seem the case, how does

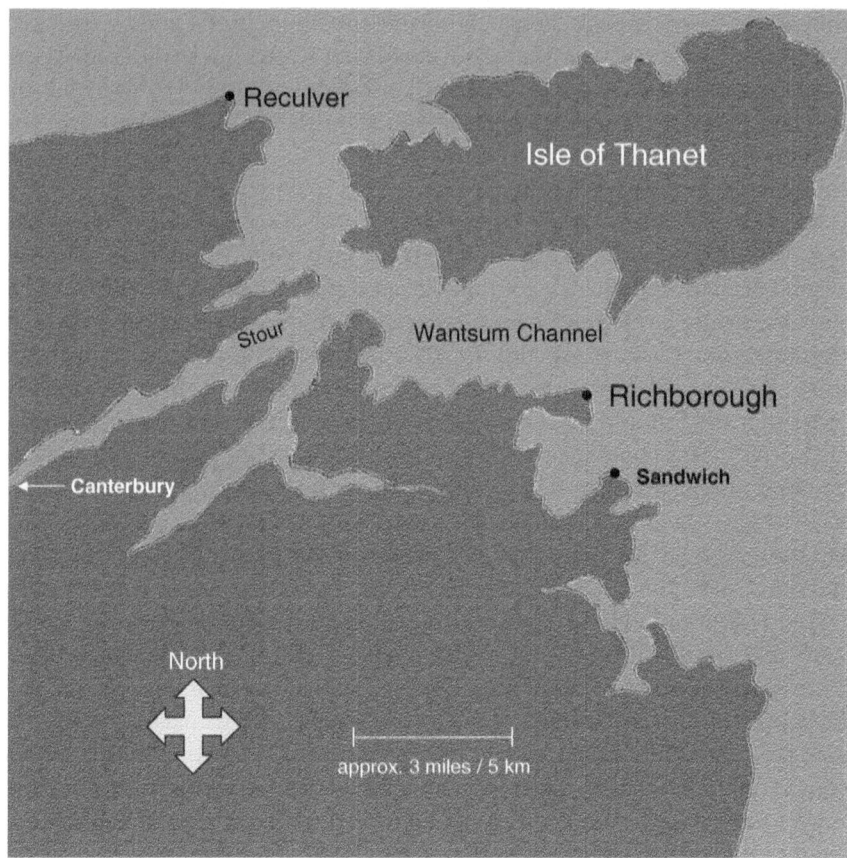

Figure 1.3   The coastline of northeast Kent at the time of the Claudian invasion.

one explain why they did not know about the visit of Narcissus and the decision finally to embark? However 'last-minute' the actual embarkation might
have been (and it would have been very time-consuming), and also bearing in
mind possible delays in receiving intelligence from the continent – and even
the remote possibility of their informant(s) deliberately not informing them (or
misinforming them) for whatever reason – and recent memories of Caligula's
abandoned invasion, it would still be extraordinarily foolish of the Britons to
abandon any assembly plans before they were absolutely sure the Romans
would not be coming. John Peddie writes:

> When the news of the unrest amongst the Romans filtered across the Straits,
> presumably to the joy of the Britons, the latter relaxed their guard. This was
> a vital failure of commission since Caratacus and Togodumnus could not

responsibly have considered themselves out of danger until they had received intelligence that the legions assembled for the assault had been dispersed. The result was calamitous for the Britons, for it allowed Aulus Plautius to achieve complete surprise.[147]

This criticism may or may not be justified, for it seems in turn based on an assumption that Dio was right in that the Britons were indeed initially planning to assemble, and that they were taken by surprise.

Foolishness, even of monumental proportions, can of course never be ruled out of human behaviour, but I personally wonder whether perhaps Dio might have misinterpreted the situation, and whether in fact the Britons ever planned to challenge the Romans head on in a pitched battle, at the landings or even possibly elsewhere. As support for my view, even for argument's sake accepting the traditional site of Richborough, I would point out that after the landings Dio goes on to refer to the Britons' strategy of avoiding engagement with the Romans:

> And even when they did assemble, they would not come to close quarters with the Romans, but took refuge in the swamps and forests, hoping to wear the invaders out in fruitless effort, so that, just as in the days of Julius Caesar, they should sail back with nothing accomplished.[148]

Perhaps indeed the Britons had learnt from Caesar's first visit, and decided not to oppose Plautius's landing, just as they had not opposed Caesar's second.

Whatever their strategy, Plautius eventually tracked them down, and in skirmishes at unknown sites (possibly near Harbledown) took on and defeated Caratacus and then his brother Togodumnus, both brothers surviving to fight on. Some (sub-?)tribes gave their allegiance to the Romans at this time. Plautius, having constructed a garrison at this forward position, then advanced further, to a river that – should the Richborough site be accepted – would almost certainly be the Medway at Rochester,[149] where the Britons were camped 'in rather careless fashion'[150] on the far bank. As with Caesar's campaigns, to the Britons' surprise, crossing the river posed no real difficulty for the Romans, with German auxiliaries in particular leading the way by swimming across in full armour. Arriving on the far bank, they concentrated not on the British warriors, but on the horses, maiming them and thereby rendering the chariots useless. Vespasian, later to be emperor, distinguished himself in this encounter – an encounter that was exceptionally hard fought and, rare for Romans, lasted into a second day (though what happened during the night is unclear).

Eventually, on that second day the Romans gained the upper hand and the Britons then retreated to the Thames (actually named by Dio), fording it at a broad part (where it emptied into the Ocean, according to Dio) through local knowledge of a seemingly complex path.[151] The following Romans had more difficulty in finding the path across (despite presumably having guides with them), but again the German auxiliaries swam across. At the same time other Roman troops managed to cross a bridge further upstream, and the Britons were attacked from several directions and forced to retreat further. It was at this point that Romans pursuing the Britons became enmired in a swamp, and lost a number of men. Togodumnus was also killed at this point or shortly afterwards.

However, submissions were not forthcoming, and British resistance continued. Plautius decided to consolidate his position and, as previously instructed, sent for Claudius. Claudius was ready to depart, and duly arrived probably some six weeks later,[152] accompanied by numerous senators – witnesses to his triumph – and, to add to the spectacle, elephants. We can understand something of the impact of the elephants on the Britons (whereas we can only guess at the impact of the senators on them) from the writing of the Greco-Roman rhetorician Polyaenus in the second century – although, as discussed in Section 1.3, he is believed to have mistakenly associated the elephant(s) with Caesar not Claudius.

> In Britain Caesar was attempting to cross a great river. The king of the Britanni, Cassivellaunus, the king of the Britons, blocked him with numerous horsemen and chariots. In Caesar's train was a very large elephant, an animal unknown to the Britanni. Caesar armoured the elephant with iron scales, raised a large tower upon its back, set archers and slingers in the tower, and ordered the animal to step into the river. The Britanni upon seeing the unknown and monstrous beast panicked. ... The Britanni fled with their horses and chariots, and the Romans crossed the river without danger after scaring off the enemy with a single beast.[153]

Miranda Aldhouse-Green refers to the important symbolism of these giant beasts: for the Romans, elephants reminded them of a heroic heritage, such as Caesar's triumphal procession in Rome in 46 BC, after victory in the Gallic Wars, through an avenue of 40 elephants, each bearing a lamp; for the Britons, they symbolised the might of Rome and the vast extent of its empire stretching into exotic lands.[154]

The exact number and role of Claudius's elephants is not clear,[155] though it does appear that they accompanied him to the British town at Camulodunum. Dio goes on to tell us that, having arrived at the camps by the Thames, Claudius took command, led the men (and possibly elephants) across the river, 'and engaging the barbarians, who had gathered at his approach, he defeated them in battle and captured Camulodunum',[156] thereby winning the submission of numerous tribes. He then departed back to Rome (again presumably with his elephants), after just 16 days in Britain, and handed command back to Plautius, bidding him to subjugate remaining districts.[157] Arriving back in Rome he received a hero's welcome, as hoped for and no doubt as planned for, and the Senate erected a victory-arch to commemorate his achievement, the inscription referring to his receiving the surrender of eleven British kings and bringing for the first time the barbarians from beyond the Ocean under Roman rule.[158]

In reality Claudius may not have fought personally in any battle, and the capture of Camulodunum was quite likely a surrender initiated by those friendly to Rome – indeed, Suetonius (without any reference to elephants) writes that 'without any battle or bloodshed [he] received the submission of part of the island'.[159] But his visit was nonetheless a success.

Claudius himself was probably involved in drawing up the basic framework of governance of this new province, which generally followed a fixed pattern. A set of statutes was drawn up, Aulus Plautius became the province's first governor, a financial procurator (who reported directly to the emperor) was also appointed, and presently *civitates* (administrative areas, based typically on tribal areas and with a main town in each) were established, and at least one *colonia* (town primarily for retired Roman soldiers) at Colchester/Camulodunum (AD 49, others later at Gloucester, Lincoln, and York). Much of Britain was soon under either direct military rule or that of client kings. Considerable territory and power was given to a king called Cogidubnus (Cogidumnus, Togidubnus), whose details are not fully clear but who appears to have been Verica's successor among the Atrebates. It is Cogidubnus who is widely associated with the renowned Roman villa at Fishbourne, though the link is not absolutely definite, and if true, it is testimony to his 'Romanisation'. One imagines that other client kings may well have had similar splendid villas.

Of course, not all Britons were pro-Roman, and some were actively anti-Roman. Caratacus, who was probably the Romans' major opponent at the time, headed west to join the Silures in what is now South Wales, and later also the Ordovices of Central-North Wales, and seems to have been accepted as leader of both in their opposition to Rome. In fact, he seems to have been the focal point for many opposed to the Romans around Britain, achieving an informal status of unifier in this regard, and eventually even being famed in Rome itself as a great fighter.[160]

However, after some years of guerilla-style attacks, in 51 he was defeated by Plautius's successor as governor from 47, Publius Ostorius Scapula, in a final battle that probably took place in or near Snowdonia.[161] Caratacus made the mistake of seeking shelter with Cartimandua, who was the ruling queen of the Brigantes and a known Roman sympathiser. Her tribe, which was probably a confederation of smaller tribes with not necessarily a universally shared similar attitude of sympathy towards Rome, occupied large territory in the northeast, mostly between the Tyne and the Humber and probably stretching to the west coast. Brigantians had briefly rebelled against the Romans in 47–48, and it may have been after this that Cartimandua was installed by the Romans as a client queen. Despite her own sympathies with Rome, Brigantian territory seemed an ongoing source of unrest, and Caratacus may have believed that anti-Roman voices among the Brigantes would outweigh her pro-Roman sentiments. But if so, he was wrong. No doubt with her own agenda of currying favour with Rome, Cartimandua promptly had Caratacus put in chains and handed him over to the Romans.[162] Her behaviour seems to suggest that she may even have tricked him with a false offer of support, in order to catch this prize and win great favour from Rome.[163] However, whatever the background, it is still surprising that a veteran survivor such as Caratacus should have been fooled. His family had been captured after the defeat in Snowdonia and perhaps his judgement was blurred by this, and he was desperate. Whatever the reason, as S. Ireland observes, the capture of Caratacus was, from the Roman point of view, a 'considerable stroke of luck'.[164] The converse to that Roman good fortune was, of course, British misfortune.

Caratacus was despatched, along with his family, to Rome, where, Tacitus observes, 'all were eager to see the great man, who for so many years had defied our power'.[165] He might well have expected to be ritually strangled, as was common with rebellious chieftains or kings, and was indeed the earlier fate of the Gaul Vercingetorix after being kept six years in Rome. However, when he was brought before Claudius he so impressed the emperor with his courage and cogent argument that he was pardoned and allowed to see out his days in peace, though kept in Rome. In his speech, according to Tacitus, he pointed out that it was essentially a matter of fortune that he was appearing before Claudius as a captive and not as a friend, and philosophically observed that 'If you Romans choose to lord it over the world, does it follow that the world is to accept slavery?'[166] After his pardon, he is said, by Cassius Dio, to have wondered aloud, while wandering through the impressive streets of Rome, '[How] can you [Romans], who have got such possessions and so many of them, covet our poor tents?'[167]

Cartimandua's husband in 51 was Venutius, and he seems initially to have been pro-Roman along with his wife. However, possibly partly because of her treatment of Caratacus, and/or partly because she divorced him in favour of his former shield-bearer Vellocatus[168] (a double insult as her new husband was of very low rank), he became hostile towards her, and presently also overtly so towards the Romans. At some point in the mid-AD 50s (possibly as early as 52), he launched an attack on her, his prime aim seemingly to displace her as monarch, and she called on the Romans for help, who did indeed come to the aid of their client queen.[169] He was narrowly defeated, but lived on to stage another uprising against her some considerable years later in 69 (no doubt taking advantage of Roman instability that year, which saw no fewer than four emperors), and this time was successful. Cartimandua again appealed for help, and Roman auxiliaries came to her aid and rescued her but were unable to quell the uprising.[170] Venutius took the throne, while Cartimandua disappeared from history, almost certainly having been taken to Rome. Tacitus famously summed up the situation: 'The throne was left to Venutius; the war to us'.[171] Though presently Venutius himself was also to disappear from history, the Brigantes were indeed to remain basically hostile and a worry to Rome for almost another century, despite temporary or partial subjugations, until more firmly defeated by Emperor Antoninus (r. 138–61), of Antonine Wall fame.

Another noted rebellion took place in 47 among the Iceni – or a least some of them[172] – of what is now East Anglia. By birth or by marriage – there are no details of her early life – this was the tribe of Boudica,[173] presently to stage a better-known and more substantial revolt of her own. The 47 rebellion was the result of attempts by the Romans to disarm not only hostile tribes, but also Rome's client kingdoms, of which the territory of the Iceni was one. It is not clear whether Boudica's husband Prasutagus was king at this stage, though it seems more likely he was installed after the rebellion,[174] but in any event the order to disarm met with great resistance. To take arms away from a Celtic male – and presumably any female armiger – was a great insult, one perhaps understandable in the case of a potential foe, but unexpected and effectively inexcusable in the case of a friendly client kingdom.[175]

As it happens the rebellion was put down relatively easily – Tacitus tells us that 'the enemy were entangled in their own defences'[176] – but the whole episode shows a Roman weakness in being too harsh on their subject/client peoples and arousing hostility in them. While it was a fact that civilians were (strictly speaking) not generally permitted to carry arms anywhere within the empire, the Romans could pragmatically have turned a blind eye to it, even just for a few more years, in the interests of good relations – certainly so in the case of those who had voluntarily submitted to Rome. In this regard Peter Salway observes that Roman insensitivity to other peoples often led them to make such mistakes, which in turn led to unnecessary wars.[177] We should also note Tacitus's view of the British sense of 'fair play':

> As for the people [Britons] themselves, they discharge energetically the levies and tributes and imperial obligations imposed upon them, provided always there be no wrongdoing. They are restive under wrong.[178]

The Romans did not learn, and were to make a similarly insensitive but far worse mistake with the Iceni again 13 years later.

1.7   Boudica and the revolt of AD 60:[179] Bold but botched?

Claudius died in AD 54, almost certainly poisoned by his wife Agrippina so that her son Nero could become emperor.[180] By inclination Nero should have been an artist-entertainer rather than emperor, and it is questionable as to what extent his energies were directed towards matters imperial. At some point he is known to have seriously considered abandoning Britain,[181] and it may have been shortly after his accession. (Venutius's first rebellion was probably around this time, and may have been a factor.)

The Romans did nonetheless persist with Britain, but, possibly growing impatient with ongoing guerilla attacks from tribes outside the southeast and perhaps occasionally inside it, their rule seems to have become somewhat harsher. Among other things, the Britons – or more probably, mostly the local Trinovantes – were soon virtually press-ganged into a massive building project in Camulodunum, the *colonia* which was seen as the Roman capital (though the procurator and governor were based in Londinium, some 60 miles away, which was actually larger). The project was a huge temple to Claudius, who had now been deified. Built in stone with a tiled roof, its dimensions were 150 feet by 78, with a height of 66 feet.[182] Not only did the Britons build it, they were also taxed for the costs. Tacitus tells us that to the Britons 'the temple to the Divine Claudius, ever before their eyes, seemed a citadel of perpetual tyranny'.[183]

Resentment must have been high, but things were to get worse, for, perhaps sensing trouble (but foolishly only adding to it if so), around AD 59–60 the Romans started calling in investment loans they had made to the tribes, but which the tribes themselves had thought of as donations.[184] The philosopher Seneca, for example, had given them the massive sum of 40 million sesterces,

Figure 1.4 A model of the Temple of Claudius at Camulodunum. (Courtesy of Colchester Museum.)

estimated to be around 50 million pounds sterling in present-day terms.[185] Immediate repayment was sought by the procurator of Britain, Catus Decianus, a favourite of Nero but certainly not of the Britons, and who might well have seen some personal gain in all this – Peter Salway refers to his 'cupidity' and 'foolishness' as among the immediate causes of the trouble that was to follow, and Joan Liversidge similarly remarks that Catus Decianus's greed was the main cause.[186]

This did not seem fair and reasonable governance. Salway is of the view that the early governors' approach to their dealings with the Britons was a 'disastrous failure',[187] and even some Romans, such as Tacitus, felt embarrassed by Roman heavy-handedness. Showing clear sympathy for the Britons Tacitus remarks, for example, that at this time the governor was violent against their persons and the procurator against their property, and goes on to refer to Roman 'avarice and lust'.[188]

But the aggravation was to continue. In AD 60 Prasutagus, client king of the Iceni, died. The Roman practice was that a client king's reign over his territory was an arrangement during his lifetime only, and that upon his death it should be left for the Romans to deal with his territory as they saw fit. They might possibly agree to another client ruler, or far more likely they might not and simply absorb the land and its people into the empire proper.[189] Prasutagus's queen was Boudica, but on the evidence we have she was a consort-queen, not a queen reigning in her own right like Cartimandua – an important but often seemingly overlooked point[190] – and not even a co-ruler. It would have been highly unlikely that the Romans would allow her to rule the kingdom after Prasutagus's death, and Prasutagus and indeed very probably Boudica herself would have known this.[191] Prasutagus thus thought it best not to make Boudica an heir, but to leave half his kingdom to their children (two daughters), and half to the emperor,[192] though what exactly the intended regnal arrangements were is not clear. His daughters appear to have been in their early teens but their age is not known for sure.[193] They may possibly have been old enough to rule without a regent, but more realistically one imagines their mother Boudica would have assumed some sort of role as regent till they came of age. Decianus the procurator, however, did not see any of this as reasonable, and insisted on claiming all the property. Though he seems to have been a greedy and not very respectworthy individual, with an eye to his own interests, technically he was following a Roman practice, and may even have been acting on direct orders from the emperor.[194] As we shall see presently, it is the manner in which he went about things that seems to have been particularly inflammatory and to have gone beyond any practice recognised by custom.

Miranda Aldhouse-Green suggests the interesting possibility that the reason for Prasutagus's omission of Boudica in his will, and of subsequent Roman violence towards her, might be that the couple did not share the same attitude

Figure 1.5   The entrance to the reconstructed Iceni Village at Cockley Cley in Norfolk. Bearing some similarity to Roman bridgehead fort gates, it has towers, a display of enemy heads, and a drawbridge operated by weighted baskets of stones. (With thanks to Cockley Cley Iceni Village.)

towards the Romans – more specifically, while Prasutagus may have been a 'staunch ally' of the Romans, Boudica may have been 'vehemently anti-Roman'.[195] There would undoubtedly have been an anti-Roman faction left over from the failed rebellion of 47, with whom Boudica may have sympathised, and with whom she may even have tried to make a bid for Icenian independence upon the death of her husband.[196] Any such attitude on her part may well also underlie the ferocity of her subsequent attacks on the Romans and those Britons she saw as too friendly towards them. Personally, I feel that if she had indeed been vehemently anti-Roman then the Romans might have detected this much earlier and done something about it. After all, a client king could lose his kingdom during his lifetime, not just at the end of it. But, if she did manage to suppress any overt expression of anti-Roman sentiment during her husband's lifetime, then Aldhouse-Green's suggestion becomes more of a possibility.

Whatever the case, Decianus's manner of enforcing his view and his authority certainly suggests something far more than a legal wrangle over rights of inheritance, and was well beyond the bounds of accepted practice. Tacitus tells us that

> Prasutagus's kingdom was plundered by centurions, his house by slaves, as if they were the spoils of war. First, his wife Boudicca was scourged, and his daughters outraged [raped]. All the chief men of the Iceni, as if Rome had received the whole country as a gift, were stripped of their ancestral possessions, and the king's relatives were [treated like] slaves.[197]

Clearly, the treatment of the king's relatives, the seizure of private property, the raping, and the flogging of a free woman were not acceptable, even by Roman standards.[198] Indeed, a case can be made that Decianus deliberately tried to humiliate Boudica, the two young royal heirs, and the Icenian nobles, as if to prove a point about who was master. In this regard, we may perhaps consider unflattering Roman attitudes towards women as a contributing factor to the particular nature and degree of violence involved in the seizure, but we should also consider the possibility that there may well have been a violent seizure even if the intended heir(s) or regent were male.[199]

The behaviour of Decianus and his men was, to use Miranda Aldhouse-Green's term, that of 'crass stupidity',[200] seemingly with little or no consideration of the repercussions. It did not take long for those repercussions to materialise. One imagines that word of the assaults would have spread quickly, and that people would have gathered around Boudica at her residence, which was possibly at Thetford in Norfolk.[201] The gathering would have evolved quickly into a centre of resistance, a mustering point for disaffected Britons, such as the Trinovantes. Boudica would naturally have been the central figure, but it is likely, especially as numbers swelled, that prominent individuals from within the Iceni and other tribes would have formed a 'war council' around her. Dio tells us that 'The person who was thought worthy to be their leader and who directed the conduct of the entire war was Boudica',[202] but it is unlikely, in my view, that she would have been sole commander.[203] She may even possibly have ended up largely as a figurehead,[204] with others making the decisions, though the Roman sources do not indicate this and do not name other individuals – but then again, the Romans, including Dio, seemed fascinated by the fact she was a woman (discussed below), and may well have focused on her to the exclusion of others, and exaggerated her role.

Boudica is said to have sought guidance from the gods, releasing a hare – a sacred animal native to Britain, as opposed to the rabbit introduced by the Romans – and judging the direction it took to be an omen in her favour.[205] It must have set off south towards Camulodunum, the notorious symbol of Roman presence, for that is where Boudica and her followers now headed, gathering supporters – including from other tribes – as they went. It would not have been a disciplined Roman-style army-march, but a slow progression – probably no more than ten miles a day[206] – of a massive collectivity of those planning to fight, and in many cases their families too, along with wagons carrying their possessions. It was not uncommon for families to spectate at battles, and one also suspects that the wagons were not just there to provide material comforts to the combatants, but also to add new possessions by way of plunder. A further reason for bringing families and possessions along was fear of reprisals by the Romans (and possibly others) on homesteads left undefended. Numbers are hard to estimate, but it could have been over 100,000, of which around a third could have been potential combatants.[207]

At this stage Cassius Dio puts an extremely long and stilted speech (complete with classical references) into Boudica's mouth, in a supposed address to her growing army about the need to resist the Romans. Almost certainly it is a product of his imagination, but it is useful as an indicator of his perception of the situation facing her and the Britons. As with Tacitus above, it also suggests in places an embarrassment over Roman excesses. The speech includes comments such as:

> You have learned by actual experience how different freedom is from slavery.... Some of you ... have been deceived by the alluring promises of the Romans ... and [now] you have come to realise how much better is poverty with no master than wealth with slavery. For what treatment is there of the most shameful or grievous sort that we have not suffered ever since these men made their appearance in Britain? ... But it is we who have made ourselves responsible for all these evils, in that we allowed them to set foot in the island in the first place instead of expelling them as we did their famous Julius Caesar.... However, even at this late stage ... let us, my countrymen and friends and kinsmen – for I consider you all kinsmen, seeing that you inhabit a single island and are called by one common name – let us, I say, do our duty while we still remember what freedom is, that we may leave to our children not only its appellation but also its reality.... Have no fear whatever of the Romans; for they are superior to us neither in numbers nor in bravery. And here is the proof: they have protected themselves with helmets and breastplates and greaves ... [while] we enjoy ... a surplus of bravery.[208]

The reference to a sense of nation would seem somewhat premature, though perhaps reflects the widespread nature of support for her, while the comment she goes on to make, to the effect that the Romans are cowards because they wear armour, would seem downright tragically silly – if, of course, she made any such comments. (In this supposed speech she also goes on to refer to the fact that armour makes the Romans less mobile, which is true and something Caesar himself had remarked upon, but then goes on further to say that the

Romans find it very difficult to cross rivers, which is again tragically far from the truth.[209])

Dio also provides us with the only known description of Boudica. In a remark indicative of widespread (Greco-)Roman male attitudes towards women, he tells the reader that she was 'possessed of greater intelligence than often belongs to women',[210] and then moves to a physical description:

> In stature she was very tall, in appearance most terrifying, in the glance of her eye most fierce, and her voice was harsh; a great mass of the tawniest hair fell to her hips; around her neck was a large golden necklace [torc]; and she wore a tunic of diverse colours over which a mantle was fastened with a brooch. This was her invariable attire.[211]

It is likely that for Dio, and no doubt most (Greco-)Roman males, Boudica was the embodiment not just of the Barbaric Other, but the Barbaric Female Other. He was by no means alone among his contemporaries in making disparaging comments about women, and indeed the fact it was a woman who was in such a prominent position in the British resistance was a source of puzzlement and potential embarrassment to the Romans. Elsewhere, in this regard, Dio states: 'All this ruin [the revolt and its destruction] was brought upon the Romans by a woman, a fact which in itself caused them the greatest shame'.[212]

Another Roman male who may have held women in low esteem (as suggested, for example, in various alleged speeches to his men) was the governor, whose role was in practice largely military and who was, apart from the procurator, the other major Roman power-holder in Britain. His name was Suetonius Paulinus (Paullinus), an experienced and successful general considered hard but efficient. Paulinus was at the time on campaign with the bulk of the Roman forces, almost as far away from Camulodunum as it was possible to achieve in Britain (minus Scotland), and that was the Isle of Mona, present-day Anglesey.[213] It was perhaps a mixed blessing for Boudica that he was away, for though she could benefit from his absence, she could probably have benefitted from joining forces with the many anti-Roman Britons whom he was about to subdue – especially Druids, for Mona was a major Druidic base, but it was also a refuge for many freedom fighters in general.

It is possible, as some historians suggest,[214] that this 'double eruption' of trouble for the Romans in such geographically widespread areas may have been planned and coordinated by the Druids, but there is no firm evidence for this and personally, I do not support the idea.[215] Tactically, had the Druids planned to draw the Romans to northwest Wales as a diversion (or respond constructively to an advance by them), it would not seem to make sense for the Britons to end up pinned down on an island from which escape was limited (but to which access would prove no problem to the Romans, as they had demonstrated in many earlier water-crossings). The argument for coordination would be greatly strengthened had it been that the British forces, centring on the local Ordovices, used their geographical knowledge to their advantage and kept leading the Romans a merry chase through the wilds of Snowdonia, as Caratacus had done (albeit ultimately unsuccessfully) just nine years earlier. As it was, on Mona they risked annihilation of a significant body of fighting Britons by the militarily superior Romans. That would not seem to be smart, regardless of whether it was part of a plan or not.

However, by way of possible mitigation, Mona was not only a spiritual home, but also a source of significant copper ores and the granary of the Ordovices,[216] and it may have been that the Druids felt they simply had to be there to defend the grain in particular – especially if, as seems a possibility, there had been a famine and grain was in scarce supply.[217] But by the same token, of course, the resources of copper and grain may have been another factor in Paulinus's interest in seizing the island.

Unfortunately for the Druids, but not unexpectedly to an objective observer, the result was effectively annihilation. Tacitus states that the Roman soldiers were initially alarmed at the fearsome appearance and wild yelling of those on Mona, who appear to have included women fighters:

> On the shore stood the opposing army of armed warriors, while between the ranks dashed women, in black attire like the Furies, with hair dishevelled, waving brands. All around, the Druids, lifting up their hands to heaven, and pouring forth dreadful imprecations, scared our soldiers by the unfamiliar sight.[218]

However, Roman discipline, aided by exhortations from Paulinus such as 'not to quail before a troop of frenzied women',[219] presently took over and they crossed to the nearby island by a combination of fording, swimming, and the use of flat-bottomed boats.[220] They soon prevailed, 'smiting down all resistance, and wrapping the foe in the flames of his own brands'.[221] Many Britons were killed, and many more enslaved. It was a major blow for Druidism as well as for Britain.

So, by what I believe to be chance – Tacitus writes that it was an act of pity by the gods[222] – there was little resistance to Boudica's army. The residents of Camulodunum appealed to Catus Decianus for help, but he sent a mere 200 lightly-armed soldiers to join the 'small force' (probably a few hundred) already there.[223] The town's defences too had been built over some time ago as the centre expanded. Prospects did not look good for the townspeople, who comprised both Romans and those Britons who, perhaps in some cases willingly, lived and worked with them. Though we should not forget that the Iceni themselves – and certainly their king and queen – would have belonged in principle to that latter 'cooperative' category till very recently, as they were a client kingdom, it was still possibly the case that in the eruption of anti-Roman sentiment, any Britons perceived as still pro-Roman, even kinfolk, might expect worse retaliatory treatment than the Romans themselves.

It would seem to me very likely that, realising the odds were against them, the great majority of inhabitants, Roman and British, fled. Many Britons, no doubt, headed north to join Boudica's army. This would surely not have been unexpected, for we have already seen that the British residents of Camulodunum were sorely put upon by the Romans. Dio refers to a 'betrayal' in the sacking of the town and Tacitus to 'secret accomplices in the revolt' living in Camulodunum,[224] suggesting that significant defections to Boudica's forces did indeed take place – perhaps a mix of planned and spontaneous, some prior to the attack and some during it.

Tacitus, in a rather confusing passage, states that these 'secret accomplices' hindered defence plans, with the result that 'neither fosse nor rampart was constructed'. He then goes on immediately to say that 'nor had they removed their old men and women', and that 'surprised, as it were, in the midst of peace, they were surrounded by an immense host of barbarians'.[225] The use of 'they' is a bit vague and potentially confusing, but more importantly, it is puzzling that they – whoever they be – should be surprised at all, for a request for reinforcements had already been sent to Catus Decianus, and his men, few as they were, had duly arrived, indicating a reasonable passage of time. And surely, even allowing for poor communications, a force of the size and composition of Boudica's could not move undetected, unreported, and unmonitored through the countryside. Perhaps we should conclude that the secret accomplices simply did their best to give false reassurances to the Romans and then struck from within once they saw the arrival of Boudica's force.

Tacitus goes on to refer to burning and plundering, but interestingly does not – at least at this point – specifically mention slaughter.[226] The burning of the town is graphically evidenced by a still-visible layer of red ash, along with melted glass, testimony to the heat and extent of the flames. Statues were defaced[227] and non-flammable buildings demolished where possible. The new stone temple to Claudius was one such non-flammable building and Tacitus tells us simply (and again without mentioning slaughter) that 'the temple where the soldiers had assembled was stormed after a two days' siege'.[228] He does not provide details of the storming, unfortunately. Given the nature of the building, with its thick stone walls and very probably a bronze door with sturdy bolts, it has been suggested that this may have been achieved by means of scaling the walls and removing the roof tiles.[229] This is of course possible, but would it have taken two days? (Though it might have been two days before someone hit on the idea.) I personally favour a determined chiselling away at the wall beside one of the doors to unhinge it – a recognised weak spot in assaults on buildings.

Figure 1.6   A (replica) bronze head of Claudius, believed to be from the statue of him destroyed in the sacking of Camulodunum. (Courtesy of Colchester Museum.)

It is also possible that civilians too were inside and that all within were slaughtered, though I repeat that Tacitus does not say so.

Camulodunum may have had a population of around 15,000 and estimates of its casualties have sometimes been put in the many thousands (even 15,000) – including indirectly by Tacitus, who refers to the total who 'fell' among 'citizens and allies' at the three sites Boudica was to attack as being, 'it appears', around 70,000, which is surely exaggerated even if it included other supposed victims along the way.[230] These figures probably reflect fairly accurately the combined population of these three sites and perhaps Tacitus just assumed all were slaughtered, since he refers to Boudica's forces throughout being 'bent on slaughter' and not taking prisoners.[231]

However, while I may again be accused of selectivity, since I do accept other figures and information from Tacitus elsewhere, the idea of a massive death toll of this magnitude seems most unlikely to me, for, as mentioned above, the slow pace of Boudica's advance, on Camulodunum and her other targets alike, would have given ample time for news to spread and people to flee, notwithstanding any obfuscatory actions by the 'secret accomplices'. Vanessa Collingridge is similarly of the view that the inhabitants of Camulodunum had sufficient warning of the attack for Catus Decianus to send his reinforcements.[232] Further evidence to support this scenario of ample time to permit flight by the residents is the apparent dearth of household possessions in the ashes,[233] suggesting either a totally rapacious pillaging by Boudica's forces or, more likely in my view, a removal of the items by the owners before those forces arrived. Nor should we forget, with regard to flight by the townspeople, that whereas Boudica's forces would have had to travel over fairly rough roads, there was a very good road between Camulodunum and Londinium.

Moreover, a very important but seemingly often overlooked point is that there is no evidence of mass slaughter in terms of skeletal remains. In fact, as Collingridge points out, there is a remarkable absence of such evidence with not a single body found despite intensive archaeological investigation, indicating that the idea of mass slaughter is almost certainly an exaggeration on the part of the classical commentators.[234] As the saying goes, 'absence of evidence is not evidence of absence',[235] and the fact that no evidence of mass slaughter has been found so far does not mean categorically that such evidence never will be, but it does raise suspicions.

Could all remains have been completely incinerated by the intense heat? Unlikely, I feel, because not all parts of the city would have been subjected to the same intensity of flame and heat. Would the Romans have come back and cremated all the alleged many thousands of corpses (including those of the Britons), as Antonia Fraser assumes?[236] Yes, they might have done that for a few hundred, namely those in the temple, but many thousands? More likely, in my view, is that Boudica's army entered a largely deserted town and that any slaughter was of a relatively small scale. Collingridge leaves open the possibility that mass graves may yet be found,[237] and of course this cannot be ruled out, but I personally think this unlikely too, because I do not believe there were any 'masses' around.

We should also note that it has recently become apparent that the scale of physical destruction at Camulodunum – as also at Londinium and Verulamium afterwards – may not have been as extensive as previously believed and was partial rather than total.[238] This lends support to a view that things have been greatly exaggerated. It does seem to me to be in the nature of human beings to dramatise, especially in matters of death and destruction.

The Roman response to the revolt included a southeastward march by men of the Ninth legion, stationed in the present-day Lincoln-Peterborough area and under the command of Petillius Cerialis (later a governor of Britain). The exact timing of this is not clear. Many scholars seem to assume it was in response to the sacking of Camulodunum, but I personally tend to favour Richard Hunt's view that, especially given the apparent role of the Ninth as a trouble-shooting legion, they would have reacted promptly to news of the revolt and set off well before Boudica's forces reached Camulodunum.[239] Thus, unless they had received later news *en route* that Boudica's army was heading for Camulodunum and changed their route accordingly to try to intercept them, it seems most likely that the men of the Ninth would be heading not for Camulodunum but for Boudica's base in Norfolk. However, though the location is unclear, what is clear is that Cerialis's men suffered a successful surprise attack by the Britons, who most likely were a substantial branch of Boudica's forces assigned to tracking the Ninth's movements and ambushing them. Caught by surprise, the Romans were unable to regroup into their usual formation and were badly defeated. Their infantry – probably some 2500 men – were annihilated, though Cerialis and his cavalry were able to escape back to their base, where, according to Tacitus, they were 'saved by its fortifications', indicating that the Britons had pursued them but presumably not in large numbers.[240]

The next target for Boudica was Londinium, a new town dating from around AD 48. It grew quite rapidly as a commercial centre and at the time of the revolt it was larger than Camulodunum, with a probable population of some 30,000. The centre of it was located on the site of the present-day City of London proper. Procurator Catus Decianus, realising that Boudica's ever-swelling army was now advancing on Londinium, fled to the continent.[241] He was very probably not alone, as those who had access to boats would surely have done likewise.

As mentioned earlier, Boudica's army did not progress with the efficiency of the Romans, who typically would have covered the 60 miles in no more than three days, or even possibly two. As her army slowly made its way towards Londinium, Paulinus, who had been informed by fast riders of the revolt, managed to return from the Isle of Mona to Londinium – possibly part of the way by boat – with a small elite force, presumably cavalry.[242] But it was not to be a case of the cavalry coming to the rescue. As a seasoned campaigner, Paulinus knew that under the circumstances the odds were against him and despite 'the tears and weeping of the people, as they implored his aid', he 'resolved to save the province at the expense of a single town', and ordered an evacuation.[243] He suggested that those who could should go with his men, who were now heading northwest up Watling Street (a major Roman-built road from Londinium to North Wales) to rejoin the main body of his forces returning from Mona. Other residents fled across the Thames into Roman-friendly present-day Sussex and Kent.

In a virtual repeat of the sacking of Camulodunum, Boudica and her forces presently arrived at what was surely another largely deserted town and put it to the torch. Once again, a layer of red ash is testimony to the destruction. And once again, we have on the one hand an assumption of huge casualties, but on the other hand a dearth of corpses.[244]

Some possible explanations suggested for these corporal absences are that the Romans later returned and cremated all their corpses (but would they have done this for collaborator Britons?) and/or that captives were taken off to other sites, such as woodland groves, for Druidic sacrifice.[245] There is indeed written evidence suggestive of some such sacrifices. Cassius Dio writes, with regard to the sacking of the (unnamed) towns on which 'indescribable slaughter was wreaked':

> Those who were taken captive by the Britons were subjected to every known form of outrage. The worst and most bestial atrocity committed by their captors was the following. They hung up naked the noblest and most distinguished women and then cut off their breasts and sewed them to their mouths, in order to make the victims appear to be eating them; afterwards they impaled the women on sharp skewers run lengthwise through the entire body. All this they did to the accompaniment of sacrifices, banquets and wanton behaviour, not only in all their other sacred places, but particularly the grove of Andate [a Celtic goddess of victory].[246]

Given that equally horrific torturings and killings have indisputably occurred even in modern times, and that skewering was a not uncommon practice long before Vlad the Impaler, and moreover given the specific particularity detailed by Dio, it is possible that some such event took place in reality and not just in his imagination of the Barbaric Other. It could indeed in particular have happened to the elite females, as Dio indicates, and especially Roman elites, though he does not indicate whether they were Romans or Britons or both. However, we should not overlook the fact that Boudica herself was an elite female, British but till recently seemingly 'doing very nicely' under Roman support. If she in any way participated in or condoned this atrocity – and one could extend this to include all the alleged mass killings of Britons – it would surely say something decidedly unappealing and unheroic about her, even taking into account her rough treatment by the Romans and a natural wish for revenge. Or was she just a product of her times, as some have suggested? As Antonia Fraser observes, Boudica seems 'curiously' to have 'remained remarkably free of the taint of atrocity'.[247] I very much agree. She is seen as the aggrieved victim fighting for justice and freedom and even somehow embodying purity and righteousness. But we should surely not distance her from atrocity while at the same time associating her with leadership of her forces. If her forces did these terrible deeds, however much she may be seen as a product of her times, then she must surely bear some responsibility even if she herself was not directly involved in them – another point made by Fraser with which I entirely agree.[248]

However, as I have suggested before, one has to question just how much she was in actual command. And one has to question the numbers. Could sacrifice really have been the fate for so many thousands of people? Logistics alone suggest otherwise. And what became of the males and non-elite females? Do we assume they were disposed of by other less-noteworthy 'forms of outrage'?

Next in line for sacking was Verulamium, present-day St Albans, lying on Watling Street. It is not clear whether Boudica had planned this from the outset or, perhaps more likely, it was a later decision, reflecting her belief that she would have to confront Paulinus and his men at some stage, preferably sooner rather than later while the momentum was in her favour, and was now heading up Watling Street to engage him, along which route Verulamium happened to lie. Once again the pace appears slow, with nothing to suggest any attempt at a swift and efficient implementation of some plan. Tacitus remarks somewhat contemptuously that her followers, who 'delighted in plunder and were indifferent to all else, passed by the fortresses with military garrisons, and attacked whatever offered most to the spoiler, and was unsafe for defence'.[249] One imagines the wagons following her forces would already have been full of plunder and one also suspects that Boudica's followers, as they went slowly northwest, burning British farms along the way, might have been settling old tribal scores. The Trinovantes in particular would probably have found some satisfaction in attacking the property of their old enemies, the Catuvellauni, in whose territory Verulamium lay and for whom it was a major centre.

By now Paulinus had sent word to the Second legion, based in present-day Exeter, to join forces with him. Its commander, Poenius Postumus, however, did not do so – Tacitus refers to his having 'contrary to all military usage disregarded the general's orders'.[250] It may have been that an actual or potential rebellion in the southwest kept him there.[251] However, rare though it might be amongst Roman military leaders, one cannot rule out sheer reluctance to enter into a confrontation against such huge forces – Boudica's followers at this stage are given by Dio as around the 230,000 mark,[252] which would probably mean some 80,000 combatants, though these figures seem excessive (see later discussion). Postumus may also have been aware and mindful of the defeat of Cerialis. In any event, the fact that Postumus was soon to take his own life suggests a profound sense of shame (discussed presently).

Verulamium, built on the site of the old Catuvellauni capital of Verlamion, was designated a *municipium*. This was one ranking below *colonia* but it was nonetheless a very significant centre, whose leading residents could normally look forward to Roman citizenship. It was considerably Romanised, but its residents were overwhelmingly British, perhaps numbering around 15,000. More specifically, one assumes, most of the residents would have been Catuvellauni, and it is perhaps surprising, given that the Catuvellauni were so opposed to Roman presence in the past, that they do not appear to feature in Boudica's forces now opposing the Romans. The relationship between the Catuvellauni and the Trinovantes seems to have been rather up-and-down and, as suggested above, there may have been some anti-Catuvellauni tribal feeling among some of the Trinovantes with Boudica, which not only motivated them to sack the town, but may also have been a factor in the Catuvellauni not joining with

Boudica. On the other hand, the Catuvellauni may simply have felt more comfortable identifying with Rome – though how they felt as Boudica's army
approached, with no sign of Roman forces coming to their defence, may be a
different matter. (One wonders, in fact, whether Paulinus, on his way up
Watling Street, might have made the same invitation to them to join him as he
had to the residents of Londinium.)

It was more of the same when it came to the sacking – another red layer as
testimony to its burning, though this was seemingly less intense, with some
structures only half burnt. And once again, in all probability, it was a ghost town
by the time Boudica actually arrived.[253] In fact this time there was probably
more time to evacuate than in the case of Camulodunum and Londinium, since
fewer coin hoards have been discovered, suggesting the residents had more time
to escape with their wealth – unless, of course, there were fewer wealthy Britons
in Verulamium than wealthy Romans in Camulodunum and Londinium.

The whole question of slaughter versus abandonment for these three centres
is, in my view, something that really deserves more attention rather than a
widespread assumption of slaughter. It has already been observed that there is
a remarkable dearth of relevant human remains at any of the centres, but this
does not seem to have been given particular importance by many scholars and
in other cases has been viewed seemingly inconsistently. For example, Graham
Webster, widely seen as the doyen of research on Boudica and the revolt, comments on the absence of human remains (and remains of portable goods) at
Verulamium as indicating that 'it can be concluded that the inhabitants had
time to remove themselves and their portable wealth',[254] though he states elsewhere (also regarding Verulamium) that the absence of human remains is not
necessarily proof that slaughter did not take place, because 'bodies would have
been collected later and decently buried'.[255] He goes on to write that 'in two
cases [Verulamium and Londinium] large numbers must have fled, even though
the disaster at Camulodunum must have accounted for almost the entire population'.[256] And yet, when referring later to Camulodunum, he remarks that
'curiously enough, few human remains have been found of the unfortunate
people who perished in the holocaust. . . . [He refers to just one mangled skele-
ton] . . . but it can be presumed that most of the bodies would have been recov-
ered and decently cremated as an act of piety'.[257] Setting aside the issue of
whether bodies were buried or cremated, my main concern is that Webster
seems to allow for large-scale flight in two cases (Londinium and Verulamium)
but not in the third (Camulodunum). Was the element of so-called 'surprise'
really that significant in the case of Camulodunum? It has been demonstrated
that there seems to have been ample time for the inhabitants of Camulodunum
as well to flee.

Returning to our narrative, Paulinus had been able to muster some 10,000
men, mostly gathered from the Fourteenth and Twentieth legions plus some

local auxiliary cavalry.[258] Vastly outnumbered, he had to use his other resources such as experience and discipline. He chose the best site he could to try to off-set Boudica's numerical advantage and waited. Presently her forces arrived. Unfortunately, despite the monumental importance of this battle, no one knows where it took place. It seems most likely to have been further northwest along Watling Street and some scholars believe it may have been near present-day Towcester, though most favour Mancetter, just a few miles northwest of Nuneaton.[259] Mancetter was a base of the Fourteenth and also has the right general topographical features, though the area was extensively quarried in the nineteenth century and so any precise site-identification is next to impossible.

The topographical site Paulinus chose was 'a position approached by a nar-row defile, closed in at the rear by a forest',[260] which would offer protection against chariots, and facing an open plain. This would mean that Boudica's

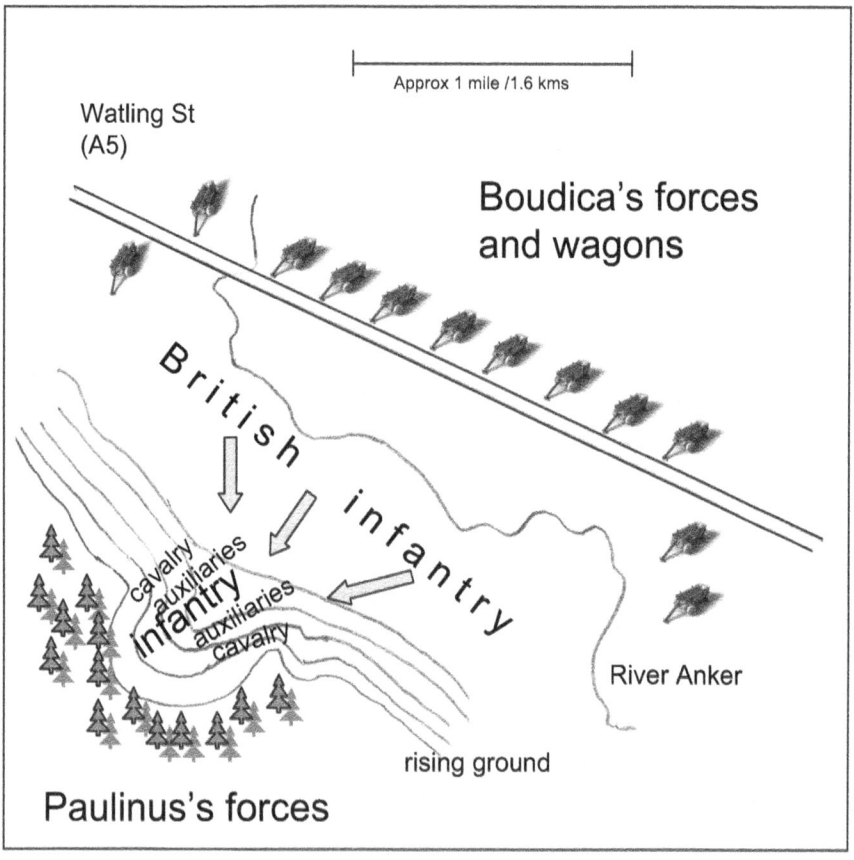

Figure 1.7 The assumed dispositions of Britons and Romans at Mancetter.

forces, though initially spread out across the plain, would, if they attacked from that position on the plain, have to funnel together to engage the Romans, meaning in turn that their numerical superiority would be in terms of depth rather than width. Webster neatly describes it as the Britons being 'forced to advance into a front of diminishing width: the greater their force, the more packed they would become'.[261] In such a face-to-face clash, with equal spread for both combatant forces, it could be assumed the Romans would have the advantage – though how long they could maintain this given the extra depth of the Britons might be another matter.

Paulinus must also have been aware that the Britons rarely made effective use of ranged weapons. Had they done so, the Romans would have been like fish in a barrel. He would have known too that they scorned armour. And he must also have known the Britons were impatient, for a patient commander, even one unskilled in the use of ranged weapons, could have waited – for days if necessary, for they had supplies enough – to draw the Romans out and thereby take away their topographical advantage. The Britons had all the time in the world and should have known through scout deployment that no other Roman forces were on their way.

And, despite the earlier successful guerilla-style attack on Cerialis's men, Paulinus would very likely have realised that Boudica (and her probable advisers) – along with many Celtic war-leaders – could hardly be considered sophisticated when it came to military tactics, at least when it came to a pitched battle. For example, he seems to have assumed that the British attack would come from the plain, despite the limitations of this, presumably because he believed the 'rash' Britons would take the most direct route to engage his men. Though one cannot be certain of the exact topography until the site is confirmed (if it ever can be), it seems likely that, given the fact it was certainly not mountainous terrain and given the large number of combatants on the Britons' side, an astute British commander could have attacked down the slopes of the defile and through the forest to the rear, as well as blocking exit to the plain. It would have meant the chariots were unusable, but, since the Britons were going to have to funnel themselves into the defile in packed conditions, the chariots were going to be ineffective anyway.

Tacitus refers to the Britons having 'a vaster host than ever had assembled' and to their 'confidently exulting' to the extent that 'they actually brought with them, to witness the victory, their wives riding in wagons'.[262] As mentioned earlier, Dio refers to a figure of 230,000, which might give around 80,000 or possibly 100,000 combatants,[263] but even with such massive numbers (though I personally believe it was a significantly lesser figure) it was by no means certain that the 'vast host' of Britons would overcome the mere 10,000 or so Roman soldiers. Indeed, Graham Webster remarks that training, discipline, and equipment – to which I would also add tactics – made a Roman force superior to any Celtic force, even if the latter had ten times as many men.[264] This would be especially so if, as seems likely, Boudica's forces had become overconfident and even more than usually rash.[265] Moreover, the drilled Romans had the ability to change their tactics very rapidly in mid-battle if necessary, using a signalling system.[266] It was a question of British quantity versus Roman quality. If the Britons were indeed going to attack from the plain – in my view foolishly – my money would be on the Romans.

Events unfolded according to the Romans' script, whereas the Britons seem to have had no script at all. In fact I believe it quite possible, if not probable, that there was a lack of consensus among Boudica's advisers and that the tactics employed were arrived at by default and aggravated by overconfidence in numerical superiority, for I find it hard to believe they could be the result of careful planning – Fraser refers euphemistically to Boudica being a typical Celt, namely 'bold', 'inspiring', but 'not calculating'.[267] Her force assembled on the plain and the two sides faced each other, the Romans some way back down the defile. Paulinus had his hardened infantry in the centre of the defile and lighter-armed auxiliaries and cavalry on the flanks, while the Britons were initially spread wide.

Tacitus, following classical convention, 'quotes' a battle-line speech by Boudica, supposedly in her chariot with her daughters. It is extremely unlikely that these were her actual words, but it is probable that she did give some verbal encouragement to her followers and possible that the gist of her words were noted by Romans or perhaps recounted later by some of the survivors. More likely, it is simply Tacitus's imagination, but, like Dio's earlier imagined speech, this still has considerable value as an indication of a Roman's perception of her situation (and one notes again a seeming focus on her womanhood).

> It is not as a woman descended from noble ancestry, but as one of the people that I am avenging lost freedom, my scourged body, the outraged chastity of my daughters. Roman lust has gone so far that not our very persons, nor even age or virginity, are left unpolluted. But heaven is on the side of a righteous vengeance; a legion which dared to fight has perished; the rest are hiding themselves in their camp, or are thinking anxiously of flight. They will not sustain even the din and the shout of so many thousands, much less our charge and our blows. If you weigh well the strength of the armies, and the causes of the war, you will see that in this battle you must conquer or die. This is a woman's resolve; as for men, they may live and be slaves.[268]

Paulinus's speech, though possibly somewhat embellished by Tacitus, is however likely to have been more accurately noted, and it was moreover a speech in substance very typical of a Roman general. We should not overlook the fact that Tacitus's future father-in-law, Agricola, may have been one of the soldiers in Paulinus's force.[269]

> There you see more women than warriors. Unwarlike, unarmed [*sic*], they will give way the moment they have recognised that sword and that courage of their conquerors, which have so often routed them. Even among many legions, it is a few who really decide the battle, and it will enhance their glory that a small force should earn the renown of an entire army. Only close up the ranks, and having discharged your javelins, then with shields and swords continue the work of bloodshed and destruction, without a thought of plunder. When once the victory has been won, everything will be in your power.[270]

The Britons, whose force very likely did include a number of women warriors, presently started to advance into the defile – some might say the jaws of death – while the Romans stood firm. Roman soldiers each had two *pila* (javelins), with specially weakened metal shafts to prevent their reuse by the

Figure 1.8   Roman equipment (replicas) including the eagle standard and *pila*, designed with a brittle neck in order to prevent reuse. (Courtesy of the Roman Army Museum [Carvoran] and the Vindolanda Trust.)

enemy, and they discharged these in quick succession as the Britons came within 30 yards or so. Being densely packed, it was now the Britons, who seemingly entirely through their own tactics, became the fish in the barrel, and it is likely that almost all the 20,000 or so *pila* found a mark. Why the Britons do not appear to have thrown spears – at least according to Tacitus – remains a mystery.

In a tight wedge shape the Romans now moved down into the Britons using the bosses on their shields to push them back and knock them down at close quarters, and their short *gladius* stabbing swords to dispatch the unarmoured foe – typically stabbing not the individual immediately facing them, but the person to that (British) individual's immediate left, whose shield would normally be in his left hand, thus exposing his right side to a diagonal thrust. The longer, cutting swords of the Britons would not have been able to be employed properly in such packed conditions.[271] Push, stab, advance – the Roman army's tried and usually true *modus operandi* proved effective once again and the Britons started to retreat. As they came down to flatter ground the Roman cavalry on the wings cut down potential flankers or escapers. It is possible some chariots were used at the rear of the retreating Britons, probably by Boudica and other leaders attempting to exhort their forces, but they could hardly have been effective.[272] In fact, vehicles less mobile than chariots were soon to present an obstacle – and a dreadful obstacle at that – to those retreating. These were the baggage wagons, carelessly drawn up in such a way that they seriously blocked any retreat, which evidently the Britons had simply not considered a likelihood. These spectators now, like the combatants, became easy prey for the Roman eagle. Tacitus remarks:

> The rest [of the Britons] turned their back in flight, and flight proved difficult, because the surrounding wagons had blocked retreat. Our soldiers spared not to slay even the women, while the very beasts of burden, transfixed by the missiles, swelled the piles of bodies.[273]

In short, it was a massacre. Tacitus, whose figures are probably more reliable than Dio's, refers to around 80,000 British dead, as opposed to a mere 400 Roman dead with as many again wounded.[274] Allowing for escapees – for surely the Romans would not have worried unduly about pursuing the fleeing camp-followers, though few actual combatants would have been allowed to escape – this would suggest the realistic British figures were possibly something like 40,000 dead combatants out of around 50,000, and 40,000 dead camp-followers out of around 100,000 (allowing for some children as well as wives being present), giving a total fatality rate of more than half of a body of 150,000 persons (as opposed to Dio's earlier mention of 230,000). Though some only lightly wounded Britons would obviously have been able to flee, perhaps with assistance, I do not believe there would have been any significant number of more seriously wounded left alive on the battlefield. Though the above is merely speculation on my part, it must be a reality that the British fatality figure was truly massive.[275]

What of Boudica? Tacitus tells us that she poisoned herself; Cassius Dio says that she 'fell sick and died' (not necessarily incompatible with taking poison), being buried with honours at some unknown location.[276] One is again inclined to take Tacitus's version, though it is unclear whether she took the poison at the battle-site or later elsewhere. I personally feel the former to be more likely, and that moreover Dio was probably right in that her corpse was taken away and given a special burial. This may have been difficult given the dreadful final scenes of the battle, but one feels that the surviving Britons would have tried very hard to prevent the Romans obtaining her corpse. It is always possible that both Tacitus and Dio were wrong and she just ended her days as one of the battle fatalities, but one suspects that had this been the case, the Romans would have made strenuous efforts to identify her corpse both as a trophy and to ensure she really was dead. Tacitus makes no such mention, which in itself suggests the Romans knew something of her death.

As to her daughters, there is no mention or any other indication as to what became of them. Antonia Fraser is of the view that Boudica probably gave them poison,[277] but I am not so sure. In my view Boudica would have had them with her, not least as symbols of Roman oppression, but probably kept them well away from the battle, among the spectators. I believe they would have been taken away to safety once it was realised that Boudica was defeated, and their identities kept permanently concealed to avoid Roman persecution of them.

As an after-note, soon afterwards the Romans brought in an extra 7000 men from the Rhine and this is sometimes seen as an indication that Roman casualties might have been higher than Tacitus stated, but these extra troops would have included replacements for Cerialis's men lost earlier. One definite Roman fatality, however, though not a direct battle-casualty as such, was Poenius Postumus, who fell on his sword, presumably out of shame.[278] Other casualties – in a figurative sense – included the procurator, Catus Decianus, and the victorious governor, Suetonius Paulinus. Both were soon replaced. Decianus was clearly not the man for the job and was replaced by Julius Classicianus, who recommended to Nero that a more conciliatory mode of governance in Britain would be more appropriate henceforth, and that the tough-minded Paulinus was not suitable for this. Among other things, soon after Boudica's defeat Paulinus had systematically laid waste to the territories of tribes participating in the rebellion, and even of some neutrals, seemingly driven by a wish for vengeance.[279] Presently, despite his great victory and obvious military talents,[280] he was replaced as governor by Petronius Turpilianus.

1.8   Thereafter

There are two paths we might briefly follow in the wake of Boudica's failed revolt – the memory or image of Boudica, as recorded in history (or not, as the case may be), and the remaining Roman occupation. Let us consider Boudica first.

1.8.1   Boudica in history

Boudica is now a very well known name – after being corrected from the earlier 'Boadicea', which was a transcription error for Tacitus's 'Boudicca', which itself should have been 'Boudica'.[281] It is synonymous with fighting spirit and the desire for freedom, and she is a great symbol both of Britain and of the strength of womanhood. Her most famous statue stands near the Houses of Parliament – the centre of power, as it were. It projects an image of a defiantly protective mother-figure seemingly sanitised of any connection with atrocity – or even ferocity – despite the spear in her hand, which seems perhaps to fulfil a symbolic role similar to a 'sword of freedom'.

Plantagenet Fry remarks that the appeal of the Boudica story is strong and that this is one of the reasons why legend has taken over at the expense of history.[282] Certainly, her story has been romanticised. But, with all respect to the renowned Fry, I feel he too may be somewhat under the spell of this 'larger than life' legend, for he also remarks that Boudica's rebellion is one of the most famous events in Britain's history and it has been remembered in literature and legend for nineteen centuries 'almost without interruption'.[283] It certainly has been remembered and famous in relatively recent centuries and no doubt a great many people would share his belief that Boudica's story has never faded, and is indeed a never-forgotten part of Britain's story itself. However, in reality, although from around AD 70 the Roman arena introduced the novelty of female gladiators riding in Celtic-style war chariots, almost certainly based on Boudica, after Dio's writings in the early third century, Boudica seems effectively to have been forgotten for over a thousand years, which is surely a significant interruption. It is true though that the rebellion itself lingered on better than its protagonist, albeit only fleetingly, indirectly, and precariously till the eventual rediscovery (and subsequent romanticisation) of the Boudica story.

The Roman priest-historian, Paulus Orosius, in his *Seven Books of History against the Pagans* of 418 (just after the Romans had left Britain), mentions Boudica's rebellion merely in one sentence, very indirectly, and does not give her name. He appears to be following Dio, since he too refers to just two sites, moreover unnamed, and to the slaughter of Romans and their allies.[284]

In the earliest relevant British written source, Gildas's *Concerning the Ruin and Conquest of Britain*, written c. 545, she does not merit a name either, but merely another brief indirect mention – though this time a handful of sentences, not just one. Gildas was not exactly a happy chap and his remarkable negativity towards almost everything, along with errors of fact, distorted his account. His basic criticism was that the Britons did not resist the Romans strongly enough, allowing the Romans to impose themselves on the land,[285] and that, even when there was a rebellion (under the unnamed Boudica), they capitulated far too easily. He goes on to refer, without specifying a name, to 'that deceitful lioness', and the shameful flight of the Britons when they faced the Romans.[286] He does not explain why exactly Boudica is 'deceitful', but the implication from the immediately preceding context, which refers to Roman ignorance of the imminence of a rebellion, seems to be that Gildas felt she had been doing very nicely as a client royal of the Romans, and was now betraying their support by attacking them. If so, it would indeed seem a strange interpretation of events on his part, suggesting he did not know the full story. One also notes in passing that Gildas seems to have empathised with the typical Roman male view of women as weak.

Bede, in his *Ecclesiastical History of the English People* of 731, closely follows Orosius and similarly makes only a very brief and indirect reference to the destruction of (two) cities, without naming Boudica, but he does differ here from Orosius in that he does not mention slaughter and adds that Nero almost lost Britain as a result.[287]

Early medieval historians tended to follow Bede very closely. Henry of Huntingdon, in his *History of the English* of c. 1129, is one such example, with an almost identical brief reference to just two sites being destroyed, Nero almost losing Britain, and not naming Boudica.[288] And Huntingdon's contemporary, that great romanticiser of British history, Geoffrey of Monmouth, who widely popularised King Arthur (well beyond the boundaries of any known fact), missed a golden opportunity to do a similar exercise on Boudica in his *History of the Kings of Britain* of c. 1136 – unless he was reluctant to fit in a queen among his kings.

Though Dio was still available, it was not till the early days of the Renaissance that Boudica was 'rediscovered', when the relevant books of Tacitus – or more exactly a manuscript copy of the originals – which had been in monastic obscurity till the fourteenth century, ended up in private hands and became more accessible. With the European development of printing a century later, Tacitus's account became far more widely read and by the sixteenth century Boudica was something of a fashion, not entirely unconnected with another powerful British queen in the form of Elizabeth I, and never again to be forgotten.[289] In fact, Boudica's story tied in nicely with a general revival of interest in the Celts. And in more recent times, of course, she was to have her statue, by Thomas Thornycroft, erected (1902) on the Embankment near the Houses of Parliament – though the blades on the chariot wheel-hubs, which she almost certainly did not have, are perhaps testimony to Fry's observation that legend has fleshed out the actual facts.

1.8.2 The continuing Roman presence

Moving on to the Roman presence in Britain, this was to continue for exactly another three and a half centuries, formally ending in 410 with the Romans' departure – though of course Roman influence lingered far beyond that. It is beyond the focus and scope of this book to examine these three and a half centuries in detail, but let us briefly consider some of the more significant events taking us up to 410, which will be the starting point of Part 2.

As mentioned earlier, after the immediate 'revenge attacks' by Paulinus, for some ten years there was a more conciliatory approach. However, with the appointment of Petillius Cerialis to governor in 71 – the same Cerialis who had suffered a bad defeat during Boudica's revolt – Roman policy firmed up again, perhaps not surprisingly as Cerialis would have had a point or two to prove. Moreover, he would have to prove it to an emperor who was also an old British hand, Vespasian, who had emerged successful from the chaotic year of 69 – the so-called 'year of the four emperors' following Nero's 'enforced suicide' the previous year.

Presently Rome decided to extend control further north. This was achieved (at least temporarily) under Tacitus's father-in-law Agricola, who arrived as governor in 77 (possibly 78). In his six or seven years (being reassigned in 84), he undertook no fewer than seven campaigns, extending Roman control in northern and western Britain by subduing (again, at least temporarily) rebellious elements among the Brigantes and in northern Wales and quite far north in Scotland. He achieved the latter by defeating the Caledonian warlord Calgacus at the Battle of Mons Graupius (widely believed to have taken place at Bennachie, 17 miles northwest of Aberdeen) in 83 or 84, which, according to Tacitus, resulted in 10,000 Caledonian dead for the loss of fewer than 400 Romans.[290]

However, while some Britons, especially among elites, were becoming increasingly Romanised, living Roman lifestyles, wearing Roman-style clothes, residing in Roman-style villas or Roman towns (which were growing), and with the Romans providing education for their children,[291] there was still unrest among many, particularly in the north. Even allowing for 10,000 dead at Mons Graupius, the Caledonians allegedly had some 30,000 in the field, meaning that the majority escaped and that opposition was not completely quelled. Indeed, within 25 years or so, the Romans had fallen back from a position probably somewhere near the Moray Firth to the more southerly Solway Firth.

It was here that, under Emperor Hadrian in the 120s (commenced c. 122), the well known Hadrian's Wall was constructed from coast to coast, some 74 miles in length from Bowness-on-Solway to Wallsend, to consolidate Roman territory. However, the backwards and forwards pattern continued, and after a further 20 years or so the Romans reoccupied southern Scotland and constructed another wall further north. This was the Antonine Wall (commenced c. 142), after Emperor Antoninus, and was not as solidly constructed or fortified as

Hadrian's. It too ran coast to coast, from the Clyde to the Firth of Forth, and at 37 miles it was exactly half the length of Hadrian's. Perpetuating the approximately quarter-century cycle, it was abandoned in 163, and Hadrian's Wall once again became the boundary marker. But from now the cycle was to be broken and Hadrian's Wall was to remain as such, despite a number of Pictish raids in which it was overrun, till the Roman occupation ceased two and a half centuries later. Though fortified, its function was not simply for military defence reasons: it also served as a border control.

In the early years of the third century, specifically 208–11, there was another push north under the personal command of the famously hard Emperor Severus. He did indeed expand Roman control further into Scotland, but died at York in 211, and the territory he had just acquired was abandoned by his successor.

Though much of the Roman Empire was in turmoil during the third century, in Britain life was relatively peaceful for most of the century, despite occasional revolts such as in 276,[292] and presently Roman forces were reduced in size. However, towards the end of the century a number of forts were built around the southeast coast (in addition to pre-existing ones). They may perhaps have been built initially to guard against raiders, who were prevalent in the Channel

Figure 1.9 Hadrian's Wall at Housesteads. The wall continues along the ridge in the distance. (Courtesy of English Heritage.)

at this time, but the main purpose may instead have been to facilitate troop movement and trade between Britain and the continent, as well as to support the Roman fleet. Unfortunately details remain unclear.[293] In the fourth century the coastal forts were extended into the northeast too, and by the late fourth century they were very likely being used, at least in part, for defensive purposes, even if that had not been their original purpose. Eventually these raiders, who appear by this stage to have included many Anglo-Saxons, became a sufficiently significant problem to warrant the high-ranking appointment of a Count of the Saxon Shore (with responsibility for the forts), though the term is not found till 408. However, it is not clear that the Anglo-Saxons themselves were raiding as early as the late third century, though they certainly were by the late fourth.

The raiders in the Channel were instrumental in an interesting episode at the end of the third century. Under the reign of Diocletian, a Menapian (a Belgic tribe) called Carausius was given responsibility for safeguarding the Channel. In 287, however, he rebelled against Diocletian and declared himself emperor, ruling in parts of northern Gaul and Britain. He was soon assassinated by a follower, Allectus, in 293, who then took the 'imperial' title for himself. However, Allectus was killed in 296 by forces led by Constantius Chlorus (who later became a 'more recognised' emperor). Britain then returned to 'normalcy', though in the final stages of Roman occupation there were to be several other self-proclaimed emperors from amongst Roman military leaders based in Britain.

Constantius visited Britain again in 305, accompanied by his son Constantine, but died at York in 306. His son was immediately proclaimed emperor. Known as Constantine I the Great, he was to be one of Rome's most famous and powerful emperors. He was to make Christianity Rome's state religion and to rebuild Constantinople.

Constantine's own religious beliefs appear rather ambivalent, for though he became a believer in the Christian God, whom he credited for a victory in 312 at Milvian Bridge over a rival, Maxentius, he continued for some time to also worship the Sun.[294] Nonetheless he proved a great champion of the Christian cause. The Christians' own position in the Roman Empire to this point was also somewhat ambivalent, for while they had gradually gained acceptance they still suffered occasional persecution. However, with Constantine's huge support, in combination with a growing need for a unified ideology and a religion that could function in a personalised, consoling capacity,[295] Christianity was fully legitimised and moreover substantially promoted. Wealth in the form of patronage and donations and suchlike was transferred from pagan temples to Christian churches. Churches were given great assets, including land, along with rights formerly conferred only on magistrates, and prominent Christians were similarly given rights and privileges. Importantly, this meant that the Church acquired a new socio-political status, and power-holders – even Roman governors – had to take the Church into consideration in policy-making and other issues.[296]

As one might expect, while many new converts were sincere, there were also those who saw the political and more immediately attainable advantages in being demonstrably Christian.[297] Accordingly, while there had been a number of Christians in Britain prior to the fourth century, such as at Verulamium, it was really from the fourth century that Britain saw a steady increase in the practice of – and in many cases actual belief in – Christianity, though clearly old beliefs and practices did not disappear overnight.[298] Christianity seems to have been especially strong among the power-holders – the villa-dwellers – though of course their beliefs would also have significant effect on those within their sphere of influence.

At a more earthly level, the fourth century also saw a reinforcement of troops in the north – tough ones too, to judge from a comment by the early sixth century writer Zosimus, on the year 386, that they were the most stubborn and violent of soldiers.[299] This was in no small part due to the fact that the Pictish tribes, including the Caledones, had united and constituted a significant threat. A number of clashes took place over some years, especially in the latter half of the century. In fact, describing the years around 360, the contemporary historian, Ammianus Marcellinus, refers to the Scots and Picts breaking their promise to keep peace and repeatedly causing destruction near the frontier.[300]

Despite a number of defeats the Picts in particular remained a 'barbarian threat' – indeed till quite a few decades after the Roman departure early in the fifth century – with a particularly serious attack in 367 in alliance with the Gaelic Scotti and the Saxons, an attack that saw a significant incursion well south of Hadrian's Wall. This represented just one of a number of barbarian threats facing Rome at this time.

It should be noted, however, that despite the disturbances of the fourth century, Britain was still producing and indeed exporting copious amounts of grain, suggesting at least enough stability for the cultivation of this. Zosimus refers to huge quantities – 800 ships' worth, moreover making repeated trips – being shipped to Germany in the year 358.[301] However, there is some evidence that the climate turned colder and wetter towards the end of the century, lasting for some centuries thereafter,[302] and that this may presently have affected harvests.

As mentioned earlier, in the final years of Roman occupation Britain saw a number of emperors proclaimed either by themselves or by their armies. This was a time when rule of the Roman Empire made for a very confused picture, with a basic division between East (based in Constantinople) and West (Rome or Milan), and with phases of plural emperors and/or 'semi-emperors' known as *Augusti* and below them *Caesars* (typically two in each category, though sometimes up to four). One of the better-known self-proclaimed emperors was Magnus Maximus, a general based in Britain who claimed the title in 383 and held it for five years. Unfortunately, in an ultimately unsuccessful attempt to gain control of the empire, he took a large number of soldiers with him to the continent who never returned. Another was Constantine III, who was proclaimed emperor by his army in Britain in 407 (holding the title till 411), and like Maximus, promptly took his men from Britain to fight in Spain, leaving the country vulnerable to raiders. The Britons appear to have expelled his administration in 409 or 410, thereby, in theory at least, coming under the rule of Honorius (emperor 395–423), who had initially treated Constantine III as a legitimate colleague but soon came to see him as a usurper (and had him executed in 411).

The combination of Christianity and barbarians was, in the view of the great eighteenth century scholar Edward Gibbon, fatal for Rome. The message from his monumental work *The History of the Decline and Fall of the Roman Empire* (1776–1788) was essentially that barbarian hordes had grown too powerful for a Rome that had had its fighting spirit weakened in part by Christianity, with its pacifism and belief in a better life in heaven than the here-and-now. Certainly, during the fourth century Rome was beset by barbarian attacks and often resorted to buying the barbarians off.

Barbarian aggression towards Rome and its empire became more intense in the early years of the fifth century, especially from late 406. Eventually, in August 410, Rome was sacked by the Visigoths under Alaric. The general view is that it seems to have been this event in particular that brought about the end of Roman rule in Britain. Around this time Emperor Honorius famously sent letters to the cities in Britain, urging them to fend for themselves.[303] This would suggest that the Romans took the initiative in leaving Britain and even perhaps that the Britons had requested help from Honorius, which, under the circumstances, with Rome and its empire beset by barbarians, he was unable to provide. But it is also possible that he sent the letters a year or so earlier, perhaps as a result of an approach to him following Constantine's removal of the army (especially given the barbarian threat to a now vulnerable Britain), and that the Britons reacted to his letters by expelling the remaining Romans.[304] This would mean that the end of Roman rule was not so much a case of Roman withdrawal but a British rejection of it, driven by frustration. Indeed, writing of 409, Zosimus states that because Constantine took the army to Spain it allowed the Germanic barbarians a free rein, of which they took advantage to make repeated raids on Britain and parts of Gaul, in turn leading the inhabitants of those places to revolt against Rome and take defence of their territories into their own hands, expelling the Roman magistrates.[305]

The 'expulsion interpretation' is further supported by the *History of the Britons*, widely attributed to 'Nennius', an early ninth century Welsh historian whose writings are at times clearly erroneous and fanciful, but who cannot be wholly dismissed. Writing of the final days of Roman rule after four centuries, he tells us that the Britons despised Roman authority in Britain, took over the government, and massacred Roman deputies.[306]

Whether through withdrawal, or expulsion, or a mixture of both, by the end of 410 the Romans had left – though it is probable that some 'Britannicised' individuals (such as Ambrosius Aurelianus discussed in Part 2) stayed on, most likely in a private or informal capacity. It may have been Rome's intention to return to Britain at some point but that was not to happen.

What did happen next is the subject of Part 2. But, before concluding Part 1, let us first consider some questions about the Roman arrival in and conquest of Britain, with particular regard to the roles of folly and fortune.

1.9   Why did things happen the way they did?

(1) *In 55 BC, could the Britons have prevented Caesar from crossing to Britain?*

The short answer is almost certainly 'no'. It would have been effectively impossible for the Britons to have dissuaded Caesar from making his first crossing to Britain. His primary motive appears to have been political ambition, which would be a very hard thing to resist. Moreover his claim that the Britons were aiding the Gauls and needed to be punished, while no doubt to some extent a pretext to circumvent the need for Senatorial approval for any conquest, was nonetheless valid. A further motive was very probably an assessment of Britain's material resources, of which he would have been aware. An overarching factor would no doubt have been simply to 'have a look' to see what the country was like, to assess how easily it might be conquered and exploited.

The British delegates who met him in Gaul could in theory have tried to assassinate him or to sabotage his boats, but this would have been suicidal on their part and moreover they may not have believed he would actually send a force to Britain.

(2) *In 55 BC, could the Britons have prevented Caesar from actually landing and establishing a beachhead?*

In my view, the short answer this time is 'yes'. The Romans were not experienced sailors and many of their vessels were not the most suitable. Nor, in my view, was the landing site the most suitable – certainly not with regard to safe anchorage. The Britons had time to assemble significant forces and had the terrain on their side, though the Romans had superior weaponry. Nevertheless the Britons were far more mobile than the Romans and should have been able to pick groups off more effectively than they appear to have done. From the moment they first heard, through Commius and others, of Caesar's idea of crossing to Britain the Britons should have learnt something of their potential enemy. In particular they should have been aware of the Romans' fear of the Ocean and of Britain as a place beyond the edge of the known world and exploited this nervousness. A more concerted and determined resistance would surely have cracked the nerves of the Romans, who at the moment of landing (and beyond) were vulnerable both physically and psychologically, despite their loyalty to their commander.

(3) *In 55 BC, even after the Romans had established a beachhead, could the Britons have driven them off and/or destroyed them?*

Again, the answer must be 'yes'. Even after the Romans had established a beachhead the Britons should have attacked this promptly and vigorously (and repeatedly if necessary) and given them no time to settle. The Romans had no cavalry with which to pursue them (except for a very few from Commius) and there should have been relentless cavalry raids by the Britons. Moreover, the Britons could perhaps have used vessels of their own to attack the Roman fleet while at anchor. Coordinated attacks could thus have been made from the front by cavalry and the rear by British vessels. There should certainly have been a more obvious attempt to threaten the Roman vessels, which were effectively the invaders' lifeline at that moment. Attacks on the vessels would have significantly distracted those defending the beachhead.

In terms of amphibious warfare (the conveyance of military forces to hostile territory),[307] which is what Caesar – or any other pre-modern force attacking any island – was waging, a key response is to disable the means of conducting such warfare, namely the vessels. This would not prevent an already landed force carrying out attacks nor would it necessarily prevent subsequent vessels arriving, but it would have devastating effect on morale, making troops feel cut off, and this would especially have been the case with the Romans in Britain who already felt they were beyond the edge of the world.

It is particularly hard to understand why, after the storm had damaged so many of the Roman vessels and driven away reinforcements, the Britons did not try more resolutely to finish off the rest. The destructive storm was on the one hand a matter of luck, but at the same time it was aided by surprising folly by Caesar, who, surely aware of the probable deterioration of the weather from this relatively late point in the season, should have ensured more sheltered anchorage for his ships. If he was not aware of any such anchorage, which seems possible, it could be argued he should not have made the expedition in the first place. To a superstitious people like the Celts it must surely have seemed, at least to some of them, as though they had spurned Fortune, which had shown them the way with the destruction of the Roman ships.

The Britons again seemed to spurn Fortune when the Romans fell into their trap, with the Seventh legion going out to cut grain. And again Fortune was helped by another surprising act of folly by Caesar, who should have brought more supplies and prevented the need for foraging. Why the Britons, according to Caesar, broke off their attack remains a mystery. And if Cassius Dio was correct and the Britons did actually cause very significant Roman casualties then the Britons had even less excuse for not having finished the others off.

There was eventually a relatively concerted attack on the Roman base-camp, which the Romans survived, but unfortunately few details are provided and it is therefore hard to comment on British tactics. Not only were the Britons repelled, they suffered the indignity of having buildings in the area being burnt. This means that some of the Roman forces must have left the base – or at least the 30 or so horsemen from Commius. But it is remarkable that those who left the base, on horse or foot, were not picked off, especially as this was a major function of British chariots.

Overall, though Caesar probably painted a more positive picture for those back in Rome than was the actual case, one still has to shake one's head in disbelief over the outcome of the 55 BC expedition. While it is true that the Romans hardly covered themselves in glory and were seemingly glad to get out, they should never have enjoyed the limited success that they did. They should have been sent packing or been destroyed. The expedition was poorly organised by Caesar's standards, he made mistakes, and the weather was seriously against him. The Britons seemed to have had so much in their favour, including the psychological edge: they were fighting against invaders who threatened their homes and freedom, whereas the invaders were having to fight in a land which didn't really belong in the world as they knew it. One can only assume that on the British side it was a combination of inferior weapons, inferior tactics, lack of cohesion, and lack of determination (perhaps indeed that Celtic fickleness referred to earlier). In my view the biggest problem was very likely the lack of cohesion, especially at leadership level. The Romans probably couldn't believe their luck in escaping with their lives. They probably also came to the conclusion, by virtue of the very fact they did escape with their lives, that the Britons were not particularly strong opposition, thereby paving the way for Caesar's return.

(4) *In 54 BC, could the Britons have prevented Caesar from crossing to Britain?*

As was the case with the 55 BC expedition, again the short answer is 'no' – in fact, more emphatically so. Caesar was in a much more determined frame of mind and could not be stopped except by assassination. He knew his previous expedition had not been exactly glorious and he would want to make amends, and he probably realised that Fortune had played with him – damaging his ships in the first place (though it was partly his fault) and then letting him off the hook by seemingly bewitching the Britons into wasting opportunities. But he probably concluded, from the self-evident fact he was still alive, that most of the gods were on his side. He also knew the Britons were beatable. And once again, to avoid any possible recrimination from Rome about an unauthorised conquest, he was able, through the non-payment of promised tribute by many of the Britons, to claim it was another punitive expedition and not a conquest as such.

(5) In 54 BC, could the Britons have prevented Caesar from actually landing and establishing a beachhead?

This time, unlike the case the previous year, the answer has to be very probably 'no'. Though the Britons would surely have been aware of Caesar's intentions, given the visible and reportable activity of preparing a large fleet, and would have had time to assemble, they may have been deterred by the scale of the force being assembled just across the Channel. Caesar's forces were indeed much bigger this time, and included cavalry. Many of the soldiers had crossed the previous year and were familiar with the area and with British tactics and fighting ability (or lack of it as the case may be). They had presumably also overcome their fear of 'the land beyond the Ocean', and would have reassured those crossing for the first time. Caesar too had learnt from the previous year and improved the manoeuvrability of his boats and also made disembarkation easier through lowering the freeboard. He had also set off earlier in the season. Moreover, though he had sent Commius the previous year and this had not been successful, this time he could count a little more reliably on some British support and very probably a guide in Mandubratius. Even though he again chose the same seemingly less than optimal landing site, the Britons would almost certainly have been overwhelmed had they attempted to fight on the beaches. It is not surprising that the landing was unopposed for one imagines the Britons, having confirmed the size of the invaders' fleet, would have preferred to pick off Romans inland using guerilla tactics and avoiding a pitched battle if at all possible.

(6) In 54 BC, even after the Romans had established a beachhead, could the Britons have driven them off and/or destroyed them?

This is more difficult to answer. All things considered, the answer would probably have to be 'no', but not as an absolute given, for had the Britons made decisive inroads into Roman strength early on, it may just have dissuaded the Romans from pursuing their incursion further. The Britons' best opportunity was when Caesar, with typical but seemingly rash use of speed, marched his men inland through the night immediately after landing, after they had already spent a largely sleepless night in the crossing and must have been weary. Admittedly it was a large force he took with him – the bulk of his men – but by the same token, the more men he took with him, the more he again left his ships relatively vulnerable. Had the Britons been more alert and more organised they could have attacked the Roman vessels at this point. Similarly, the Britons could have attacked immediately after the storm that came a couple of days later, again wrecking ships, except for the fact that by this stage a significant British force had already been defeated at Bigbury, which proved useless as a defence, as had also their resistance at the Stour River engagement. The Britons could not have known, of course, that a storm was in the offing, but had they kept to guerilla tactics rather than foolishly taking on the Romans in a set engagement or equally foolishly retreating to a fixed defensive site, they would have had men enough to launch an attack.

Another opportunity for the Britons was during their guerilla attack on the Romans when the tribune, Laberius, was killed, before the engagement at the River Thames. It was clear that Caesar was exasperated by the British tactics, and had they continued with these tactics they may well have discouraged the Romans. As it was, the Britons suffered desertions when things did not go too well for them following a counter-attack the next day (again, the Celtic fickleness?) and then played even more into the Romans' hands by trying to confront them in a set battle at the Thames. It seems the Britons had not learnt from the earlier engagement at the Stour. After the almost inevitable defeat at the Thames they did revert to guerilla tactics, but seem to have suffered from a loss of men (both as casualties and as deserters) and of morale, and were not noticeably successful.

Belatedly, they did now send a force to attack the vessels and their limited Roman guard – but *after* defences had been erected by the Romans. Since four sub-kings were involved the British forces must have been reasonably substantial, but were still not enough to defeat the relatively small guard left with the ships.

It is quite evident that, as seen in Cassivellaunus's despair, the Britons were sorely afflicted by desertions and defections, which in any combat situation affect morale as well as numbers. Given as well the existence of certain British leaders who were pro-Roman from the outset, the Britons seem to have found difficulty in mustering full forces. Even when assembling reasonable numbers their cohesiveness and commitment were open to question. Cassivellaunus may have had overall command, but the degree of loyalty to him must have varied.

And he may not have been the wisest leader. The Britons did not help themselves by questionable tactics. Why they did not continue with their guerilla attacks, which so disconcerted the Romans, is a mystery. Again we see missed opportunities. Of course, guerilla warfare can, by its very nature, be protracted, and it can leave towns and other settlements – where families would be – relatively vulnerable. But if guerilla warfare is conducted properly and on a large-scale, with constant intelligence reports and monitoring of the enemy's movements, relocating non-combatants from site to site is not necessarily impossible. As mentioned earlier, it was far riskier to engage the Romans in a set battle, even across a river with stakes set in its bed. Nor was retreat to a fixed defensive site a good option.

(7) In AD 43, could the Britons have prevented Claudius's forces from crossing to Britain?

As with Caesar's campaign, driven by ambition, the answer must be 'no'. It was admittedly a close call because in the many years since Caesar's expeditions the fear of the Ocean seems to have returned among the Romans, and the soldiers came very close to not going. However, this was not a matter in which the Britons could have any control or even input. And with the emperor system now in place, there was little scope for recourse to technical appeals regarding authorisation of invasion – not that any was needed, for on the face of it Rome was helping an ousted king in distress, Verica, at his request.

(8) In AD 43, could the Britons have prevented Claudius's forces from actually landing and establishing a beachhead?

As with Caesar's landing in 54 BC, the answer is very probably 'no'. Plautius was a veteran and actually seems to have done a better job than Caesar. The landing site – wherever it was and whether it was a single site or the main site of several – was certainly better than Caesar's. The force was again large and would have been extremely difficult to repel. Some of the Romans, despite Narcissus's persuasive skills, may still have been nervous about going to the land beyond the edge of the world, but at the same time they were with many thousands of auxiliaries, from the continent and elsewhere, who did not share their fears and would surely have reassured the more nervous among them. It is hard to believe Dio's explanation for the unopposed landing as being that the Britons had dispersed because they had not expected the Romans to come: far more likely in my view, as I have argued, is that they decided on guerilla tactics from the outset.

(9) In AD 43 or very shortly afterwards, even after the Romans had established a base, could the Britons have driven them off and/or destroyed them?

More clearly so than was the case in 54 BC, the answer is probably 'no'. If there had been a combination of cohesiveness and commitment on the part of the Britons and persistent use of guerilla tactics alone, and more leaders in the mould of Caratacus, it is possible though unlikely that the Romans could have been forced to leave before they became firmly established. But again we find the Britons ending up in fixed battles with Romans, again seeming to hide across rivers (which presented no real obstacle to the Romans at any point be it under Claudius or Caesar), and again losing men and morale. And as in Caesar's case in 54 BC, there were a number of pro-Roman British leaders.

We should note however that, in the years between Plautius's arrival in 43 and Boudica's revolt in 60, there may have been an opportunity to get rid of the Romans. Had Cartimandua been assassinated at an early stage and replaced by Venutius, and had he joined forces with Caratacus and had the Brigantes become more determinedly anti-Roman, along with the hostile Ordovices and Silures, then the combined resistance from the north and west – even though it was beyond the southeast area the Romans saw as the real province of Britannia – may have persuaded the Romans to pack up. We are not sure at what stage Nero (from 54) considered abandoning the province, but such a for-midable resistance might well have decided it for him. Cartimandua's betrayal of Caratacus was certainly a major blow to British resistance.

(10) *In AD 60, could Boudica's revolt have driven the Romans from Britain?*

In my opinion, absolutely 'yes', this could and indeed should have happened. The Romans were proving themselves harsh and sometimes unjust rulers and had upset both ordinary people and some of their client kings. This is evidenced *inter alia* by the numbers Boudica appears to have had flock to join her.

Even allowing for gross exaggeration, Boudica clearly had large numbers and should have made better use of them. She was fortunate that Paulinus was away in Anglesey when her revolt started and that she was able therefore to wreak considerable havoc at three major sites – though, as I have argued, I believe the fatalities have been greatly exaggerated. The defeat of Cerialis's men, seemingly as part of Boudica's revolt, also shows that the Romans could be beaten with the right (guerilla) tactics. Dio may well have accurately described Boudica's thinking with regard to her alleged view that the British were, though unarmoured, more mobile, but it is a pity that this advantage was not put more into effect. Boudica's followers were so numerous that, unfortu-nately for her, her force as a whole was slowed down and lost much of the advantage of mobility. The worst thing that could happen for the Britons was to be forced to face the Romans in a pitched battle, and yet this is exactly what they ended up doing. She would have done better, I believe, if she had left the baggage wagons and family-followers behind – with some guard of course – and taken a force of properly mobile fighters to harry Paulinus's men as they returned from Mona.

But, even if that was not possible, and she had no choice but to confront the Romans in a set battle, with such massive advantages in terms of numbers and supplies and motivation (for they were fighting for their freedom and homes, unlike the Romans), she should still have won convincingly. The British tactics in the 'Battle of Mancetter' (assuming this location for convenience) were fool-ish and disastrous. Having said that, I have argued that Boudica was almost cer-tainly not the sole commander and should not bear sole responsibility for this. Though she may possibly have had some sort of supreme designation, I am sure that in practice she would have had a number of advisers/co-leaders. She had no battle experience, for her sackings of the three sites were not engage-ments proper. There must have been, alongside her, men who had actually fought, such as those who successfully attacked Cerialis and those who had fought at the time of Claudius's arrival. At the very least there would have been a Trinovantian leader. I believe it probable that a lack of consensus led by default to the poor tactics that were actually employed.

First, the enemy was allowed to choose the ground, and, from what we can tell, it was a good choice on their part (at least, given their assumptions about British tactics). For the very reason that the enemy had made a good choice, she could have held back. The Britons had time on their side, presumably aware that no relief force was on its way (at least in the short term), and with supplies aplenty in the many baggage wagons that accompanied her forces. They could even have starved the Romans into desperation and forced them to come out from the defile. With woods behind and steep hills to the sides, the Romans would probably have come out prematurely onto the plain in front where the Britons could use their extra mobility to their advantage, encircling them for a start. And if the Romans had tried to get out over the more difficult terrain of the hills or through the woods, the British could pick them off.

Alternatively, if she wanted for some reason to hurry to engage the Romans, why did she not use her men's mobility to attack over the sides of the defile and through the woods at the rear? Of course this would not permit chariots, but it should not have prevented infantry or cavalry (or perhaps more exactly 'mounted troops'). These were hills not mountains and it would surely have been possible for men and horses – certainly men – to climb the outside flanks of the hills forming the defile. And once on top, they could wreak havoc on the Romans below. At the very least they could have caused a distraction in the Roman rear and flanks, thereby limiting available backup for the Roman front line.

And one wonders why ranged weapons were not used more by the Britons. The Romans were effectively backed into a corner and volleys of arrows loosed from the tops of the hills and from the rear – and even from the front – would have been murderous, however much the Romans might form their testudos or reuse British missiles. (In fact, puzzlingly, bows and arrows seem to have played little part in British warfare throughout early history, not being used effectively until the Middle Ages. I return to this issue in Part 2.)

What was particularly foolish about the British tactics at Mancetter was their apparent readiness to do exactly what the enemy wanted, which is a major weakness in any military engagement. It would seem they nullified much of their numerical supremacy by funnelling themselves to attack the Romans in the defile across an equal front, moreover ending up in such cramped circumstances that their swinging swords were almost useless while the Romans' stabbing swords were ideal. It is also puzzling why they persisted with this when they should surely have seen early on that it was disastrous and then pulled back. They would still have had enough men left to cope with the Romans. This all suggests poor planning and/or poor communication and/or poor discipline. Perhaps alcohol played an unfortunate role. Cockiness certainly did.

To have left the baggage wagons obstructing retreat to the rear was surely one example of foolish cockiness, for any army should, where at all possible, allow an uncluttered escape route should things go against them, however unexpectedly. Moreover, the Britons seem to have retreated rather readily, though – sad to say – this was not untypical based on what we have seen so far.

In sum, based on available evidence, we have to conclude that it was a disastrous defeat, one that was truly pivotal in history since it confirmed Roman superiority and their right – by the standards of the day – to occupy the territory of the vanquished. Boudica almost certainly should not take the blame for this alone, for I am sure she was just one of a number of leaders and was possibly even relatively powerless. I believe that poor planning amongst these leaders – probably reflecting overconfidence in their numerical superiority and perhaps a lack of consensus at leadership level – was a major factor in the defeat, together with cockiness, poor choice of weapons, scorning of armour, and repeatedly disastrous tactics. It may also have been compounded by the oft-remarked fickleness that is often the reverse side of cockiness. Richard Hunt seems to refer to the Boudican period as something that we (British) should 'gloat over and treasure'.[308] For the life of me, I cannot see why.

1.10   Conclusion

We have seen in Part 1 how Rome finally brought Britain – or much of it – into its empire. It was not done quickly, and it was not done easily. Though the individuals behind the conquest – particularly Caesar and Claudius – were driven by their own personal agendas, for Rome it had a special significance in that it almost literally expanded the Roman worldview to an acceptance that there was land and life and riches beyond the dreaded Ocean.

For the Britons, incorporation into the empire also had a geographical significance, for it drew Britain into a southern sphere of influence and kept it there for more or less half a millennium – till the arrival of the Angles, Saxons, Jutes, and Vikings took it north again for half a millennium, when in turn the Normans and Angevins took it back south once again for another half-millennium. For Romanisation meant not only enjoying a degree of sophistication, with fine roads and buildings and institutions, and of course support for the causes of those friendly to Rome, it also meant adopting the ways of a southern people, certainly more southern than the contemporary Britons. Such an orientation did not necessarily suit everybody, particularly the Picts to the north, and in general these northerners successfully avoided incorporation into that southern realm.

But, with their 'divide and conquer' approach and their building of walls as boundary markers, the Romans also brought disunity – or more exactly, added to an already existing disunity. Had there been more unity amongst the tribes of Britain, it is probable that the Romans would never have succeeded. Militarily, despite the Roman advantages in weaponry and discipline and tactical ability, the Britons had advantages numerically and in terms of knowledge of terrain, as well as in many cases motivational advantage. Under the circumstances, in my view they should have persisted with guerilla tactics and avoided pitched battles. They could and should have repelled the Romans on a number of occasions, such as Caesar's first expedition in 55 BC and in particular on the occasion of Boudica's revolt in AD 60. Although the latter culminated in a pitched battle and not a guerilla engagement, it should still have been won easily by the Britons, and now stands as a showcase of how foolish tactics at one point in time and place can change the course of history – though Boudica is by no means alone in such determining of history, as we shall see in subsequent chapters.

The tactical folly at Mancetter is a particular shame because Boudica had succeeded in bringing together a greater mass of Britons than had ever been achieved before, yet ironically, a cocky overconfidence deriving from that very numerical superiority was very likely a major factor in her defeat. Moreover, it seems likely that Boudica was just one of a number of British leaders on that day, and that the tactics were arrived at by default through lack of consensus – again, perhaps an ironic reflection of the large numbers.

We must remember that, despite the idealised sense of nationhood that Dio attributes to Boudica, the concept of Britain as a nation was, at this stage, at best embryonic, probably limited to an awareness of certain commonalities such as Druidism and linguistic overlaps and an overarching 'Celtic' cultural framework. Yet such commonalities did not guarantee unity, and did not define national boundaries, as seen in the fact that Celtic culture spanned many geographical areas that are now separate nations, and that not a few tribes had branches both in Britain and the continent. Tribes in Britain did what they thought was best for themselves and many obviously felt it was better to go with Rome than go against it.

That, ironically, is freedom – sort of.

2
The Coming of the Pagans

2.1 Introduction

After the departure of the Romans Britain was left vulnerable to the continued raids of barbarians, particularly – at least initially – the Picts. However, other raiders, principally from what is now northern Germany and southern Denmark, were soon to prove a more serious threat. These were a grouping of various peoples nowadays known collectively as the Anglo-Saxons. Their threat went beyond mere raiding and turned into occupation and settlement, at the expense of the Britons.

Remarkably, the Anglo-Saxon Advent (*Adventus Saxonum*) is often blamed largely on one man, Vortigern, a British overlord who, probably around the middle of the fifth century, and following a Roman practice of using barbarians against barbarians, invited a group of Anglo-Saxons into Britain to help fight off the Picts. The invitees did not go away, seizing land allegedly on the grounds that Vortigern had broken his agreement to compensate them, and thereby opening the way for others to follow. In Part 2 we will, *inter alia*, investigate just how culpable – and foolish – Vortigern may or may not have been.

The establishment of the Anglo-Saxons was not an overnight affair. It took around 150 years for them to dominate what is now England, with many Britons seemingly being driven principally to Wales and the far southwest, and others subjugated – though the degree of subjugation, and indeed the nature of the Anglo-Saxon Advent itself, are much disputed. Unfortunately this important period of confrontation between Briton and Anglo-Saxon is the least documented period in British history subsequent to the departure of the Romans.

But that does not mean that it is not widely written about. Looming large in later literature about the period is the figure of 'King' Arthur in particular. In contrast to the paucity of contemporary historical documents, there is indeed a massive later (mostly much later) literature on Arthur, some of it contributing to the legend, some of it commenting on the legend. I personally feel it likely that there was a real Arthur, though almost certainly far removed from his image in legend. However, claimed historical fact about him is so flimsy (some would say there is none at all) and demonstrable fiction is so great, that to discuss him in Part 2 would give a disproportionality to this book, which after all is a book dealing primarily with the themes of folly and fortune. At the same time I do not wish, unlike some historians, to ignore him, so I have therefore compromised by assigning treatment of Arthur, brief as it must necessarily be, to Appendix 1.

The entrenchment of Anglo-Saxon occupation, probably from around the end of the sixth century though some would argue for an earlier date, coincides with the spread of Christianity among them. However, it was not enough to unite them, for there was much internecine strife between the regional Anglo-Saxon kingdoms. As a very rough generalisation, the eighth century was dominated by Mercia, in whose history King Offa is particularly prominent, while the ninth and tenth centuries were dominated by Wessex, in whose history Alfred is prominent. Although Alfred is seen widely as 'the Great', and does indeed deserve credit for a range of achievements, not a few historians feel his reputation has been excessively boosted by panegyrists – including writers in the *Anglo-Saxon Chronicle* – and this is something we will touch upon. In any event, during the tenth century Wessex was sufficiently dominant to provide the kings of a reasonably united England.

Of course, the ninth and tenth centuries – as too the early part of the eleventh century – are also dominated by incursions and settlement by the Vikings, a mix of mostly Danes and Norwegians and to a much lesser extent Swedes. The nature and causes of the expansion of the Viking world, which saw incursions and settlement in many countries and not just Britain, are still matters of some dispute. We will consider these, their raids, their later settlement, and their eventual attainment of the throne of England under Cnut. The role of the Anglo-Saxon king Aethelred – the supposed 'Unready' – in the 'loss' of the kingdom to the Vikings is a matter we will examine in more detail, to try to establish just how 'unready' or 'poorly advised' (the latter being the correct meaning of his by-name) he actually was. The results might be surprising to some readers.

Though the perils of oversimplification should be borne in mind, there seem to be a number of interesting broad 'parallels' between the history in Britain of the Anglo-Saxons and that of the Vikings. When the Anglo-Saxons arrived they were pagan and were confronted by a (partly) Christian people in the Britons, but presently became Christians themselves. When the Vikings arrived they were pagan and were confronted by a (largely) Christian people in the Anglo-Saxons, but presently became Christians themselves. In an age of providential interpretations of events, both sets of invaders were widely seen as barbarian manifestations of the Lord's wrath, and of course they were invariably vilified in the records of those suffering the invasions. The Anglo-Saxons originally came to Britain to raid for booty or 'tribute', including slaves, but eventually settled. This was the same pattern the Vikings followed. It took the Anglo-Saxons almost two centuries to become established and dominant, and only slightly longer for the Vikings. The Anglo-Saxons were a mix of various northern European peoples, and so too were the Vikings. And, as will become clear, and setting aside for the moment finer arguments about causality, both Anglo-Saxons and Vikings did what they did because they wanted to and they could.

However, one can see some degree of difference with regard to political power and geographical occupation. The Anglo-Saxons were to displace many Britons from what is now England (though to what extent is still debated) and establish political dominance but, though the Vikings were to displace some (but by no means all) Anglo-Saxons during the heyday of the so-called Danelaw in the east and north of the country, the Anglo-Saxons did not lose their land to the same extent that the Britons had, and they retained more political power.

Another difference is that the Viking monarchy was not to endure in England to the same extent that the Anglo-Saxon monarchy did. Though Cnut was arguably one of England's strongest rulers there was very little in the matter of Viking succession after his death in 1035. His two sons, Harold Harefoot and Harthacnut, were both dead by 1042 after very short reigns, and a (paternally) Anglo-Saxon monarch (whose mother was Norman), Edward the Confessor, then assumed the throne. Alas for the Anglo-Saxons, after his reign ended in 1066, followed by the brief rule that year of the (paternally) Anglo-Saxon Harold Godwineson (whose mother was Danish), Normans were to prevail, as we shall see in Part 3. The Normans were themselves of relatively recent Viking descent, so it could be argued that Norman rule was in an indirect sense Viking rule, but in practice the Normans were treated as French rather than Viking, just as many of the Danes who had settled in East Anglia, for example, were presently treated as English rather than Viking.

2.2 The Anglo-Saxon 'guests'

The fifth and sixth centuries in Britain were a significant transitional phase between the departure of the Romans and the establishment of a dominant new presence in the form of the Anglo-Saxons. The term 'Anglo-Saxon' – or even just 'Saxon' – is used as a recognised, if simplistic, shorthand for diverse Germanic peoples who included Angles, Saxons, and Jutes,[1] as well as smaller numbers of Frisians, Swabians, and Franks, and some Scandinavian peoples. Their exact inter-relations are now lost to us, but they do seem to have been generally allied rather than foes, even though conflict – particularly power struggles – occurred not infrequently.[2] It has been suggested, cynically but in my view realistically, that it was the search for loot that brought them together, and that they were subsequently kept together by the acquisition of land and the defence of it.[3]

These two centuries are often referred to as (the onset of) the 'Dark Ages', the 'Post-Roman Period', or, less frequently and perhaps somewhat confusingly, the 'Sub-Roman Period'.[4] The boundaries are sometimes seen more specifically as the 'formal' departure of the Romans in 410 and the arrival of St Augustine in 597, the latter bringing Christianity directly to the pagan Anglo-Saxons and in a sense, through recognition by the pope (Gregory the Great), conferring a degree of legitimacy on the authority of Anglo-Saxon power holders.

Unfortunately for the historian, this period was most definitely not a time of great literary output. Known British documentary sources categorically attributable to fifth and/or sixth century authorship are extremely few.[5] There are really just two British authors, St Patrick (c. 390–c. 460), and the cleric Gildas (widely but not unanimously accepted as c. 500–c. 570). St Patrick is believed to have lived in the Carlisle region before his abduction in his teens by slavers from Ireland (from where he presently escaped, only to return). His writings include a letter and his *Confession* (*Confessio*), but they tell us relatively little for our purpose. Gildas is popularly believed to have been the son of a Strathclyde king named Caw and to have been educated in Wales, though in later life he was possibly based in Wiltshire or Dorset.[6] He is effectively the only contemporary British writer to comment on the advent of the Anglo-Saxons, in his work *Concerning the Ruin and Conquest of Britain* (*De Excidio et Conquestu Britanniae*). There are, however, significantly differing views as to the dates of Gildas and his work. The most widely accepted date for his birth is around 500, and for his *Ruin of Britain* as around 540–5. However, it has been argued controversially that he may have been born much earlier, around the mid fifth century, and that the work may have been as early as c. 480;[7] while on the other hand he may have been born as late as c. 516 and his work written as late as c. 560.[8] Moreover, his writing is skewed by his 'fire and brimstone' sermonising about how the arrival of the Anglo-Saxons was Divine Punishment for the sinfulness of British kings. He is also somewhat frustrating through his frequent reluctance to name names, while on some matters he is demonstrably unreliable, such as his erroneous dating of the Roman walls.[9] He cannot be ignored, but he is surrounded by vagueness and controversy, which inevitably are inseparable from questions regarding the dating of the Anglo-Saxon Advent.

Later texts making retrospective reference to this time frame, such as the *Anglo-Saxon Chronicle*, first compiled in the late ninth century though drawing on certain earlier material, and the early ninth century *History of the Britons* (*Historia Brittonum*, c. 829), long attributed to a Welsh cleric named 'Nennius' but the authorship of which is now queried,[10] are similarly not necessarily reliable for this period. The same can be said of the Anglo-Saxon cleric Bede, who wrote his *Ecclesiastical History of the English People* (*Historia Ecclesiastica Gentis Anglorum*) in 731 and used much of Gildas's material as well as other sources now lost. Though he is relatively more trustworthy and respected as a historian than Gildas or 'Nennius', he still shows a bias towards his own Anglo-Saxons – as opposed to his 'profound contempt for the Britons'[11] – and puts an appropriate spin on some of Gildas's material.[12]

As a result of these literary limitations, our knowledge of these two centuries is more than usually dependent on archaeology, epigraphs (such as tomb inscriptions), toponymy (the study of place-names), and occasional written sources outside Britain itself. There have been valuable findings in these fields, particularly archaeology, such as excavations at Tintagel in Cornwall, which have revealed trade links with the eastern Mediterranean and North Africa as well as Gaul, and excavations at a number of Roman or earlier sites which have revealed re-fortification. But even archaeology is hampered by the apparent absence of new coins – an important item for the archaeologist-historian. Thus this period remains the least understood in British history.

What little information that can be gleaned from the scanty literature is often contradictory, even within the same text, and errors of fact (including mathematics) by the authors are all too frequent. Even establishing a clear and definite timeline is next to impossible, not helped by the fact that there were several dating systems in use at the time, and at a finer level, by the fact that years did not necessarily begin in January.[13] Moreover, elements of legend and myth are mixed in with the real and are not easily separable. A number of seemingly real figures of this time may in fact be mythical – including 'King' Arthur. Some of the names of the protagonists are also usable as titles, and one is sometimes unsure whether it is the same individual being referred to. In short, as has been famously observed, it is not a period to choose if you wish for certainty and firm ground in history.[14]

Some scholars believe that it is not possible to write a narrative history of this period.[15] This is certainly true, at least with our present state of knowledge. However, if one sets aside the matter of precise dates and does not dwell too much on the identity of specific individuals, the broad sweep of events does seem to become at least relatively clearer. Fine detail and exact sequencing are often impossible, and much interpretation is necessarily speculative, but there is generally widespread agreement about broad outlines.[16] Let us consider, then, the outlines.

After the Romans left, many of the dozen or so British kingdoms, which did not necessarily always enjoy harmonious relations with each other, or share the same attitudes towards Rome, seem to have tried to maintain basic Roman infrastructures in some matters, such as local administrative systems and even Roman lifestyles. Understandably, however much Romans may have ended up being treated with contempt and perhaps even being expelled, there was nonetheless, for some Britons at least, a tempting expedience in maintaining their systems and structures. But how long this might have continued, had there not been external intervention, is debatable. John Blair, for example, is of the view that even if there had been no Anglo-Saxon arrivals, Roman civilisation was too fragile to endure.[17] The fact that no new coinage seems to have been minted or imported, which must have had an adverse effect on the economy, would certainly help raise doubts as to the durability of a Roman *status quo*. On the other hand one could of course argue that Christianity was a major exception to this and remained an enduring Roman legacy.[18] This does not mean, however, that Christianity dominated religious beliefs in immediate post-Roman Britain. Scholars recognise that Christianity had a significant presence, but there is considerable diversity of opinion as to the degree,[19] and we may never know for sure.

A number of Roman settlements, such as Viroconium (Wroxeter) and some sites at Hadrian's Wall, were maintained and sometimes modified or even refortified. As late as the mid fifth century an (unsuccessful) appeal for help against barbarian raids seems to have been made to the Roman consul Aetius,[20] and there was probably, at least for the first few decades, some expectation that the Romans might return at some point. Life must have been made very difficult by these frequent barbarian raids, which were a major problem even when the Romans were present and were obviously far more so in their absence. The raiders were Picts, Anglo-Saxons, and to a lesser extent the Gaelic Scotti (Scots) from Ireland, the latter having made inroads into the coastline of Wales and having established a kingdom known as Dalriada on Scotland's west coast.

The Anglo-Saxons had been periodically harassing Britain from at least as early as the late fourth century. Their interest in Britain not unnaturally increased after the Roman departure, and, given the reality of eastern barbarian incursions into their own or nearby lands, plus increased flooding of their low-lands as a result of apparent climate change,[21] it was surely not just as a raiding target but as a possible new home – a view supported by evidence of depopulation from the mid fifth century in some areas of the Anglo-Saxon homelands.[22]

However, as is clear from Gildas – for there is no reason to doubt him here – the greatest immediate post-Roman threat to the Britons was from the Picts (and to a lesser extent the Scots), not the Anglo-Saxons.[23] And it was not just in the north, for Gildas refers to their 'canoes' (or 'coracles'), indicating that the Picts were seaborne, with the result that they were even plundering southern coastal regions. This led a mid fifth century British king known as Vortigern (literally meaning 'leader', and possibly used as a title), who appears to have had over-king status in the southeast, to employ Anglo-Saxons to help resist the Picts, promising land and other remuneration. The Anglo-Saxons (more specifically Jutes in this event) duly arrived, initially in a mere three boats, under their 'divine' leaders, the brothers Hengist (Hengest) and Horsa,[24] and were invited to settle in Thanet. They do seem to have been successful in suppressing Pictish raids for a while, but requested reinforcements, resulting in more arrivals and the granting of more land in Kent – a process probably repeated more than once.

This, then, is the start of what is known as the '(Anglo-)Saxon Advent', generally but not universally believed to be around 450 (discussed presently). It would seem to have been initially a continuation of a Roman practice of employing potentially hostile barbarians as mercenaries (known as *foederati/federati*), sometimes relocating entire peoples, to fight against more immediately threatening barbarians. In Rome's case this was not ultimately helpful to the employer and was indeed counter-productive, and this was to prove the case also in Britain. All went well for a time, but presently, unsatisfied with their rewards, and/or realising that land and other easy pickings were there for the taking, the Anglo-Saxons seem to have turned hostile towards the Britons, apparently even making a temporary pact with the Picts.[25] The invited residents had now effectively become invaders.

In the coming years more Anglo-Saxon leaders arrived and played their part in the expansion of the Anglo-Saxon power base. These included, around 477, Aelle, associated in particular with present Sussex (i.e. the land of the South Saxons), and, around 495, Cerdic, in the Hampshire region. Cerdic's British name suggests either that he was British but had thrown his lot in with the Anglo-Saxons, or that he was part-Saxon and part-British, or that he was from a Germanicised expatriate 'ethnic British' family. In any event he was to become, at least in legend, the founder of the kingdom of Wessex.

Vortigern, which name and/or title may refer to two (and possibly successive) individuals,[26] was presently replaced as over-king – or at least as *de facto* leader of the Britons – by Ambrosius Aurelianus, a man with whom he had not enjoyed the friendliest of relationships. Ambrosius seems to have been a real figure, based either in the southwest or in Wales, and of recently ennobled Roman descent.[27] But in this case too there may possibly have been two successive figures, an 'Ambrosius the Elder' and an 'Ambrosius the Younger'.[28] A series of battles ensued against the Anglo-Saxons (and occasionally Picts and combined Pict-Saxon forces), with victory sometimes going one way and sometimes the other, led either by Ambrosius (probably 'the Younger' if there were two) or possibly Arthur, who may have been a general under Ambrosius's command. Aggressive Anglo-Saxon expansion at this time seems to have been a major factor in the departure of many Britons to Armorica in northwest Gaul, later known as Brittany, with some going further afield to what is now Bretona in Spain.[29]

Around the turn of the fifth century into the sixth, again probably led either by Ambrosius or Arthur, the Britons gained a substantial victory over the Saxons at Badon Hill, widely but not universally believed to be a hill in the immediate vicinity of Bath.[30] This seems to have earned a respite for some half a century, and even the departure of some Anglo-Saxons back to the Continent, which may indicate a view among at least some Anglo-Saxons at that point in time that further territorial acquisition was not very feasible.[31] Most scholars believe that it was during this peace-time in the first half of the sixth century that Gildas lived and wrote, but nonetheless his writings make it clear that the Anglo-Saxons were a strong presence. However, despite the interlude of peace, the Anglo-Saxons did presently manage to reassert themselves and push back British resistance to Cornwall, Wales, and the far north. The resurgence of the Anglo-Saxons in the latter half of the sixth century is sometimes linked to a plague around the mid-500s (just as there was a plague in the mid-400s), but logically one would have expected that the Anglo-Saxons would be similarly afflicted. More likely perhaps, it may have been aided by a British relapse into internecine conflict, perhaps exacerbated by pressure on food resources as a result of prolonged bad weather causing poor harvests.

By this stage the Gaelic Scotti had been removed from Wales by the Britons, not necessarily just by local Britons but possibly with the assistance of the Votadini (Gododdin) of present southeast Scotland.[32] However, Dalriada in western Scotland was to remain a major power base for the Scotti till it was attacked by Vikings in the mid ninth century, when the Dalriadians appear to have expanded eastwards under Kenneth MacAlpin and taken over control of Pictish territory. This is seen as the start of unification of the land that presently took its name from the Scotti. The relationship between the Scotti/Gaels and the Picts had been a changeable one, with fluctuations in power holding. The Picts had mixed fortunes against the Anglo-Saxons too, or more particularly the Angles, who during the later part of the sixth century established powerful kingdoms in the northeast, namely Bernicia between the Tweed and the Tees, and Deira to Bernicia's south, reaching down to the Humber. These two kingdoms were to fuse into Northumbria by the early seventh century, though occasionally old divisions still resurfaced. The Picts were to enjoy occasional victories against the Northumbrians, notably in the late seventh century, but in general they were held in check and kept further north.

Further south, in the various Anglo-Saxon kingdoms in what was to become Angleland/Aenglaland and eventually England (for some time excluding the far southwest), increased unity was achieved and a seemingly informal practice of overlordship emerged in similar fashion to that of the Britons. The so-called 'heptarchy' of kingdoms – though there were in fact more than seven – in the sixth century were Sussex, Wessex, Essex, Kent, East Anglia, Mercia (including Middle Anglia, and at some times including Lindsey, disputed with Northumbria), and Northumbria (initially comprising Bernicia and Deira, and at some times Lindsey).[33] The first recorded Anglo-Saxon overlord – later termed *brytenwalda/bretwalda*, literally 'ruler of Britain', though this is a confusing term[34] – was the earlier mentioned Aelle of Sussex (r. 488–c. 514). That there was then a break of around 50 years till the reign of the second overlord, Ceawlin of Wessex (r. 560–91), perhaps suggests a setback in Anglo-Saxon fortunes, consistent with the long peace said to have followed the substantial triumph of the Britons at

Badon Hill. From Ceawlin on there was unbroken continuity till the middle of the seventh century, with the overlordship being rotated among the kingdoms, possibly as a deliberate policy but more likely by chance, as *bretwalda* does not seem to have been a formally specified position, but rather an informally recognised pre-eminence – *primus inter pares* – amongst the various regional kings.

The third overlord, Aethelberht of Kent (r. 591–c. 616), had a Frankish wife, Bertha (daughter of the Merovingian king Charibert I), who was Christian. In 597 she welcomed a visit from a Christian mission, headed by Augustine (later Saint Augustine) and instigated by Pope Gregory the Great.[35] Her husband Aethelberht was initially hesitant to trust the Christian delegation and insisted on meeting Augustine in the open. However, he increasingly came to be impressed by Christianity, and became the first Christian king among the Anglo-Saxons.[36] Others soon followed suit. Through Aethelberht, an abbey was established on his land at Canterbury and Augustine became the first Archbishop of Canterbury.

The main British kingdoms in the sixth century comprised Gwynedd (larger than at present and occupying most of north Wales), Powys in central Wales, Dyfed in southwest Wales, Gwent in southeast Wales, Dumnonia in the Devon-Cornwall region, Elmet in the central north around present Leeds, Rheged in the northwest around Carlisle (once the kingdom of Coel, better known as 'Old King Cole'), Strathclyde in the southwest of Scotland, and Gododdin (the kingdom of the Votadini) in the Lothian area south/southeast of Edinburgh.

The expansion of the Anglo-Saxons has been subjected to a range of interpretations. While there is broad agreement that the phenomenon was a gradual process rather than sudden, some see it as one of integration and adaptation with merely occasional hostilities, while others see it as substantially more invasive and violent. This latter view is sometimes referred to as the 'traditional view', but it is by no means defunct. David Starkey, for example, in his recent popular television series on the British monarchy, argues that DNA tests show that large numbers of Anglo-Saxon males displaced as many as 90 per cent of British males in some areas and mated with their British women in what he terms 'ethnic cleansing at its most savagely effective'.[37] In some contrast geneticist Bryan Sykes, while conceding the possibility of partial or localised elimination or displacement of the indigenous males, argues overall for a much smaller impact in the case of male chromosomes, and even less in the case of female mitochondrial DNA, which still remains overwhelmingly British.[38] Presumably, as the DNA strongly suggests, males would have greatly outnumbered females among the Anglo-Saxons in Britain, reflecting their arrival as warriors (at least initially), but it should also be borne in mind that there may well have been a surplus of British females – or more exactly a relative paucity of British males – owing to depletion of British males through casualties in frequent fights against the Picts. Moreover, those who favour an early date of 428 (discussed presently) for the Anglo-Saxon Advent might also argue for the further lingering effect of the depletion of males during the final years of the Roman occupation, such as when Constantine III took large numbers overseas with him in 407, in turn following a similar depletion under Maximus some 20 years before that.[39]

Gildas himself, never at a loss for dramatic terminology, is very firmly in the 'violence' camp and describes the havoc wrought by the Anglo-Saxons (though, as mentioned earlier, if writing in a time of relative peace he himself probably did not see much of it):

> The sword gleamed, and the flames crackled around them [fleeing Britons] on every side. Lamentable to behold, in the midst of the streets lay the tops of lofty towers, tumbled to the ground, stones of high walls, holy altars, fragments of human bodies, covered with livid clots of coagulated blood, looking as if they had been squeezed together in a [wine-]press; and with no chance of being buried, save in the ruins of the houses, or in the ravening bellies of wild beasts and birds.[40]

Even allowing for Gildas's penchant for the dramatic, as well as his intent to portray his fellow Britons as hopelessly sinful and weak and thoroughly deserving of God's punishment through the agency of the heathen Anglo-Saxon barbarians,[41] this does not paint a picture of peaceful integration and adaptation.

It is of course possible that the violence came in cycles and that some or even most of the expansion was more or less peaceful but went unrecorded. After all, peace is generally less 'newsworthy' than violence. In recent times, though Starkey and others would evidently disagree with this, there has been a growing belief in a less violent expansion with less displacement, based on lower estimates of Anglo-Saxon numbers[42] – though Francis Pryor's seemingly tongue-in-cheek dismissal of the Saxon Advent as a largely fiction-generated myth in which 'a few 'Anglo-Saxons' (or people like them) probably did come to Britain in the post-Roman period' would seem a little extreme.[43] As indication of at least some peaceful co-existence there is indeed some archaeological evidence of Britons living alongside Anglo-Saxons and adopting Anglo-Saxon culture, such as the well known site at Wasperton in Warwickshire. On the other hand, Norfolk, for example, provides little evidence of fifth century British graves, only Anglo-Saxon cremation sites, suggesting displacement of the Britons and no reoccupation by them.[44] Clearly, there would seem to have been different population mixes in different localities, and very probably different relationships.

However, an important factor is that, for Britons in Anglo-Saxon territory, while there are of course exceptions, in general there seems less evidence of *egalitarian* co-existence than of progressive Anglo-Saxon dominance, particularly in the central and southeast areas. The widespread Anglo-Saxonisation of

British place-names is one such illustration. It could be argued that Britons' adoption of Anglo-Saxon culture, as at Wasperton, is in itself a demonstration of this dominance, as also the fact that so few Brythonic words survived in southeast England. Is this not a form of displacement? Gildas talks of Britons who had been unable to escape to remoter British territory in Wales or overseas as being either murdered or enslaved,[45] and it would seem that the Britons within Anglo-Saxon territory were generally second-class. John Blair, for example, has termed the Britons 'subservient', with their society 'shattered', while Hugh Kearney refers to a 'catastrophic decline' for British culture.[46]

But at least it would appear that the Britons who stayed in Anglo-Saxon territory were not all exterminated, as some earlier scholars believed – though this still does not rule out the possibility of localised or partial extermination – and that there was a 'British Survival' outside Wales, Scotland, and Cornwall.[47] Moreover, it is probable that, even if Britons generally did form an underclass, the fact that there were a number of socio-cultural commonalities between Britons and Anglo-Saxons would have helped this British Survival, and we can think in terms of certain continuities rather than a complete break. For example, these include the warrior ethic, the election of leaders, loyalty of retainers to leaders, the aversion to absolute power being held by those leaders, a grading of social status reflected in different compensatory payments for death or injury inflicted, reciprocity and obligation, the importance of kinship, and so on.[48] (There were differences of degree, however, as will be discussed presently.)

However, I have to stress that I myself do not think that, for the Britons, it was a case of 'scraping a draw' rather than suffering a defeat. I believe it more appropriate to talk of their losing, for most certainly they lost land and power. Even if there were fewer Anglo-Saxons than initially believed, and even if they were a small minority during their establishment,[49] at the end of the day they still achieved dominance, and created Anglo-Saxon kingdoms throughout England, with their language prevailing.[50] I find it hard to accept that the Britons as a whole somehow willingly acquiesced in this. It is surely a major challenge for scholars to ascertain how exactly a seeming minority, with no obvious technological or other advantage, could achieve such dominance – certainly political dominance in terms of power holding – whether it be by peaceful means or otherwise. Depletion of British males could be one factor, and very likely disunity among the Britons another, but there is surely a need to find other factors, especially if the elimination of British males was indeed less than first thought. Adoption of another language can sometimes be for reasons of prestige,[51] but would the Anglo-Saxons have seemed that prestigious to the Britons? Minority power holders can also sometimes force their language on majority subjects, but there is usually evidence of strong resistance.[52] As with the arrival of the Romans, it is possible that some local British leaders pragmatically accepted Anglo-Saxon overlordship and were allowed reasonable autonomy (particularly in the north), and even that some individuals genuinely aspired to things Anglo-Saxon just as some had aspired to things Roman.[53] Moreover, not a few British women may have been quite prepared to take Anglo-Saxon husbands. But nevertheless, while things may not always have been quite as extreme and confrontationist as Gildas and others portray them, I cannot see the overall picture as a particularly happy one for the Britons.

2.3   Vortigern the 'host': Villain or scapegoat?

With regard to the role of folly and fortune in all this, what is perhaps of most relevance in this post-Roman period is the invitation made by the Britons to the Anglo-Saxons to assist in defence against the Picts – a request for help that turned sour and saw the rescuing allies become invading foe. This seems to have been made by Vortigern. Unfortunately the date is unclear because there are at least two principal possibilities for the onset of the Saxon Advent: 428 or 449–55.

Put briefly, 'Nennius', in his *History of the Britons*, gives a date identifiable as 428, from his mention of it being in the fourth year of Vortigern's reign, the start of which reign he links to the consulship of Theodosius and Valentinian, which according to Roman records can only be 425.[54] By contrast Bede, in his *Ecclesiastical History*, gives a date of 449–55.[55] Similarly 449 (with no further entry till 455) is also given in the *Anglo-Saxon Chronicle* (Ms A and E). The late eighth century Northumbrian (and Anglo-Saxon) scholar Alcuin, in a letter of 793,[56] states that he is writing nearly 350 years after his ancestors first came to Britain, clearly endorsing the c. 450 date, though he may have been influenced in this by Bede. The pros and cons of both dates are much debated, with the 428 camp having support such as entries in the *Gallic Chronicles* for 452 and 511 that refer to Britain being under Saxon rule by 441, whereas the c. 450 camp have *inter alia* the greater bulk of archaeological evidence, the dates given by Bede and Alcuin, and the possibility that the lack of success in the appeal made to the Roman Aetius in 446 or slightly later was a trigger for an appeal instead to the Anglo-Saxon 'guests' represented by Hengist and Horsa.

It is also quite possible, of course, that two significant requests were made, perhaps even by the same Vortigern, and that both dates are valid to a greater or lesser degree, perhaps with separate requests ending up conflated in later records. And anyway, given that the Saxon Advent would appear to have been a gradual process, building on earlier incursions dating back a century or so, it may be of mere academic interest to try to establish a precisely fixed given point in time for it. To all intents and purposes, it may be better just to think of the increase in Anglo-Saxon presence and aggression as matters of degree.

Many commentaries on the Saxon Advent have cast Vortigern in a very bad light, suggesting he foolishly and greedily failed to honour his agreement to reward the Anglo-Saxons sufficiently, and that it was only natural that the Anglo-Saxons would react the way they did. For example, in another recent popular television series, the *History of Britain*, Simon Schama takes this line, and refers to Vortigern's behaviour as 'one of the more spectacular blunders in British history'.[57] Michael Holmes similarly observes that Vortigern's action was a 'major error of judgment', with 'disastrous' consequences.[58] Charles Thomas, though he has doubts about the veracity of the story, refers to the reality of Vortigern passing into legend as 'the archetypal national mistake-maker'.[59]

But is it fair and appropriate to dump all the blame on Vortigern? If it was indeed Vortigern who broke the agreement, through sheer avarice or bloody-mindedness or similar failing, then of course he would have a case to answer, for his own behaviour at least. However, even assuming this, one would have to wonder why it is that, once the consequences of his error were clear and the Anglo-Saxons started on their rampage, there seems no evidence of any belated attempt, either by Vortigern himself or by any group of Britons, to make good the agreement immediately, apologise, pay the Anglo-Saxons, and offer them generous 'penalty payments' by way of compensation. It would seem more plausible that the Anglo-Saxons were intent on making a land-grab anyway and may have been looking for an excuse to legitimise their actions. This is in fact what Gildas himself suggests about the Anglo-Saxon motive, notwithstanding his criticism of Vortigern and the council for their naivety:

> The barbarians being thus introduced as soldiers into the island, to encounter, *as they falsely said*, any dangers in defence of their hospitable entertainers, obtain an allowance of provisions, which, for some time being plentifully bestowed, stopped their doggish mouths. Yet they complain that their monthly supplies are not furnished in sufficient abundance, and *they industriously aggravate each occasion of quarrel*, saying that unless more liberality is shown them, they will break the treaty and plunder the whole island. In a short time, they follow up their threats with deeds.[60] [my emphasis]

Perhaps it was convenient for the Britons to see Vortigern as a scapegoat, a specific and easily blameable embodiment of what might have been a more widespread error of judgement in inviting the Anglo-Saxons into Britain in the first place. In this regard it is interesting that Gildas did not blame Vortigern alone and treated the advent of the Anglo-Saxons as Divine Punishment for the sinfulness of most of the British kings, of which Vortigern was just one example. And, very possibly also mindful of the Roman invasion some centuries before, he also blames internal conflict in the country – and one notes his concept of nationhood, albeit perhaps somewhat premature – for leaving Britain vulnerable to external threat: 'It has always been a custom with our nation . . . to be impotent in repelling foreign foes, but bold and invincible in raising civil war.'[61]

As regards that invitation itself, two points are worth noting. The first is that Vortigern was following a common practice of the later stages of the Roman Empire by employing (and even relocating) barbarians to defend against other barbarians. C. Warren Hollister makes the same point that while many historians have proclaimed Vortigern's decision an act of folly, this is 'scarcely a fair judgment', for Vortigern was simply following Roman tradition.[62]

Indeed, more specifically, the Romans had not infrequently employed Germanic groups, including in Britain.[63] As mentioned earlier, this practice of using *foederati* was risky and not ultimately to Rome's advantage, but it did sometimes work quite effectively. For example, a large group of several thousand Sarmatian cavalry (from the area to the northeast of the Black Sea) were incorporated into the Roman forces in the late second century and sent to help defend Hadrian's Wall against the Picts.[64] By all accounts they did their job very successfully over a lengthy period of some 20 years or more, working in well with local tribes friendly to Rome such as the Votadini – whose territory, between Hadrian's Wall and the more northerly Antonine Wall, seems to have been used by the Romans as a buffer zone between territory under Roman control and territory that was not. Moreover, the local Britons and Romans alike may have learnt certain cavalry techniques from them. After their period of service many of the Sarmatians seem to have settled in the area and married local British women.

The second point, often overlooked, is that Vortigern did not make the invitation alone, but in discussion with a council. This too is clear from Gildas, and again we have little reason to doubt him on this – even bearing in mind his seeming intent to blacken the British as a whole, which might be undermined if all the problems could be attributed to one individual alone:

> A council was called to settle what was best and most expedient to be done [with regard to the Pictish/Scottish threat], in order to repel such frequent and fatal irruptions and plunderings. . . . Then all the councillors, together with that proud tyrant Gurthrigern [Vortigern], the British king, were so blinded that, as a protection to their country, they sealed its doom by inviting in among them (like wolves into the sheep-fold) the fierce and impious Saxons, a race hateful both to God and men, to repel the invasions of the northern nations. Nothing was ever so pernicious to our country, nothing was ever so unlucky. . . . Foolish are the princes.[65]

We do not know whether the decision was unanimous, or even whether Vortigern may have defied the majority wish of the council, but if the latter were true one would have expected it to have been noted and indeed highlighted in Gildas's work as a dramatic example of the sinfulness of kings. It is possible he persuaded the council, as is suggested by a later Anglo-Saxon text, the *Chronicle of Aethelweard*,[66] but that would not absolve the council of shared responsibility. More likely, it was a joint decision, reflecting one of the differences between Britons and Romans in that British rulers were not generally accorded the degree of power and authority that Roman rulers were. But if it is true that it was a joint decision by a council to invite the Saxons, one wonders why that same council did not ensure that Vortigern – or someone – honoured the agreement in order to avoid Anglo-Saxon belligerence. Was Vortigern too powerful to be directed? Were the councillors just 'yes-men' used to legitimise his decision? This is not impossible, but again one would have expected Gildas to note this.

All things considered, on the evidence we have, it seems to me that to blame Vortigern for the Anglo-Saxon Advent would be overly simplistic.[67] He may perhaps have been foolish, and a contributing factor, but it seems far more likely that by around the mid fifth century (or indeed earlier) the Anglo-Saxons had decided for themselves, moreover with firm conviction, that they wanted a piece of Britain, ideally a very large piece. And, by the end of the sixth century, they had pretty well achieved this, occupying almost all of what is now England with the exception of a few outlying regions such as the far southwest (which remained British till the ninth century).

Yet it is clear that an attempt was indeed made to make Vortigern solely responsible, and it is to be found in the early ninth century *History of the Britons* by 'Nennius'. Though a Briton like Gildas, 'Nennius' had different aims with his work. Whereas Gildas castigated the Britons as a whole, 'Nennius' tried to restore their prestige by shifting the blame for the Saxon Advent from the people to the evil individual, Vortigern.[68] According to 'Nennius',[69] Vortigern was guilty of the following: he was too friendly with these strangers from the start, was besotted with Hengist's attractive daughter and ended up, in a drunken state, falling into Hengist's trap and receiving her in marriage in return for guaranteeing Hengist land in Kent; he was a terrible man whose lust knew no bounds, even that of incest, and also married his own daughter and fathered a son (Faustus) by her; his behaviour was so bad that the virtuous St Germanus, who was visiting Britain, came urgently to him to 'reprove' him, and ended up taking the child away from the unfit Vortigern so that he (Germanus) could act as father to the boy;[70] his behaviour continued to be so bad that St Germanus prayed for him over 40 days and nights; and, foolish man that he was, Vortigern was later duped into attending an Anglo-Saxon banquet along with three hundred British nobles, all unarmed, who were then murdered by their hosts, leaving Vortigern alone to live – his survival helped by massive gifts of land extracted from him – with a tormented conscience. His final days were, according to one account in the *History*, spent as a wandering outcast, despised as a fool and traitor, till he finally died of a broken spirit. In another contradictory account in the same book, after fleeing to the remoteness of Wales and building a castle, he perished in it shortly afterwards when it burnt down, seemingly an act of God. We should also note that another son of Vortigern (not one born of incest), Vortimer, is starkly contrasted with his terrible father as being a 'valiant' and God-fearing man who tried to atone for the sins of his father, but one who met an early honourable death in battle.

Even discounting at least some of these stories, and appreciating the spin put on the more credible of them, Vortigern's popular image continues to be very negative, seemingly forever linked to the Anglo-Saxon 'takeover' of Britain. If he is not seen as the devil incarnate, he is seen as stupid. On the plus side, relatively speaking, there is some if limited evidence to suggest that there were actually people who thought positively of Vortigern. This is to be found in a very faded inscription on the Pillar of Eliseg near Llangollen, a ninth century record of the royal dynasty of Powys. As Nick Higham points out,[71] this provides a hugely different image from that of the *History of the Britons*. With no mention of an incestuous relationship or marriage to Hengist's daughter, Vortigern is said to have been married to the daughter of the warrior-emperor Magnus Maximus, Severa, who bore him a son Britu. And he is said to have been blessed by St Germanus. The whole entry is one of pride in having such an illustrious ancestor.

Given the contrast between these two sources, it is probably safer to treat both of them as being of questionable reliability. I will return to the question of Vortigern's actions in the questions at the end of Part 2.

2.4   The English make themselves at home

We move now into a time-span of 400 years or so between the establishment of Anglo-Saxon rule at the end of the sixth century and the establishment of Viking rule in the early eleventh century, and this can be conveniently split into two halves. The first two centuries can be seen as a period of entrenchment for the Anglo-Saxons, and the remaining two centuries as a period increasingly involving the Vikings, whose raids on England started in the late eighth century. We will consider the generally troublesome relations between Anglo-Saxons and Vikings in the next chapter.

Unsurprisingly, Anglo-Saxon relations with the Britons, certainly in the seventh and eighth centuries, do not seem to have been all that cordial. Notwithstanding some degree of adaptation and commonality, Hugh Kearney, for example, is still of the view that the relationship between the Anglo-Saxon and British cultures was one of colonists and colonised, and was 'permanently antagonistic'.[72]

In terms of commonality of values, as mentioned in a previous chapter, we might cite the warrior ethic, the election of leaders as opposed to automatic acceptance of a successor, loyalty of retainers to leaders, the aversion to absolute formal power being held by those leaders, a grading of social status reflected in different compensatory payments for death or injury inflicted, the importance of kinship, and so on. But if we examine some of these a little more closely, we can find points of difference in degree – though of course these are always open to question as they are not absolutes.

As some examples, kinship was important to both Britons and Anglo-Saxons, but the Anglo-Saxons seem to have tended to focus more on immediate kin, while the Britons, as reflected in their range of terminology, had a more extended concept of 'family'.[73] This may in turn be felt to suggest that the Anglo-Saxons had a stronger concept of individualism, especially in the later stages of the period.[74] Loyalty to leaders, at least early on, seems to have been more extreme and personal among Anglo-Saxons than among the Britons, in the sense that leading retainers (presently known as thegns) were expected to live mostly with their lord in his great hall, rather than on their own estates, and fight to the death for him; but at the same time their loyalty was paradoxically more fragile, because – reflecting the importance of gifting in Anglo-Saxon culture – it could be affected by a drying up of rewards should the lord experience ill fortune. (Indeed, by the later stages of the period, it can be argued that Anglo-Saxon individuals had more interaction with the organs of state than with their lord.[75]) The gradation of social status reflected in compensatory *wergeld/wergild* ('man money', to use the Anglo-Saxon term) was more detailed and developed in the case of the Anglo-Saxons – for example, a thegn could be worth up to six times as much as a ceorl (a changing term that typically meant free peasant, the lowest free status in Anglo-Saxon society and also the most numerous class).[76] Kevin Crossley-Holland remarks of the Anglo-Saxons that their society was 'rigidly stratified'.[77] Perhaps in connection with this stronger sense of social hierarchy, the Anglo-Saxons seemed more prepared to support the institution of slavery – slaves themselves being ranked hierarchically in various categories, including a differentiation between Welsh (i.e. British) slaves and English.[78] Moreover, it was not difficult to end up a slave: for example, the *Laws of Ine, King of Wessex*, of c. 690, refer to entire families being enslaved if the male head of the house steals with the knowledge of the other family members.[79] Barbara Yorke refers to around 10 per cent of the recorded population of Wessex being slaves, and remarks that slave trading was a feature of life throughout the Anglo-Saxon period.[80] R. I. Page states unequivocally that Anglo-Saxon England was a 'slave state'.[81]

Other value differences include a seemingly stronger sense of vengeance among the Anglo-Saxons, leading to the notorious blood feud (though this was not specifically confined to Anglo-Saxons, for other peoples in Europe and elsewhere had similar practices). In the epic seventh/eighth century poem *Beowulf*, for example, we find Hengist determined to carry out the 'duty of vengeance'.[82] In some cases feuds could be settled by *wergeld*,[83] and in fact as time passed rulers often tried to encourage this and thereby exercise some degree of control over the 'management' of violence and the administering of justice. Indeed, *wergeld* – often in the extended sense of fines for a range of 'criminal' behaviour, not just compensation to victims or their kin[84] – was stipulated in law codes as early as the reign of Aethelberht of Kent (r. 591–c. 616), and again notably under Ine of Wessex (r. 688–726). Naturally, in a warrior age, there were not a few cases of individual acts of revenge,[85] but, as Richard Fletcher points out,[86] while the instinct of revenge was an underlying factor in the blood feud, the feud often went beyond the individual and became something shared by a group, usually kin, moreover governed by social conventions (as evidenced by the reference above to 'duty of vengeance' in *Beowulf*), and also having associations with justice, equity, and – paradoxically perhaps – order. This involvement of the group is seen for example in some law codes, which oblige kin to take at least some of the responsibility for paying *wergeld*[87] – though with time, and the increased codification of the blood feud, it became easier for kin to disown a wayward individual.[88] As context for all this feuding, Fletcher argues[89] that, while the idea of feuding does seem violent, peace was not the natural order of the society of the day and had to be brought about, meaning that peace was in that sense a construct and that the feud played a part in its construction.

It may have been this frequent violence, especially given the demands of risking one's life for one's lord and/or in a blood feud of one's own, that endowed the Anglo-Saxons with what Kevin Crossley-Holland terms 'an acute sense of fate'.[90] Indeed, the way a man accepted his fate, which governed his entire life, was important to his subsequent reputation, with dignity and even humour being seen as desirable attitudes.[91]

This extended to the battle-field, where the Anglo-Saxons were far from being the only people to have such values – the Japanese samurai being one classic example – and indeed warriors in general would probably espouse such ideals, but, without demeaning the valour of the Britons, we can perhaps see this fatalism in clearer definition among the Anglo-Saxons than the Britons.[92]

A more obvious difference between Britons and Anglo-Saxons is seen in religious beliefs, with the Britons including many Christians while the Anglo-Saxons were pagan till the end of the sixth century and not substantially converted to Christianity till the end of the seventh century. Christian conversion was not a simple 'overnight' matter either. Kings and their subjects were increasingly to follow Aethelberht of Kent's lead and take up Christianity, but some of them – such as the East Saxons and the Northumbrians – then renounced it, though in all cases only temporarily. It was in fact priests from Ireland, where Christianity was more deeply rooted, who were instrumental in reconverting many of those (especially in the north) who lapsed from the faith. Some of these Irish priests were based in Dalriada on Scotland's west coast. One such priest, (St) Aidan (d. 651), helped to establish the Lindisfarne monastery. Christianity was also widely promoted through the country by the example of powerful kings such as the Northumbrians, Oswald (r. 633–41) and Oswy (r. 641–58). Certainly, Christianity spread with the passage of time. For example, King Penda of Mercia (r. c. 626–55) was pagan, but his sons Peada (r. 655–6) and Wulfhere (r. 658–75) became Christian. In effect, England could be called Christian by the end of the 600s.

The uptake of Christianity had a number of effects. For one, it helped to further unity among the various peoples making up the Anglo-Saxons, especially in its monotheism as opposed to diverse and potentially particularistic (and hence potentially divisive) polytheism. It also led to churches and minsters gradually spreading through the country, centres that were to become villages and towns in the future. Moreover, the power of the church, in both the abstract and physical senses, soon became very considerable: in the late seventh century *Laws of Ine, King of Wessex*, it was decreed that if anyone liable to the death penalty reaches a church, his life is to be spared, and similarly that if anyone liable to be flogged reaches a church, the flogging is to be remitted.[93] Such sanctuary, the breaking of which was deemed extremely abhorrent and serious,[94] was surely a very great inducement not to stray too far from a/the church, and must have contributed to agglomeration of population in church centres. Oaths – an important matter in many societies – seemed to acquire a greater gravity when sworn in the name of God or the saints or relics or similar Christian icons, with the penalty for breach being concomitantly graver (as King Harold was to experience some centuries later, as discussed in Part 3). Christianity also encouraged greater literacy, seemingly more so than was the case with the pre-Advent Britons. This resulted in greater control and stability and efficiency, such as in the codifying of laws – as seen directly above – and diffusion of (relatively) consistent and accurate information. And very importantly, as had started to happen in the late Roman period, the spread of Christianity and its representatives, especially those in high office, came to represent an authority other than that of the warrior-ruler – indeed, an authority that could, in some cases at least, hold in check and even admonish a wayward king. In connection with this, kingship itself was to acquire a degree of sacredness, in that kings were deemed to rule only by the grace of God, as symbolised by formal religious coronation.

For the historian it also led to an increase in written resources for the seventh and eighth centuries, which include royal charters, laws, and similar documents, and not a few letters. In this time frame Bede becomes contemporary and more reliable, though he can still be accused of some bias against Britons. There is also a relatively greater reliability in the *Anglo-Saxon Chronicle* entries for this period, though not compiled till the late ninth century. Further authors include the Northumbrian scholar Alcuin (c. 735–804), who was a tutor and adviser to Charlemagne, and is recognised as arguably the leading intellectual in Europe at that time. We also have heroic poems, of which *Beowulf*, probably

Figure 2.1   Anglo-Saxon kingdoms (in bold) and British territory around 600.

written in the eighth century or possibly late seventh century, is the best-known and is the earliest major epic poem in English. As one might expect, the written sources for the seventh and eighth centuries are overwhelmingly Anglo-Saxon.

Aided by these enriched sources, we can say that the seventh century saw the firming up of kingdoms, relatively and informally united throughout much of England under a *bretwalda* (overlord). After Aethelberht of Kent (r. 591–616), the third *bretwalda* and as we have seen the first to become Christian, the *bretwaldas* were Raedwald of East Anglia (r. 616–27), Edwin of Deira (r. 617 [*sic*]–33), and the above-mentioned Oswald of Bernicia (r. 633–41), and Oswy of Northumbria (r. 641–58). From that point on the title *'bretwalda'* seems to have been applied somewhat inconsistently, not necessarily reflecting actual power status, and should be approached with caution if approached at all.[95] The principle of informal overlordship, however, remained valid in practice.

One indication of entrenchment of political power and permanent presence is the practice of burial of elites in prominent barrows, a relatively new practice for the Anglo-Saxons dating from around 600.[96] Raedwald is the most likely candidate for the powerful and wealthy figure buried at the well known Sutton Hoo barrow, near Woodbridge in Suffolk. The finds there indicate trade links with the Mediterranean and beyond, as well as links with Sweden, and they include an array of excellently crafted Anglo-Saxon items, often of gold, such as ornaments, jewellery, and utensils. The objects also indicate a mix of pagan and Christian, reflecting a transitional period in religious beliefs – which would fit particularly well with Raedwald, who according to Bede was eclectic in his religious beliefs and was 'serving both Christ and the gods whom he had previously served'.[97]

Despite overlordship and other factors giving a degree of unity, relations between the various Anglo-Saxon kingdoms were by no means always harmonious, and the various power struggles can seem a kaleidoscopic array of names and dates and places. For example, in 633, Penda of Mercia, a kingdom yet to provide an overlord, allied with the British king Cadwallon of Gwynedd (r. c. 625–34), and defeated Northumbrian forces, killing Edwin. However, it was a short-lived success. Oswald restored Northumbrian power the following year and Cadwallon was killed. More than 20 years later, in 655, Penda was killed by another Northumbrian, Oswy. However, Mercia continued to grow in strength, and a few years later Mercians overthrew Oswy, with Penda's son Wulfhere (r. 658–75) coming to power. By the 670s Wulfhere himself appears to have become effectively an overlord, though his power in the south was soon challenged by a resurgent Wessex, under the short reign of Caedwalla (r. 685–8) and the much longer reign of his son Ine (r. 688–726).

It was however Mercia that was presently to prevail under long-reigning monarchs, Aethelbald (r. 716–57) and particularly Offa (r. 757–796), the latter being seen as the most powerful king before Alfred a hundred years later – but frustratingly, among the major monarchs of Anglo-Saxon England, also perhaps the most obscure.[98] Though Mercia was dominant throughout much of England at the end of the eighth century, including loosely over Wessex, it did not prevail over Northumbria. While Offa was powerful enough to style himself *rex totius Anglorum patriae* (king of all the land of the English), and in 794 to order the execution of a king of East Anglia,[99] a letter sent to him by Charlemagne, while treating him as an equal (in fact Offa was the only king that Charlemagne did recognise as an equal), nonetheless refers to the 'two kings' in England, Offa himself and Aethelred of Northumbria (reigned twice, 774–c. 779, 790–6).[100]

Offa is of course associated with Offa's Dyke, a massive continuous barrier between Wales and England that originally stretched some 120 miles, of which about 80 miles remain. Consisting of a ditch and an adjacent 8 feet high mound, and up to 60 feet wide (including the ditch), it was probably for defence but may have been a forward offensive fortification. One key factor to note is its reflection of the breadth and depth of Offa's power, in being able to muster and mobilise the resources necessary for the Dyke's construction, and in broader terms it also suggests a considerable sophistication of administrative mechanisms.[101] It would seem though that his exercising of power may well have been aided by a certain ruthlessness and use of violence. Alcuin, for example, writing to a Mercian friend in 797, refers to the great bloodshed Offa caused, in this case in killing off rival claimants so as to secure the succession for his son Ecgfrith (whom Offa consecrated as joint king in 787, some nine years before his own death in 796, but who survived his father Offa by just 141 days before being murdered), and treats this as a foolish act that was bad for the kingdom of Mercia.[102] However, on the other hand Offa also earns praise from the same writer – admittedly addressing his subject directly, which may have influenced his terminology – for his enthusiastic promotion of education, so much so that he is 'the glory of Britain'.[103] Staying on the positive side, he is associated with the first English coronation that involved consecration and anointment with holy oil (for his son Ecgfrith as mentioned above) and with the first major minting of the silver penny – though in fact coins had started to come back into use from around 600, being minted at Canterbury and London.

The apparent duality of good and bad in Offa is also described by William of Malmesbury in his *Chronicle of the Kings of England* (*Gesta Regum Anglorum*) of c. 1125. He describes him as a man of great ambition, but who shifts unpredictably between 'vice and virtue':

> When I consider the deeds of this person, I am doubtful whether I should commend or censure. At one time, in the same character, vices were so palliated by virtues, and at another virtues came in such quick succession upon vices that it is difficult to determine how to characterize the changing Proteus.[104]

William of Malmesbury may have had some bias towards the negative, as he refers to Malmesbury itself being among the considerable church land that Offa appropriated,[105] but even so, by all accounts it would seem that Offa's 'overlordship' was more a case of direct control through force than one of diplomatic forging of alliances for the sake of the emerging nation. Perhaps rather like the later William the Conqueror, he seems to be a case of 'cross me at your peril'.

Figure 2.2 Offa's Dyke just south of Knighton, looking south. The dyke here, which curves round in front of the forest, is in Wales (Powys), the present border being a mile or so to the east.

There are a number of similarities between Offa and the 'other king' mentioned by Charlemagne, Aethelred of Northumbria. Like Offa, Aethelred too had a record of bloody disposal of rivals, certainly in regaining his throne in 790, and he too was not a man to be crossed. Again like Offa, his life ended in 796. And again like Offa, who has an enduring association with the physical monument of the Dyke, Aethelred also has an enduring association, though of a less constructive nature, and that is with the notorious Viking attack on Lindisfarne, in his kingdom of Northumbria, in 793. This was not the first Viking attack on England, for Vikings had caused bloodshed at the Isle of Portland (Dorset) in 789,[106] but it was the first significant attack, moreover with evidence of plunder, and was a particularly ferocious one that resulted in the slaughter of numerous monks there. The *Anglo-Saxon Chronicle* records:

> Dire forewarnings came over the land of the Northumbrians, and miserably terrified the people: these were excessive whirlwinds and lightnings, and fiery dragons were seen flying in the air. A great famine soon followed these tokens, and a little after that, in the same year, the havoc of heathen men miserably destroyed God's church at Lindisfarne, through rapine and slaughter.[107]

In the following chapter, we pursue these raiders – figuratively speaking – and examine their impact on the newly established Anglo-Saxons.

2.5   The uninvited Vikings: Bad boys or bad press?

It is common practice nowadays to refer to the seaborne Scandinavians of the eighth to eleventh centuries as 'Vikings' – the exact meaning of the name is unclear, though it perhaps relates to 'those entering bays', or to 'plundering', or to the area of Viken (a historical term for the land around the Oslo Fjord) – but in those days they were usually known as 'Norsemen' or 'Danes' (and no doubt other more colourful names). This was an accurate description of the two main groups, who were indeed Norwegian and especially Danish, though the terms themselves often seem to have been used indiscriminately – in some but not all cases perhaps reflecting combined forces. (Moreover, the demarcation between these 'nations' was not necessarily as clear at this time as it is now.) There were also a smaller number of Swedes, though during their period of expansion most moved eastwards into Russia and elsewhere rather than westwards to Britain. The Vikings had been visiting Britain as traders since the sixth century or even earlier, but around the end of the eighth century their visits became more aggressive in purpose, namely raiding rather than trading. In general, the Norwegians attacked to the north and west, the Danes to the south and east,[108] but there were many exceptions to this, including, as mentioned above, combined attacks (such as at Maldon in 991, as will be discussed presently).

The exact reasons for the emergence of this 'Viking Phenomenon', which came to include a Viking presence as far afield as Vinland (North America) and North Africa and the Black Sea, are much debated and still not clear.[109] Theories span the political (instability in Scandinavia), the economic (trade), the geographic (easily accessible rich lands nearby), the demographic (overpopulation), the religious (reaction to encroaching Christianity), and the climatic (deterioration in Scandinavia),[110] though none has absolutely prevailed, but one 'bottom line' explanation that few scholars could disagree with is the likelihood that the Vikings did what they did because they wanted to and they could. This may sound rather flippant, but it does make sense. Technologically their longships were very efficient, their navigational skills were excellent, and they were people noted for their sense of adventure, their ability to endure hardship, and their physical prowess as fighters. Like the Anglo-Saxons and others – and we should bear in mind that they were not that far removed from the Anglo-Saxons, with a particular proximity in the case of the Viking Danes and the 'Anglo-Saxon' Jutes – they were no doubt attracted by the rewards of plunder, especially if the pickings were rich and easy.[111] Perhaps one can say that their initial trading intent became increasingly aggressive and 'raptorial' – to use Lawrence James's term[112] – to the point of just taking and not paying, which led in turn into simply turning up and intimidating the opposition into buying them off. But presently, just like the Anglo-Saxons, their thoughts would turn to acquisition of land – especially fertile land, which England had in plenty – and settlement (which tends to suggest relative unhappiness with their homelands).

On that matter of Viking settlement, we should note that here too there is still no firm consensus about scale, or about impact. One of the major figures in Viking studies over the last half-century, Peter Sawyer, is noted for taking a minimalist view regarding settlement scale and impact (in England), but he has been widely challenged, particularly in terms of linguistic evidence that strongly suggests a large scale settlement and linguistic impact, such as place-names and personal names as well as lexical items and even grammar.[113] Settlement impact in other regards may have been less, with Scandinavians in many cases taking over existing structures and institutions.[114] Of course, churches and monasteries (and their libraries) were to suffer, but this was generally early on and at the hands of raiders rather than settlers.

We should also bear in mind that 'the Vikings', rather like the 'Anglo-Saxons', are typically grouped together for convenience of reference, but in actuality did not necessarily have any binding common ethnic identity. It is more likely that war-bands and settlers represented a mix of regional locations and affiliations, and that solidarity was by no means permanent.[115] The same principle can be applied to the two 'waves' of Viking incursions and presence (to be discussed presently), in that the second wave of Vikings could not necessarily rely on support from descendants of the first wave.

Another important matter to bear in mind is that the British (and other nations') view of the Vikings is heavily coloured by accounts written by clerics of the day, who tended only to portray the incidents of aggression, and that more positive Viking achievements have been overlooked as a result.[116] In fact, in recent years there has been increasing recognition of this and scholars have tried to approach the study of the Vikings in a more open-minded way, though one has to say that to treat them as 'maligned and misunderstood victims of a Christian press',[117] or as 'cultivated men with elevated thoughts and honourable intentions'[118] might be overly generous. Lawrence James notes these recent attempts to 'rehabilitate' the Vikings, with a positive emphasis being put on their trading activities and their shipbuilding and navigational skills, but realistically adds that men with names such as Eric Bloodaxe and Thorfinn Skullsplitter were probably not interested in merely picking up a bargain or wanting nothing more from life for their followers than to grow corn in East Anglia.[119] One tends to agree. Surely sobriquets such as these are not simply examples of negative labelling theory put into practice by a Christian press!

Unfortunately the Vikings were of limited literacy (or at least made limited use of literacy) and left no contemporary written accounts of their own.[120] Their famous rune stone inscriptions, dating mostly from the late-tenth and eleventh centuries, cast little light on their raids and overseas settlement.[121] The somewhat later Icelandic saga writers could be said to represent a recorded Viking voice, but, as Else Roesdahl observes, they tended if anything to elaborate on the violent accounts of the clerics in order to try to establish a 'dramatic national identity'.[122]

It is fair to point out that the Vikings have a limited press of their own through which to make their case, but it is equally fair to point out that the Vikings did do their bloody deeds. Obviously they were by no means the only people in history to do so, for such behaviour was commonplace, but in terms of degree they would surely not be at the lower end of the list. However, looking on the positive side, as suggested above, we should indeed also note some of their more constructive achievements, which included impressive artwork, superb seamanship and boat-building, and widespread trade and exploration. Among other things, they were the first recorded Europeans to reach 'Vinland' (North America), around the year 1000.[123]

Roesdahl goes on to refer to their subsequent settlement and integration in lands they had conquered (such as England), their contribution to the establishment of trading centres, their employment as imperial guards in Byzantium, their employment – and rewards – as defenders against other Vikings (as in the French land granted to Rollo in 911 which subsequently became Normandy), and their attainment of elite status in some lands (such as Russia).[124] We should indeed bear these attainments in mind, but in a balanced context.

Returning to their recorded deeds in Britain, specifically (for the moment) the early raids, Logan reminds us that, given the backdrop of the violence of Anglo-Saxons against each other, in both extent and frequency, the early Viking raids were nothing special in that regard, but what did make them different was the fact that the perpetrators were foreign.[125]

As mentioned in the previous chapter, the first clear Viking aggression in England was in 789, at Portland in Dorset. The *Anglo-Saxon Chronicle* records that

> [There] came three ships of Northmen from Haerethaland [Hordaland in western Norway]. And then the reeve rode thereto and would drive them to the king's vill [town], for he knew not what they were; and they there slew him. These were the first ships of Danish men [sic] [*Deniscra manna*] that sought [*gesohton*] the land of the English race.[126]

The *Chronicle of Aethelweard*, believed to have been written c. 985 by a Wessex ealdorman and obviously drawing on a source other than the *Anglo-Saxon Chronicle*, adds that upon hearing of the arrival of three 'speedy vessels', the reeve, named Beaduheard and based in nearby Dorchester, rode to meet them with just a few men, thinking they were merchants with no aggressive intent, and spoke to them in an 'authoritative manner'.[127]

Given the apparent sharp attitude of the reeve, there may have been some provocation leading to his fatal misfortune, but this does not exonerate the Viking aggressors. Moreover, the reference to 'speedy vessels' clearly suggests longboats (known as *drakkar*, meaning 'dragon') rather than the slower *knarr*, which was the typical Viking trading vessel. This in turn would strongly suggest that they came with belligerent rather than mercantile intent, and thus it is quite possible that the reeve's realisation of this may have caused his harsh attitude. Unfortunately, we have no firm record of what happened next and what became of these three boatloads of Vikings, despite their important role in history.

As mentioned in the previous chapter, it was the attack on Lindisfarne four years later – specifically 8 June, 793[128] – that really signalled deliberate Viking aggression. Alcuin for one was personally devastated, and very shortly after the attack wrote a number of letters of condolence-cum-exhortation. To the Bishop of Lindisfarne, Higbald, he encouraged steadfastness in the face of this 'calamity' in which the pagans had desecrated God's sanctuary, shed the blood of saints, and trampled on the bodies of saints as if they were 'dung in the street'.[129] To King Aethelred of Northumbria, he lamented the unprecedented terror caused by the pagans and that such a holy place had become 'prey to pagan peoples'.[130] He then, in a manner reminiscent of Gildas two and a half centuries earlier, advised Aethelred that the terror was likely linked to corruption, particularly with regard to inequality of wealth between nobles and commoners, and that the attack on Lindisfarne was God's judgement, so Aethelred should set an example and defend his country by prayer, justice, and mercy.[131]

In an age when so many events were seen as God's judgement, it is inevitable that apparent contradictions occasionally surfaced. While Alcuin suggests that God was using the Vikings as agents of His wrath, Symeon of Durham (the church at Durham having its roots in Lindisfarne), writing around 1110, gives a graphic description of the slaughter and then writes (twice) that God soon punished the Vikings for killing holy men during the attack, for the very same Viking raiders were shipwrecked and killed the following year, their leader meeting a particularly 'cruel death'.[132]

Alcuin's letter to Aethelred contains a number of interesting observations. For example, several times he condemns extravagant dressing among the wealthy and also observes that in the matter of beard and hairstyles they have consciously and naively sought to imitate the pagans.[133] It is difficult to judge how long a fashion trend lasted in those days, but clearly Alcuin indicates an emulation among the Anglo-Saxons of those who had now attacked them, such emulation presumably indicating in turn reasonably positive attitudes towards the Vikings and reasonably cordial relations with them up till 793, notwithstanding the 789 incident.

Alcuin also refers to seemingly widespread surprise at the logistics of the attack, for it had been believed that such a seaborne assault could not happen.[134]

Given that the Anglo-Saxons themselves had a history of launching seaborne attacks, his comment indicates an acknowledgement of the superiority of the Vikings in this regard. He was certainly concerned enough to send a letter also to the monks at Jarrow to be on their guard – advice well-merited, for Jarrow was indeed attacked the following year of 794. This was followed in 795 by an attack on the monastery at Iona, on the west coast.

It was as if a pattern was emerging of annual attacks on major Christian centres, though what exactly lay behind this apparent strategy – other than the fact that they were relatively lucrative and easy targets – is unclear. It may indeed have been just that, namely that they were lucrative and easy targets, or it may have been a response to the perceived encroachment of Christianity, or perhaps it was a mix of both motives, or even perhaps it was just a case of literate clerics not surprisingly highlighting attacks on holy sites more than on other sites.[135]

There is an interesting commentary by Eric Oxenstierna on the attack on Lindisfarne. He is clearly a staunch flag-flier for the Vikings, *inter alia* referring positively to their 'exuberant lust for action', and the 'fascination of their exploits'.[136] His commentary can be seen as a defence of sorts, and is worth quoting at some length. Having mentioned the slaughter of monks and cattle and the seizing of monastic treasure, he writes:

> But what really happened? Men who have been on the open sea for weeks have to go on land from time to time to rest and find provender. Very often the alien native population doesn't welcome them. Fresh meat and water have to be gained by force. . . . On that summer day in Lindisfarne, the Norsemen acted according to the old seafarer's law. It is indicative that they slaughtered the cattle and took the carcasses with them. With that bit of information, the written sources give us the true purpose of the landing. To murder the monks, who did not defend themselves like men, and to take booty was just too tempting and therefore irresistible.[137]

I am tempted to use my teenage son's favourite phrase of 'Yeah, right', but I will merely draw attention here, in scholarly fashion, to the fact that it represents an extreme manifestation of the point made above about the Vikings taking easy pickings because they could. What all this might say about human nature, among other things, is an issue for another day. Oxenstierna goes on to remark, less controversially, that once these men returned home with their booty, the message soon spread about how easy it was to obtain, 'completely unguarded on the British coast'.[138]

Obviously, others in Scandinavia did get the message. Along with Jarrow and Iona, other 'easy targets' were attacked on a number of occasions in the coming years, in addition to some more demanding targets. However, in general, the

Vikings – particularly Norwegian Vikings – left England alone and concentrated on Ireland for the first few decades of the ninth century, the first attack there taking place in 795 at Innismurray on the northwest coast. Dublin, for example, was founded by the Vikings in 841, and became a major Viking centre and a base for attacks on Wales and other western territory – though in 838 the Britons of Cornwall actually allied with the Vikings in an unsuccessful attempt to defeat the Anglo-Saxons of Wessex under King Egbert (r. 802–39).[139] Other attacks took place on the continent, presumably also deemed soft targets, such as Aquitaine in 799, Frisia in 810, and Aquitaine again in 820.[140]

As Egbert's activities might suggest, during this first half of the ninth century Wessex reasserted itself, including over Mercia, and was recognised as the most powerful of the English kingdoms. Offa's effective successor, Coenwulf (Cenwulf, r. 796–821),[141] had retained Mercian control of Kent, Essex, and Sussex, and to some extent East Anglia, but he lost Wessex to Egbert in 802. After Coenwulf's death Mercia was plagued by instability in its leadership, which undermined its own strength and its ability to control other kingdoms. Coenwulf was succeeded in 821 by Ceolwulf I (r. 821–3), who was succeeded by Beornwulf (r. 823–5), succeeded by Ludeca (r. 826–7), succeeded by Beornwulf's son Wiglaf (r. 827–9, and again 830–40). Under Beornwulf Mercia was defeated by Egbert in 825 at the Battle of Ellendun (near Wroughton in Wiltshire), which saw the start of a shift in power to Wessex. As a result of the defeat Mercia lost control of the southeast territories to Wessex, while Egbert became the eighth king to be termed *bretwalda*. Worse was to follow for Mercia in 829, when Egbert drove out Wiglaf, with Mercia itself coming under the control of Wessex. However, Mercia very quickly fought back under Wiglaf, and he regained his throne the following year, along with autonomy for Mercia. Thereafter Mercia achieved some stability in its leadership, with Wiglaf's second reign spanning ten years, and with another of Beornwulf's sons, Beorhtwulf (r. 840–52), then reigning for 12, and then Burhred (Burgred, r. 852–74) reigning for 22 years, but it was unable to regain its former status as leading kingdom. That status now lay with Wessex.

In Wessex there was somewhat greater stability, at least during the time Mercia was not stable. Egbert, having reigned 37 years, was succeeded in 839 by his son Acthelwulf (r. 839–58), who reigned another 19 years. He was father to four kings, including the renowned Alfred (r. 871–99). Alfred followed his three elder brothers Aethelbald (r. 856–60), Aethelberht (r. 860–5), and Aethelred (I) (r. 865–71). However, the House of Wessex too was to have its share of acrimony, with for example Aethelbald obliging his father Aethelwulf to share the throne with him from 856, and Aethelred's son Aethelwold contesting his uncle Alfred's assumption of the throne. Nevertheless, among the Anglo-Saxon kingdoms, if the eighth century was dominated by Mercia, then the ninth was dominated by Wessex.

However, Wessex, along with other kingdoms, had a greater threat than from Mercia, and that was from the Vikings, who had resumed raiding England from around 835. In 850 the Vikings had, instead of withdrawing to their homeland after the 'raiding season' of clement weather, decided to overwinter in Thanet. This was ominous, portending other overwinterings and the threat of a more permanent presence. And the portents proved meaningful: for example, in 854/5 there was another overwintering, this time on Sheppey, followed by a number of other attacks, and then, in late 865, the so-called 'Great Army' landed in East Anglia, led by the brothers Halfdan (d. 877) and Ingwaer (d. 873), sons of the legendary Ragnar Lodbrok.[142] Numbers are not clear, but it must have been a very significant force. Whatever its numbers, it did not go away. Far from it, in 866 the Vikings of the Great Army raided extensively in East Anglia, securing a significant foothold, and later that year, aided by dynastic discord, achieved the conquest of Northumbria, establishing a major base at York (Jorvik, November 866). The following year they also took control of the eastern part of Mercia and wintered in Nottingham. After a return to York for a year they came back to East Anglia in 869 and consolidated their control of it, killing the East Anglian king Edmund. However, an attempt to encroach into Wessex the following year was thwarted on the Berkshire Downs by a force under the brothers Aethelred and Alfred, representing the first significant defeat for the Vikings. In April 871 Viking reinforcements arrived, possibly under Guthrum (d. 890), and in a year of numerous clashes – the *Anglo-Saxon Chronicle* for that year records nine major battles[143] – they prepared once again to invade Wessex. At this point Aethelred died, and Alfred, in his early twenties, assumed the throne of Wessex.

He was challenged by (those representing) Aethelred's sons, Aethelwold and Aethelhelm, particularly Aethelwold, who appears to have been the elder. Aethelhelm's claim does not seem to have been very vigorously pursued and was soon discounted, while Aethelwold's claim was probably thwarted on two counts. First, though his exact date of birth is not clear, he must have been a child at the time. Second, Alfred had long been seen as the heir-apparent, reflecting the wishes of their father Aethelwulf, and Aethelred himself respected this.[144] However, Aethelwold should not be written off, for as we shall see presently, he was to make a further and stronger claim upon Alfred's death in 899.

Alfred's early years as king were not particularly successful. He suffered a number of minor defeats and ended up buying off the Vikings.[145] He was not the first to offer money for peace (and nor was this the only time he did so), either in England or elsewhere in Europe – for we should not forget that the Vikings were also raiding in countries on the continent, and were causing huge problems there as well as in England. For example, in the 860s the monk Ermentarius of Noirmoutier referred to the massacres, burnings, and plunderings of the 'all-conquering' Vikings across much of France, including Bordeaux, Périgeux,

Limoges, Angoulême, Toulouse, Angers, Tours, Orléans, Rouen, Paris, Beauvais, Meaux, Melun, Chartres, Evreux, and Bayeux.[146]

As for examples of payments outside Britain, in 810 in Frisia the Vikings were paid 100 pounds of silver as tribute and in 845 Charles the Bald, King of France, paid a very large sum of 7000 pounds of silver to Ragnar Lodbrok to take his Vikings away from Paris.[147] As a pre-Alfredian English example, the men of Kent had offered to buy off the Vikings in 864–5 – but the Vikings, while promising to accept the offer, in practice continued their ravaging. In his *Life of King Alfred* of 893, the contemporary Welsh bishop Asser – though his authorship has been seriously challenged and the author may in fact have been a later hagiographer[148] – comments on this incident, and seemingly also as a general principle, that stealing booty was more profitable for them than making peace regardless of any 'peace-money' paid.[149]

The Kentishmen's experience shows two things: one, that the Vikings were not necessarily trustworthy; and two, that any payment to them would have to be very significant to outweigh the potential gains from raiding. Presumably therefore, though we do not know the sum, Alfred's payment must have been very large, for Wessex was apparently left in peace for some four years. During this time the Vikings turned their attention to Mercia, conquering it (or at least the eastern part) in 874 and expelling Burhred. Then once again they turned towards Wessex, though with reduced forces since many of their men, under Halfdan, instead headed north to York to settle. The force that now headed to Wessex was led by Guthrum. Their attacks in 875 and 876 were largely unsuccessful – though Alfred appears to have made payment to them again[150] – and they retired to Mercia. Here another group split off to settle in parts of the north and east midlands. Yet once again, early in January 878, Guthrum and his men attempted to take Wessex, and this time, despite greatly reduced strength, they had surprise on their side and made major inroads.

As is so well known, Alfred was forced to retreat to a refuge in the marshes of Athelney in Somerset, with which he had been familiar since childhood, though whether he actually did burn those cakes or not – a story first noted in the late-tenth century[151] – is a matter of debate. Whether true or not, the story is surely indicative of his state of mind, understandably distracted given that he was beset by persistent and rampant invaders and in danger of losing his kingdom in Wessex along with the bigger prize of the country as a whole. Many in his position might have given up at this stage, but, showing great patience and perseverance and tenacity, Alfred steadily regathered his forces and then in May launched a decisive and successful attack on Guthrum near Edington, near Westbury in Wiltshire. According to Asser, Guthrum and his men were forced to retreat to their 'stronghold', which Alfred besieged for 14 days till the Vikings came out and sued for peace, offering unprecedented terms such as an unlimited and non-reciprocal offer of hostages.[152] Epoch-making though these terms might have been, Alfred pressed home his advantage even further. He not only took hostages, he seems to have pressed Christianity upon the Vikings (or at least their leaders), in addition to an understandable withdrawal from Wessex. The upshot was that peace was agreed upon, and Guthrum and some 30 of his leading men were presently baptised by Alfred himself.

This was to be followed by a wider adoption of Christianity by the Vikings through the following century – in their homelands and other settlements as well as in England.[153] However, this must be tempered by the apparent fact that many (though not all) Vikings treated 'conversion' to Christianity very lightly. Indeed, it was not uncommon for Viking mercenaries in Christian employ, or Viking merchants in Christian countries, to adopt Christianity at a nominal level, in a practice known as 'provisional baptism' or 'prime-signing' (*primasigna*), for the benefit of expediency (such as better access and better treatment), while in practice often openly retaining their original religious beliefs.[154]

Guthrum withdrew his army from Chippenham to Cirencester and eventually to East Anglia. The exact expectations of where they would finally withdraw to are not clear at this point, but it would seem that Alfred recognised their right to some territory in England.[155] We can note Alfred took London from the Danes in 886, and it was perhaps following this that a treaty was drawn up with Guthrum (obviously sometime before the latter's death in 890), which resulted in a division northwest from London to the northwest midlands.[156] The eastward side of this was recognised as basically Danish, and was later, stretching roughly as far as the Tees, to be known as the Danelaw. English people living in the Danelaw became subject to the Danes.[157] Though obviously inter-marriage between Danish male and English female would have been frequent, it would seem that presently significant numbers of Scandinavian women and children also arrived in England, showing clear Viking intent to settle.[158] Danish settlements are reflected in the number of towns ending in '-by' or '-thorp(e)'. (By contrast, Norwegian settlements are represented by '-thwaite' and Anglo-Saxon by '-ham', -'ing', '-borough', '-ford', '-worth' and so on, typically following a person's name, such as Birmingham meaning 'the home [ham] of the followers [ing] of Beorma'.[159]) However, despite Scandinavian influence, English seems to have remained the major language.

This was by no means the end of hostilities, however. For example, in 893 a large Danish force sailed into the Thames and over the next two or three years caused considerable damage by raiding, though not as effectively as in earlier years, and particularly ineffectively in the case of Wessex. To combat an ongoing threat from the Vikings Wessex and western Mercia had formed an alliance, strengthened through the marriage – probably in 886 – of Alfred's daughter Aethelflaed (c. 870–918) to Aethelred of Mercia (d. 911), and continued to conduct joint campaigns against them.

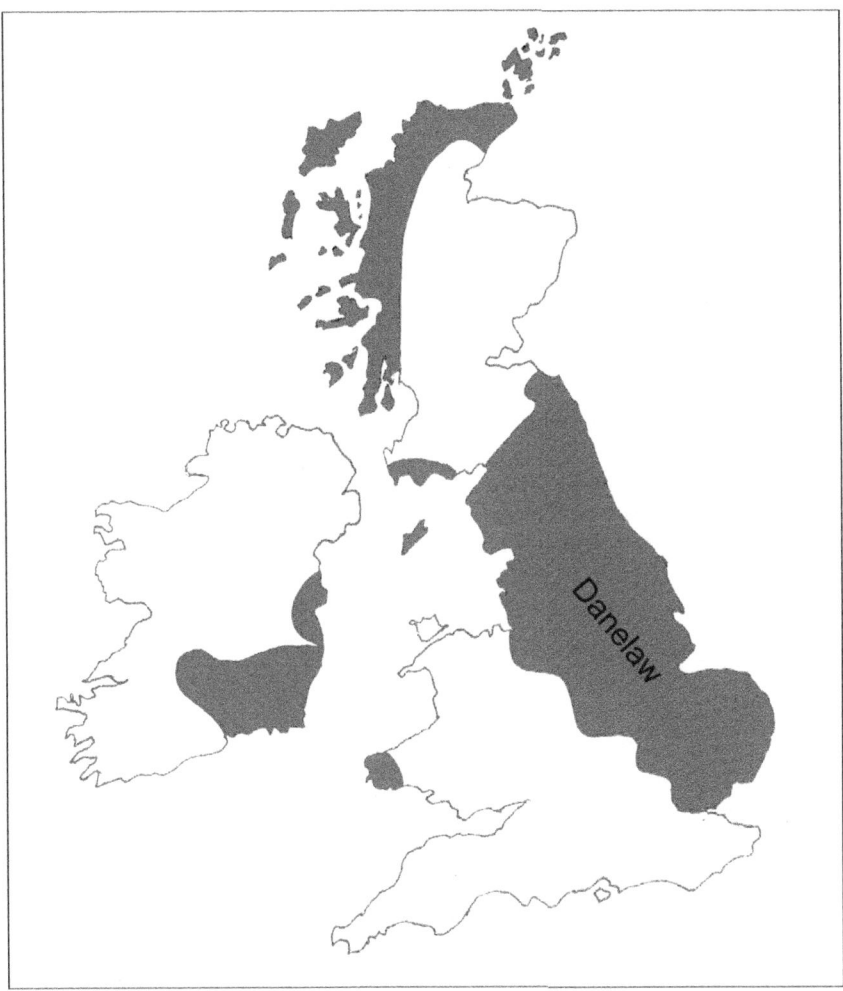

Figure 2.3 Viking influence in the late Anglo-Saxon period.

To further help defences, Alfred constructed a network of 30 or so *burhs/burghs* (boroughs), or fortified towns, situated in such a way that virtually nobody in Wessex was more than a day's walk – 20 miles – from one. In an early example of town planning, each was designed on a systematic grid pattern. In many cases these were built upon former Roman centres, such as Winchester, and in some cases they also became important centres of commerce. He also arranged for their defence to be maintained through a local administration system. Furthermore, he reformed military service in such a way that instead of the whole army being called up for service, only half was on service at any given time, which proved more efficient. This was the forerunner of the *fyrd*. And with a view to dealing with seaborne raiders before they reached land, he built up a formidable navy, moreover designing many of the ships himself.

We have to bear in mind that Asser's *Life of King Alfred* – the first biography of an English king – paints a positive picture of him, as does the *Anglo-Saxon Chronicle*, in the compilation of which Alfred appears to have been instrumental. These positive portrayals make him seem the perfect king – and for many the perfect Englishman – and have evidently swayed many later interpretations, particularly in nineteenth century England. In actuality, he would almost certainly, like any other king in those days, have had a less wonderful side to his character. David Bates, for example, writes that to achieve what he did Alfred must have been 'extremely ruthless', that his declaration that he was king of the English denied such a claim from others, and that his seizure of London (a Mercian town) and monastic lands show his readiness to override existing property rights if it suited him.[160]

In similar vein Barbara Yorke refers to resentment by the people of Wessex towards Alfred's demands upon them for military service, public works, and contributions towards tribute to be paid to the Vikings, and remarks that he was able to get away with this by claiming it was in the interests of the kingdom, though she concedes that he must also have had a reasonable support base.[161] F. Donald Logan also expresses reservations about Alfred, including his alleged military skills and the claims that he saved England. He points out that he bought off the Vikings in 871 and again in 875 rather than fighting them off, made no move to help Mercia in 873–4, was still initially unprepared in 878, and ended up ceding a large portion of England.[162] I myself would add that Alfred's much lauded conversion of Guthrum and his men to Christianity may well not have been all that meaningful, as discussed earlier.

But for all that undoubted occasional harshness and self-centredness, Alfred does seem to have been a multi-talented and energetic individual in many regards, his wide-ranging accomplishments and activities perhaps all the more noteworthy because he seems to have suffered for most of his life from a succession of illnesses, including chronic pain from the age of 19.[163] Those accomplishments are said to include a number of inventions such as candle-clocks, the personal designing of ships for his strengthened navy, and the promotion of education and literacy. The latter included pressing literacy upon his nobles, and he himself contributed in no small measure to this by his translation of Latin texts into English. As mentioned above, he is also believed to have taken a role in instigating the compilation of the *Anglo-Saxon Chronicle*, appreciating the value of records – and perhaps, a cynic might add, propaganda. In fact, he is the only English monarch before Henry VIII to have written books. He was respected for his talents in matters ranging from military (at least to some degree) to scholarly, and was also seen – in general, but by no means universally – as a fair and just ruler. This had the advantage of bringing a certain natural unity under his leadership. Alfred Smyth observes that Alfred's real strength was not so much in an ability to excel in any one field, but in his possession of 'the qualities of a great all-rounder'.[164] It is a significant testimony to his accomplishments and the perception of him by people at large – and again perhaps to his panegyrists – that he has been in recent centuries the only English king to be referred to consistently as 'the Great',[165] though the later monarch Cnut (r. 1016–35) is sometimes referred to as 'Cnut the Great', albeit no doubt in recognition of his rule over other nations as well as England (England 1016–35, Denmark 1019–35, and Norway 1028–35).[166] In a broader context this places him alongside figures such as Charlemagne (Charles the Great), a monarch similarly recognised for his promotion of education and learning as well as his military and political strengths – though Barbara Yorke observes that Alfred was not quite the same towering monarch that Charlemagne was.[167]

Let us conclude that we should take a balanced view of him, as does Christopher Brooke. After commenting on the dangers of idealising Alfred, Brooke observes that he was after all human and that his wish for a better life for his subjects has something of the heroic about it.[168]

Alfred died in October 899, still in his early fifties. Though this might be felt to be a somewhat premature death, it can be said – as indeed Douglas Woodruff has[169] – that Alfred might even have been looking forward to it, in the sense that his intellectual curiosity had once moved him to remark that it would be a foolish person who did not 'long to reach that endless life' – i.e. the afterlife – 'where all shall be made clear'.

On this mortal coil, Alfred was succeeded by his son Edward the Elder (r. 899–924). Nick Higham, along with many others, feels that Edward has long been neglected and deserves better recognition for his 25-year reign that saw an expansion of England.[170] He attributes this neglect in large part to unflattering comparison with his father Alfred, particularly in the matter of learning, along with a lack of documentation.

However, Edward was like his father in that his succession was contested by Aethelwold, his cousin, who had been unsuccessful in his claim to the throne in 871. This time it was a much closer affair. One can feel some sympathy for Aethelwold, as he was the victim of an arrangement between his father Aethelred and his uncle Alfred with respect to the wishes of their father Aethelwulf. As mentioned earlier, this arrangement had facilitated Alfred's succession as Aethelred's brother – or more exactly as Aethelwulf's son – over Aethelred's son(s). But in addition, the terms of the arrangement stipulated that, while the children of the brother who died first would be well provided for by the surviving brother, when it came to succession the surviving brother could pass over his nephews in favour of his own children.[171]

That is exactly what Alfred did in leaving the kingdom to his son Edward. But, whether intentional or not, the situation was made even worse for Aethelwold because he was given fewer and lesser estates than in 871, as is clear from Alfred's will.[172] Keynes and Lapidge remark that Aethelwold would have had cause to feel aggrieved by this.[173]

Not surprisingly, Aethelwold rebelled. The *Anglo-Saxon Chronicle* records that upon Edward's succession Aethelwold seized a number of manors and then, pursued by Edward, '[Aethelwold] stole away by night and sought the [Viking] army in Northumbria and they received him for their king and submitted to him'.[174] He appears to have spent a year or so overseas, presumably in Denmark itself, for he was termed 'king of the Danes', and returned leading a great fleet.[175] He then mustered great support in East Anglia (or at least a part of it under the rule of a little-known king called Eohric) and Essex, in addition to his Danish forces – presumably from both Northumbria and Denmark. His forces raided into Mercia. Then, laden with booty, they were pursued by Edward as they returned. The armies clashed somewhere in the fens of the southern Danelaw, and Edward was victorious. Both Aethelwold and Eohric were killed in the battle, of which we have few details, but which almost certainly took place in either 902 or 903.

Though Aethelwold's rebellion is not a particularly widely known matter, it is an important one. James Campbell writes that Aethelwold may well have become 'one of the greatest figures' in British history but for the fortunes of battle.[176] Campbell also observes that he had a good claim to the throne of Wessex; he was accepted or at least influential in much of the east and north and may have brought about a less violent unity,[177] presumably through his acceptance by the Vikings.

Edward, after Aethelwold's death, was able to consolidate his position. He worked together against the Vikings with Aethelred of Mercia, who had married Edward's elder sister Aethelflaed. Aethelred's health deteriorated over some years and the kingdom was in effect ruled by Aethelflaed, who became known as the Lady of the Mercians. She is sometimes seen nowadays as a latter-day Boudica in her determination and willingness to fight. She and Edward successfully helped resist a major Viking raid on Mercia in 910 and then went on the offensive, attacking the Danelaw from the south. She became reigning queen of Mercia after her husband Aethelred's death in 911[178] and was kept busy on her western frontier by the Welsh, on the northwest by renewed Norwegian Viking attacks from Ireland, and on the east by the Danelaw Vikings. Using her father's system of *burh* establishment, she not only made a successful defence, but also was able to take Derby in 917 and Leicester in 918, occupying the Vikings sufficiently for her brother to make major advances in the southern part of the Danelaw. Aethelflaed seems to have been a formidable character. William of Malmesbury writes:

> Ethelfled, sister of the king and relict [widow] of Ethelred, ought not to be forgotten, as she was a powerful accession to his party, the delight of his

subjects, the dread of his enemies, a woman of an enlarged soul, who, from the difficulty experienced in her first labour, ever after refused the embraces of her husband; protesting that it was unbecoming the daughter of a king to give way to a delight which, after a time, produced such painful consequences. This spirited heroine assisted her brother greatly with her advice, was of equal service in building cities, nor could you easily discern whether it was more owing to fortune or to her own exertions that a woman should be able to protect men at home and to intimidate them abroad.[179]

Fortunately, the English reoccupation of the Danelaw was helped by the wish for peace of many of the Scandinavian settlers there, who were weary of fighting and simply wanted to get on with life under a strong leader who could ensure stability. But on the reverse side of fortune, Aethelflaed died in the summer of 918, shortly after taking Leicester (without bloodshed) and seemingly just as she was about to receive the promised submission of the people of York. The *Anglo-Saxon Chronicle* tells us, in the entry for 918:

> In this year, with the aid of God, in the early part of the year, she got into her power peacefully the burgh at Leicester; and the greatest part of the [Viking] army which belonged thereto became subjected to her. And the people of York had also promised her, and some given a pledge, and some confirmed by oaths, that they would be at her disposal. But very soon after they had agreed thereon, she died at Tamworth twelve nights before Midsummer (June 12th), in the eighth year from the time she rightfully held the lordship over the Mercians.[180]

Aethelflaed's contribution to the survival and indeed expansion of England was very significant, in stark contrast to the disaster under Boudica, and in my personal view it is a shame that she does not enjoy anywhere near the degree of fame that Boudica does. She is, like Boudica in a 'Celtic' context, sometimes seen in an Anglo-Saxon context as evidence of positive attitudes towards women that included acceptance of them as leaders. Be that as it may, as Barbara Yorke points out, this view has to be tempered by the fact that both her father Alfred and brother Edward had their own political ambitions towards Mercia, and indeed shortly after her death Edward simply brushed aside her daughter Aelfwyn and took control of the kingdom for himself.[181]

The *Anglo-Saxon Chronicle* states, 'Aethelflaed his sister died at Tamworth, twelve nights before midsummer. And then he [Edward] took possession of the borough at Tamworth, and all the people in the Mercians' land, who had before been subject to Aethelflaed, submitted to him.'[182] 'Submitted' may seem a harsh term, but in fact, though some Mercians would seem to have been prepared to have Aelfwyn as their ruler,[183] it is quite likely that more Mercians may have preferred Edward. As Maggie Bailey observes, Aelfwyn was not well established, had limited support, and was faced with ruling over a recently enlarged territory, whereas Edward was an experienced military commander well disposed towards Mercia.[184]

Thus Aethelflaed goes down in history as the last independent ruler of Mercia, and Aelfwyn disappears from Mercia with a brief and somewhat intriguing entry in the *Anglo-Saxon Chronicle*:

> In this year also the daughter of Ethelred, Lord of the Mercians, was deprived of all power, and conveyed into Wessex, three weeks before Midwinter. She was called Aelfwyn.[185]

Despite this entry following shortly after the entry about her mother Aethelflaed, and despite her father Aethelred having been dead for seven years at the time of her mother's death, she is nonetheless referred to as 'daughter of Aethelred' not 'daughter of Aethelflaed' – perhaps further tempering of the view that Anglo-Saxons had positive attitudes about women leaders.

To what fate was Aelfwyn led, following what Bailey terms 'her enforced Christmas vacation in Wessex'?[186] Aelfwyn was not married in 918, when she would be around 30 years of age, and it seems likely she did not marry subsequently, for there is no record of this. In fact, Bailey believes that she became a lay sister – a woman who had not taken full religious vows – and that a grant from King Eadred (see below) in 948 to 'Aelfwynn, religious woman' is this same Aelfwyn(n), aged 60 or thereabouts, who may well have ended her days at the nunnery in Wilton.[187]

By 920 the Vikings had been pushed north to the Humber by Edward. He was however unable to take York, which in 919 had fallen to Raegnald, a Norwegian based in Ireland. By this stage there seems to have been a significant rift between the Norwegians, especially those based in Ireland, and the Danes,[188] for it seems that the Irish-based Norwegians were keen to seize the northern Danelaw. Edward had also received the submissions of the kings of Gwynedd and Dyfed, and in 923 he similarly received the submission of the king of the new nation of Scotland, along with Northumbria and even – albeit very temporarily – Raegnald of York. This did not mean their surrendering of independence, but rather their acceptance of his overlordship, and it was not necessarily eternally binding.

Edward died in 924, succeeded by his son Athelstan (r. 924–39),[189] who had been raised by his aunt Aethelflaed of Mercia. Athelstan can in effect be called the first king of England,[190] but nonetheless relatively little is known about him. David Dumville describes him as enigmatic but remarkable and capable, and terms him 'the father of medieval and modern England'.[191]

In 927 Athelstan achieved control of York (which had been lost briefly the previous year) and in 937, with his younger brother Edmund, plus 300 Viking mercenaries under the Norwegian brothers Thorolf and Egil, achieved victory over a combined force of Scots (under Constantine) and Vikings (Norwegian, under Olaf Guthfrithsson), also including many Irish and Welsh, at the battle of Brunanburh (at an unknown northern site).[192]

This was a rare occasion for the *Anglo-Saxon Chronicle* to include poetry, of 70 or more lines. Space precludes giving the full poem here, but perhaps a few excerpts might convey something of its 'nationalistic' flavour:

> King Aethelstan, lord of earls, ring-giver of warriors,
> and his brother eke, Eadmund aetheling,
> life-long glory in battle won . . .
> . . . Edward's offspring,
> as was to them congenial from their ancestors,
> that they in conflict oft, 'gainst every foe,
> should the land defend, treasure and homes . . .
> The foes lay low,
> the Scots' people and the shipmen
> death-doomed fell . . .
> . . . Five lay on that battle-stead,
> young kings by swords put to sleep . . .
> . . . Constantine, hoary warrior . . .
> his son he left on the slaughter place, mangled with wounds . . .
> . . . Departed then the Northmen . . .
> . . . o'er the deep water, Dublin to seek, Ireland once more,
> in mind abash'd . . .
> . . . No slaughter has been greater in this island . . .
> . . . since hither from the east Angles and Saxons came to land . . .
> . . . the Welsh o'ercame, the country gain'd.[193]

Brunanburh was an attempt to curb Athelstan's power in the north, but it failed. Alfred had ruled the Angelcynn – 'the English kin/folk' – but, as mentioned earlier, it could be said of his grandson Athelstan that he was now effectively the king of England, including people other than Anglo-Saxon, such as in the Danelaw. Coins minted in his reign carry the title *rex totius Britanniae* – 'king of all Britain', and they show a crowned head. His reign also saw many sophisticated laws and charters, strong diplomatic links with foreign powers in Europe, and, as seen above, a growing sense of nationalism.

Athelstan died in 939 and was succeeded by his young brother Edmund (r. 939–46). Edmund was only around 17 at the time, but had seen action at Brunanburh. It may have been his age that counted against him, but very shortly he was forced to surrender York, and considerable territory in the northern Danelaw, to the Norwegian Olaf Guthfrithsson, king of Dublin, who had been among those on the losing side at Brunanburh. Fortunately for Edmund, after Guthfrithsson's death in 941, he was able to regain much of that lost territory, including York, helped by the fact that many of the local inhabitants preferred Christian Anglo-Saxon rule to that of the Vikings (even though York itself was largely a Norwegian town). However, Edmund's potential was not to be realised, for in 946 he was tragically murdered while trying to help his steward in a private dispute.

Edmund was succeeded by his brother Eadred (r. 946–55), the third of Edward the Elder's sons. Eadred was a devout Christian, was generous, and was administratively efficient, but he was plagued by serious ill-health and a seemingly anxious disposition. Unfortunately his reign is characterised not just by its relative brevity, but by the fact that much of it had a shadow over it in the form of one Eric Bloodaxe (d. 954), who in 947 seized power in York – which in those times was experiencing a maelstrom of rulers. Bloodaxe lived up to his colourful name and was an extremely violent man, among other things killing his own brothers. For a short time he had been King of Norway, but had been expelled in 946. He was expelled by the Northumbrians too, in 948 and again in 954, after having regained control of York two years before. After his second expulsion, as Eadred was marching towards him, he was betrayed to his enemies and killed by them.[194] He was the last ruler of an independent York.

Probably few would have wept over Eric's demise. It may not even have been necessary for Eadred to confront him, for he seems to have been his own worst enemy. No doubt, after experiencing life under Eric, the inhabitants of York would have welcomed Eadred with open arms. They were never again to have a Viking ruler. Unfortunately for Eadred, he was only to enjoy one further year free of Eric, for he died in 955. In his will, perhaps reflecting both his generosity and his anxiety, he left money to buy off future Viking incursions, thereby continuing to encourage a widespread but questionable practice.

Eadred's death was followed by a brief period which could have resulted in a serious setback for the new nation. He died without issue, and left the throne to his nephews Eadwig (r. 955–9) and Edgar (r. 959–75), sons of his brother Edmund. Eadwig, the elder, was around 15 when he inherited the throne. Nowadays he enjoys a mixed reputation, some seeing him as an unpleasant and incompetent figure, while others feel he was subsequently blackened by his brother Edgar's supporters.[195] He did treat certain individuals harshly, particularly those associated with his brother Edgar, confiscating their property and/or exiling others, such as (St) Dunstan, but it is not clear whether there was provocation. In 957 his brother Edgar, despite being only 14 at the time, was made king of Northumbria and Mercia following a revolt in Mercia, thereby partitioning the kingdom and halving Eadwig's realm of authority. Clearly Eadwig was not fully in control, and forces were at work against him. Civil war became a possibility, but, conveniently perhaps, he died in 959 and Edgar became the sole king. Most historians seem to accept his death as attributable to natural causes – and there were certainly many premature deaths through illness in those times[196] – but one might feel an open verdict is more appropriate (as indeed in other 'convenient deaths').[197]

The *Life of St Dunstan*, written in the early eleventh century, and which unsurprisingly paints Eadwig in a very bad light, records him as having deserted God and dying a miserable death, enabling the popular Edgar to succeed to the full throne.[198] There is no specific mention here of any illness or attempted treatment. Similarly a document written shortly after Edgar's death in 975, *King Edgar's Establishment of Monasteries*, also heavily criticises Eadwig for among other things giving church land to 'rapacious strangers', and states that God was on Edgar's side, ensuring that Eadwig's life ended prematurely.[199]

With Eadwig's premature death, through natural means or foul, the kingdom was once again united under a single monarch, the divinely favoured Edgar, and the churches fared better.

Edgar's reign was essentially one of peace and consolidation, aided by a lack of Viking belligerence at this time. His by-name, in fact, is 'Edgar the Peaceable'. He had a formal 'second' coronation in 973 at Bath, much of which ceremony was retained for coronations thereafter. Shortly afterwards he met with eight kings of Britain at Chester, who rowed him on the River Dee to indicate their submission to him. During his reign progressive laws were passed, such as recognition of Danish practices in the areas in which they lived. A major reform of coinage was enacted. Regional government became shaped around shires and counties that were essentially to remain in place until the latter half of the twentieth century. He worked closely with the church and was instrumental in Benedictine reforms aimed at improving moral standards and furthering links between king and church. (In fact, according to some scholars, his second coronation in his thirtieth year had a religious rationale in that this was the minimum age for ordination to the priesthood.) Regular assemblies of nobles and other dignitaries into a royal council known as the *witangemot* ('meeting of the wise') came into prominence, not exactly a parliament but at least a step in that direction – though of course we must not forget that this was not entirely new, for as early as the fifth century Vortigern was advised by a council.

So, by the mid 970s, all seemed reasonably well. Wessex had prevailed as the dominant kingdom and its kings were effectively kings of the nation of England. Compared with a thousand years before, when Caesar first appeared, the country was more cosmopolitan, with not just Britons but the various peoples of the Anglo-Saxons and Vikings. It was true that some of the Britons in Wales and some peoples in Scotland were not entirely happy to accept English kings and the Irish were not really in the equation, but at least in general there appeared to be a greater stability, certainly in England itself, than in Caesar's day. James Campbell remarks that by this stage there was, despite demonstrable diversity, a still greater degree of uniformity, unity, and a sense of nationhood among the English.[200] Perhaps ironically, it can be argued – and has been – that English unity was prompted by the Viking attacks, without which England might well have stayed as four independent states: Wessex, Mercia, East Anglia, and Northumbria.[201] Though a counter-argument can be made to the effect that there was increasing unity anyway, such as through exogamous marital inter-connections, it would seem unreasonable to deny the unifying effect of an external threat.

Whatever the contributing factors, at this stage all seemed fairly rosy for England. Was the first millennium going to be seen out in such a positive state? We shall see.

2.6   Aethelred and the 'New Wave' Vikings: Poor king or poor luck?

Upon Edgar's sudden death in 975, at just 32 years of age, the succession was disputed by his two young sons, Edward (b. c. 963) and Aethelred (b. c. 968) – or more exactly by the factions which grouped around them, for Edward was only around 12 years of age, and Aethelred just 7 or so. They were in fact half-brothers, with different mothers. Edward's mother seems to have been Aethelflaed Eneda ('White Duck'), though some sources suggest a nameless virgin seduced by Edgar.[202] Aethelred's mother was Aelfthryth, who married Edgar in 964. Interestingly, unlike the case with Eadwig and Edgar in the late 950s, when the kingdom was deliberately split between brothers, there was no apparent move to do likewise with a split rule between Edward and Aethelred. Perhaps Aethelred was considered just too young[203] to participate in shared rule, or perhaps the country had grown accustomed to the idea of regnal unity – even at the expense of fraternal unity – through the 16 years or so of Edgar's sole reign.[204] At the time succession was not based on a simple principle of primogeniture: a suitable candidate had to be throneworthy. As Simon Keynes points out, there were probably three reservations against Edward: doubts about the legitimacy of his birth; the apparent fact that, even if his birth was legitimate, the marriage between Aethelflaed and Edgar had not been consecrated; and the 'reputed severity' of Edward's character.[205] However, it was Edward's supporters who prevailed, perhaps because he was the elder, but more importantly perhaps thanks to the endorsement of Edward by the powerful Archbishop Dunstan (c. 909–88).

Alas for Edward and his supporters, he was murdered shortly afterwards in 978 (18 March), allegedly stabbed by Aethelred's supporters while on a visit to his younger brother and step-mother Aelfthryth in Corfe.[206] He was later canonised as a martyr, while his brother Aethelred's reward – insofar as he was fully aware of it at the age of ten or so – was more immediate and terrestrial, for he became king.

Figure 2.4 Coins (replicas) depicting Offa and Aethelred Unraed, two of the best-known figures in Anglo-Saxon history.

The assassins remain unknown. Though it is unlikely Aethelred himself had any actual part in the murder, or any knowledge of it beforehand, the affair may have had some effect on his subsequent state of mind and behaviour. He may indeed have felt some guilt at inheriting the throne as a result of his brother's murder (regardless of who did it). Some would argue it might perhaps have been more specifically over his mother's possible involvement. Nick Higham points out that it is strange that he appears not to have taken any steps to try to find the culprit and avenge his half-brother's murder, even though there was a strong moral and legal obligation on him to do so, and sees this as a pointer to his mother's probable involvement.[207] Aethelred's own legislation in later years (1008) set 18 March as Edward's commemoration day,[208] and this is often cited as evidence of his feelings of guilt, but Ann Williams points out that this would appear to be a later interpolation of c. 1018, suggesting it was by Cnut.[209] Nonetheless Aethelred does appear to have promoted veneration of Edward, and Williams refers to him as possibly the biggest sponsor of his brother's sanctity and feels that this might reflect some 'residual guilt'.[210] This veneration included the establishment of a monastery in Edward's honour at Cholsey in Berkshire.

There would seem to be no firm evidence that Aethelred was deemed personally culpable by his contemporaries,[211] at least in his early years. However, the fact that he soon came to earn an enduringly bad reputation, including being deemed guilty of the crime, is clear from his blackening by early historians such as William of Malmesbury and the emergence of apocryphal stories.[212] More particularly, the subsequent Viking invasions came to be seen by some earlier historians as divine punishment for his crime.[213] And of course one has to consider his later popular and indeed ongoing designation as 'Ethelred the Unready' – though this reflects criticism of his later reign and is not particularly related to possible involvement in Edward's murder. The epithet is in fact a mis-interpretation, probably through an intermediate form 'Ethelred the Unrede', of 'Aethelraed Unraed', this being a twelfth century pun on his name 'Aethelraed', meaning 'noble counsel', by linking it with its opposite 'Unraed', meaning 'no counsel' – in linguistic terms, an oxymoronic appellation, with poetic metre.

But many would perhaps prefer to treat Aethelred as a moron than an oxymoron, and as unready rather than inadequately advised. But unready for what? Unready for the Danes, according to Sellar and Yeatman in 1930 in their well known humorous account of British history, *1066 And All That*. We might indeed find it a useful approach to consider their humorous description of him first – for Aethelred's association with unreadiness and other negative attributes is so well entrenched in our consciousness that it is difficult to approach him without this image – and then compare it against the real Aethelred, insofar as we can arrive at something close to reality. (I will make a specific comparison in the questions at the end of Part 2.) They write – and I quote the entire entry, with their spelling and capitalisation:

> Ethelread the Unready was the first Weak King of England and thus the cause of a fresh Wave of Danes. He was called the Unready because he was never ready when the Danes were. Rather than wait for him the Danes used to fine him large sums called Danegeld, for not being ready. But though they were always ready, the Danes had very bad memories and often used to forget that they had been paid the Danegeld and come back for it almost before they had sailed away. By that time Ethelread was always unready again. Finally, Ethelread was taken completely unawares by his own death and was succeeded by Canute.[214]

Aethelred had a long reign, from 978 to 1016, with a short break towards the end (discussed below). During the course of that reign he was to show a certain competence in administration, implement – or at least oversee – some excellent legislation, strengthen the navy, and give substantial support to the church. However, overall it was an unfortunate reign which, put bluntly, ended with the loss of England. The principal agent of his misfortune was the return of the Vikings, in what is sometimes called 'The Second Viking Age' or 'Second Viking Wave'. It was a series of incursions seemingly aimed initially at extorting silver, perhaps to make up for a reduction in silver obtained from the east,[215] though, as with the 'First Age', thoughts were presently to turn to establishing a more permanent presence.

Though this 'Second Viking Age' was not confined to attacks on England alone and occurred elsewhere in Western Europe, in England it was felt by some, in the fashion of Gildas, to be divine retribution for Aethelred's perceived involvement in his brother's murder. Though it was more likely to have been a combination of coincidence and political circumstance in Scandinavia, such as the revival of Danish power under Harald Bluetooth and his son Swein Forkbeard,[216] it is still quite possible, if not probable, that there was indeed a Viking awareness that particularly easy pickings might be had in England under a young boy-king, who had moreover acceded to the throne in somewhat dramatic circumstances and may not have had the full support of his subjects. Certainly, England was the principal target for these renewed attacks.[217] The assertive Danish king Harald Bluetooth had gained control of Norway by the 970s. Under him, Viking attacks on England recommenced in 980, starting at Southampton, followed that same year by Thanet and Cheshire. These were coastal raids for plunder, with small fleets – seven vessels, for example, in the case of Southampton. Harald was displaced in 988 by his son Swein Forkbeard, and the attacks intensified.

In 991 a particularly serious attack occurred involving a raid on Ipswich and then a major battle near Maldon in Essex, Maldon being the site of a mint and probably targeted for that reason. The Vikings in this particular campaign were possibly led by a Norwegian, Olaf Tryggvason,[218] who was keen to free Norway from Danish control (and indeed presently succeeded in so doing, becoming King of Norway), and it may well have been that if he was indeed present and in a leading role, he was co-leading the force with the Dane Swein Forkbeard.[219] The Anglo-Saxon force under the aged Byrhtnoth, Ealdorman of Essex and a leading magnate in the kingdom,[220] was defeated in what might be deemed truly tragic circumstances, in the literal sense of the protagonist bringing about his own demise.

At this point in time Anglo-Saxon opinion was divided as to whether to continue the old practice of buying off the Vikings or to fight them off. Byrhtnoth was of the latter view, and by all accounts a great patriot. In August that year, after raiding Ipswich, a large Viking fleet of some 90 vessels[221] sailed into the mouth of the Pant (Blackwater) River, berthing at the little island of Northey, which at ebb tide was linked to the (west) bank by a narrow but fordable causeway. These were raiders, not intending settlers, and they demanded payment or else. Byrhtnoth refused to buy them off – at least without a fight first. The Vikings then tried to attack Byrhtnoth's forces, but were easily kept at bay on the causeway by his men – though from a tactical perspective, why arrows were not used more effectively by either side (particularly the English) to pick off what would have been relatively static targets is puzzling. (I return to this in the questions section.) In what seems bizarrely similar to the modern-day complaint that 'It's not cricket, chaps', the raiders appear to have asked Byrhtnoth to allow them unopposed passage to the bank so that they could have a proper fight. He did so, and got beaten, losing his own life in the process – for it was most certainly not a game of cricket.

The battle was commemorated in a well known Anglo-Saxon heroic poem, *The Battle of Maldon*, in its genre rated second only to *Beowulf*. It is believed to have been written very shortly after the battle, very probably based on an

Figure 2.5 The causeway to Northey Island at low tide at Maldon, Essex, where (on the mainland side) Byrhtnoth was defeated by the Vikings in 991. It is on private land, but access is permitted.

account from a survivor. As a work of literature it has its limits as a reliable item of historical evidence, such as in the matter of quoted speeches, selection of incidents, degree of emphasis, value-laden terminology, and so forth. Nevertheless the degree of specificity and the accurate description of many details such as the names of individuals and mode of warfare suggests it can give the reader a reasonable and impactive idea of what the engagement was like, and in a broader sense, of life in those times. Some literary historians consider it fiction, but it should be borne in mind that whoever wrote it had a detailed knowledge of his topic and was very likely writing for people who also had knowledge. It occupies 325 lines, so I will quote just a few passages (from the translation by Donald Scragg). In response to the Viking spokesman's request for payment – 'money in exchange for peace'[222]

> Byrhtnoth made a speech. He raised his shield,
> waved his slender spear, spoke out with words,
> the angry and resolute one [Byrhtnoth] gave him answer:
> 'Sea raider, can you hear what this army is saying?
> They intend to give all of you spears as tribute,

deadly points and tried swords,
payment in war-gear which will be of no benefit to you in battle.
Messenger of the seamen, report back!
Tell your people a much less pleasing tale,
that here stands with his company an earl of unstained reputation,
who intends to defend this homeland,
the kingdom of Aethelred, my lord's
people and his country. They shall fall,
the heathens in battle. It appears to me too shameful
that you should return to your ships with our money
unopposed, now that you thus far in this direction
have penetrated into our territory.
You will not gain treasure so easily;
spear and sword must first arbitrate between us,
the grim game of battle, before we pay tribute.'[223]

The Vikings presently attempted to cross the causeway, but

When they recognized and saw clearly
that they had come up against unrelenting guardians of the causeway there,
then the hateful visitors started to use guile:
they asked to be allowed to have passage,
to cross over the ford, to advance their troops.
Then because of his pride the earl set about
allowing the hateful race too much land.[224]

Byrhtnoth was presently slain after valiant defence and, as with *Beowulf*, the
poem is then replete with examples of his men's determination to fight to the
death to avenge their lord, such as Leofsunu's vow:

'I vow that I shall not from here
flee the length of a foot, but I intend to push forward,
to avenge my lord and friend in the struggle.
Steadfast warriors around Sturmere will have no cause
to taunt me with words, now my beloved one is dead,
that I travelled home lordless,
turned away from the fight; but a weapon must take me,
pointed spear and iron sword.' He advanced furiously angry,
he fought strenuously, he scorned flight.[225]

There were, however, some who fled. One of the first of these was a man called
Godric, who 'leapt on the horse that his lord had owned',[226] and galloped off.

This seems to have been a telling moment, for as Offa, one of the more loyal retainers, says:

> Us Godric has
> betrayed, one and all, the cowardly son of Odda:
> too many men believed, when he rode away on the horse,
> on the prancing steed, that it was our lord:
> because of that the army became fragmented here on the battlefield,
> the shield-fort smashed to pieces. Blast his action,
> that he should have put so many men to flight here.[227]

This incident, in its specificity, appears very much to have a ring of truth about it and would have been a serious – and indeed possibly fatal – setback to the Anglo-Saxons in the battle, with seemingly considerable numbers of men believing their lord had left the field and that it was appropriate that they too should therefore retreat.

Was Byrhtnoth's charitable act foolish, or at least an error? Many might say so,[228] but on the other hand it did have heroic intent, and one cannot question his valour. It is also important in this case to appreciate that these Vikings were raiders, and had Byrhtnoth denied them passage to the bank, or possibly even if he paid them, they would very likely have moved on somewhere else and potentially caused even more damage. We have no reliable knowledge of numbers of men or casualties, but it is at least clear that Byrhtnoth's armed men were able to inflict some casualties, which might not have been possible had the Vikings attacked a softer target elsewhere. We will return to Maldon in the question section at the end of this Part 2.

Despite Byrhtnoth's valiant demonstration of his will to fight and refusal to pay, the raiders were eventually bought off. The same happened in 994, 997, and 1002, and various other times, and the payments were not small either. For example, the *Anglo-Saxon Chronicle* and other sources tell us the raiders of 991 were paid 10,000 pounds (the first such payment under Aethelred), a payment in 994 was 22,000 pounds, another in 1002 was 24,000 pounds, one in 1007 was 36,000 pounds, and one in 1012 was 48,000 pounds – massive sums in those days, in the latter stages beyond the entire normal tax-take for the kingdom. So massive, in fact, it is possible that the chroniclers exaggerated these latter sums, or that the payment of tribute proper (*gafol*) became conflated with other types of payment, such as from local magnates, or payment of a stipendiary army (*heregeld*), but even so the payment to the raiders must still have been enormous, even if we might question the specific sums. (The term *Danegeld* is actually a post-Conquest reference to *heregeld*, though in modern times it has been popularly used of payments to the Danes in general.)

It is important to remember that Aethelred did not initiate the practice of payment, which had been employed since at least the days of Alfred. Indeed, the same practice of buying off invaders had been used by the Romans too, in the latter stages of the Western Empire, with payments to Attila the Hun and others (and with the same ultimate lack of success). Moreover, Aethelred did not make any such payments by his decision alone. In the case of 991, for example, he authorised the payment on the advice of Archbishop Sigeric rather than by his own initiative.[229] The payment in 994 was similarly on the initiative of Sigeric and others, as is clear from the treaty that year between Aethelred and the Vikings, wherein Clause 1 explicitly refers to Archbishop Sigeric (of Canterbury), Ealdorman Aethelweard (of the Western Provinces), and Ealdorman Aelfric (of Hampshire) obtaining permission from the king to 'purchase peace'.[230] Clause 7.2 confirms the payment made for this truce was 22,000 pounds in gold and silver.[231]

However, even if Aethelred was passive rather than active in these matters of payment, taxes had to be levied to keep making them. And as all taxpayers can readily imagine, this did not exactly enhance Aethelred's image. Nor did his general passivity, or his readiness to authorise payments, do anything to improve that image. We have seen that William of Malmesbury was not exactly an admirer of Aethelred, but he may speak for many – particularly those in the mould of Byrhtnoth – when he writes (in connection with the 991 payment and thereafter):

> Thus a payment of ten thousand pounds satisfied the avarice of the Danes. This was an infamous precedent, and totally unworthy of the character of men, to redeem liberty, which no violence can ever extirpate from a noble mind, by money. They [the Vikings] now indeed abstained a short time from their incursions; but as soon as their strength was recruited by rest, they returned to their old practices. Such extreme fear had seized the English, that there was no thought of resistance.[232]

He adds that the situation was not helped by apparent traitors such as Ealdorman Aelfric of Hampshire, who in 992 was in command of the navy but who, instead of confronting the Vikings (the same force that had stayed on since Maldon), became a turncoat on the eve of battle: '[Aelfric], instead of trying his fortune, as he ought, in a naval conflict, went over, on the night preceding the battle, a base deserter to the enemy, whom he had appraised, by messengers, what preparations to make.'[233] This was not the only time Aelfric appears to have let his king down, as we shall see presently. Nor was he the only person to do so, as we shall also see.

Even though Aethelred strengthened the navy on more than one occasion, it was ineffective, seemingly badly managed by those who should have been coordinating England's military response to the Vikings. In 999, for example, facing another attack from the Vikings, the *Anglo-Saxon Chronicle* tells us that

> [T]he king with his *witan* resolved that they should be opposed with a naval force and also with a land force. But when the ships were ready, then they [the English forces] delayed from day to day, and distressed the poor people who lay in the ships. And ever as it should have been forwarder [earlier], so it was later, from one time to the next, and ever they let their foes' army increase; and ever they [the English forces] receded from the sea, and ever they [the raiders] went after them. And then in the end neither the naval force nor the land force was productive of anything but the people's distress, and a waste of money, and the emboldening of their foes.[234]

Ann Williams, in her study of Aethelred, helpfully points out that the frequently cited E manuscript for this period of the *Anglo-Saxon Chronicle*, along with C, D, and F, was composed, with regard to coverage of 983–1016, after the 1016 Viking conquest of England (but before 1023), and thus it paints a particularly gloomy picture of Aethelred and English resistance.[235] Indeed, she states that more than any other source the *Anglo-Saxon Chronicle* has contributed to Aethelred's reputation for cowardice and foolishness. She further observes that by contrast with E, Ms A, though for the period between Maldon and the end of Aethelred's reign it has only an entry for 1001, nonetheless has a more positive tone for that year than the other manuscripts, even though it covers the same engagements and the same outcomes. As Williams cautions, we have to be careful to avoid uncritical acceptance of the lamentation in other manuscript versions and to appreciate that the *Anglo-Saxon Chronicle* does show subjectivity and partiality. This is sound advice, and should be heeded. At the end of the day, it is deeds and outcomes that matter more than tone, but here too – as I have discussed in the Introduction and elsewhere – we need to appreciate that in many if not most (or arguably even all) cases subjectivity can also affect the very selection of deeds in any given account and the interpretation of outcomes. That said, Simon Keynes reminds us that the 'sorry tale of military disaster' in the *Anglo-Saxon Chronicle* cannot be seen as a complete misrepresentation of the truth.[236]

Another significant Viking attack occurred in 1001, launched from Normandy where the Viking fleet had been sheltering. Normandy had been established in French territory in 911 by Rollo (Rolf) the Viking, and was not necessarily hostile in itself towards England, but did obviously have Viking connections, despite its adoption of French language and many French customs – including, as 1066 was to show, the French use of cavalry, which was very un-Viking. In what seems to have been at least in part an attempt to reduce the risk of further Viking attacks from that quarter, Aethelred married Emma of Normandy, daughter of Duke Richard I and great grand-daughter of Rollo himself, in 1002. This may also have given him a certain sense of alliance with the Viking world. It was to no avail. The attacks continued, though not from Normandy.

Perhaps exasperated and desperate,[237] perhaps 'pushed over the edge' by a high-ranking Dane called Pallig breaking his oath of loyalty to him,[238] or, conversely, perhaps with his spirits raised by his marriage to Emma,[239] or perhaps genuinely learning of a plot against him, in the autumn of 1002 Aethelred 'commanded all the Danish men who were in England to be slain. This was done on the mass day of St Brice [13 November], because it had been made known to the king that they would plot against his life, and afterwards those of all his *witan*, and then have his realm without any gainsaying.'[240] Whatever Aethelred's specific motivation might have been, this decision too was made with the advice of others, and its (partial) implementation must have had substantial and widespread support. Moreover it was almost certainly aimed at recent arrivals, particularly potentially dangerous mercenaries[241] and not at those already established Danes in the east and northeast of the country, some of whom would have had roots going back several generations and were now well intermingled with the English – and indeed were often to suffer as well from this second wave of Viking attacks, suggesting that the later Vikings felt little affinity with them. (His omission of Norwegians as targets – unless these were subsumed under 'Danish men' – would seem to indicate that relations with the Norwegians were at this stage relatively good.) In practice a genocidal extermination as such did not eventuate, but nonetheless a significant number of Danes were killed, including in a massacre in Oxford where citizens burnt down a church in which Danes were seeking refuge. This was the Church of St Frideswide, and a diploma of Aethelred's of 1004 – sent out with 'the counsel of his leading men' – renewing its title-deeds confirms in his own words that he had decreed that the Danes, 'sprouting like cockle amongst the wheat', were to be destroyed by means of 'a most just extermination', and also that the Danes, fleeing for their lives, had entered the church to seek the 'sanctuary of Christ', only for their pursuers, unable to get them out, to burn the church, along with its precious objects and books.[242]

The sanctioning of the extermination of Danes – which in this particular case seems to have been taken even to justify the breach of church sanctuary – naturally provoked a backlash. The violation of church sanctuary would have outraged sincere Christians, and some of this outrage would probably have been directed towards Aethelred, though he does not seem to have explicitly authorised such violation. And obviously it must have alienated possible support for Aethelred from those Danes who had already settled in England,[243] let alone any newer non-belligerent arrivals. Henry of Huntingdon tells us that the Danes were justifiably angry, 'like a fire which someone had tried to extinguish with fat', and links this to the fierce attacks the following year, under King Swein Forkbeard of Denmark.[244] It is often said that a particular and more personal provocation for Swein was that his sister Gunnhild, married to Pallig, was one of the casualties of the St Brice's Day Massacre (along with Pallig himself and their child). However, as Ann Williams argues, this is almost certainly a misunderstanding of the date (used by William of Malmesbury) and that the murder of Gunnhild should be linked if anything to Swein's visit in 1013, not his visit in 1003 (both discussed presently), but in fact she questions the entire existence of Gunnhild, and certainly her alleged marriage to Pallig.[245]

Swein did come with a major raiding-army in 1003, and the *Anglo-Saxon Chronicle* tells us that

> [T]hen was gathered a very large [English] force from Wiltshire and from Hampshire, and very unanimously marched towards the [Viking] army. Then should the ealdorman Aelfric have led the force, but he drew forth his old artifice; as soon as they were so near that one army could look on the other, he feigned himself sick, and began retching to vomit, and said that he was sick, and so deceived ['betrayed' in some versions] the people that he should have led.[246]

We see Aelfric once again making a dubious contribution to the cause of Aethelred and England, for his men dispersed – though obviously this cannot be blamed entirely on Aelfric – and Swein and his army went on to raid in East Anglia in particular, not leaving England till 1005. It is possible, as some have argued, that Aelfric was genuinely sick, through nerves on the battlefield.[247] He may well have been a less than courageous individual, for as we have seen he is also said to have deserted on the eve of battle in 992. However, the apparent fact that, according to the *Anglo-Saxon Chronicle* (and William of Malmesbury), he had deliberately warned the enemy in the case of 992[248] suggests something more than timidity.

But, treachery aside, the possibility of battle-leaders being too timid to be effective is an important issue. Ryan Lavelle, for example, observes that there was a major weakness in a system that put ealdormen in charge of local defence, for ealdormen were not necessarily generals.[249] Indeed, as he goes on to say, at this point in time the ealdorman's position was very important and he was expected to be many things, including tax collector, representative of the king's justice, and unfortunately for Aelfric, a war leader.[250] Thus it behoved a king to pay very close attention to the all-round qualities of anyone before appointing them to such an office, and so – though of course it is difficult to make such pre-appointment assessments, and other factors would enter into the appointment – it is perhaps the case that Aethelred had some culpability in appointing Aelfric in the first place. (By the same token, of course, though he might have more advisers than an ealdorman, a king too was expected to fulfil many roles, including that of leader in major battles.)

Nor was Aethelred helped in the latter part of his reign by another of his senior counsellors/councillors, Eadric Streona, Ealdorman of Mercia (from 1006), who is said to have been profiting handsomely from taxation – 'Streona' actually being a nickname meaning 'acquisitor'. Eadric was later to be seen as a cowardly traitor, and was executed as such by Cnut in 1017. John of Worcester, from whom we obtain most of our information about him, tells us that he was quick-witted, smooth-talking, and unsurpassed in 'malice, treachery, arrogance and cruelty'.[251] Eadric was in later years to become Aethelred's son-in-law, marrying (probably around 1012) his daughter Eadgyth. Not only did he contribute to Aethelred's financial woes and hence his (Aethelred's) poor reputation, he also seems to have given some substance to Aethelred's nickname of 'Unraed', or 'ill-advised'. Simon Keynes sees him as playing a major role in the fate of England and the reputation of Aethelred.[252]

The navy was often plagued by problems at command level, be it defections by leaders such as Aelfric, or squabbles, or just poor command. And sometimes Nature itself combined with human nature to deal a double blow. In 1008, for example, showing commendable administrative vision Aethelred divided the country into naval districts to help the building and operating of a new large fleet. This was completed the following year, and Aethelred had his vessels – said to be some two to three hundred[253] – stationed off Sandwich to guard against the Vikings, and possibly in particular one expected attack, under Thorkell the Tall (see below). Aethelred himself was with his ships. Then one of his commanders, Beorhtric (Brihtric), a brother of the seemingly treacherous Eadric Streona, denounced a rival, Wulfnoth Cild, a Sussex thegn (and the future King Harold Godwineson's paternal grandfather), accusing him to the king of a certain crime – though we do not know the details of this accusation. Wulfnoth rebelled and left with 20 vessels, possibly at least in part his own contribution to the fleet. Beorhtric pursued him, taking no fewer than 80 vessels with him – more than his own contribution. A terrible storm blew up (as it had twice for Caesar in those waters) and drove almost all 80 vessels under Beorhtric's command onto the shore, badly damaging them. The survivors seem to have set off inland, leaving the wrecks unguarded or at best lightly guarded. Wulfnoth's vessels weathered the storm, perhaps because his sailors were from Sussex and more familiar with the sea than Beorhtric's Mercians. Looking to his own safety, Wulfnoth presently took the opportunity to burn all the beached ships, before they could be repaired. If we take the figure of 200 for the total number of ships, then the loss of these 80 or so vessels, plus (presumably) Wulfnoth's 20, this represented around half of the fleet, or around a third if we take the larger figure of 300. This was a great blow, and the *Anglo-Saxon Chronicle* records that this just seemed to shatter everyone's morale:

When this was thus known to the other ships where the king was, how the others had fared, it was as if all counsel was at an end, the king and the ealdormen and the high *witan* went home and thus lightly left the ships; and the people then who were in the ships brought the ships again to London; and they let the toil of all the nation thus lightly perish.[254]

The chronicler laments, with almost a mournful fatalism regarding the fortunes of his country's naval defence, that 'We had not yet the happiness [some versions give 'luck'], nor the honour that the naval force should be useful to this country, [any] more than it had often been before.'[255] However mindful one is of the need for caution regarding the expression of lamentation in the *Anglo-Saxon Chronicle*, it must indeed have seemed like the hand of cruel fortune that those vessels, so purposefully and laboriously constructed, should be doubly destroyed, by storm and by fire – moreover fire from an Englishman – before they could be put to any use. Aethelred must have felt he was doomed to lose, even though he did still have probably the majority of his fleet left intact.

Very shortly afterwards, fate twisted the knife in his wounds, and yet another major Viking raiding-army landed unopposed in Kent. In fact, Aethelred may have been aware in advance of this force, hence his stationing of the ships at Sandwich. When the fleet was partly destroyed, he may well have felt he had insufficient ships left to block the Vikings, and hence fell back to London. This raiding-army was led by Thorkell the Tall (Thurkil, d. 1023), and was to stay around in England for three years, causing significant death and destruction. During this three-year period, much of the remainder of the English fleet was effectively blockaded in London, for the Vikings under Thorkell had set up base downstream on the Thames, though the exact location is not clear.

The whole nation was called to arms by the king later in 1009, but was ineffective on land as well, allegedly in part through the notorious Eadric Streona, though it would be inappropriate to blame all on him:

> The king commanded all the nation to be called out, that they [the Vikings] might be resisted on every side; but lo! they went, nevertheless, how they would. Then on one occasion the king had got before them with all his force, when they would go to their ships, and all the people were ready to attack them, but it was prevented through the ealdorman Eadric, as it ever yet had been.[256]

Management of the land-army (the *fyrd*) seems to have been as bad as with the navy, at least according to the *Anglo-Saxon Chronicle* entry for 1010:

> when they [the enemy] were east, then was the force [English land-army] held west; and when they were south, then was our force north. Then were all the *witan* summoned to the king, and they should then decide how this country could be defended. But though something was then resolved, it

stood not for a month: at last there was not a chief man who would gather a force, but each fled as he best might; nor even at last would any shire assist another.[257]

The exact movements of the raiders on land are not fully clear, though the *Anglo-Saxon Chronicle* for 1011 enumerates their conquests by that year:

> They had overrun 1st East Anglia, and 2ndly Essex, and 3rdly Middlesex, and 4thly Oxfordshire, and 5thly Cambridgeshire, and 6thly Hertfordshire, and 7thly Buckinghamshire, and 8thly Bedfordshire, and 9thly half Huntingdonshire, and 10thly much in Northamptonshire; and south of the Thames, all Kent, and Sussex, and Hastings, and Surrey, and Berkshire, and Hampshire, and much in Wiltshire.[258]

We can very likely add Somerset and Dorset to this list, too.[259]

In that same year of 1011 Canterbury was sacked, aided by the treachery of a certain Aelfmaer, and the following April, refusing to be ransomed, Archbishop Aelfheah was brutally bludgeoned to death by the Vikings. As Ann Williams observes, it was bad enough that Canterbury, the centre of Christianity in England, should fall, but it was the murder of the archbishop that gave the event its 'peculiar horror'.[260]

The earlier-mentioned massive payment of 48,000 pounds succeeded in bringing about the departure of the Vikings in 1012, though Thorkell himself, with some 45 ships, stayed behind and entered Aethelred's employ. His reasons are not fully clear, but he does not seem to have had a particularly strong commitment to Swein Forkbeard, and may also have felt some remorse over Aelfheah's death.[261] But this development did not reduce the need for funds to be raised for payment: instead of – or in addition to – payment to the raiding Danes there was now payment to maintain a standing Danish militia (this latter payment continuing in Cnut's reign too).

Perhaps in reaction to Thorkell's move to Aethelred's camp, or perhaps in conjunction with the murder of his supposed sister Gunnhild, Swein returned to England in the summer of the following year (1013). Though he initially landed at Sandwich, he skirted the East Anglian coast and landed finally in Northumbria. The size of his force is unknown, but, as Else Roesdahl observes, it would have been easy to gather people for expeditions to England, both in 1013 and 1015, for by that stage everyone in Scandinavia knew of England's seemingly inexhaustible and easily obtainable wealth.[262]

Swein was thinking of more than just seizing wealth – just as Cnut would be too in 1015 – for he had eyes on conquest of the kingdom. His strategy this time – as opposed to his ravaging in East Anglia on his earlier visit – appears to have been to win over the Northumbrians, many of whom were of Danish (and

Norwegian) descent, and moreover by diplomacy, not force, for he forbade his men to pillage in that region. He was successful in this, and next proceeded to gain the allegiance of Anglo-Saxon leaders in the southwest after a brief but convincing display of violence. That he generally avoided the southeast, and Thorkell, is intriguing, but unfortunately we have little information on this, or on Thorkell's activities at this stage. By the end of the year Swein's forces had somehow also gained the submission of London, though Thorkell's fleet was still at Greenwich. Emma fled back to Normandy, taking her sons Edward (later King Edward the Confessor) and Alfred. Aethelred stayed on a while but presently followed in her wake to Normandy. His sons by his first (or possibly second) wife Aelfgifu,[263] Athelstan (the elder) and Edmund ('Ironside'), remained in England. In effect, Swein was now King of England, though he was not universally recognised as such, and even in the present day seems to be treated rather ambivalently with regard to that title.[264] It would perhaps seem best to treat him as a *de facto* king, but not a *de jure* king, with an informal title of 'King of England' rather than a formal one.

It was in any event the briefest of 'reigns', for he died in early February the following year, his son Harald succeeding to his Scandinavian realm and his younger son Cnut staying in England as head of the army, seen as king (of England) by his followers. However, and perhaps somewhat surprisingly, Aethelred now returned (to the southeast) at the conditional request of his councillors, who, despite misgivings, seemed to prefer him to a Viking monarch. The *Anglo-Saxon Chronicle* tells us that 'then resolved all the *witan* who were in England, ordained and lay, that King Aethelred should be sent after, and said that no lord was dearer than their natural lord, if he would govern them more justly than he did before', to which Aethelred promised (through the medium of his young son Edward) that 'he would be to them a kind lord and would amend all the things which they all eschewed, and all the things should be forgiven which had been done or said to him, on condition that they all, unanimously without treachery, would turn to him', and both parties also 'pronounced every Danish king an outlaw from England for ever'.[265] In spring, strengthened by Thorkell's contingent and also that of another leading Viking, Olaf Haroldsson, whom Aethelred had recruited while in Normandy, he launched an offensive against Cnut, who was based in Gainsborough and had arranged for the people of nearby Lindsey to join him for a raid. In this venture at least, Aethelred could not be considered 'unready' – on the contrary, according to the *Anglo-Saxon Chronicle*, he attacked Lindsey 'before they [the townspeople] were ready'.[266] Cnut, similarly taken by surprise, withdrew (temporarily) to Denmark. Before he left, he cut off the hands, noses, and ears of the English hostages he held.[267]

Numbers are unclear, but these hostages were almost certainly from noble families of Wessex and Mercia, and probably young sons, which was the norm of the day. Ryan Lavelle comments poignantly on their mutilation that it was not only a brutal act on Cnut's part but an enduring 'visual reminder' of what can happen when a hostage holder – certainly one with the determination of Cnut – feels betrayed, and the dreadful price the hostages and their families might have to pay.[268]

It was around this time that the scholarly Wulfstan, Archbishop of York (1002–23), who drafted many of the laws of Aethelred and later Cnut, gave his famous 'state of the nation' address, known as the *Sermon of the Wolf to the English*. (Lupus, 'the wolf', was the literary alias of Wulfstan.) It does not make for happy reading. He laments the sinfulness of the English and urges that they mend their ways, for they have incurred the wrath of God and merited the miseries that now afflict them. He clearly intends the Vikings when he refers to 'heathen peoples', and it is also clear that he believes they now hold dominion over the English. In the matter of *wergeld*, for example, if an Englishman kills a Viking – even an escaped English slave who has joined up with the Vikings – he has to pay, but in practice never the other way round.[269] God has given Vikings, as agents of punishment for the wicked English, great strength, so that one Viking can put ten Englishmen to flight. It is shameful that the English suffer such degrading treatment as having to watch their wives or daughters violated by as many as a dozen Viking 'pirates', along with suffering their plundering and ravaging and burning. This is all a clear sign of God's anger. The English need to stop their oathbreaking and disloyalty, their sexual perversions, their killing and stealing, their perjury, their selling of their own family members into slavery, their deceit and their fraud, and their other sins and misdeeds, and return to godly ways.[270]

If this sounds reminiscent of Gildas, this would only be natural, for Wulfstan refers specifically to him. He remarks how Gildas had written of the sins and misdeeds of the Britons, which were so extensive they angered God to the point where He allowed the army of the English to conquer their land and to destroy many Britons. Wulfstan points out the need to take warning from this precedent, for he feels the English have been guilty of 'worse deeds' than the Britons.[271]

There does indeed seem to the present-day observer an irony in the apparent parallel experiences of the Britons and the Anglo-Saxons. This would be even more so if – as was the norm in those days – such events were interpreted as God's will. The Anglo-Saxons (or at least the clergy) must have had a particularly strong sense of a fall from grace, plunging from having once upon a time – in their heathen days – been God's agents in punishing sin to ending up as objects of punishment by new 'heathen' agents. (In fact, many Vikings were Christian, at least nominally. As early as the 950s Harald Bluetooth had – probably for political reasons – declared Denmark a Christian country.)

God's will or not, and despite the earnest prayers of the English – seen by Keynes as a 'defensive strategy'[272] – Cnut was to return in the autumn of the following year, 1015. By this time a series of events had started by which Aethelred's son Edmund 'Ironside'[273] – Athelstan having died in June 1014 – took control of much of the northern Danelaw. The circumstances behind this are not the clearest, but it looks very much as though a seemingly unwise act by his father Aethelred was part of it – an act Ann Williams refers to as a 'serious error of judgment'.[274] Aethelred had summoned a great *gemot* (assembly) in early summer that year, at which two leading northern magnates, Sigeferth (Siferth) and Morcar from the Five Boroughs (Nottingham, Derby, Stamford, Leicester, and Lincoln), were treacherously murdered. The murders seem to have been done through the agency of Eadric Streona, but Aethelred then claimed the land of the two victims, and imprisoned Sigeferth's wife.

This strongly suggests Aethelred's complicity in the murders, his motives perhaps being related to the ready acceptance the two magnates had shown towards Swein Forkbeard two years earlier in 1013, followed by their initial acceptance of Cnut – they may well have been leaders of the people of Lindsey who were planning to resist Aethelred – and/or the fact that they were relatives of Aelfgifu of Northampton, whom Cnut had married (probably 'Danish-style', similar to 'common law') around 1013. Even if Sigeferth and Morcar had indeed been leading the people of Lindsey, for Aethelred to act against them would seem to represent a breach of his promise made on his return that he would forgive those who had acted against him in the past, although it is possible he suspected them of treachery subsequent to his return, which would legitimise his actions on the basis of the condition to that effect that he had attached to his return. But in any event it may have been better to extend the spirit of forgiveness to the two magnates, while prudently 'keeping an eye' on them. Edmund for one seems to have reacted badly, and virtually rebelled against his father, releasing Sigeferth's widow from prison without his father's consent, and indeed marrying her, and also issuing diplomas in his own name, which was really the king's prerogative – one diploma being explicitly for the redemption of Sigeferth's soul.[275] Edmund rode north by early September, took possession of both Sigeferth's and Morcar's (or arguably now his father Aethelred's) estates, and was seemingly accepted by the people there.

It was at this point that Cnut arrived with some 160 or so ships, attacking not the northeast but the southwest. Aethelred was now lying ill in nearby Hampshire. Edmund raised a force from the north, and Eadric Streona a force from Mercia, their forces being supposed to join to repel Cnut. However, neither commander trusted the other, and the forces dispersed. Eadric then defected to Cnut, 'enticing forty ships from the king'.[276] It is not clear whether these ships were vessels Eadric had brought with him as the contribution from Mercia, or whether perhaps he had persuaded Thorkell to switch allegiance to Cnut and bring his fleet with him. The word 'enticing' might perhaps suggest the latter, but if so it is perhaps odd that the *Anglo-Saxon Chronicle* does not mention Thorkell by name. The *Eulogy for Queen Emma* (*Encomium Emmae*

Reginae), written some 30 years later, states that Thorkell had sailed to Denmark some months earlier to pledge his allegiance to Cnut, though this account is widely seen as unreliable.[277] In any event, wherever the 40 ships came from, the West Saxons followed Eadric's suit, allying themselves with Cnut and moreover providing horses for his force. That force must have already been quite considerable, bearing in mind Else Roesdahl's comments earlier about England being seen as a rich and easy target.

In the winter of 1015/16 Cnut and Eadric raided southern Mercia (Eadric's own base being northern Mercia). A national force was summoned to tackle them, and formed under Edmund, but then disbanded, seemingly because the king and his London-based forces would not join them. It later formed again, with Aethelred's presence, but then he himself left the force when he was told that some of his supporters wanted to betray him. He returned to London and the force again disbanded.[278] There is a frustrating lack of detail here, and we are very largely dependent on confusing entries in the *Anglo-Saxon Chronicle*, but what does seem to emerge is that once again there was poor management of the army. Perhaps Aethelred's state of mind was affected by his illness, but the situation also shows that at this stage Edmund seemed unable to wield the necessary authority to unify the English, who very probably were not keen to tackle Cnut and his men anyway.

Edmund then joined forces with his brother-in-law Uhtred of Northumbria, and they attempted to attack northern Mercia, presumably to draw Eadric away from Cnut. However, Cnut, showing great tactical wisdom, attacked Uhtred's Northumbria by skirting through the eastern part of Edmund's recently acquired territory. Uhtred was obliged to return to Northumbria and submit, along with his territory. He was then killed, seemingly on the advice of Eadric.[279]

Activities then moved south. Cnut was back with his ships (apparently still in the southwest, perhaps at Poole) by the beginning of April, and Edmund returned to his father Aethelred in London. On 23 April, Aethelred died there in London, of illness – very probably the same illness he was said to have been suffering from when Cnut arrived some six months ago – and Edmund became king.

Reflecting on Aethelred's unfortunate reign, Ann Williams writes that his failures were largely political, especially in his ability to control his counsellors/councillors and to keep out of their power plays. She feels this may to some extent justify his by-name of *Unraed* ('no counsel'), but on the other hand she also feels he did on occasion receive good counsel.[280]

Christopher Brooke acknowledges similar problems and adds that it was a combination of inability to command united loyalty and his own temperament that made him indecisive and ineffective as a leader. But, importantly, he is also of the view that Aethelred was 'very unlucky' in a number of ways, notably the manner in which he became king, the renewed intensity of the

Viking attacks from such an early point in his reign, and even more so in the fact that the Viking leaders of this new wave of attacks were so strong and capable.[281] Indeed, as Sean Miller observes, Aethelred's inability to keep the Vikings out of England may well have had more to do with the Vikings' strength than with Aethelred's supposed incompetence.[282]

Simon Keynes, while acknowledging that Aethelred is widely seen as a figure of fun and bad rulership, feels that Aethelred's critics should appreciate the difficulty he faced with the Viking invasions.[283] He also feels that, while it is understandable, Aethelred has unfortunately been judged very much on the last decade of his reign, 'when matters went progressively from bad to worse to calamitous'.[284] And in this regard he observes that, based on the 'dismal tale of recurrent treachery, cowardice, incompetence, and defeat' told in the *Anglo-Saxon Chronicle*, the 'ubiquitous villain' is not Aethelred but Eadric Streona.[285] We shall return to an assessment of Aethelred in the questions section.

Cnut's force arrived to lay siege to London in the second week of May. By this stage Edmund had left the city, probably leaving Queen Emma in authority there, and headed west to enlist those West Saxons and Mercians who had not allied with Cnut. Cnut's fleet arrived at Greenwich, Thorkell's base, but was clearly unopposed by him, so it would seem by this stage at the latest he must have switched his allegiance to Cnut. He may have done this upon Aethelred's death two weeks earlier, but one wonders why he did not continue to serve Edmund as Aethelred's successor. But then again, as seems to be the case with many figures of this time, he may simply have been an opportunist who could read the way the wind was blowing.

Edmund had some success in raising troops, particularly in Mercia, and then returned to London, successfully relieving the siege and causing Cnut to decamp. Presently Cnut's forces returned and Edmund engaged them, driving them off again. While giving chase, at Aylesbury he was met by Eadric Streona, but not in battle – rather, Eadric had come to make overtures and offer his services to Edmund. With remarkable naivety – or more exactly, on the face of it, foolishness – Edmund accepted his offer, despite the fact that he had already indicated his distrust of Eadric, and moreover had seen that distrust well founded. The *Anglo-Saxon Chronicle* remarks that 'never was greater evil counsel counselled than that was'.[286] Perhaps, because he appeared to have had the upper hand at that particular point, Edmund may have thought that Eadric, unprincipled and untrustworthy opportunist that he seems to have been, would now throw his lot in with him (Edmund) as the perceived victor in the inevitable looming confrontation with Cnut, and that self-interest rather than honour and loyalty would keep him – and his men – in line.

By this stage Edmund does appear to have increased his authority and ability to unite men for his cause, and his confidence must have increased. He caught up with the Danes at a hill in Essex called Assandun, and battle was joined on

18 October. It is not clear whether this is Ashingdon (the traditional choice as the site) or Ashdon (which is being increasingly favoured in recent times). Whatever the site, it saw a reversal of fortune for Edmund, for it was a Danish victory – blamed by the chroniclers yet again on Eadric Streona, said to be the first to take flight. A number of leading English magnates died in the battle, including the notorious Ealdorman Aelfric of Hampshire and the valiant Ulfcytel (Ulfcetel) of East Anglia.[287] Edmund retreated to southern Mercia and Cnut pursued him.

There may possibly have been another engagement in the Forest of Dean, but the next major development was an agreement that Edmund and Cnut should meet to try and work something out between them. The irrepressible, mercurial, and ubiquitous Eadric Streona is said to have been instrumental in this. It took place at Alney, near Deerhurst. The outcome was a split of the kingdom, in very similar fashion to that between Eadwig and Edgar: Cnut was to reign over territory north of the Thames, and Edmund Wessex.[288] And inevitably, there was to be a payment to Cnut. Edmund may have retained the formal crown of the realm,[289] but this is not clear. It is probable that there would have been some agreement to the effect that upon the death of one the other would succeed to the whole kingdom, though that might invite assassination. As it happens, within a few weeks, on 30 November, Edmund died, and Cnut did indeed become ruler of all the land, at around a mere 21 years of age, while Edmund's two young children were taken into exile in Hungary.

It is not clear how Edmund died, though it was not of old age, for he was no older than 30. It is possible he received a wound at Assandun, and that this became fatally infected. However, no source mentions any such battle wound – but then, no source really tells us anything reliable on this matter.[290] In my own irrepressibly cynical view I believe it very possible – though not definite – that Cnut had him murdered. The relevant passage in the *Eulogy for Queen Emma*, which seems to me an almost tongue-in-cheek 'explanation', refers to God 'taking away' Edmund, and 'commanding that he should die', because He did not want to see a divided kingdom, which could lead to renewed conflict, and favoured Cnut.[291] If such was really God's will, then, with Edmund's death and Cnut's accession to an undivided kingdom, His will was done.

2.7   Vikings rule: And how Cnut got his feet wet

While there may be some uncertainty about the regal status in England of his father Swein, Cnut's reign as king of England (in addition to later being king of Denmark and king of Norway), regardless of questions about how exactly he became sole king, is undisputed. He reigned from 1016 to 1035, in the early stages disposing of potential troublemakers – Trow refers to a 'hit list'[292] – and in the summer of the following year also marrying Aethelred's widow Emma.

The practice of a victorious king marrying the widow of a defeated king, regardless of age difference – Emma was at least five years older than Cnut, more likely ten[293] – was not an uncommon practice, even if the king was already married (Cnut having a wife Aelfgifu of Northampton). He helped to gain himself widespread acceptance by keeping a number of Anglo-Saxons in high office, the best-known being Earl Godwine of Wessex (who will be discussed further in Part 3). He also entrusted various military campaigns in Scandinavia to Godwine and arranged for him to marry his (Cnut's) sister-in-law Gytha, a Danish princess. Thus their famous son, Harold Godwineson, was not an Anglo-Saxon commoner, as often believed: he was paternally Anglo-Saxon, but maternally Danish, and had royal blood through his mother. (Again, more on this in Part 3.)

Cnut, the Viking ruler of England, was in fact one of England's better kings. Roesdahl remarks that, notwithstanding his responsibilities in Scandinavia, Cnut became 'above all an English king', and further comments that he was an 'exemplary king'.[294] Going somewhat further still, M. K. Lawson expresses a view that by the standards of his day, Cnut was the most successful of all the pre-Conquest rulers in Britain.[295] Certainly, as Lawson points out, Cnut was also king of Denmark, Norway, and parts of Sweden; was to have a daughter married to a Roman emperor; and to attend an imperial coronation in Rome. We can also say that his reign was characterised by general peace, after some initial disturbances. He was strong, authoritative, efficient, reasonably just (or perhaps we should say 'not the most unjust'), supportive of the church,[296] mentally sharp, and certainly nobody's fool. It is a strange quirk of fate that he is so often popularly but incorrectly associated with extreme vanity and foolishness in a supposed attempt to hold back the waves as a demonstration of his power. The story of the waves, which may or may not have a factual basis (many believe it happened at Bosham in Sussex, territory associated with Godwine), was first written down by the twelfth century historian, Henry of Huntingdon. Huntingdon clearly depicts Cnut as reacting humbly to flattery and making a deliberate demonstration of the limits of his power, not the enormity of it. As depicted by Huntingdon, Cnut also intended to show the limits of the power of earthly kings in general, for Cnut believed only God could command the waves:

> When he was at the height of his ascendancy, he ordered his chair to be placed on the sea-shore as the tide was coming in. Then he said to the rising tide, 'You are subject to me, as the land on which I am sitting is mine, and no-one has resisted my overlordship with impunity. I command you, therefore, not to rise on to my land, nor to presume to wet the clothing or limbs of your master.' But the sea came up as usual, and disrespectfully drenched the king's feet and shins. So jumping back, the king cried, 'Let all the world know that the power of kings is empty and worthless, and there

Figure 2.6 Bosham seafront in Sussex, a base for Earl Godwine and also where Cnut is said to have demonstrated to his flatterers the limits of his powers by failing to stop the incoming tide. Present-day residents still seem happy to follow his example.

is no king worthy of the name save Him by whose will heaven, earth, and sea obey eternal laws.'[297]

If the story is indeed true, it is possible that Cnut chose the sea for his demonstration, as opposed to trying to stop the sun setting or similar, as a result of the idea of supposed Viking mastery of it. However, if another story is also true, that Cnut had an eight-year old daughter drowned in the millstream at Bosham (seemingly by 1022),[298] this tragedy may have had a bearing on his choice of a watery master.

Cnut may not have been able to command the waves, but he certainly had considerable terrestrial power in England, as well as in Scandinavia. From the perspective of British history, his reign represents a pinnacle of Viking achievement. We should not overlook the general context of Viking power at this point, around the turn of the millennium, for it was an age in which Viking influence as a whole could be seen as being at a pinnacle, extending from the Black Sea to Iceland and Greenland and even Vinland (North America). Cnut's reign in England was but one part of the Viking world, though it was a very important one. Certainly, England at this time should be thought of as Anglo-Danish rather than simply Anglo-Saxon.

Viking rule in England was not, however, to endure. Upon his death in 1035 – seemingly through natural causes[299] – there were two rival successors, Harthacnut (b. c. 1019, r. 1040–2), his son by Emma, and Harold ('Harefoot', b. c. 1016, r. c. 1035–40), his elder son by his first 'Danish-style' wife Aelfgifu of Northampton. Cnut preferred Harthacnut as successor to all his kingdoms, and thus Harthacnut also succeeded to the throne of Denmark, where he had all his time taken up by a serious military threat from Magnus of Norway. Regarding England, Harold felt he had the greater claim, and presently there was an agreement to split the kingdom, with Harold taking the north and Harthacnut the south, but with Harold ruling on his behalf in southern England as regent. However, in 1037 Harold took the crown for himself, becoming Harold I. (Harold Godwineson, of Hastings fame, was thus Harold II.) However, he was to die in 1040, upon which Harthacnut became king. After just a year, in a rather mysterious move, he invited his stepbrother Edward (the Confessor, b. c. 1005, r. 1042–66), the son of Emma by Aethelred and who was still in Normandy, to co-rule with him informally (Edward was not considered a formal king during this time). Harthacnut himself was to die suddenly in 1042, and this left Edward as king.

Table 2.1   Edward's genealogical connections to Alfred

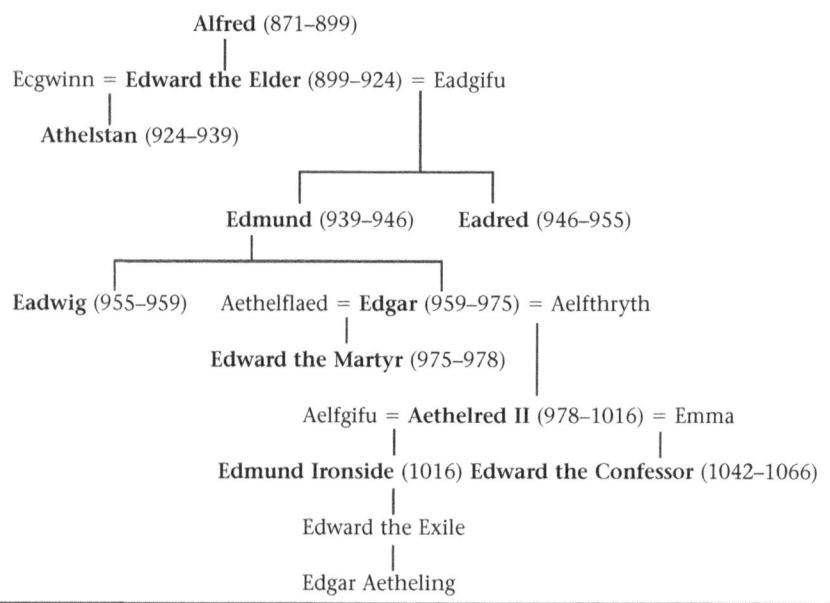

Edward had only the weakest of links to any Viking lineage, in that his mother Emma was a Norman and thus of 'Norseman' descent, going back a century to the creation of the duchy by Rollo in 911. But in this respect she was little more Viking than William the Conqueror. Both Emma and William were Norman-French. Edward, for his part, was seen as Anglo-Saxon through his father Aethelred, though he spoke French as his main tongue as a result of so many years spent in Normandy, and in some regards was more Norman than English. Any other association he might have felt was Norman-French too, and not Viking, again reflecting his many years spent in exile in Normandy, as well perhaps as the fact that his mother was Norman. (The relationship between Edward and his Viking half-brother Harthacnut must have been a curious and fascinating one.) Upon Edward's death in January 1066 the crown was to go to Harold Godwineson, son of Earl Godwine of Wessex. Harold is often seen as the last Anglo-Saxon king, and this is true with regard to his paternal lineage, which usually prevailed over the maternal. However, as mentioned earlier, it is important to appreciate that through his mother he was actually half Danish and, as will be discussed in Part 3, a distant blood relative of Cnut, not just a relative by marriage. So with Harold's death at Hastings, in that fateful year of 1066, we see an end not just to Anglo-Saxon rule, but also – with the tenuous exception of the Viking origins of the Normans – the end of Viking rule in England.

There was the occasional subsequent and unsuccessful Viking attempt to regain some or all of England, notably in 1066 under Harald Hardraada (just prior to Hastings, and discussed in Part 3), and an attempted invasion in 1069–70 by Harold Godwineson's Danish cousin Swein Estrithsson – though interestingly, William the Conqueror seems to have 'bought him off' by allowing him to take away 'treasures' his men had seized, and no one could accuse William of being weak.[300] There was also an attempt in 1075, and in 1085 Swein's son Cnut organised a very large fleet with a view to invasion, causing William to transfer huge numbers of men from Normandy to England, but the invasion never got under way due to problems on Denmark's southern border that caused a delay. The fleet dispersed, apparently contrary to Cnut's wishes, and those who had returned home were punished so severely that it provoked a rebellion, leading to Cnut being killed the following year in the church of Odense. This was a factor in his eventual canonisation, meaning that, as Roesdahl remarks, the unfulfilled dream of taking the English throne ended up making Cnut into Denmark's first royal saint.[301] There were no further Scandinavian attempts to conquer England.

When thinking of the end of Viking rule in eleventh century Britain one really has to refer specifically to England, not Britain as a whole, for Viking rule was maintained much longer in certain geographical regions of the present-day British Isles, such as the Shetlands and Orkneys (till 1469 and the marriage of Margaret of Denmark and Norway to James III of Scotland) and the Isle of Man and the Western Isles of Scotland (till 1266, though actually a mix of Norse and Gael in both rulers and people). However, in general Viking influence waned in Scotland and Wales (where it had never been strong despite numerous raids), and in Ireland too it was severely curtailed through the exploits of King Brian Boru (d. 1014), though it continued after a fashion till the Anglo-Norman conquest of Ireland in the 1170s. In broader terms, from the mid-late eleventh century on, especially after Stamford Bridge (Hardraada's demise) and Hastings, we can say that the Viking heyday had passed. As Else Roesdahl observes, if one date has to be chosen to mark the end of the Viking Age, 'it has to be 1066'.[302]

Their legacy in England is not just a matter of vivid images of Viking raiders, images not necessarily of the sort Else Roesdahl would like, and probably wrong in many regards, such as the horned helmet as a tangible example, and at a less tangible level perhaps an overweighted (but not wholly misplaced) focus on violence and cruelty. As mentioned earlier, it includes many place names, such as those ending in '-by' or 'thorp(e)' from the Danes and '-thwaite' from the Norwegians. The northwestern town of Wigan represents a more direct toponomical legacy, for its very name is a variant of 'Viking'. The legacy also includes a large number of diverse words of Scandinavian origin, such as 'cast', 'knife', 'take', 'window', 'egg', 'ill', and 'die', and grammatical elements such as the plurals 'they', 'them', 'their', etc.[303] And most importantly perhaps, the Viking legacy left many of us British with some degree of Viking blood in our veins. I do not mean to pursue the old-fashioned idea of biological race, or for that matter 'nations', but in figurative and possibly romantic terms describing descent, many of those in the northwest will have some Norwegian blood, and many of those in the east and northeast Danish blood, and some, of course, both, and maybe even a little Swedish. For the majority of those with Viking blood, it no doubt mingles with Anglo-Saxon blood, and in many cases Brittonic Celtic blood, and/or Gaelic Celtic, and/or Pictish Celtic, and maybe even a little Roman blood. And a few of us may also have some Norman/French blood, which leads us on to Part 3, and the account of how it got into our veins.

However, before concluding Part 2, let us consider some of the more questionable elements of this period from the perspective of folly and fortune, including of course Aethelred.

2.8   Why did things happen the way they did?

(1) *Was Vortigern foolish in inviting the Anglo-Saxons into Britain, and how instrumental was this in the Anglo-Saxon Advent?*

I believe the answers to this two-part question are 'no' and 'not very'. As discussed in the text, I think history has been unkind to Vortigern and treated him as a scapegoat. In inviting the barbarian Anglo-Saxons into the country to ward off Pictish attacks, he was simply following the Roman practice of employing one group of barbarians to protect the empire against other less tractable barbarians. This eventually turned out to be an unwise policy both for Rome and for Britain, though at the time of his invitation the full extent of the damage to the Roman empire may not have been apparent to Vortigern, for the Western empire did not collapse till some decades afterwards in 476. And there had after all been some successes with this Roman policy, not just failures, as evidenced by the effective use of Sarmatian cavalry against the Picts at Hadrian's Wall in the late second century.

A further factor in Vortigern's thinking may have been that the Anglo-Saxons too had been doing a lot of raiding, as well as the Picts, and that he could perhaps 'kill two birds with one stone' by playing them off against each other. Certainly, he could at least hope that by employing the Anglo-Saxons he would establish friendly terms with at least some of them and thereby prevent or reduce their raiding.

We should also bear in mind that it is clear that Vortigern was acting, in true Celtic fashion, with the advice of a council. If it was indeed an error to invite the Anglo-Saxons, then it is unfair for him alone to take the blame. He may well have been the king and perhaps it could be argued that, to use a modern term, the buck stopped with him, but then again he was not an absolute king, merely an informal overlord.

Having arrived, the Anglo-Saxon invitees presently began complaining that Vortigern had broken an agreement, seemingly involving promises of material supplies and also money and land. If he did blatantly break some specific contractual arrangement, without due cause, then he could be considered culpable to some extent – but surely only to a limited extent. Unfortunately the sources do not provide sufficient reliable detail for us to judge. However, even assuming the worst case scenario, and that he did break an agreement, it would seem a considerable overreaction on the part of the Anglo-Saxons to use this as justification for a reputedly bloody invasion. Rather, as Gildas suggests, it would seem far more likely that the invitees had acquisitive intent from the outset.

And anyway, at the end of the day, Vortigern's invitation to the Anglo-Saxons was not in my view particularly causally instrumental in their subsequent invasion, though it may have played a certain part. He merely opened the door. Given especially the wealth and fertility of Britain and the pressures in their own homelands, I feel that they would have broken the door down if it had not been opened. We need to be ever mindful of the reality of life in those days, insofar as we can tell, to the effect that violence and conquest were even more the norm than they are today. The strong consumed the weak, and gentility and pacifism would very likely risk being seen as failings.

If we are looking for causes for the Anglo-Saxon Advent, I would suggest a combination of Anglo-Saxon desire and British weakness; the former arising from the attractiveness of Britain relative to their homelands and the latter principally from lack of unity among the Britons, along with some of the tactical weaknesses I raise below with regard to the possibility of the Anglo-Saxons repelling the Vikings, such as failure to focus on vessels. Perhaps, if we are looking to blame Vortigern for anything, we could focus more on the lack of British unity under him, though he seems to have gone part of the way in achieving at least an overlord status. But then again, we know so little about Vortigern (or possibly the Vortigerns), or indeed the state of Britain at this time, that above all else we should keep an open mind, and not confine our thinking to a scapegoating of this unfortunate and much maligned man.

(2) Could the Anglo-Saxons have prevented the early Viking attacks and subsequent settlement?

All things considered, the realistic answer is probably 'no', though I think they could have put up more effective resistance. The Vikings could be said to have been in a phase of strong ascendancy, and were difficult to deal with. Though not the happiest of bedfellows, the Norwegians and Danes, at least initially, seem to have been bonded by joint interest – or more exactly greed, first for loot, then for land. In this regard they followed the precedent of the Anglo-Saxons, and it is an irony of fate that the Anglo-Saxons should receive much the same sort of treatment that they themselves dished out to the Britons.

In the early days, when the Vikings were raiders rather than invaders – that is, seeking portable plunder rather than land acquisition and settlement – it is possible that attacks on their vessels could have been effective. As discussed in Question 3 of Part 1 with regard to Caesar, the Viking raiders were waging amphibious warfare and could have been seriously immobilised or even neutralised by the destruction of their means of waging that warfare, namely their vessels. The potential for an effective English naval response in those days was not that great, for even if they had had a large and coordinated fleet the English vessels in general were technologically behind the longboats of the Vikings. In fact, even after Alfred strengthened the navy, it does not seem to have been particularly effective in suppressing Viking raids (and we have also seen the ill fortune that accompanied Aethelred's later attempts to strengthen the fleet). Nonetheless, in my view any hostile vessel close to the coast, and particularly upon entering a river, should, whenever within range, have been harried by arrows from the shore (or possibly from small, fast, and manoeuvrable craft that could carry archers), ideally burning arrows to catch sails and wood. Other arrows should have been focused, wherever possible, on leaders. Vessels are concentrated targets, and in those days they were for the most part unprotected. (It was the sixteenth century Korean admiral Yi Sun-shin who first developed a fully armoured vessel that could properly resist ranged weapons.)

Another possible opportunity for destruction of their boats would have been when they were beached or at anchor while raiding parties went ashore, even though they would have been guarded.

Rightly or wrongly, I get the impression that not enough was done to focus on the conveyances. The target seems too often to have been the men, not their means of transport and mobility, despite the great advantages in targeting the latter – as the Romans showed in Part 1, in the battle at Medway in AD 43, when they deliberately maimed the Britons' horses and thereby rendered their chariots useless. Perhaps in Anglo-Saxon times it was considered unmanly to target something other than the man. But this would seem rather like the simplistic, Hollywood-driven idea that, in the 'Wild West', the cowboys and Indians always tried to shoot the man, not the horse, however desperate the chase, and however difficult a target the man might present. True, there would be occasions when targeting the rider might be the more appropriate course of action (a horse was after all a valuable thing), but anyone who only ever did that would at some point deserve to lose. Even the Japanese samurai, with their much vaunted (and idealised) code of bushido, with its focus on man-to-man combat, nevertheless appreciated that when faced with a mounted adversary it is a pragmatically good move to break the horse's legs. And if the English really did do the equivalent of a 'Hollywood' with the Vikings and their ships, then perhaps they deserved to get beaten. It is ironically unfortunate that the clearest display we have of the Anglo-Saxons destroying vessels was that of their own, through Beorhtric in 1009.

After the Vikings landed in force, and especially after they had started to settle, it obviously became more difficult to dislodge them. They were by all accounts fierce and determined folk, and on occasion capable of an extreme ruthlessness and brutality – though some of their supposed sadistically cruel punishments have been exaggerated.[304] In terms of warrior values, they were in many respects very similar to the Anglo-Saxons (and no doubt many other peoples): Roesdahl refers to courage, strength, delight in weapons, the splendour of battle, loyalty to one's fighting comrades, and faithfulness to one's lord unto death.[305] And they were numerous, and kept coming and coming and coming. But the fact, as mentioned earlier, that Norwegians and Danes were not always the best of friends, even though they shared the same aims and might on occasion have the same king, could perhaps have been used as the basis of a systematic policy of divisiveness. From an early stage of Viking settlement there were localised geographical divisions, even quite odd ones such as the town of York being largely Norwegian whereas many of its environs were Danish, and it would seem these could have been exploited more purposefully.

The policy of staving off attacks by payment was perhaps useful as a short-term expedient, such as when Alfred was on the back foot, but nonetheless it was a very dangerous policy, that clearly got out of hand under Aethelred in particular. From a military perspective, and to an extent also a political one, it symbolised weakness and fear, and endowed England (and other places with a similar policy) with a 'defenceless victim aura'. More materially, it also sent out signals that not only was England wealthy enough in the first place to consider such buy-offs, it also could continue to make them frequently and at an ever-increasing rate.

Once again, we can look to a lack of unity among the English kingdoms as a factor facilitating Viking attacks, despite the informal overlordship of the *bretwaldas*. Even during the prominence of Wessex in the ninth century, it was not until Alfred in the later part of that century that a meaningful degree of unity was achieved, and by then the Vikings had already settled in much of the north and east of the country.

(3) Was Byrhtnoth foolish in allowing the Vikings to come ashore, and how instrumental was his defeat in the Viking rise to dominance in England?

I believe the answers to this two-part question are 'no' and 'significantly but not wholly'. As mentioned in the text, the Vikings who sailed up the Blackwater in 991 were raiders not invaders, and had Byrhtnoth of Essex not engaged them they would almost certainly have simply gone elsewhere to do their raiding. That might have solved the problem for Essex, but not for the kingdom as a whole. As a very high-ranking ealdorman (equivalent to and effectively interchangeable with 'earl'), Byrhtnoth was in the *witan*, that early form of national assembly, and would surely have been thinking in nationwide terms rather than local. As we saw in the heroic poem *Battle of Maldon*, he – or more exactly the poet – does indeed refer to himself and his men as defending the country.

His men were armed and could at least inflict some damage on the Vikings, whereas a target elsewhere may not have been able to arm and this could have led to even greater English casualties. We do not know the numbers for certain, but 93 vessels suggest a very significant force – possibly several thousand, for some of the longboats of this period could carry up to a 100 men,[306] though 40 or so was more usual – and he may also have felt that the depletion of such a significant force was an urgent task, even if his own force was outnumbered and he suspected they might be doomed. (There are not a few examples in history of such self-sacrificial actions.) However, this is speculation, and he may well have believed he would win.

Also, his action had a symbolic effect in showing the Vikings that at least some of the English were prepared to fight, and presumably to the death, whether or not they believed themselves doomed from the outset. From a present-day perspective we would normally consider any unnecessary loss of life as tragic, and that once the tide of battle had turned against the English they should if possible have withdrawn, awaited reinforcements, and regrouped to challenge the Vikings again. However, the values in tenth century England were not necessarily the same. Though there were of course always exceptions, there was a widespread and even fatalistic expectation that warriors would fight on to the death, especially if their leader was killed.

It could be argued that Byrhtnoth should have harried the Vikings to try to prevent a successful landing, but since their ships would have been on the seaward side of the Isle of Northey, this may have been logistically difficult. They were very probably out of arrow range from the shore. Nevertheless, small and manoeuvrable boats carrying archers could perhaps have been used to get within range of the ships.

At the risk of digression this leads me to a large and persistent reservation I have regarding British/English military weapon-based tactics from 55 BC through to 1066, and that is the inadequate utilisation of ranged (missile) weapons, particularly the bow and arrow. (And this reservation also applies to some of their foes.) The spear – often doubling as both throwing spear and thrusting spear[307] – was not uncommon, but obviously had limited range relative to the bow and arrow. The heyday of the highly efficient longbow proper was still some way off, but nonetheless bows of one sort or another had been in use for some 10,000 years and there were certainly reasonably effective bows (such as the self-bow) available in England in the late tenth century. It is puzzling why they were not used more. Indeed, Matthew Strickland, in a specialist paper on Anglo-Saxon weaponry, remarks that the Anglo-Saxons had 'a long tradition of archery' but 'its military application remains obscure'.[308] The *Battle of Maldon* does make an occasional reference to the bow and arrow being used by the English (and the Vikings) in the battle. For example, the Northumbrian Aescferth 'loosed forth many an arrow; sometimes he shot into a shield, sometimes he ripped open a man; every now and again he inflicted a wound'.[309] Given the explicit record here of its efficacy, it is all the more puzzling. The Vikings too could have used ranged weapons, particularly the bow, to deal with the men defending the causeway.

There is perhaps a clue to the bow's under-utilisation in another reference to arrows in the early part of the poem, when the Vikings were still on the island (the tide being in at this stage), with both sides lined up for battle, but 'not one of them could harm another except where someone was felled by the flight of an arrow'.[310] This, in combination with the above quotation that mentions only 'wounding' and not killing (though being 'ripped open' seems potentially fatal.), appears to suggest that arrows were considered lightweight and not very effective as weapons, perhaps only thought of as irritants that could for the most part merely wound rather than kill or seriously disable. Moreover, it was likely that the bow was considered an 'unmanly' weapon not fit for a truly effective warrior, and that there was thus a status factor.[311] It appears the case that 'real warriors' preferred the sword (or axe),[312]and where possible to face each other closely in man-to-man combat.

But the reality is that, though they might seem 'lightweight' relative to a sword, it would be patently wrong to say that arrows could not kill or disable. The Mongols, for example, used their horn bow with enormous and fatal effects. There must surely be other reasons for avoidance of the bow and arrow by some societies. And that is, in my view, related to stability in the social structure – or more exactly maintenance of an elite warrior class. Ranged weapons meant that a great and noble warrior, highly trained in swordsmanship and in peak physical condition, could be felled by a missile (especially an arrow) from a weak and lowly serf – of either gender. That is, like the gun in the 'Wild West', the bow was a potential leveller, but the difference in context was that in the West it became a symbol of widely desired equality, whereas in early Britain equality was not at all desired by those at the top, and was probably largely undreamt of by those lower down. I myself think it must have been a shared and probably unspoken understanding among warriors – at least in Celtic and Anglo-Saxon societies, and also to a lesser extent Viking – that too much encouragement of the bow and arrow could undermine warrior culture and cause major societal upheaval, and even affect concepts of maleness.[313]

And yet, within the next century, it was the bow that was to prove so decisive in two major English battles, Stamford Bridge and Hastings, and thereafter the bow was to become more widely accepted. The failure of the British/English to use the bow and arrow more systematically at earlier points in history must be considered foolish to some extent – especially if, as at Hastings, the enemy was making substantial use of them – but this also needs to be assessed in a socio-cultural context. Failure to make more use of ranged weapons was not necessarily a failing on the part of Byrhtnoth alone, though a later general might have behaved differently and more successfully.

Reflecting on the result of the battle itself, we need to bear in mind the unfortunate incident of Godric's fleeing on Byrhtnoth's horse, causing many to think it was Byrhtnoth himself in flight. Had this not happened, the outcome might have been different. As shown in the poem, the heroic death of a commander in battle – as opposed to his being 'picked off' at an early stage by a sniper or similar,[314] which I have advocated earlier as a desirable tactic – could actually inspire his followers, but the sight of a commander in flight obviously had the opposite effect. Had the incident not occurred, not only would the morale have been better, the English would have retained greater numbers of men, and the shield-formation might not have been broken.

Regarding the significance of his defeat, one has to say that this was reasonably considerable. Though it did not signal an end to armed resistance, it did mark the renewal of the practice of buying off the Vikings. Maldon was a 'showdown', in which the English lost. It could be argued that even if Byrhtnoth had won and set the Vikings back, there would have been other raids by them in due course, but nevertheless their victory must have been a catalyst for the subsequent plethora of raids. And of course, in this regard, Byrhtnoth's defeat did not help Aethelred's image. Had Byrhtnoth won, Aethelred might – though on balance it is unlikely – subsequently have had a peaceful reign, or at least a period of peace.

(4) *Just how foolish was Aethelred, and to what extent was he responsible for the loss of the kingdom to the Danes?*

Again, another two-part question, and I believe the answers to be 'somewhat but not enormously' and 'partly but by no means solely'. Let us start by reconsidering the caricature of Aethelred by Sellar and Yeatman, point by point.

They refer to him as 'the first weak king'. Yes, he was weak militarily, and probably weak in his endless payments to the Vikings, but he was almost certainly not the *first* weak king, even at national rather than local level. His great-uncle Eadred is one who springs to mind. But in terms of weakness, it is hard to make a case for the defence. Highly respected scholars such as Frank Barlow feel there is no question that he was 'an incompetent ruler',[315] and there is considerable evidence of his shortcomings. I will return to this presently.

They say his weakness caused a fresh wave of Danes. This may be partially true, for he was very young and far from popular at his succession, and opportunistic Viking leaders may have scented particularly easy pickings. Certainly, these later raiders did constitute a 'new wave' (of Norwegians as well as Danes), but the initial arrival of the wave in 980 could hardly be attributable to Aethelred personally. However, a stronger king may have prevented the wave from coming back on so many occasions later in his reign.

They say he was always unready. We know that 'unready' is not really the right word, and that he should more accurately be known as 'Aethelred the Ill-Advised'. And ill-advised he must have been on occasion, with counsellors such as the seemingly traitorous and self-seeking Eadric Streona. But like Vortigern, Aethelred acted on advice, so it is hard to blame him alone. Indeed, not all his advisers were bad, and it was, for example, Archbishop Sigeric – seen as one of a number of men of 'considerable calibre' around Aethelred in the 990s and early 1000s[316] – who advised payment to the Danes. And even if, for argument's sake, we do take the term in the meaning of 'unready', we could hardly accuse him of it in the sense of being taken by surprise, for he would surely have come to expect the Vikings on a very regular basis. But perhaps he should have been more ready to put up armed resistance and readier with his preparations. He did make preparations in the form of strengthening the navy, a navy which does not seem to have been particularly effective and may perhaps justify accusations of unreadiness, but it is hard to blame that directly on the king, as we saw in the text. Another area where he might perhaps be accused of being unready was in his assumption of the throne at such a tender age, but that was hardly of his making. Almost certainly he would, at least in the early years, have had decisions made for him, and this may possibly have impaired his later ability to make decisions. However, this is mere speculation – a similar experience did not deter William the Conqueror, for example, who became Duke of Normandy at the age of seven and became one of the most decisive figures in history.

Sellar and Yeatman also say that he was forever paying the Danes, so often it seemed they were paid before they'd even left. Yes, we could say they are right on this one. The frequent and large payments, especially in the latter years of his reign, must have caused a haemorrhage in English coffers – and would have caused apoplexy in the likes of Byrhtnoth, who in one sense was fortunate to meet his end before the payments really started. But we should not overlook the fact that payments to the Vikings were not a creation of Aethelred's, nor were they necessarily associated with weak kings. Alfred the Great and other monarchs also made such payments (though perhaps not with the same frequency), and they could hardly all be called weak. In fact, given Aethelred's weakness as a general, which even he himself must surely have been aware of, it might even be argued that paying off the Vikings was a sensible ploy that minimised disruption to the country,[317] certainly relative to total invasion and possible annihilation or enslavement of the English. And the frequent nature of the payments is to some extent understandable: though there were certain prominent Viking figures who feature in numerous raids (such as Swein Forkbeard), it can be argued that there was such a diversity of forces and leaders that paying off one force/leader on one occasion did not by any means guarantee that a different force/leader would not attack and demand similar payment.[318]

Finally, with particular facetiousness Sellar and Yeatman say he was caught unawares even by his own death. He died of illness, and however sudden this may have been, it would not have been instantaneous – in fact, his illness seems to have spanned at least six months – and he almost certainly would have had some perception that he might die, even though he was only in his late forties. How wisely he used this time to make constructive plans for the succession and thereafter is not so clear.

Moving on to a broader assessment, one matter in which Aethelred might be called foolish – Audrey MacDonald refers to it as 'considered a cardinal blunder'[319] – was his part in the decision in 1002 to exterminate all Danes in England. One can appreciate that it was very likely an act born of desperation and a feeling of 'enough is enough', and that it was a decision taken 'with the counsel of leading men and magnates', but it was inevitable that it would escalate hostilities by causing a backlash. However, once again, while the decision to exterminate the Danes would seem a reflection of Aethelred's frustration and desperation, and he may perhaps have been the first to voice it, it is hard to believe that its attempted implementation was purely driven by Aethelred himself. As Keynes points out, a violent act of such scale must have had widespread support – certainly those in Oxford seemed to carry out the directive with some enthusiasm.[320]

Similarly, his behaviour in 1014, after his return to England, when he seized the lands of Morcar and Sigeferth and may indeed have been involved in their murder, was another unwise act. As mentioned in the text, he may have been better advised to show forgiveness, and certainly not to claim their lands even if he had them executed. We do not know all the details and he may have been reacting to some other threatening behaviour of theirs, but on the face of it, he does not emerge with much credit. In fact, bearing in mind also his order in 1002 for extermination of the Danes, he may be felt to have shown on occasion a certain erraticism, volatility, and overreactiveness, sometimes with violent consequences. Ryan Lavelle, for example, states that Aethelred's reign may have been characterised by a 'bi-polar mixture' of sensitivity and severity.[321] But perhaps, when it comes to an assessment of Aethelred's character, we should most safely follow Simon Keynes and conclude that the more one learns about Aethelred the more frustrated one becomes about trying to understand what he was really like.[322]

But the fact that he did return in 1014, moreover apparently at the request of his councillors, must have meant that he was not seen as a total 'write-off' as a monarch. He was at least, among his councillors, relatively preferable to Cnut at that point, though it is debatable how much this was due to positive thoughts towards Anglo-Saxon continuity rather than Aethelred personally, and more particularly one has to consider the councillors' fears for their assets and possibly even their lives should Cnut take the throne. Paying the Vikings was bad enough, but having a regime-change from Anglo-Saxon to Viking could be disastrous.

In passing one might also perhaps wonder why, if Aethelred was really such a bad king as his reputation suggests, he did not join the list of those kings who died 'conveniently'. Of course, it could be argued that being weak meant that he was manipulable by others for their own interests, and that may have been a factor in his survival. However, it does make one wonder why someone who was supposedly responsible – in the minds of some – for upsetting God through involvement in the death of Edward the Martyr to such an extent that He sent the Vikings to plague the whole nation, should be allowed to survive. Wouldn't someone somewhere have entertained the idea that sacrifice of the sinner might bring redemption for the nation? The apparent fact that nobody did try to murder him – in an age when murder was common – would seem to support further the idea that, while Aethelred was obviously not particularly admired, he was not seen by his contemporaries as thoroughly bad.

Some scholars have criticised Aethelred for his marriage to Emma, on the grounds that it blurred loyalties, a blurring compounded ten years later in 1012 when, as mentioned above, Aethelred recruited the Viking leader Thorkell the Tall and his men (and his 45 ships), and similarly his enlisting in 1014 of another leading Viking, Olaf Haroldsson. Barlow comments that Aethelred did not help his own cause by blurring ethnic loyalties, thereby making it easier for English nobles to desert him and switch allegiance to the Scandinavian invaders.[323] It might perhaps be counter-argued that having Vikings on his side might have helped dissuade other Vikings from attacking. Indeed, Barlow's argument might equally be applied to the Vikings, for by employing some Vikings and fighting other Vikings, Aethelred – though probably not as a conscious policy – could be said to have blurred loyalties and associations among the Vikings. Moreover it was a very old practice, going back to Roman days, to employ one group of barbarians against other barbarians, even if those others were from the same people as those employed.

Fleeing overseas was not the bravest thing to do, and would certainly have contributed to his reputation as a weak king, but at the same time it was tactically successful, for he and his children by Emma did survive. Moreover he did return, albeit only after Swein's death, and it is possible – though unlikely – that he may have retrieved the situation to some extent had his life not been cut unfortunately short by illness. At least his son Edmund did succeed to the throne, albeit one of the briefest reigns in English history, to be followed eventually, and unexpectedly, by another son, Edward. In this latter case it could be said that fate bestowed good fortune rather than ill fortune on the House of Aethelred – just as it could be argued that fate allowed Aethelred a 'second chance' with the death of Swein.

In my view it was really fortune rather than foolishness that characterised Aethelred's reign. If I might use an awful pun, he certainly paid the Vikings a fortune. His fortune in the sense of luck and fate was overall very much on the bad side rather than the good, as we have already seen suggested in the text. C. Warren Hollister, for example, is so moved by Aethelred's being 'the victim of nearly hopeless circumstance', particularly with regard to the relentless and intense Viking attacks, that he is prompted to lament 'Poor wretch!'[324] The weather was not kind to Aethelred in his attempt to strengthen and employ the navy, and he also had the misfortune to have a number of less than reliable counsellors (/councillors) and commanders in the control of which he may have been considered deficient. Certainly, regional rivalries and his inability to get on top of these and keep reasonable relationships with all his magnates, contributed to an unhelpful lack of internal solidity. The lack of loyalty to him was instrumental in the weakness of his position. However, in my view the main agents of his ill fortune were the Vikings. Had they not renewed their belligerence after a period of relative quietude, Aethelred's reign would obviously have been recorded differently in the history books. In a time of peace his administrative competence (albeit not shown consistently), his fine legislation (admittedly with the help of others), and his support for the church may have prevailed in the creation of his image, which would probably have been of an overall positive nature.

As seen in the case of Vortigern, it seems an unfortunate and simplistic part of human nature to seek out scapegoats to explain away adversity. However unhelpful the behaviour of an individual might be, it is highly unlikely they are solely responsible for the outcome – though in terms of degree they might play a major role, as we will see in Part 3. It is easy to blame Aethelred for the loss of England, and he certainly did play his part in it, and moreover a significant one. A stronger, more active king may have helped bring about a different outcome, though I repeat that the Vikings would very likely have persisted with their raids and intended settlement even if Byrhtnoth had initially beaten them, and by the same token even if there had been a stronger king in place than Aethelred. We must also remember that technically it was Edmund who lost England, not Aethelred, though it would be even more unfair to make Edmund a scapegoat – and no one has, to judge from his enduring byname of 'Ironside'. He was, after all, in a parlous position from the moment he became king. His father Aethelred must take some serious blame for the loss of England, but, as I have argued, others need to shoulder some responsibility as well, particularly his counsellors/ councillors. And we must not forget the strength of his opponents and the role of fortune. We can perhaps also question the idea of loss. Though I do not mean at all to downplay the loss of life and land and liberty amongst the English, England itself was not lost. To use a dreadful euphemistic cliché from the harsh world of business takeovers and restructuring, it can be argued that it simply 'came under new management' – moreover, as it would turn out, 'temporary new management'.

2.9   Conclusion

We have seen how England was beset by waves of pagan incursions following the departure of the Romans, though we should not forget that such incursions were also taking place in the latter part of the Roman occupation. The main early threats were from the Picts in Scotland, but very soon their primacy as threat gave way to that of the Germanic Anglo-Saxons. Employed as defenders of Britain against the Picts, they soon became hostile to their employers and established a presence in England, apparently driving many Britons into Wales and the far southwest, and subjugating many others.

We have seen that Vortigern was instrumental in their arrival, in that he was (evidently) the first Briton to employ the Anglo-Saxons, but he should not be blamed for that, or for their subsequent entrenchment. He may perhaps – though we cannot be sure – have defaulted to some extent on promised rewards, but that is insufficient cause for what followed. The Anglo-Saxons invaded Britain – or more exactly the area to become known as England – because they wanted to and they could.

As they settled and established dominance they also became increasingly Christian, though this was insufficient to unite them to the point of ceasing warfare between the regional kingdoms. Among those kingdoms, Mercia, especially under Offa, was dominant in the eighth century, and Wessex thereafter. In the tenth century, Wessex supplied the kings of what was effectively (but not wholly) a united nation we can call England, in part undeniably thanks to Wessex's most famous figure, Alfred, although the exact extent of his contribution is subject to question.

Alfred has been seen to be, to a considerable extent, an example of the effect of subjectivity – and concomitant bias – in the documenting of history. His deeds were generally presented in the best possible light, in contrast to Aethelred, who seems – not unlike Vortigern half a millennium earlier – to have soon been scapegoated for the loss of the English kingdom to the Vikings.

The Vikings themselves have been seen, in many regards, to have done unto the Anglo-Saxons that which the Anglo-Saxons did unto the Britons,[325] though not to the same extent, for the Anglo-Saxons at least retained most of their land, though they may have had to live under Viking kings for a while. Indeed, we have looked at a number of parallels, including the conversion to Christianity. And we should also recognise that, although English unity and national consciousness would seem to have been developing steadily through the Anglo-Saxon period, the external threat posed by the Vikings in the later half of the period would very probably have helped that unification – the end-product being a unified England that could absorb the Viking threat.

As suggested above, one result of these various waves of invasion is the rich and diverse bloodlines of many present-day English, and another, of course, is the basis of our present-day English language, basically Anglo-Saxon but enriched with Viking words. Another major element in present-day English, namely French, was to follow in the wake of the major event discussed in Part 3, the Norman Conquest.

3
The Improbable Norman Conquest

3.1 Introduction

1066 was arguably the most fateful of years for the English. It started with the
death of Edward the Confessor and the accession of Harold Godwineson, seemingly designated by Edward himself on his deathbed. However, his assumption
of the crown was disputed by Harald Hardraada of Norway, a renowned and
much feared Viking warrior, and in particular by the similarly feared Duke
William of Normandy.

William claimed that Edward had already promised him the throne during an
alleged visit by William to England in 1051, and moreover that Harold had
sworn on oath to support his (William's) claim to the throne during a sojourn
Harold had with William in 1064, though Harold appears to have protested that
he was forced to take his oath under duress and that it was therefore invalid.
Moreover, if Edward, on his deathbed, did indeed promise the crown to Harold,
then, as with wills, that latest designation should have superseded any earlier
promises or oaths in support of them. Certainly, the circumstances around all
this are at the very least unclear.

William planned to cross to England to do battle with Harold for the crown,
and assembled a large fleet – having to build much of it – for that purpose.
Harold assembled his army and his own fleet on the south coast to await and
repel his arrival. William's fleet was ready in late summer, but contrary winds
delayed its departure for England till late in September, by which time Harold,
low on provisions and at the end of the recognised time-limit for keeping the
levies assembled, had been obliged to stand down his army, and also sent his
fleet back to base. Moreover, just a week or so after standing his forces down earlier that month, Harold had received news of an invasion in the northeast of the
country by Hardraada, accompanied by Harold's rebel brother Tostig (Tosti).
Tostig had been exiled late the previous year; he blamed his brother Harold for
it and seems to have been bent on revenge rather than specifically the crown.

Assembling what men he could, and with his personal guard of housecarls, Harold moved rapidly north, took Hardraada and Tostig by surprise, and won a memorable victory at the Battle of Stamford Bridge on 25 September. Both Hardraada and Tostig were killed.

Within a week after his victory, apparently while still in the north, Harold learnt that William had landed at Pevensey on the south coast on 28 September. And so, with the remains of his army he headed south again, once again gathering more men as he went. William, meanwhile, had moved to nearby Hastings and was harrying the area, which happened to be the ancestral territory of the Godwinesons. His strategy appears to have been to lure Harold into a premature engagement. Certainly, William was clearly staying put in the Hastings area, for to have moved inland would have stretched his supply and communication lines and been risky. Rather, he was prepared to risk all on an early engagement with Harold.

While still waiting for some levies to join him, Harold set off for Hastings on the 10th or possibly the 11th of October, arriving at the neck of the Hastings Peninsula on the evening of the 13th or in the small hours of the 14th. Instead of surprising William, it was Harold and his men who were taken by surprise the following morning when William's men appeared before the English were ready.

A daylong battle ensued, with the English essentially fighting a defensive battle against charges by William's cavalry. Though accounts of the battle vary considerably, it seems that shortly after sunset Harold was killed, apparently being injured by an arrow in the eye and then finished off by four charging knights. The English shield wall had given way by this stage. William had won the day and in effect won the crown. There were no real challengers, with Harold's brothers also dead at Hastings and with Edward's great-nephew Edgar, who many felt should really have succeeded Edward, still a child. William was crowned at Westminster Abbey on Christmas Day.

The key question asked by almost every historian is why Harold chose to engage so early, when all he had to do was play a waiting game. To use a sporting metaphor, he could afford to draw whereas William had to win, but he does not seem to have used this advantage effectively. Thus Part 3 pays particular attention to Harold's actions.

As mentioned above, it is difficult to work out exactly what happened at Hastings. One reason for this is the vagueness and variability of the primary sources. I discuss the general problems with these at the beginning of my treatment of the battle (Section 3.5: 'October and Hastings'), and illustrate just how much interpretations can differ. Here I merely note very briefly that the main primary sources can basically be divided into English and Norman/French, though there are also some Germanic and Scandinavian sources that add light on particulars.

Among the main English sources, we have the anonymous *Anglo-Saxon Chronicle* (in various manuscript versions), the *Chronicle of John of Worcester* (completed c. 1140), Eadmer's *History of Recent Events in England* (*Historia Novorum in Anglia*, c. 1123), William of Malmesbury's *Chronicle of the Kings of England* (*Gesta Regum Anglorum*, c. 1125), and Henry of Huntingdon's *History of the English People* (*Historia Anglorum*, c. 1129). Some of these authors, notably Malmesbury and Huntingdon, were Anglo-Norman and did not necessarily follow a pro-English line.

On the Norman/French side, the main sources include the *Bayeux Tapestry*, probably commissioned by William's half-brother Odo some time before 1082, though very probably made in England. In literary form there is the *Song of the Battle of Hastings* (*Carmen de Hastingae Proelio*), widely attributed to Guy of Amiens and possibly written as early as 1067; the *Deeds of the Norman Dukes* (*Gesta Normannorum Ducum*), in large part written by William of Jumièges by the mid-1070s and subsequently added to by Orderic Vitalis and Robert of Torigni; and the *Deeds of William* (*Gesta Guillelmi*) by William of Poitiers c. 1077. Orderic Vitalis, born in England but raised in Normandy, added to the *Deeds of the Norman Dukes* c. 1109, and then wrote his *Ecclesiastical History* (*Historia Ecclesiastica*) c. 1142, which included a treatment of Hastings. Around 1110 there appeared the *Brief History of the Most Noble William, Count of the Normans* (*Brevis Relatio de Guillelmo Nobilissimo Comite Normannorum*), thought to be written by an anonymous Norman monk. There is also Wace's long poem *Story of Rollo* (*Roman de Rou*), of c. 1175.

There are a number of other primary sources of varying degrees of relevance, such as the *Life of King Edward* (*Vita Edwardi Regis*, c. 1100), attributed to a monk at St Bertin, which is very useful for pre-1066 material, and the *Life of Harold* (*Vita Haroldi*, c. 1200), which, despite its promising title, is only occasionally relevant.

3.2   January 1066: Contested succession, past deeds

Edward (later 'the Confessor'), the half-Saxon, half-Norman king who had reigned since 1042 and been married since 1045, died childless at Westminster in the early hours of Thursday, 5 January 1066, following an illness of several weeks that had left him semi-comatose. According to the *Life of King Edward*, written shortly after his death, at his bedside were his queen Edith (Harold's sister), Harold himself as the king's most powerful earl (called sub-regulus or 'under-king' by some), Archbishop Stigand of Canterbury, the royal steward Robert fitzWymarc, and a few unnamed others.[1] Although Edward's fitness of mind at that point has been questioned, he is said to have told Harold that he commended the kingdom to him,[2] and that Harold should obtain an oath of fealty from those Normans who had served Edward himself, or else let them return to

Normandy. Though not fully explicit, this does strongly suggest that Edward was designating Harold as his successor. Indeed, the *Anglo-Saxon Chronicle* states with more explicitness that 'Harold succeeded to the kingdom of England just as the king had granted it him.'[3]

Moving with extraordinary speed, the *witan* (a convocation of magnates that was effectively the 'parliament' in those days) met later that same day to endorse Harold's accession. He was duly crowned the following day, the 6th, straight after Edward's funeral and moreover in the same place – Edward's pride and joy, the newly consecrated (as of 28 December 1065) Westminster Abbey. Despite scenes in the *Bayeux Tapestry* – probably English-made, but Norman propaganda – which suggest Stigand carried out the coronation, Harold may well have been crowned by Ealdred (Aldred), Archbishop of York.[4] This would have been in order to avoid any claims that the coronation was invalid on the grounds that Stigand's appointment as archbishop was at that time uncanonical.[5]

Criteria for kingship at this point in history were rather vague.[6] Generally, the preferred heir should have a close blood claim, ideally being a son of the preceding monarch but not necessarily the eldest. Depending on circumstances a grandson or sibling too could be a good candidate, and to a lesser extent so too a nephew or cousin, especially with a paternal link. Again with circumstances permitting, the incumbent monarch was allowed some latitude to designate a preference for successor among a range of appropriate persons, with their latest-stated choice having the strongest claim. However, choice of heir was also subject to popular acclaim, usually expressed in the form of approval by the *witan*. And of course, right by conquest was also necessarily recognised, as seen in the case some 50 years earlier of the Dane Swein Forkbeard and particularly his son Cnut.

Harold appears to have satisfied two of these criteria, namely designation and popular acclaim, and he was related closely to Edward through marriage (being his brother-in-law), but he did not have a blood claim – or at least not a strong one, for it is argued by some scholars that Harold was in fact a distant descendant through his father's line of the Anglo-Saxon king Aethelwulf (r. 839–58).[7] More definitely, those who try to discredit Harold as an outright commoner are mistaken, and here again Cnut plays a role. Cnut had been a strong supporter of Harold's father Earl Godwine of Wessex, and in 1019 had arranged a marriage for him to Gytha Thurgilsdottir, Cnut's own sister-in-law (strictly speaking the sister of Cnut's brother-in-law Ulf, who was married to Cnut's sister Estrith).[8] Gytha was moreover a distant blood relative of Cnut, and was certainly of royal blood of some standing, being the granddaughter of the Swedish king Styrbjorn and great-granddaughter of Cnut's grandfather the Danish king Harald Blatand (Bluetooth). Thus her son Harold too carried royal blood – though admittedly not of English royalty except through a tenuous link to Cnut.

Table 3.1 Harold Godwineson's ancestors and descendants

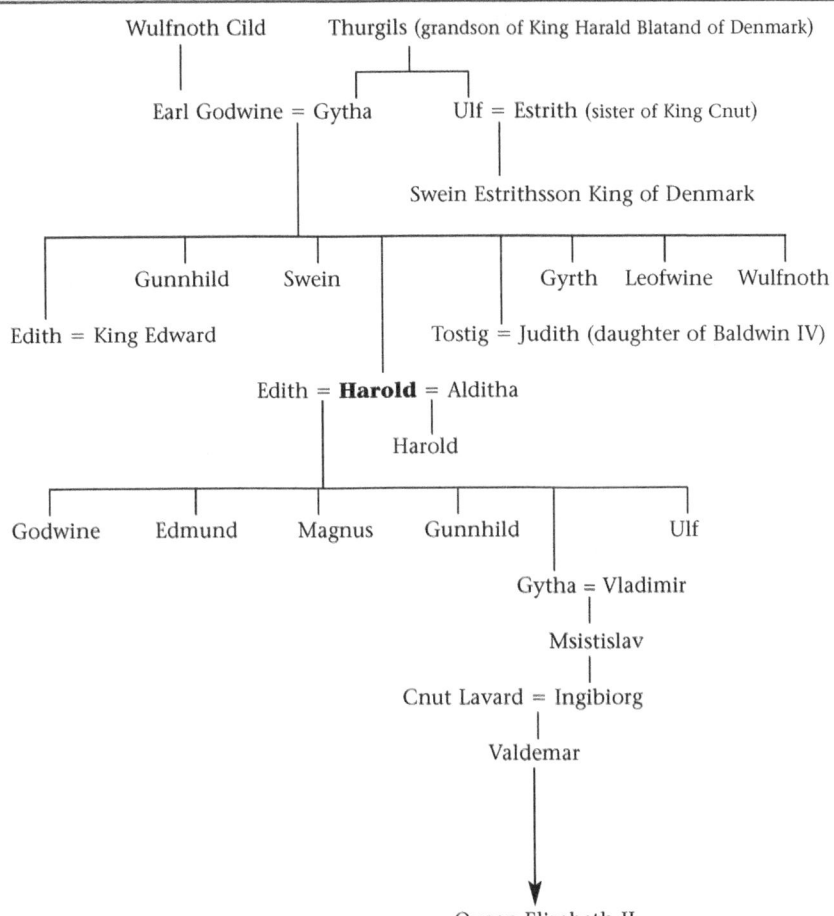

Given that Edward died without progeny and moreover with no surviving siblings or even nephews (of the first degree, at least), and given the nature of his 'last gasp' unwritten and somewhat inexplicit designation of Harold, a man with a very limited blood claim, it was highly likely that the succession was going to prove contestable. As Pauline Stafford has said, noting the complexities and vagueness of the situation, the succession in 1066 will always produce more questions than answers.[9]

In theory the crown should probably have gone to Edward's great-nephew Edgar the Aetheling, who had a relatively strong blood claim as son of Edward the Exile, in turn the son of King Edmund 'Ironside', in turn the son of Edward's own father, King Aethelred Unraed. That is, Edgar was the grandson of Edward's half-brother Edmund. This sounds somewhat distant, but his claim seems stronger if he is considered rather as the grandson of a former king. It is also worth noting that the term 'a(e)theling', meaning 'throneworthy', was applied to Edgar by Edward himself.[10]

The son of a former king would have an even stronger claim, and indeed Edgar's father, Ironside's son Edward the Exile (sometimes known as the 'Lost King'), had been brought back to England in 1057 from obscurity in Hungary (where he had been in exile following Ironside's death and Cnut's assumption of the throne in 1016), seemingly at Edward the Confessor's request,[11] specifically as an early pre-emptive solution to Edward's inauspicious lack of offspring to that date. John of Worcester states explicitly that Edward had decided that his namesake should be established as his 'heir and successor to the realm'.[12] However, within days of landing in England, before he could meet King Edward and have the succession confirmed, he had died mysteriously – indeed very suspiciously[13] – leaving his young son Edgar as apparent next-in-line. Edgar's date of birth is not clear, but was at the latest 1055, and was possibly as early as 1051. This makes him at least ten years old in 1066, and this was certainly old enough for him to accede to the crown, even if only under a regent.[14]

Harold, who had effectively been the principal player in affairs of state since the death of his father Earl Godwine in 1053, could easily have taken up a regent's role. His sister Queen Edith could probably also have done likewise. Though Edgar's mother Agatha was still alive, the boy had largely been brought up in the Royal Household, treated by the childless Edith seemingly as if he were her own son.[15] He seemed well-liked, including by Edward, and was apparently sound in mind and generally in body – though he was said by some, perhaps conveniently, to be in ill-health at the time of Edward's death. The fact that Edith seemed cold towards her brother Harold in 1066[16] possibly suggests she may have reacted negatively towards his sidelining of her 'almost-son' Edgar – and perhaps thereby her own chance of becoming regent. On the other hand, her coldness towards Harold was no doubt also due at least in part to his treatment a few months earlier of their brother Tostig, to whom she was particularly close,[17] and of course it may also have been for other unknown reasons. Tostig will be discussed presently.

It is worth noting that, after Harold's death at Hastings, Edgar was belatedly designated by the remnants of the *witan* as King Elect later in 1066. However, he was once again sidelined, though this time by William, who simply dismissed Edgar's elect regal status and had himself crowned, on Christmas Day and at Westminster Abbey, as King William I. (After a long adventure-filled life, including an attempt or two to take the crown off William, Edgar was to die many years later in Scotland, known as the 'Forgotten King'.)

One possible reason why Harold and the *witan* may have ignored Edgar's strong claim in January 1066 was that the kingdom was in peril (such as with regard to Northumbria, to be discussed presently) and needed a mature, strong, and experienced leader to respond to a number of threats. However, there is no reason why Harold could not have done this as a regent, as for example William Marshal was later to do for the young Henry III. It could also be counter-argued that one or more of these threats resulted from Harold's very assumption of the crown, which in that regard means his action could be seen as generating rather than preventing trouble. One has to conclude that he and his supporters did sideline Edgar. Was this because Harold was genuinely seen by the *witan* as the best man for the job? Was he dutifully obeying his dying king's words? And, one wonders, did Edward himself have anything to say about Edgar? Did he and Harold discuss him? Or, did Harold and/or his supporters put undue pressure on Edward to designate Harold himself? Or was there some other factor? We will probably never know.

On his deathbed Edward was said to have also spoken of a vision in which God's wrath would result in the imminent destruction of the kingdom,[18] and while this vision was probably greatly exaggerated with hindsight and possibly with a view to claims for Edward's sainthood,[19] there could indeed be some truth to the idea that on his deathbed he expressed a dire warning. If he did, it may well have been because of a troubled conscience on his part, for he himself had contributed greatly to the peril by indecision and apparent vague promises regarding the succession.

Most significantly of all, Edward appears to have given Duke William of Normandy the impression that he was his designated heir. Examination of this requires us to go back some 15 years or so to 1051/2, then a little further back to 1036, then forward again to 1051/2 and on to 1064. (It was indeed a complex situation.)

William's alleged designation was seemingly in 1051, and according to Norman sources[20] it was supposedly in recognition of the hospitality Edward had been shown during his long exile in Normandy away from Danish rule, from 1013, when Edward was around eight years old, till his return to England in 1041.[21] This designation of William is said to have been recognised by the magnates of the kingdom,[22] and it is also said that hostages were given to support this pledge by Earl Godwine, namely his youngest son Wulfnoth and his young grandson Hakon (son of Godwine's eldest son Swein). Some sources – curiously the *Anglo-Saxon Chronicle* (Manuscript D, but no other version) and the *Chronicle of John of Worcester* (following D), but no Norman document – refer to a visit by William to Edward in England in late 1051,[23] which may have been an opportunity for any such designation. Given the troubled state of affairs in Normandy at the time, it is unlikely, but not impossible, that William made such a visit. Even if he did, it is open to question whether Edward made an explicit formal designation[24] and equally whether the earls would have approved any such designation anyway – although, as discussed below, it was a time of great tension and the earls may have been under considerable pressure. Certainly, there is no reference to anything being put down in writing. Yet it would appear a fact that William ended up, within a year or so, with Wulfnoth and Hakon as hostages.

What may perhaps have happened, in my own interpretation of events, is that Edward grew thoroughly frustrated with being surrounded and dominated by the ubiquitous and sometimes troublesome Anglo-Danish Godwine family,[25] and was especially weary of being dictated to by the patriarch Earl Godwine himself. He had a deep lingering dislike of Godwine, suspecting him of the earlier torture and murder of his (Edward's) elder brother Alfred, who in 1036 had made a forlorn attempt to claim the English crown following the death of Cnut.[26] He therefore may well have decided finally to 'put his foot down' and break loose from Godwine's grip, making the most of a timely (possibly suspiciously so) incident.[27]

The incident in question was a fracas between the townsfolk of Dover and the troops of Edward's brother-in-law Count Eustace of Boulogne (the second husband of Edward's sister Goda), during a visit to England by Eustace in July that year (1051). There were a dozen or so casualties on each side, and sources agree that Eustace's men struck the first blow. However, hereafter specifics vary according to source. According to the *Anglo-Saxon Chronicle*, Manuscript E, Eustace made a very one-sided complaint to Edward, and Edward believed him completely, refusing to listen properly to anyone other than those on Eustace's side.[28] Edward deemed the townsfolk to be at fault and demanded that Godwine, in whose earldom Dover lay, should punish them severely. Godwine refused, since it seemed clear that it was the Count's men who had started the trouble by throwing their weight around and rudely demanding accommodation – in fact, Ms E records that Eustace's men put their armour on before riding into Dover, suggesting it was a deliberate provocation that may have got out of hand.[29] The situation at Edward's court then escalated and presently led to the brink of armed confrontation between Godwine on the one hand and the earls Siward (Northumbria) and Leofric (Mercia), whom Edward had called upon to help him, on the other.

By contrast, Manuscript D states[30] that it was Godwine who was the angered party, rather than Edward, being enraged that Eustace and his men had acted so violently in his earldom and forcefully demanding of the king that Eustace should be handed over to him, thereby bringing the situation to the brink of armed confrontation.

Either way, it is very possible for Eustace's actions to be interpreted as a deliberate provocative act. If it was indeed a deliberate provocation, it may be thought unlikely to have been of Edward's making,[31] for despite his shortcomings he does not seem to have been a schemer or deliberately dishonest, at least as far as we can judge. More likely, one imagines, it would have been a joint scheme by Eustace and the Norman Robert of Jumièges, the newly and controversially installed Archbishop of Canterbury who had returned from Rome a few weeks earlier and was strongly opposed to Godwine.[32] Edward may have been 'egged on' by Jumièges, who seems to have reminded him about Alfred and made other accusations against Godwine such as unlawful seizure of church land, and even that Godwine was planning to kill him (Edward).[33]

Whatever the specifics, Edward certainly ended up in a stand-off with Godwine, accusing him of treasonous insubordination, and it was probably at this point that Godwine handed over the hostages to him as a pledge of good faith towards him. However, Edward apparently refused to give hostages in return[34] and was completely implacable, refusing to listen to any words in support of Godwine.[35] It could have ended in civil war, which would not have been helpful to the country, but in fact the result was that the Godwine family – Godwine, his wife Gytha, his sons Swein, Harold, Tostig, Gyrth, and Leofwine, and his second daughter Gunnhild – went into exile in September, with Godwine's first daughter Queen Edith being sent to a convent.

Soon afterwards, perhaps in a fit of pique, or perhaps fearing a return of the Godwine family and a possible civil war that might see him deposed, in some desperation – and very possibly on the advice of Jumièges – Edward may have turned for moral and no doubt potential military support to his familiar 'other home' of Normandy, despite his long-standing dislike of his seemingly unloving Norman mother Emma[36] and the apparent fact – already noted – that he had not necessarily been happy for much of his time in Normandy. Though he had very probably not seen William since the latter's early teens, he would have known of his growing reputation and may indeed have at that point promised the crown to him[37] – possibly even largely to spite the Godwines. But the fact remains that nothing was put down in writing (that we know of), and we simply do not know exactly what happened.

It is also important to take into account that it was as early as 1054 that King Edward sent for Edward the Exile to be his successor,[38] though it took some years for the latter to be found and brought back to England (only to die almost immediately afterwards, as already noted). This does not say much of Edward's support for any promise he might have made to William regarding the succession. And one wonders what William thought of the approach to the Exile – if he knew. Again as already noted, if he did know, he may perhaps have been connected with the Exile's sudden death. Here too we can merely speculate. We should also note that William of Malmesbury has Edward promising William the crown not in 1051 but after the death of Edward the Exile in 1057,[39] though there is similarly no known record of this either, and moreover it overlooks the Exile's son Edgar, who appears to have been very well liked by Edward. Malmesbury's date is not widely supported, with the great majority of scholars feeling that, if William was indeed promised the crown, it would have been in 1051.

Though it may be a premature comment on personality we might observe here that Edward was seemingly an immature and erratic man with little real wisdom or perspicacity – a man described by his chief biographer Frank Barlow as 'a mediocrity' whose actions lacked proper purpose and thoughtful policy, a simple man but one who tended to be both rash and inflexible.[40] The whole business – if the above account is reasonably accurate – would indeed seem to smack of childish petulance on Edward's part, and may not have happened with a stronger, more mature-minded, and consistent monarch.

The Godwine family, by contrast, could not be accused of weakness. Having regrouped with the help of sympathisers in Ireland and on the continent, the family returned,[41] almost exactly a year later in September 1052, moreover with considerable armed and public support. Civil war did not break out, Edward relented, the family was given back all its lands, Queen Edith was restored to favour, and William was conspicuous by his failure to do anything other than to house Jumièges and certain other Normans who were dismissed by Edward and felt it prudent to flee to Normandy. It was probably at this stage, rather than 1051, that Jumièges took with him the two hostages previously entrusted to Edward and delivered them to William,[42] possibly just as an expedient to guarantee his own safety *en route*, or possibly at Edward's suggestion as a 'just in case' safeguard of Godwine's behaviour. And just to stir things up against the Godwines, he may have maliciously reinforced – or even implanted – the idea that William was Edward's chosen successor. (Jumièges died the following year, and left no clarification on this point.)

The idea of William being designated as Edward's successor was apparently made no more mention of until it was rather bizarrely reinforced more than ten years later, this time by Harold himself. For unknown reasons (discussed presently), sometime in 1064, Harold was on a small vessel in the Channel with very limited armed support. The weather was adverse and he ended up shipwrecked on the coast of Ponthieu. Count Guy of Ponthieu seized him and his men and imprisoned them, intending to hold them for ransom.[43] However, one of Harold's men managed to avoid capture and got word to Duke William in neighbouring Normandy, who promptly turned up and obtained the release of Harold and his men. For some months thereafter Harold was a somewhat reluctant houseguest *chez* William, who was evidently by one means or another detaining Harold and trying to use the opportunity to win Harold's support for his claim to be heir to the English throne.[44]

Among other events he took Harold with him on an impressive campaign against the wayward Count Conan of Brittany, and, again showing opportunistic skills, used a chance incident to help bind Harold's support. On crossing the dangerous River Couesnon, two of William's knights fell into quicksand and Harold, bravely and showing quite remarkable strength, pulled them out and saved their lives. In return, William knighted Harold – an occurrence which not only showed William's assumption that he was of higher rank than Harold, but also to some extent bound Harold to him through fealty. Later, just to ensure his point was made, he also 'persuaded' Harold to take an oath on sacred relics to support his cause in England, though Harold probably felt he had little choice in this matter.[45]

Indeed, the *Life of Harold* asserts that brave as he was, Harold was merely human on this occasion and feared for his life, seeing no way out of the situation other than taking the oath, moreover being urged to do so by 'certain friends who were with him' (presumably those who had set sail with him).[46]

In any event, the reality was that Harold did take the oath, and thus it was that William was able to make such a strong complaint when Harold took the crown that he (William) was expecting. Moreover it is generally agreed that he was able to appeal to Rome and obtain important papal endorsement and even a papal banner for his cause (discussed later, though it should be noted here that not all scholars agree that he obtained this support), since perjury of an oath made on sacred relics was viewed very severely. Papal support – assuming it was given – may also have had something to do with the apparent fact that the pope who granted the endorsement, Alexander II, was politically indebted to the Normans (who also had colonists in southern Italy).[47]

The reasons for Harold being in the Channel in the first place remain unclear. It has variously been suggested that he was on a fishing trip (!) and got caught out by the weather;[48] that he was actually intending to travel to Wales (!);[49] that he was planning a grand tour of the continent to study the statecraft of continental rulers; that he was going to visit William in Normandy to confirm Edward's designation of him (William);[50] that he was going to visit William to discuss a possible marriage alliance (perhaps of his daughter Gytha to William's son Robert, though some scholars[51] feel it may have been regarding a betrothal of William's own very young daughter Agatha to Harold himself, even though Harold was older than her father William); or, least unlikely of all in my personal view, and as asserted by Eadmer in his *History of Recent Events*,[52] that he was making a personal visit to William to plead for the release of the two hostages who were still being held by him. Certainly he came back from Normandy with his nephew Hakon, though his brother Wulfnoth was sadly doomed to spend the rest of his life, till his death in 1094, in imprisonment, not even released upon William's death in 1087 (whereupon virtually all prisoners held by the Normans were pardoned and released).

If redemption of the hostages was indeed the reason, then one has to wonder why Harold had left it for 12 years, unless perhaps he had also made unrecorded unsuccessful attempts in the meantime to redeem them, and had now finally decided to petition William face-to-face. The *Bayeux Tapestry* shows Harold in discussion with Edward immediately prior to the trip, but whether Edward is asking him to do something or advising him not to is unclear, though

Figure 3.1   A scene from the Bayeux Tapestry appears to show Edward admonishing a contrite Harold after his ill-fated journey in 1064. (By special permission of the City of Bayeux.)

a subsequent scene of Harold after his return facing Edward with head bowed and downcast expression seems to suggest the latter.[53] This in turn might suggest it was a private trip, moreover against the King's advice (though Edward was generally not noted as a source of sound advice, and Harold may not have been swayed by it).

We should also note that the fact that Harold's man got word to William may suggest that William was the person they were intending to visit, though it may just have been that he was the closest and/or most realistic source of rescue. Nor does it seem likely to have been a formal, pre-arranged visit. One imagines that if William had known beforehand of Harold's visit and was expecting him, then Harold needed only to have mentioned this to his captor Count Guy and he would surely have been escorted to William immediately with apologies, for Guy would have been foolish to have waylaid one of William's guests and thereby incurred his wrath. This strongly suggests that Harold's trip was indeed private, and possibly somewhat impromptu.

As mentioned above, my own interpretation is that it was a private trip in an attempt to redeem the hostages, a trip which Harold discussed with Edward beforehand and proceeded with despite Edward's telling him it would be futile. I believe that Harold had made a number of unrecorded and unsuccessful approaches to William beforehand, and was now going to raise it with him face-to-face, moreover making the visit unannounced to try to maximise impact. This would be a bold move, but Harold had very recently (August 1063) finally put an end to long-standing trouble in Wales in a triumph over the formidable Gruffydd ap Llywelyn, was at a peak of his strength and standing, and was no doubt feeling confident, if not overconfident.[54] This scenario is plausible and fits with all the known facts, but nonetheless the whole episode seems stranger than fiction, and remains a puzzle.

Two important points remain to be stated about the threat posed by William following Harold's coronation on 6 January 1066. The first is that, following his above experiences in 1064, and messages of protest sent by William during January,[55] Harold would have been left in no doubt about William's indignant belief that he was the designated heir to the English throne, and he would similarly have been aware that William was not a person to upset. Though an attempted Norman invasion of England would be a very risky and logistically difficult business, Harold would surely still have felt that it was very possible that the intrepid and affronted William would nonetheless attempt one – though almost certainly later in the year, as he would have to assemble and in large part build a much larger fleet than Normandy currently possessed.

The second point is that, while Edward does not seem to have paid great attention to any promise he might have made to William – he made similar promises to others (to be discussed later), and once again we should remind ourselves how he instigated the return of Edward the Exile and made much of Edgar Aetheling – William himself very much appears to have genuinely believed in his designation. It is not clear how aware he was of other designations, but even if he was he seems determined to believe it was his own claimed designation that should take priority. He seems simply not to have believed that Harold's similarly claimed designation had any validity. While it is a theoretical possibility that he made up the whole business as some sort of false justification for an expansionist conquest of England – for Normandy certainly was expansionist – in practice this would be extremely unlikely. As mentioned above, it was a highly risky and difficult business, and if he lost, it would almost certainly result in his death. Moreover, it was not just a case of opposing Harold: he would also have to be able to assert his claim over that of others, notably Edgar. As it turned out, that is what he ended up doing, and met with little resistance in doing so, but prior to the venture the idea of other claimants would surely have seemed a far greater obstacle. He did have an indirect blood link to Edward in that his paternal grandfather, Duke Richard II, was a brother of Emma, Edward's mother, making him a cousin-once-removed of Edward. However, this distant blood claim to the throne was not as strong as Edgar's, and does not seem to have featured noticeably in William's claim, which was overwhelmingly based on the supposed designation.[56] On balance, it seems one can only conclude that his decision to move against England was substantially driven by an extreme sense of self-righteous indignation, perhaps fuelled further by a personal competitive wish not to let Harold get the better of him. That he was to succeed in cajoling or coercing so many others to accompany him on such a risky and indeed life-threatening mission, in many

Table 3.2 The linkages between the various royal families

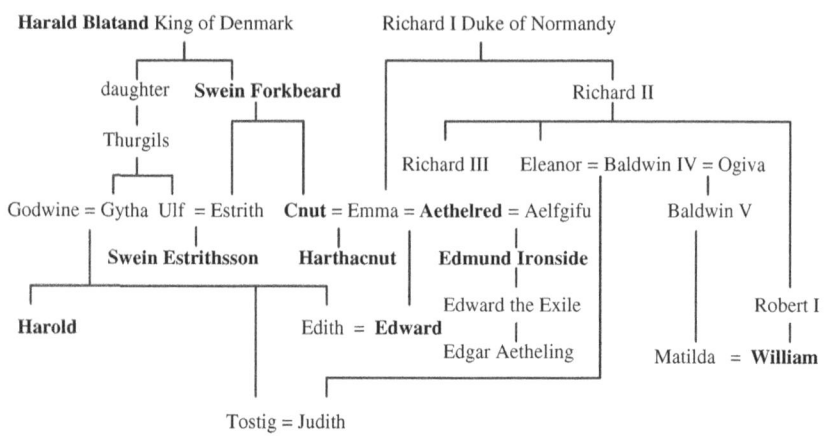

Notes:

1) Children, spouses and siblings not directly relevant are not shown, and those shown are not necessarily in order of birth or marriage.

2) Also not shown is Harold Harefoot, Cnut's son by his first wife Aelfgifu of Northampton (not shown either, and not to be confused with the Aelfgifu who was married to Aethelred).

3) Norwegian (including Hardraada) and Swedish genealogical connections are complex and indirect and are not shown here.

Some points of interest:

a) Harold's great-great grandfather on his mother's side, King Harold Blatand of Denmark, was the paternal grandfather of Cnut, thereby establishing a distant blood relationship between Harold and Cnut.

b) Harold's cousin Swein Estrithsson was the nephew of Cnut.

c) The wife of Harold's brother Tostig, Judith of Flanders, was the step-aunt of William's wife Matilda.

d) William's aunt Eleanor was the (second) wife of Matilda's grandfather Baldwin IV.

e) William's paternal great grandfather Duke Richard I was the maternal grandfather of Edward.

cases contrary to their better judgement, suggests a charisma of truly extraordinary proportions. One imagines that the papal endorsement was instrumental in this regard.[57]

William was not the only actual or potential threat facing England in January 1066. As mentioned earlier, at various stages Edward appears to have made promises about the succession to others, including one just after his own succession in 1042,[58] to Swein Estrithsson, who was to become King of Denmark in 1047 (till his death in 1076).[59] Swein was the son of Ulf, the brother of Harold's mother Gytha, and was therefore a cousin of Harold. And since his mother was Estrith, a sister of Cnut, he was also Cnut's nephew, and therefore also had a strong blood claim through the Scandinavian line – and we must bear in mind that England was at this point Anglo-Danish. He was indeed not only a strong claimant to the throne in 1066 – in fact, felt by some scholars to be the strongest[60] – he also seems to have had a stronger claim than Edward to the throne in 1042 (apparently being unable to force his claim as he was busily occupied in Scandinavia). He therefore had no particular liking for Edward, who had moreover at least once refused to help him in his protracted fight against the belligerent King Harald Hardraada of Norway.[61] However, just two years earlier, in 1064, Swein had finally achieved a peace with Norway when Hardraada withdrew his claims on Denmark. Swein was not entirely predictable, but as it happens he got on well with his cousin Harold – in fact, he appears to have sent men in support of Harold, men who also fought at Hastings[62] – and was probably not a particular worry in Harold's mind. Moreover, the fact that the peace with Hardraada was uneasy very much helped keep him in Denmark (though it should be noted that he did attempt an invasion of England in 1069, by which stage Hardraada was dead, in support of his claim to the English throne).

By contrast, Hardraada was indeed a worry. For a start he could claim that Harthacnut, the son of Cnut and Emma and Edward's half-brother and predecessor on the English throne (r. 1040–2), had promised the English throne to Magnus, Hardraada's own predecessor as king of Norway, should he (Harthacnut) die childless. Harthacnut did indeed die childless, but the throne went to Edward instead. It is not exactly clear why Magnus did not pursue the claim, but it probably had something to do with the fact that at around the same time as Harthacnut's untimely death in 1042 Magnus became king of Sweden, in addition to retaining the throne of Norway. That is, he too was occupied by affairs in Scandinavia. Upon Magnus's death in 1047, Hardraada took the Norwegian throne but not the Swedish, and similarly seems to have had his work cut out for many years with affairs in Scandinavia. But now that he had been thwarted in his attempt to take Denmark, he could well use Edward's death as an opportune time to enforce, as Magnus's successor, the promised Norwegian entitlement to the English throne.

Moreover, if he did so decide, he would be an extremely formidable foe. A giant of a man (reputedly almost seven feet tall, which may not be much of an exaggeration),[63] he was arguably the single most feared Viking warrior. Warlike by nature – though ironically the half-brother of a man later declared a saint, Olaf – in his younger days he had achieved what was perhaps the most respected position for a warrior, captain of Empress Zoe's Imperial Varangian Guard in Constantinople.[64]

Yet another threat came from within Harold's own family in the form of Tostig, his next younger brother and until recently Earl of Northumbria. He had been given the earldom in 1055, but perhaps partly because he was a southerner with no northern roots or connections, had not been well received. Worse, he had been overzealous in applying law and order and meting out harsh punishments for minor offences. At the same time, his own adherence to the law was questionable. He was accused with some apparent justification of several murders, one of them that of Gospatric in late 1064, possibly involving complicity with his sister, Queen Edith.[65] In addition he had progressively increased taxes to what the Northumbrians deemed an intolerable level. This all culminated in a large-scale rebellion against him in October 1065 by the Northumbrian nobles, who seized control while he was away south hunting with Edward (as he often was).[66]

Edward had always treated Tostig as his favourite, and sent Harold to negotiate with the rebels in an attempt to restore him to his earldom.[67] However, the rebels remained firm. Harold desisted from any thoughts of military action against them when he saw their determination. He seems to have wished above all to avoid a civil war, and to an extent he could probably genuinely feel sympathy with the rebels' cause against his sometimes extremist brother. Such thinking was widespread, as it turned out, for when Edward tried to call out armed forces nationwide to Tostig's aid his call was ignored[68] – the first time ever a royal command of such nature had been ignored, and incidentally evidence too of Edward's weakness and how he was viewed at large.

Tostig for his part felt betrayed by Harold, and went so far as to accuse him before the king of inciting the rebellion in the first place.[69] This was almost certainly an untrue accusation, but something that Tostig seemed to believe; though one must also bear in mind that Tostig was apparently jealous of his elder brother, probably also felt rather eclipsed by him, and seemed prone to overreaction and possibly also vindictiveness of the most brutal type.[70] Harold denied the accusation on oath, but Tostig was not satisfied, and Edward was unable to resolve the matter. The rebels, realising that neither Harold nor the army was going to oppose them, and that the king was powerless without Harold, insisted that Tostig be banished from the entire kingdom, not just his earldom.[71] To add to Tostig's rage, at the rebels' request and agreed to by Harold, his earldom was now given to someone he did not at all like, the young Morcar (Morkere), brother of Edwin, Earl of Mercia.[72] Thus it was that he and his wife Judith (and probably also two illegitimate teenaged sons of Tostig, Skule and Ketel) left the country for Flanders in November to seek shelter with Count Baldwin V, Judith's half-brother, swearing revenge against Harold and Northumbria.

Harold must surely have been anticipating some reaction in the near future from Tostig. He was not as fearsome a foe as William or Hardraada, but he was still a courageous and experienced military leader (having shown this in recent successful campaigns with Harold against the Welsh) and one to take seriously. It would be especially dangerous if he could gather allies. Baldwin himself, who could muster a reasonable force, was something of a dark horse, friendly to some of the Godwinesons but not necessarily Harold. Worse, Tostig (with or without Baldwin) could end up allied with William, with whom he was related

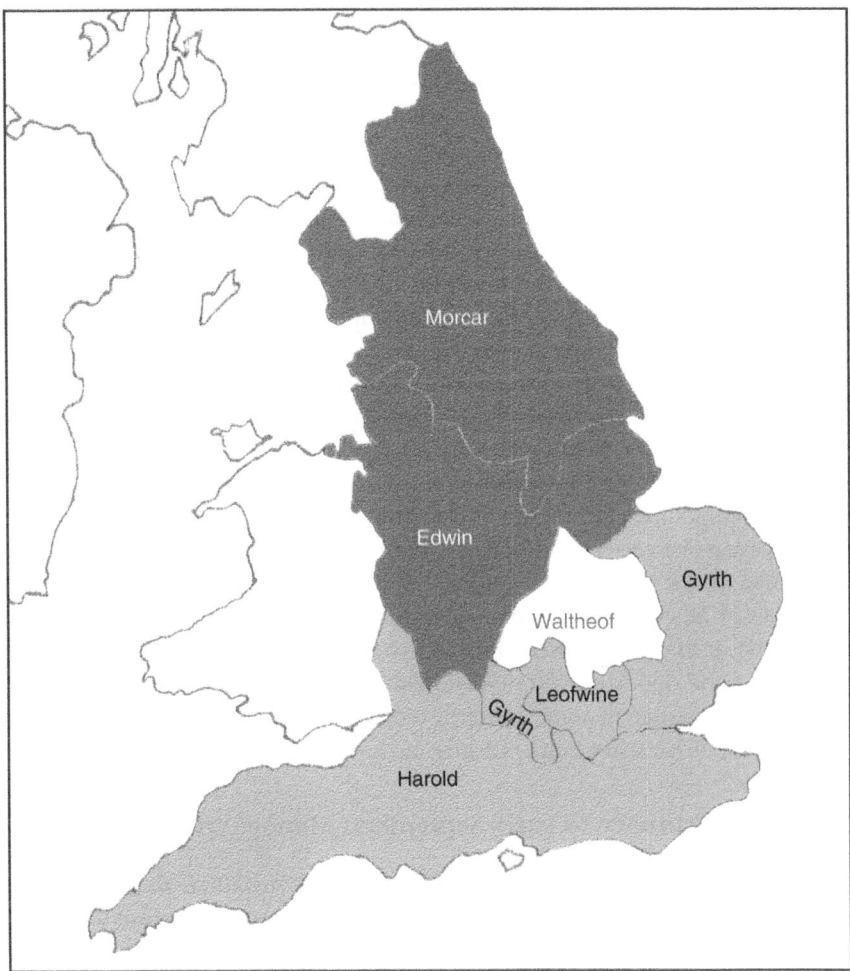

Figure 3.2   The earldoms of England on the eve of Harold's reign. The light grey areas are those under direct control of the Godwinesons.

by marriage through Judith. Tostig had married Judith in late 1051, coincident with the Godwine family's exile and with William's marriage to Matilda, who was a daughter of Baldwin V and thus a step-niece of Judith's. William and Judith were in themselves related by blood anyway, sharing a common grand-father in Duke Richard II of Normandy. And in addition to Flanders and Normandy, Tostig could also find ready support from his sworn friend Malcolm Canmore (Malcolm III), King of the Scots. Though not possessing a massive force, Malcolm was nonetheless another leader to be respected, among other things having triumphed over Macbeth.

As another worry, despite Morcar having been given the Northumbrian earl-dom, and his brother Edwin holding the earldom of Mercia, Harold was still not fully sure of their support, for there had traditionally been considerable rivalry between the northern earls and the Godwine(/son) clan in the south. There were three other major earldoms at the time, Wessex, East Anglia, and East Midlands, and as of 1066 Harold held Wessex while his younger brothers Gyrth and Leofwine held East Anglia and East Midlands respectively. It was a fairly even match between north and south, with the two sets of brothers hold-ing approximately half of the kingdom each. If Edwin and Morcar were sud-denly to decide to throw in their lot in support of say, Edgar (even if only nominally), or worse, strike a deal with an outside attacker in return for recog-nition of Northumbria as an independent kingdom, Harold would have serious internal problems as well as external ones. (We should remember that the con-cept of nationhood was still relatively weak at this time, and that as recently as 50 years earlier England had been divided – albeit briefly – into northern and southern kingdoms under Cnut and Edmund.)

In a very worst case scenario, it was not impossible that Harold might face a combined attack from Tostig, Baldwin, Malcolm, and William (plus any num-ber of lesser allies of theirs, such as Eustace of Boulogne), plus an attack from Hardraada, plus opportunistic resistance from the northern earls, and though unlikely, some opportunistic involvement by Swein of Denmark, and maybe even the emergence of some hitherto hidden support for Edgar, perhaps with the backing of his sister Edith. Clearly, he had to proceed very cautiously.

3.3 Early February to early September: Manoeuvrings

As we move on now to the progression of events in 1066, we can see that Harold did indeed show caution in many cases, though unfortunately, as we shall see, not always.

Later in January or early in February Harold replied in the negative to irate messages from William exhorting him to give up the throne,[73] Harold no doubt claiming (as noted earlier) that the oath he made in 1064 was made under duress, which was indeed in theory a sound defence for invalidating an oath. By the standards of the day, breaking an oath was permitted when an oath was made under duress, or in order to avoid bloodshed.[74] William did not accept this, and Harold in turn would probably not have expected him to.

A good example of his prudence was shown shortly afterwards. Though most of the kingdom seems to have supported his enthronement, the north was still unsettled, perhaps through a fear that now that he was king he might try to reinstate his deposed brother Tostig as earl. He answered this suspicion by trav-elling north to York in February in order to reassure the northern sceptics.[75] This was the first time since 1031 that an English king had travelled north of

Thomas Thornycroft's statue of Boadicea (Boudica), near Westminster Station.

A reconstructed Iron Age farm, at the Archaeolink Prehistory Park near Inverurie. Bennachie, the assumed site of the Battle of Mons Graupius in AD 83–4, is in the background to the right. (Photograph by Mark Keighley)

The entrance gate to Lunt Roman Fort, at Baginton near Coventry, from the inside. Lunt was a 'bridgehead fort' (wooden and usually a temporary base in enemy territory), built around AD 60 and almost certainly in response to Boudica's uprising. (Courtesy of Lunt Roman Fort and Coventry City Council)

Viroconium (Wroxeter), near Shrewsbury, was a major Roman centre subsequently occupied for some time by Britons. It is believed by some to have been a main base for King Arthur.

The helmet believed to have belonged to the early seventh century king Raedwald, reconstructed from remaining fragments at Sutton Hoo. Replica at Sutton Hoo Centre. (Copyright and courtesy of the National Trust Museum and Sutton Hoo Centre)

External view of buildings at the West Stow Anglo-Saxon Village in Suffolk. The house with the eaves down to the ground was experimental and showed that such sunken buildings were unlikely. The three buildings at the back are, from the left, hall, living house (for up to ten people), and workshop. Anglo-Saxon buildings tended to be rectangular, as opposed to Celtic round huts. (Courtesy of St Edmundsbury Borough Council and West Stow Anglo-Saxon Village Trust)

King Alfred's best-known statue, in Winchester.

The Middleton Viking Cross in St Andrew's Church, near Pickering in North Yorkshire. The cross clearly shows a Viking with pointed helmet, shield (top right, not to scale), spear, sword, knife (at belt), and axe. (With thanks to St Andrew's Church)

the Humber,[76] and moreover he travelled with only a small party including his old friend Bishop Wulfstan (c. 1009–c. 1095, later Saint Wulfstan, and not the Archbishop Wulfstan of Part 2), clearly showing his lack of intent to use force. He stayed in the north till early April, and duly obtained a pledge of allegiance.

Though the exact date is not clear, it is almost certain that it was at this time that, to cement relations formally with the northern earls, he married Alditha (Ealdgyth), the sister of Edwin and Morcar and the widow of the recently killed Gruffydd ap Llywelyn. This was despite the fact that Harold already had a 'common-law' wife of over 20 years' standing, Edith Swansneck ('Edith the Fair'), who had borne him six children,[77] and whom, by all accounts, he loved dearly, faithfully, and devotedly.

More exactly, Edith was his wife *more Danico*, that is to say in the traditional semi-formal Danish style, in which the union lacked a church blessing. It was not held in the same low regard as outright illegitimacy such as in Duke William's case, but it was still not as positively viewed as a formal church-blessed wedding, and was in fact to be declared an invalid form of marriage a century later. In the eleventh century, however, it was still not uncommon among leading figures, especially with Danish connections, since it conveniently allowed for a marriage of love and at the same time kept the door open for a possible second marriage of a political nature. On the other hand, it could obviously create inconvenience and disputation regarding inheritance and succession. In the case of Harold, it would seem likely that any of his children by Alditha would be expected to have priority over his children by Edith, even if the latter were 20 years or more older, and this would have been understood by all concerned in the arranging of the marriage. Harold's marriage to Alditha clearly ensured the loyalty of the northern earl brothers to Harold as king, for they would be uncles to any future king. (A son was indeed born, as will be discussed later.)

Edith and Harold must have anticipated from long ago that such a second marriage might happen (even perhaps if Harold had only remained an earl), but nevertheless they must have been greatly saddened when it did, for it seems theirs was a solid and loving relationship. As with the case of Cnut's mutilated hostages seen in Part 2, this is another of many examples of the human tragedies in the unfolding of history. Edith was certainly not cast aside, and remained wealthy and cared for, as also her children, but she would have had to cede her 'husband' Harold to Alditha. That Harold could take this sacrificial measure, hurting not only himself but also his beloved Edith, is an indication of how much importance he placed on the alliance and the internal security of the kingdom. It is also highly likely that he had been aware of the necessity of such an event even as he took the crown.

In the meantime the everyday machinery of state, and the king's duties such as the issuing of writs and appointment of abbots, continued as usual, for after all Harold was already familiar with such matters, and moreover kept more or less the same personnel that Edward had employed. Nothing in these regards appears to have been controversial or irregular, including Harold's order for new coinage to be struck bearing his own image. On the obverse, the word *pax* no doubt indicated his sincere wish.

Accompanied by Queen Alditha, Harold returned to London from the north in time to celebrate Easter on 16 April,[78] which similarly passed with nothing out of the ordinary. But shortly afterwards, on 24 April, something very much out of the ordinary did happen, with the appearance of the 'long-haired star' – Halley's Comet. It was visible for some two weeks and seemed ominous to many. Curiously, although biblically it might be expected that a heavenly body would be seen as a good sign, in the Middle Ages, characterised by an eschatological fear that the end of the world was nigh, it was generally the opposite case.[79] But whether good or bad, it was surely a sign that great events were to unfold.

And sure enough, just as if great powers of Fate (or God) were indeed at work, just a few days after the disappearance of the heavenly omen, in its stead came the appearance of the somewhat less heavenly but still decidedly ominous Tostig. Baldwin had provided him with some 60 ships and Tostig used these to harry the southern coast from the Isle of Wight to Sandwich.[80] His exact purpose is not clear, for he seems to have displayed a confusing mix of trying to win support on the one hand but also seizing money and provisions and generally causing trouble on the other, but I will return to this presently.

On hearing of this attack Harold promptly sent the fleet to the south coast, called out the land forces, and rode towards Sandwich at their head. He may possibly have initially thought it might be an advance attack by William,[81] but would very rapidly have realised it was Tostig, and that William was not in evidence. In turn hearing of Harold's forces being called out, Tostig promptly sailed northwards, unsuccessfully trying to win support from his brother Gyrth, Earl of East Anglia, and then continuing on, raiding the coast at various points up to the Humber mouth. He was met in combat in north Lincolnshire by Earls Edwin and Morcar and soundly routed, fleeing north with just 12 remaining ships to seek refuge with his sworn brother Malcolm in Scotland, where he appears to have remained for the summer.[82]

Tostig's movements before his appearance on the south coast in early May are not clear. He would almost certainly not have made any move until some weeks after Harold's coronation, in case Harold reinstated him in his earldom. He probably resolved to attack when this did not happen, a resolve no doubt reinforced when Harold married the sister of Morcar, the man who had replaced him in Northumbria. His first move was to seek allies – in addition to the support he had received from Baldwin – for an attack on the kingdom. Specifically, as potential and powerful combatant allies, he appears to have approached Swein Estrithsson, Harald Hardraada, and William – and probably in that order. (Malcolm was also an ally but gave limited military support.)

Given that Tostig was being hosted by Baldwin, who was William's father-in-law and a supporter of William's planned invasion, it would have been understandable for him to visit William first. However, it is probable that he actually visited Swein first. Scandinavian sources – though one has to be wary of their reliability – state that he went to visit Swein from Flanders, and do not indicate that he had visited anyone else first.[83] Though unfortunately the date is not clear, late February or early March might seem likely. Since there was a good relationship between the Godwinesons and Swein, Tostig would probably have felt personally more comfortable approaching his friendly cousin first, rather than William or Hardraada. Moreover he may have felt that Swein would be the most enthusiastic of the three, perhaps because Swein's claim to the throne, which included a strong blood claim, might have appeared to him (Tostig) as the most justified.

But he was to be disappointed, for the same Scandinavian sources make it clear that Swein was not prepared to become involved (at least at that stage), and that this refusal sorely tested their hitherto friendship. *King Harald's Saga*, after remarking that Tostig had no joy in trying to persuade Swein to join him in an invasion of England, tells us the following:

> Earl Toste said [to Swein], 'The result of my errand here is less fortunate than I had expected of thee who art so gallant a man, seeing that thy relative is in so great need. It may be that I will seek friendly help where it could less be expected; and that I may find a chief who is less afraid, king, than thou art of a great enterprise.' Then the earl and king parted, not just [exactly] the best friends. . . . Toste turned away then, and went to Norway, where he presented himself to King Harald [Hardraada].[84]

Of course, while we must question the verbatim speech, the outcome seems realistic enough – no deals with Swein. It would seem probable that Tostig next went to Hardraada, not William. The only record we have of a visit by Tostig to William – that of Orderic Vitalis – suggests strongly that this visit to Normandy occurred immediately prior to his harrying of the south coast in early May.[85] This would place the visit to William in April, meaning that he probably visited Hardraada in mid- or late-March and left him before mid-April. In fact, *King Harald's Saga* refers to Tostig leaving Hardraada in spring, which we might take as a departure in early- or mid-April.[86]

It should be noted that Tostig would have realised he could not enlist the support of both Swein and Hardraada. Despite their recent uneasy peace the two Scandinavians hated each other and could not be expected to work together.[87] Of the two he is very likely to have preferred Swein, for Hardraada was not only unrelated to him but also had a fearsome reputation, and Tostig may have been somewhat nervous about approaching him. Nevertheless, he persuaded Hardraada to join him – Hardraada probably not needing much persuading – and 'he [Hardraada] took the resolution to proceed in summer to England, and conquer the country'.[88]

It is said that when Tostig visited William, the Duke was aware (either beforehand or through being informed by Tostig) of Tostig's involvement with Hardraada, and possibly also their plan.[89] If so, William would probably have had mixed feelings, for on the one hand he must have been disturbed by the likelihood that if Hardraada defeated Harold then he too [William] would have to confront the fearsome Viking, but at the same time he must have been heartened by the realisation that, whoever was the victor out of Harold or Hardraada, their forces would have been significantly depleted by the battle between them. Overall, he would probably have supported it.

As mentioned, only one source, Orderic Vitalis, reports a visit to William by Tostig. Orderic's work contains numerous errors of fact and is often considered unreliable, but there is no logical reason to doubt that a visit itself happened. Tostig seems to have been determined one way or another to see Harold deposed, or at least compromised, and the more people he could persuade to attack him the better. He may perhaps have had in mind some sort of two-pronged attack and subsequent division of the kingdom, though one suspects above all that he simply wanted his earldom back. In any event his visit to William came to nought. According to Orderic, Tostig mildly chided William for not having already acted against Harold and apparently left in some frustration, albeit with William's blessing.[90] William was evidently not interested in any joint venture with Tostig.

One does wonder what was going on in Tostig's mind with regard to William at this time – assuming this visit did actually take place – for he must have realised that if he and Hardraada were successful in their invasion of England, it was highly unlikely William would have simply shrugged his shoulders and left them in peace, disbanding his forces and not bothering to make use of the fleet he was going to such lengths to assemble (though this may not have been very far advanced when Tostig visited). As suggested above it seems possible that Tostig might have proposed some sharing of the kingdom, at least to the extent of getting Northumbria back. But did he change his thinking after William's apparent lack of interest in partnership? Did he keep Hardraada informed about William? We simply do not know.

To return to Tostig's alliance with the formidable Hardraada, one extreme view is that there was no approach made by Tostig at all, and that their fleets met by chance in Scottish waters (for Hardraada came down via the Orkneys), or off the north-east English coast.[91] However, that there was no prior arrangement seems most unlikely. The *Anglo-Saxon Chronicle*, Ms C, for example, states that when Hardraada sailed into the mouth of the Tyne 'Earl Tostig came to him with all that he had got, *just as they had before settled*' (my italics).[92] And we have seen that *King Harald's Saga* mentions Tostig visiting Harald in Norway and agreeing on a joint attack in summer,[93] though some scholars doubt that such a visit happened. It is also possible that Tostig conducted some of his dealings with Hardraada, including perhaps also the initial approach, through a friend and ally, Copsig,[94] who was at the time based in the Orkneys – then under Hardraada's control – and who brought his own small fleet of 17 ships to join Tostig.[95]

Unfortunately, there is much that is unknown, including the specifics of their strategy. It could well be that they decided that as a diversionary tactic Tostig should harry the south coast of England before their attack in order to test Harold's defensive reactions and/or draw his forces and attention to the south and away from the north, as well as trying to garner support where possible (such as from Gyrth).[96] And the attack on the east coast (as opposed to the south) may have been to keep Harold guessing and/or to test out the defences on that part of the coast – in which case, Tostig must have had an unpleasant surprise, for he was surely not expecting such spirited resistance from the two young and inexperienced earls.

This scenario would explain the nature of Tostig's behaviour in early May. However, if so, why would Tostig attack so early on, given that in actuality their attack took place well into September? The value of drawing troops to the south and away from the north risked being wasted the more time passed before the main attack, for those troops could be disbanded and/or sent elsewhere. Perhaps the main attack was actually supposed to have taken place earlier that summer, but was delayed for some unknown reason, and had to be rescheduled. We have seen earlier that the attack was indeed planned for summer, and September does seem rather late to be termed 'summer'.

One also has to consider factors such as communications and intelligence gathering. It is questionable as to just how much the protagonists knew about each other's activities, be they friend or foe. Messages could not always be conveyed speedily, even in friendly territory. Spies of course play a part in the information business, and these were most definitely used very frequently in the eleventh century;[97] and indeed an English spy was discovered at Dives while William was busy building his boats, and was apparently sent back to England to tell Harold how powerful William's fleet was and to confirm William's intent to attack.[98] But it is very difficult to gauge their effectiveness, particularly with regard to the speed with which they could convey intelligence. Military leaders of the day were often left with little choice but to proceed in relative ignorance, far more so than in modern warfare.

Back in England, as we have seen, Tostig's harrying of the south coast in early May did indeed result in Harold calling out the *fyrd* (conscript army). Even though he soon realised it was Tostig and not William, he may have felt it better to keep the troops there as a defence against William if and when he came.

There was in theory a two-month limit on *fyrd* duty, supposedly even in times of warfare, though in practice extensions were possible. As a legacy from Alfred, there were two *fyrds* Harold could call on in turn, giving a cumulative theoretical final stand-down date of early September. Time-wise this seems to have been what was to happen, with the *fyrd* (and the naval forces) being stood down on 8 September,[99] but seemingly on the practical grounds that provisions had run out rather than the technical grounds of completion of the compulsory service period.[100]

As time went on William was proving successful in his gathering of support, and would very probably have been helped in this by news of papal endorsement, though it is not clear at what precise point this was received.[101] He was also proceeding with assembly of his invasion fleet. Though there is huge variation in estimates of its size,[102] it seems reasonable to conclude it may eventually have comprised around 700–1000 ships and 12,000 or so men, of whom about 8000 were combatants. Possibly a third or so of these were knights, as there were apparently around 3000 horses. Some vassals and allies provided ships, but William still needed to build several hundred, and engaged busily upon this task at Dives – a relatively sheltered bay with a broad and firm beach suited to the task – during May, June, and July. The logistics for this were an enormous challenge,[103] but, whereas Harold appears to have had insurmountable logistical problems regarding provisions, William fared better. The fleet was ready to sail from around early August, but was seemingly prevented by contrary winds for about a month (I shall return to this below), and he was not able to set sail till 12 September.

3.4   Mid to late September: The arrival of Hardraada and William

The date of William's departure from Dives, 12 September, was four days after the *fyrd* had been stood down, and it is perhaps possible that William knew this. Any contrary winds that had kept him at Dives till the 12th would have been more favourable to any informant sailing from England on say the 9th. It is tempting to think that William was aware of this limitation on *fyrd* service (which he may possibly have been), and thus deliberately delayed his invasion till after the second *fyrd* was stood down. However, while William was no doubt delighted that the *fyrd* was stood down, it is questionable to what extent this was actually factored into his planning. Among other things, it would be hard to accept that William would not imagine Harold could use some emergency means to keep the *fyrd* assembled beyond the theoretical stand-down date if he thought it necessary, and similarly hard to accept that the fyrdmen themselves would be overkeen to disband, or at least to disband completely. After all, the *fyrd* was there not just at the whim of the king, but for the genuine defence of the realm. Moreover, unless William was kept informed of the plans of Tostig and Hardraada, which is not entirely impossible but unlikely (especially if there was a hitch with their timing), then he would have expected Harold himself, along with many hundreds of housecarls or more,[104] to remain in the south even after the disbanding of the *fyrd*, which could moreover be reassembled in haste while Harold's permanent housecarls engaged William's men.

Scholarly views are divided on this question of a planned departure time, but certainly many – myself included – feel that William would have sailed to England as soon as possible, and that therefore he simply had luck on his side in his timing.[105] I would add that, if the timing of his departure was deliberate, then surely his panegyrists would have made much of this in order to display his great wisdom, but they do not. Rather, Poitiers, despite doing his usual best to praise William, actually confirms the view that it was winds: 'presently the whole fleet, equipped with such great foresight, was blown from the mouth of the Dives and the neighbouring ports, *where they had long waited for a south wind to carry them across*, and was driven by the breath of the west wind to moorings at Saint-Valery' (my italics).[106] If, by contrast, it was planned, then I repeat my view that his omission to state this represents the wasting of a very major opportunity to sing William's praises.

As it happened, having set sail, William landed not in England but some 150 miles northeast along the coast at St Valery-sur-Somme, and here again we have a division of opinion. Not a few scholars assume that William intentionally sailed there from Dives to make for a shorter Channel crossing,[107] but this is questionable. William's panegyrist Poitiers does not appear to refer to this as a planned move, but rather (as seen in the quotation above) describes the fleet being blown to St Valery by adverse weather, clearly suggesting it was not the intended destination, which surely, judging from his words 'to carry them across', could only have meant across the Channel to England. He also immediately afterwards refers to some loss of lives and ships *en route*, and to William secretly burying corpses – presumably to avoid disheartening the others. Given that this all casts William in a not particularly flattering light, it is not what a panegyrist might be expected to write unless it was true and moreover widely known at the time to be so – or unless, some might argue, it masked something even worse.

There is a brief and curious sentence in Manuscript E (and E alone) of the *Anglo-Saxon Chronicle* for 1066 referring to Harold going out against William with a ship-army, though no month is specified.[108] It is possible to speculate that this might indicate a skirmish, and even perhaps that this was the cause of William's casualties, which obviously he would want to cover up. My own view is that the chronicler is referring to the situation in which, as mentioned earlier, Tostig started his raids in May, and Harold called out the army and the fleet, initially seeming to think that it was an advance raid by William himself, and then, after realising it was only Tostig, leaving them there against any future attack from William. There was perhaps an actual engagement with Tostig, for the *Deeds of the Norman Dukes* states that Tostig, having been sent to England by William, was driven off by Harold's fleet.[109] It is of course possible that a naval attack of some sort on William's fleet itself did happen,[110] but we cannot infer this from the *Anglo-Saxon Chronicle* reference.

In any event, William was kept at St Valery a further fortnight – this time indisputably by continuing adverse winds – till the evening of 27 September, when a sudden change of weather seemed to bring a sudden change of fortune and consequently a hasty departure with the late afternoon tide. Though this may just be a fictional eulogy of William, *en route* his fast ship is said to have become separated from the others in the darkness, and that when this was realised at dawn (a few miles off the English coast) William reassured his anxious companions by calmly ordering and eating his breakfast as if nothing was amiss, after which the other vessels duly came into sight.[111]

If this story is true, William was indeed fortunate that no English vessels seem to have been patrolling the coast, for he would have been an easy prey in isolation, and the whole expedition – and the course of history – could have been affected as a result. William may well have gone down in history not as a conqueror but as a fool for allowing himself to get isolated, for it was not stormy weather and his sailors should never have lost sight of the fleet, who should have had lanterns during the night. It is easy to dismiss the story, but one wonders what the source and/or purpose of it was, for if it is an invention of Poitiers, it portrays William in a bad light of poor generalship more than a good one of calmness. Anyway, as it happened, the landing was made at Pevensey, unopposed, around 8 a.m.

Before William left St Valery on 27 September it is possible, if not probable, that he had received news of the landing of Tostig and Hardraada in northeast England, which surely would have pleased him for the reasons outlined earlier. Tostig and Hardraada rendezvoused as planned at the Tyne mouth on or around 8 September – a fateful day, it would seem.[112] Tostig only had his 12 remaining ships, though possibly some also from Malcolm, and Copsig his 17. Hardraada by contrast appears to have had some 300 vessels and around 10,000 or more men. (He had fewer non-combatants and horse-transports than William, and hence a higher combatants-to-ship ratio.) It was obviously an uneven partnership in those regards. Tostig's real value was surely his local knowledge and no doubt a claimed support-base. But if so, the latter certainly rapidly proved an exaggeration, for when shortly afterwards they landed on the Cleveland coast, they met spirited if doomed resistance from the townsfolk of Scarborough.

After four or five days of pillaging in the region, with no significant organised resistance, they sailed further south, again unopposed (the king's fleet being still in the Thames area), entering the Humber and Ouse rivers to land at Riccall, some ten miles south of York, a site convenient for also covering the

Wharfe River (which joins the Ouse just above Riccall). Several days later, on 20 September, the Earls Edwin and Morcar opposed them in the Battle of Fulford Gate, two miles out of York, having gathered what forces they could (though the size is unclear). The invaders prevailed. Morcar may have been slightly injured and possibly Edwin also, both of them perhaps underestimating their opponents after their crushing rout of Tostig a few months earlier. Hardraada, of course, made a critical difference.

The young earls have been criticised for rashness in leaving the heavily fortified city of York rather than waiting for reinforcements from the south. According to the *Anglo-Saxon Chronicle*, news of the invasion had been sent by a messenger to Harold but seemingly only following the landing at Riccall.[113] (If so, one is left wondering why word was not conveyed to Harold a week earlier when the invaders first landed north of Scarborough. This may partly be explained by the same *Anglo-Saxon Chronicle*, which states that 'it was announced to King Harold in the south when he came from off ship-board',[114] indicating that following the disbanding of the *fyrd* on the 8th he had returned to London with the fleet, which was held up by bad weather. That is, he may have been out of contact, even if an earlier message had been sent.) However, a major defence of the earls' apparent rashness in not waiting for Harold and reinforcements before engaging with the enemy is that they were simply not expecting Harold for some time, and presumably in their view could not afford to let the pillaging and slaughter of the locals continue unchecked. Had news been conveyed to Harold earlier than it apparently was, and had they known this, or had they known of his expeditiousness, then they would no doubt have been more inclined to wait.

Although Harold could not, according to the accounts, have heard the news before the 16th or thereabouts,[115] and although he had just a week earlier disbanded the *fyrd*, he responded extremely quickly. He is believed to have regathered what he could of the recently disbanded troops, presumably also finding extra provisions from somewhere, and then to have taken his forces the 200 or so miles north in record time, travelling day and night,[116] to arrive at Tadcaster, just eight miles southwest of York, on the 24th. He had his personal elite-warrior housecarls with him, possibly as many as some 3000 mounted men. In addition he presumably gathered men along the way north, no doubt sending fast messengers ahead to alert local thegns, who may already have been alerted to the invasion by the messengers on their way south to Harold, and who had responded by assembling local forces. These may have comprised the bulk of his army, the size of which is not recorded. Estimates for the numbers involved vary greatly, for both sides, and it may be pointless to speculate, but it is nonetheless worth noting that in terms of relativities the near-contemporary Henry of Huntingdon stated that the English force had 'superiority in numbers'.[117]

Even if one allows for the possibility that, contrary to the *Chronicle*, Harold had received news of the invasion earlier than their landing at Riccall, he could not have known earlier than about the 12th or so – most certainly after the disbanding of the *fyrd* – and it would still be an outstanding feat of speed and efficiency. Obviously mounted troops could progress faster than those on foot, but it is not clear how many were mounted, and the force as a whole is usually referred to by modern commentators as 'marching', suggesting that the bulk were on foot and that presumably the mounted troops had therefore to adjust to their pace. However, this remains an open question, to which I shall return presently.

The invaders were, undeniably, genuinely unaware of Harold's arrival in the area. They would obviously have been expecting word to have been conveyed to him and for him to appear at some point soon, but clearly not as soon as he actually did. This shows not only a misplaced complacency on their part, but a serious failure to use scouts to provide advance warning of his arrival.[118] There were relatively few routes an army could follow, and Tostig with his local knowledge should have had them all watched.

Also remarkably, they were still ignorant of his presence the following day.[119] It had been arranged that on this day, the 25th, they would receive the formal submission of the local leaders, along with hostages, at Stamford Bridge on the river Derwent, about eight miles east of York and a massive twelve miles from their main encampment by the ships at Riccall. It is not clear why this seemingly distant site was chosen.[120] Hardraada did not take all his forces, leaving a third with the ships, presumably as a guard.[121] So relaxed and unprepared for battle were the invaders that, it being a warm day, they left their armour behind.[122] One can easily imagine their shock when, instead of the local leaders, Harold and his army appeared – and they would have appeared very suddenly, topping the ridge at present-day Gate Helmsley just a mile west from the battleground, leaving little time for the Vikings to organise a defence.[123]

There is little recorded detail about the actual progression of the battle, though it is apparent that the Vikings constructed a shield wall, perhaps triangular as was not uncommon, and that this was gradually worn down by the English over the course of the day, seemingly – and very unusually for the English – even using cavalry charges (discussed below). More importantly the element of surprise, plus the fortunate fact that Hardraada's men had no armour, and moreover that they were not at full strength and indeed seemingly outnumbered, were key factors in the English victory. Another factor was that Hardraada himself seems to have been killed relatively early, by an arrow in the throat.[124] Tostig then took over, and presently was also killed, possibly similarly by an arrow (though this is less certain) and possibly also even to the head.[125] The invaders had sent for the remainder of their troops from Riccall, and these arrived towards the end of the battle, putting up a firm fight but to no avail.

Figure 3.3   Gate Helmsley seen from the east side of the River Derwent running through Stamford Bridge. Harold's men would have appeared suddenly over the upper ridge, perhaps a mile or so away from the main Viking forces.

The English won, the invasion was over, and Harold was – for the moment at least – a hero. C. Warren Hollister sees it as arguably the greatest military triumph in Anglo-Saxon history.[126] Certainly, it was a major turning point in history, for it signalled the end of Viking aggression in English history, and was a significant factor in the end of Viking expansion in broader terms.

There are several other points to note about the battle. The first is Harold's use of rapid movement, a very effective tactic reminiscent of Caesar. Harold had used this to great effect a few years earlier in his campaign against the Welsh prince Gruffydd ap Llywelyn. The downside, of course, is that rapidity, especially when sustained, exhausts men and horses, and it is testimony to Harold's leadership that he could extract so much from his resources – and of course, it is also testimony to those resources, notably his men.[127]

A second point is the role of the English archers, which is not really very clear. Though the English in those days made very little use of archers,[128] obviously there were some present and most definitely in Hardraada's death and possibly also Tostig's, they were instrumental in the victory. Yet there is also an incident – surprisingly, recorded in English sources rather than Scandinavian[129] – which

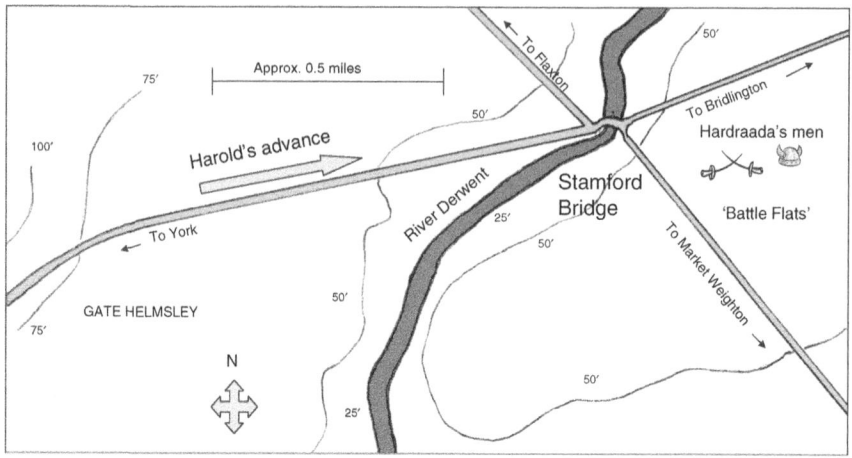

Figure 3.4   Assumed dispositions at the Battle of Stamford Bridge.

suggests the use of archers was not very good. Apparently the English forces, arriving at the narrow bridge at Stamford from the west,[130] were delayed significantly from attacking Hardraada's forces on the east by a solitary 'berserker' Viking defending the bridge, who is said to have killed more than 40 Englishmen with his axe.[131] The most widely accepted account has him finally killed by an Englishman with a spear getting into a small boat, manoeuvring under the bridge using the cover of willows, and impaling him through a gap in the planks.[132] There is an alternative account that he was killed by a thrown spear,[133] but this may be a later misinterpretation of the basic fact that he was killed by a spear, which one would indeed normally expect to be thrown under the circumstances – but in this case may have been a dedicated thrusting-spear. If it was a throwing-spear, it should surely have been thrown a lot earlier.

The story of the attack from under the bridge is so unusual it suggests it may well be true, but whatever the means of dispatching him, one has to wonder why it took so long to remove this warrior – William of Malmesbury found it incredible, stating that 'however reluctantly posterity may believe it, one single Norwegian for a long time delayed the triumph of so many'.[134] Even allowing for heroic exaggeration, this lone individual seems to have caused disproportionately numerous casualties and a disproportionately long delay, which gave time to the Norwegians to draw up formations – though one wonders why they did not capitalise on this delay more effectively by providing support for the lone berserker or, more sensibly, destroying the bridge if at all possible. Admittedly he was one of the few who had insisted on taking his armour (the *Anglo-Saxon Chronicle* refers to his 'mail-coat'), but even so it remains puzzling as to why he was not simply taken out very quickly by an archer, or a spear-thrower. Arrows might have been relatively ineffective against chain-mail, but surely an archer could have approached very close if necessary – he was, after all, a static target with no missile weapon of his own – and hit him in the head or some other exposed part. The *Anglo-Saxon Chronicle* does say that 'an [*sic*] [one] Englishman aimed at him with an arrow, but it availed naught',[135] leading to the need for the 'impaler' to do his deed, but it is puzzling why there does not seem to have been a more concerted and efficient use of arrows. There is a possibility, of course, that the whole business was not merely exaggerated but totally invented, perhaps to enhance the valour of Harold's opponents and thereby the merit of the English victory, but as mentioned above the particular circumstances suggest something like it probably happened. *Prima facie,* it suggests the English were making only partial and possibly haphazard use of ranged weapons, and that their leadership in this regard was less than admirable.

A third point is the apparent use of cavalry, and in association with that the use of horses in broader terms. One has to distinguish here between, on the one hand, cavalry proper, in which men fight on horseback and use particular group tactics associated with this (as opposed to isolated single combat between mounted warriors), and on the other hand those mounted troops – typically including housecarls – who merely ride to battle and then dismount to fight on foot. The English to this point in history had overwhelmingly used horses merely in the latter way, as transport. However, if Scandinavian sources can be believed – and it is undeniable that they do make many obvious errors (such as having Morcar as Harold's brother) – it is apparent that at Stamford Bridge there were cavalry tactics proper employed against the Viking shield wall, including a feigned retreat. *King Harald's Saga,* for example, records:

> For although the English rode hard against the Northmen, they [the English] gave way again immediately, as they could do nothing against them. Now when the Northmen thought they perceived that the enemy were making but weak assaults, they set after them, and would drive them into flight; but when they had broken their shield-rampart the Englishmen rode up from all sides.[136]

Since these accounts were written some time after the battle, and it was a known fact that the English did have horses with them, it is possible to argue that the idea of cavalry charges and feigned retreats was imposed on this battle by the saga-writers on the assumption that the English use of horses was similar to that of the Normans, who certainly seem to have used such tactics at Hastings.[137] If the English were indeed using cavalry, then it was perhaps the mounted house-carls who had been trained in basic cavalry moves. It is also apparent from these accounts that the English all too frequently had their horses shot out from under them by the Norwegian archers – incidentally further testimony, if any is needed, to the importance of ranged weapons as well as recognition of the importance of taking out the means of conveyance rather than the man. Cavalrymen cease being cavalrymen when they have no horses – though if the English 'cavalry' at Stamford Bridge were actually housecarls more accustomed to fighting on foot, it may ironically have advantaged the English.

The Scandinavian accounts refer not only to cavalry tactics, they also refer, just prior to the battle, to Hardraada's men spotting a force *riding* towards them,[138] as opposed to marching, which would suggest that at least a substantial part – possibly even the bulk – of Harold's forces were actually mounted. Though, as mentioned earlier, the balance between mounted soldiers and foot soldiers is a debated point, it is possible that the bulk of Harold's forces were mounted and not on foot, and that this was one reason why he was able to move so quickly from the south. He and his housecarls may have ridden much of the way, gathering local mounted men *en route*, but only starting to pick up infantry, which would slow the pace, in the latter stages of his ride to Tadcaster. That is, contrary to popular assumptions, Harold may not have gathered infantry from the start of his journey north, but only towards the end. However, he would have had to move at a slower pace over the 15 or so miles from Tadcaster to Stamford Bridge, if he wanted his infantry to keep up with him.

This raises questions – which we probably can't answer – as to the role of the English infantry. It is hard to catch an army by surprise when attacking on foot even if one has the protection of topography till a mile from the site. Infantry may have run – rather than walked – some of the distance from the ridge at Gate Helmsley to the battle site but very probably not all the way (especially bearing in mind they had marched from Tadcaster), and would surely have taken at least ten minutes to cover that mile, whereas mounted men could have done it in two minutes or so. In my view it is quite possible that Harold's mounted men may well have kept infantry pace till they came to the ridge at Gate Helmsley, beyond which they would be in the open, and that from that point, to maximise the element of surprise, the mounted men (cavalry?) went in at the gallop as an advance 'shock' wave. The slower infantry would be following as quickly as they could, but there might have been a significant time-lag before their arrival. However, if indeed most fighting was to take place on the far side of the river, then the use of speed to maximise the element of surprise would have been significantly wasted by the failure to dispose promptly of the defender on the bridge – and could even have cost them victory had the Norwegians made more effective use of this apparently long delay.

A fourth point is the questionable account in *King Harald's Saga* of a brief parley between the brothers Harold and Tostig.[139] Harold is said to have come forward just prior to engagement, with just a few companions, to offer Tostig the return of his Northumbrian earldom in return for peace, to which Tostig replied with anger (and some justification) that if Harold was now prepared to do so he should have done so well before setting this train of events in place, for it was now too late, and he (Tostig) now had Hardraada to consider. When Tostig asked what offer his ally might receive, Harold replied with some black humour that he would give him 'seven feet of English ground, or as much more as he may be taller than other men'. Tostig refused and as Harold rode away Hardraada, who had been watching but was unaware of the Englishman's identity, asked Tostig who the cocky fellow was. When told it was Harold himself, Hardraada said angrily that he should have been told this so that he could have taken the opportunity to kill him. Tostig agreed that it was incautious of Harold to have exposed himself to such a possibility, but said that he did not want to act dishonourably by revealing his brother's identity.

If this account is indeed true, it says much about the personalities of the protagonists. If it is not true – for it does seem rather difficult to reconcile with the more convincing story of the single defender on the bridge, and with the idea of Harold using the element of surprise for a speedy attack – it still has value in showing the perceptions of the protagonists' personalities by the writer(s) of the sagas.

And on the matter of personality, a fifth point to note is the magnanimity shown afterwards by Harold towards the surviving defeated Norwegians, including Hardraada's son Olaf, who had stayed with the ships at Riccall, and Tostig's sons Skule and Ketel, who had fought alongside their father. Harold allowed all survivors to proceed in safety back to Norway – such being the casualty rate that they needed a mere 24 ships, as opposed to the 300 or so they had come in – in return for a pledge never to attack his kingdom again.[140] Olaf was sincere in his gratitude, and showed this a few years later by providing long-term refuge for Harold's namesake young son, who had fled with his mother Queen Alditha from England. In an age of all-too-frequent treachery, this is a heartening exception.

Within a week or so of this memorable victory in the north, Harold was given news of the Norman landing in the south. One cannot help feeling sympathy for him. However much he may have been guilty of misjudging William's manner and movements, and of leaving the south too vulnerable, the news must have been devastating for him, and he may well have felt himself a victim of Cruel Fate; and even perhaps that God Himself was against him. He would have gained confidence following his victory over Hardraada, but the victory also cost him many men, including not a few of his housecarls. It was going to be a hard time ahead against William.

William, meanwhile, having arrived initially at Pevensey[141] on 28 September, promptly moved the next day to the neighbouring peninsula of Hastings, which after consideration he had felt to be better ground for his purposes. The citizens of Hastings had little choice but to accept his demand for their surrender. Among other things William then reinforced existing ancient fortifications,[142] possibly remains from a Roman 'Saxon Shore' fortification or similar, as well as erecting fortifications of his own known as motte-and-bailey (essentially a wooden fortress on a mound), much of the material for which had been brought with him from Normandy in 'kit-set' form.[143] Two sources say that he then destroyed his own boats, just in case any of his men had second thoughts, but in my personal view this destruction is very questionable.[144] He was unopposed militarily all this time, in which regard he was either very lucky or very cleverly benefitting from knowledge that, although Harold had left some men in Romney and Dover, he had withdrawn them from Pevensey and Hastings.[145] Very probably it was a day or so after his move to Hastings that he was informed by the English-resident Norman Robert fitzWymarc (formerly Edward's steward) of Harold's triumph at Stamford Bridge.[146]

William's strategy was evidently to lure Harold as soon as possible into a decisive battle,[147] obviously risky but less so than the alternatives. Certainly William had relatively mobile forces through his use of horses – indeed actual cavalry – and initially he could cause reasonably significant damage in those southern coastal regions. However, he would have realised that sooner or later, given that he had very limited support in England, and could not necessarily count on reinforcements from Normandy (which might be hard to muster,

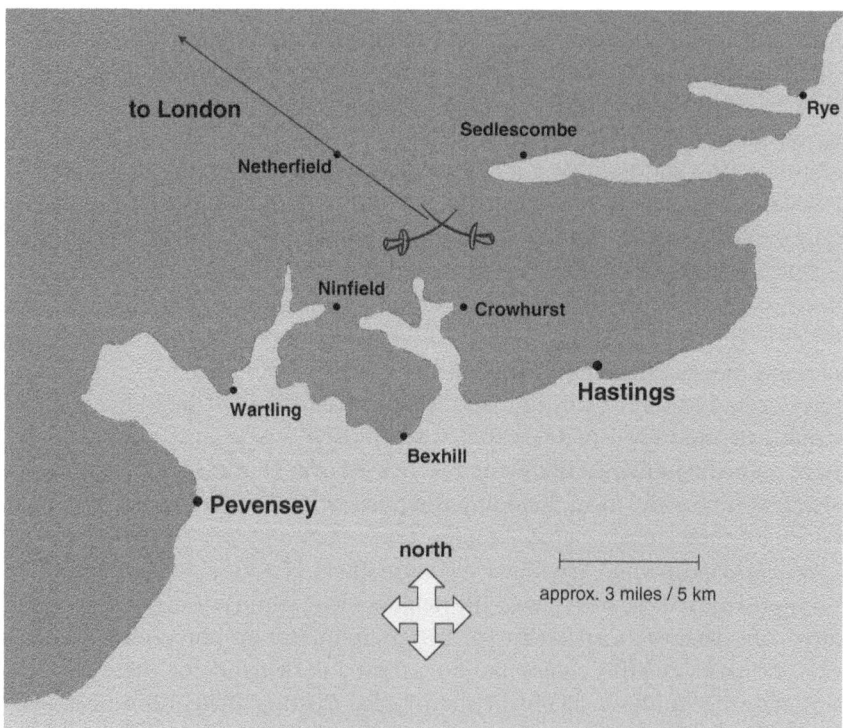

Figure 3.5 The coastline of the Hastings area in 1066.

and harder still to convey to England given the weather and the English fleet, though in actual fact more men did arrive from Normandy shortly after Hastings), he would expect that the more he moved his force out and about the more vulnerable he would become. This would be especially true if he tried to spread out to occupy territory, thereby thinning his numbers and stretching his lines of communication. And, even if he survived a probable ambush or two while on the move, he would very likely end up suffering attrition, having his lines of supply and communication and retreat cut off, and defeat.[148] He was adventurous, but militarily astute. Thus he confined himself to the peninsula, ships perhaps at the ready in case of a forced withdrawal – though it is extremely unlikely he would actually have resorted to the ignominy of withdrawal – but more probably just to guard against any English landings to his rear.

In the meantime, he raided and ravaged the immediate locality, partly to supplement his supplies (which were apparently quite meagre at this stage), and partly to incite Harold, especially given that this was the Godwine(/son) family's traditional territory.[149] By all accounts a ruthless man – characterised *inter alia* by what has been termed a 'wanton disregard of human suffering'[150] – William may well have been playing on what he saw as a relative weakness in Harold's character.[151]

To sum up the military situation at this point in time: William was employing an effective strategy in staying close to his ships, knowing his forces would be in danger should they stray too far inland while Harold and his forces were at large. He aimed to bring Harold to him as quickly as possible – for a delay would be to Harold's advantage – and then, almost certainly, planned to attack him as soon as he arrived, probably hoping to catch Harold by surprise in so doing. Thus he ravaged the nearby territory, which happened, to the good fortune of William, to be Harold's own territory, which added a further incentive for Harold to arrive sooner rather than later. Moreover, he very probably knew of Harold's impetuous nature.[152]

William was laying bait, hoping to catch a formidable but seemingly vulnerable prey. We shall see in the following chapter how effective or otherwise his apparent strategy was to prove.

3.5 October and Hastings: Human error or the fortunes of war?

When it comes to the battle in particular, we should remind ourselves of the limitations of the primary sources.[153] For a start, even an eyewitness commentator on a major battle is likely to have at best an incomplete picture of events, for battles are extremely confusing affairs and one cannot see all aspects, or always establish precise chronology or precise identification.

Moreover, as mentioned earlier, the writers of the day, however objective they might have tried to be (though not all did try at all times), nevertheless had their preferences and prejudices. As might be expected, the Norman writers such as Poitiers typically favoured William, moreover very strongly so, and while the English might be expected to have typically favoured Harold, or at least the English side, they did not actually always do so, perhaps in some cases because of their mixed Anglo-Norman blood and/or a wish not to upset the Norman rulers. John of Worcester and Eadmer (though the latter is a relatively minor source regarding 1066) could be said perhaps to show the strongest pro-English tendencies.

One matter to consider is that of textual error. Sometimes a text draws to a greater or lesser degree upon another earlier and possibly now lost text. This may be felt to increase the authority of the later text in terms of indirect proximity to the events it describes, but on the other hand, in the days of copying by hand, later copies are prone to deviation through omission or transcriptional error. We saw an example of the latter in Part 1 with regard to the spelling of Boudica. As a possible further example, in texts relating to Hastings, references (as in the *Deeds of the Norman Dukes*) to Harold being killed in the first onset of the battle, which seems highly unlikely, could be based on a miscopying of the Latin term 'in *postremo* militum congressu' ('in the final attack') as 'in *primo* militum congressu' ('in the first attack').[154] A later writer might also deliberately modify an earlier text, not just for dramatic or political purposes but also in the sincere belief that they are making a correction to an error, when in fact they are the one making the error. But even if it can be demonstrated that a given writer was wrong in one or more particulars, it does not mean that all their comments can be disregarded – though inevitably some sources have acquired, rightly or wrongly, reputations for reliability or lack thereof. Wace, for example, is one who has widely acquired a rather negative reputation. And the fact that multiple authors might state the same thing does not automatically mean that they are right and some discrepant lone voice wrong, for those multiple authors might have based their accounts on the same flawed text.

I mentioned dramatic purpose, and this is another matter to consider. Especially as we move into the twelfth century, when storytelling became very prominent, we find increasing fiction (or what appears to be fiction) woven into accounts. There is also explicit reference to and comparison to classical heroes and events, and as a result it seems likely that accounts of Hastings and its protagonists might have been subject to distortion to some degree. Certainly William was likened to classical heroes by his panegyrists. But does this mean that all events that are in some way similar to some Golden Age precedent should be treated with scepticism, when they might actually be merely coincidentally similar? For example, are accounts of Harold's mother Gytha offering William her son's weight in gold for his corpse (discussed presently) merely fiction, or exaggeration, in order to parallel Priam's similar offer to Achilles for his son Hector's body?

Another point to consider is that of reported speech. The present-day reader is often left wondering what the ultimate source is for such matters. Speeches made in front of reasonably large numbers of people may end up transmitted reasonably accurately to a scribe not actually present, for the scribe can call on those who were present and cross-check one person's account with another. However, one wonders about, for example, conversations between Harold and his brother Gyrth. The Norman sources seem to esteem Gyrth over Harold, and portray him as wiser. He may well have been, but just who was witness to their conversations? We simply do not know, and so we must always proceed with caution. But we can at least conclude that, even if such speeches are fiction, they nevertheless express a particular view present at that time.

As a result of the sources' diversity and vagueness – and indeed occasional downright contradiction – it is possible to produce a wide range of interpretations of the battle. Of course the 'solid facts' would seem to be that it took place on the Hastings Peninsula on Saturday, 14 October 1066 (though see the list of bullet points below), that the armies fought for much of the day, that Harold and his brothers were killed, that the English lost, and that William triumphed. Some scholars add as an 'assumed fact' that the 'hard fact' that the battle lasted all day indicates an even match in terms of numbers, but, while I personally agree with this, I would nonetheless point out that it is still open to question. We do not know numbers (figures in the sources range enormously), and it could well be that one side had considerable numerical supremacy but did not use this advantage effectively, or conversely that the smaller force fought with greater commitment or with some other advantage on their side. It is also sensible to assume that the victors would tend, if anything, to overstate the number (and by the same token the military merits) of their opponents in order to emphasise the heroic nature of their victory.

Using the sources one could variously construct accounts whereby:

- the battle took place on 14 October, or 22 October (the latter given by John of Worcester but treated by almost all scholars as a clear and simple error of fact);[155]
- Harold and his men arrived at the battle site late on Friday the 13th, or alternatively early in the morning of the 14th;
- the English spent the night riding/marching, or sleeping, or carousing;
- Harold intended to catch William by surprise, or not;
- Harold planned to fight a defensive battle, or an offensive one, or a mixed-phase of defensive followed by offensive;
- William's men were stationed at or near Hastings and marched up to the battle site (some five or six miles away) early on the 14th, or they were already at or very near the battle site;
- pre-engagement messages were exchanged, or not exchanged;

- William did, or did not, warn the English they would be excommunicated if they fought him, and similarly the papal banner played, or did not play, a significant part;
- Harold had a larger army than William, or a smaller army, or one of equal size;
- The earls Edwin and Morcar were present, or were absent;
- Harold had time and/or inclination to construct field defences, or he did not have time and/or inclination to do so, or he only managed partial construction;
- Harold's battle array was confined to the top of a ridge, or it extended down into an adjacent valley (possibly even also occupying a separate hillock);
- as a battle preliminary the Normans sent forth a warrior on a 'suicide mission' to the English shield wall to taunt them, or no such thing happened;
- the well known retreat by the Bretons attacking the English right flank was deliberate, or feigned;
- Harold did, or did not, order or permit pursuit of the fleeing Bretons;
- Gyrth or Leofwine did, or did not, order or permit pursuit of the fleeing Bretons;
- subsequent Norman retreats were feigned, or not feigned, or a mix of both, or did not take place at all;
- William's cavalry played a major role, or did not;
- William did, or did not, slay Harold's brother Gyrth;
- Gyrth and Leofwine fought and died alongside their brother Harold, or fought and died together elsewhere in the field, or all three brothers died in different places;
- Harold himself was killed early on, or late in the day, or even not killed at all;
- Harold was felled by an arrow, or by knights, or by both;
- the knights who attacked Harold included William, or did not;
- numerous Norman knights who fell to their death in the ditch known as Malfosse while in pursuit of retreating English late in the day were lured there deliberately, or it was by pure chance;
- Harold's body was buried on the shore, or at Waltham, or Bosham.

There are something like 65 significant variables here – and this is just a sample – so one can see that the chance of 100 per cent consistency across texts is extremely remote. Obviously, it follows that interpretations will differ accordingly.

That makes me feel better about saying that in the following account I necessarily do what every other historian has necessarily also done, however sure and certain they might seem, and construct a tentative narrative of what to me personally seems to be a plausible scenario that fits reasonably well with some sources and with some recognised interpretations. I do so principally based upon the primary sources (albeit necessarily selectively), but also with an awareness of other scholars' interpretations, plus some knowledge of military studies, reasonable knowledge of textual deconstruction, and hopefully with a degree of common sense and a healthy scepticism. Moreover, despite this book's thematic interest in folly, I do not deliberately seek this out *a priori* to the point of losing my conscious objectivity – as I trust I have demonstrated in my defence earlier in this book of certain historical figures popularly deemed foolish.

Another fast ride, this time back down to London, saw Harold there on around 6 October, where he waited a few days for forces to join him. Again, he had to scramble together what forces he could, having once again sent messengers ahead to alert the local thegns to muster what they could. Though figures are again not clear, he was accompanied or followed by some from Stamford Bridge, but as mentioned earlier he had lost a lot of valuable men there. Edwin and Morcar, who were still regrouping their surviving men (and may have been slightly injured), were very probably not among those present,[156] but were to follow as soon as they could.

On the 10th or possibly the 11th, having arranged for the fleet to move to Hastings to cut off any possibility of William's retreat, for unclear reasons (though I shall return to this presently) Harold decided he should wait no longer, and set off on the 60-mile overland march to Hastings. He took as many men with him as he had at that stage, and arranged for those following later to meet with him at the 'hoary apple tree', a well known landmark at the (inland) top of the Hastings Peninsula. He must have assumed that his total force at that stage, which may have been roughly equivalent in number to William's force, would be sufficient, for there was no compelling deadline he had to meet. It is puzzling why he left at that point, despite allegedly being advised to wait by his brother Gyrth – who is also said to have suggested that he (Gyrth) should lead the battle and that, to protect the interests of the kingdom, Harold should stay out of the fight, to which Harold reacted very angrily.[157] And it is especially puzzling when one realises that the levies from the Home Counties were apparently due to be with him in London within 24 hours.[158] As it was, he simply left orders for them to follow him to the apple tree.

Harold and his accompanying men probably arrived at the said tree late on Friday the 13th – not the most auspicious date to later generations – or possibly in the early hours of Saturday the 14th. We should bear in mind that this was Harold's home territory, and he would be familiar with its topography. The tree was on Caldbec Hill, the highest in the area, but it was not necessarily the best site for any defensive battle. Senlac Ridge, half a mile or so further into the peninsula, was of lesser height but had a steeper angle of drop ahead of it – a 1 in 15 gradient – making a frontal advance against it a very uphill job. Its easterly (English left) flank was much steeper than the front, and effectively very hard to assail, though the westerly (English right) flank was easier, indicating a relative potential vulnerability. It was indeed Senlac where the battle was to take place.

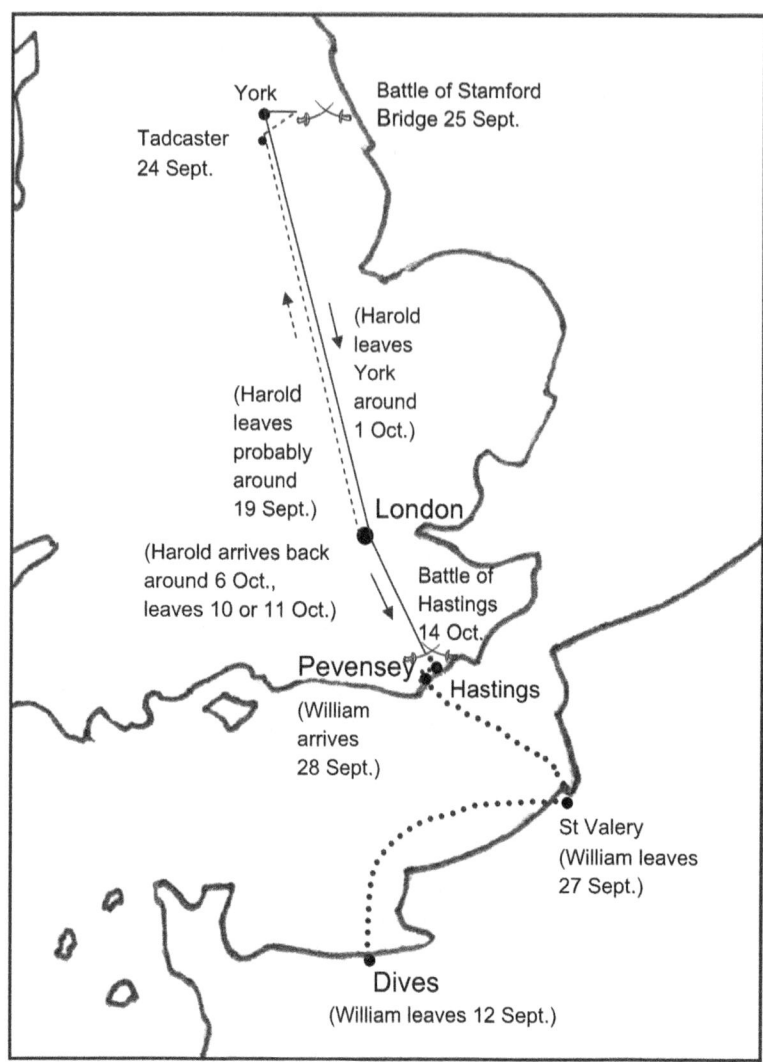

Figure 3.6   The routes taken by Harold and William from mid-September to mid-October.

Senlac was, as mentioned, a good site for a defensive battle, but it is not fully clear what type of engagement Harold had in mind. Given that William's force was effectively pinned down on the peninsula, with retreat to some degree blocked off by Harold's fleet and/or increasingly bad weather, Harold could in theory easily defeat him – or at least repel him – simply by blockading him till his supplies ran out, though in practice this would very likely have become a

Figure 3.7   The slope that confronted the Normans. The British were lined along the top, where trees and Battle Abbey now stand. Harold was to fall just beyond the tall dark tree with the curved top, in a line with the lady looking at the sign.

defensive battle for one cannot see William being so passive. A message had in fact been sent to offer William the chance to withdraw, and it had been curtly dismissed.[159] But would Harold have attempted an offensive battle? Perhaps we cannot rule that out.[160] But even if Harold wanted to finish off William as a threat once and for all and actually kill him, he could still achieve this without engaging in any offensive battle at this particular moment. Harold had time and seemingly most of the odds on his side, though on this occasion, unlike Stamford Bridge, he would not have the element of total surprise, nor would he be facing unarmoured opponents.

It is true that he would not have wanted the inhabitants of the peninsula to suffer, which would inevitably be the case in a blockade as William would obviously sooner have the locals starve than his own men. Nevertheless, callous as it may seem, a general endeavouring to save a kingdom would have to expect 'tolerable collateral loss'. In that regard he could also have expected that William, noted for cruelty, might even resort to torturing and killing some of the inhabitants in sight of his foe, as he had done before on campaigns,[161] but the same principle remained. (I will return to this in my discussion of Harold's actions.)

However, Harold would most likely have expected a defensive battle, for having spent time with William on campaign, he would have realised it was simply not William's style to stay pinned down for long. William was not the sort
of man to suffer a blockade in quiet passivity. More importantly, strategically,
he must have known that William's best chance was to engage him and defeat
him in battle – not simply in order to break out from the peninsula, for he had
had ample chance over the previous fortnight to do that if he so wished, and
moreover it carried the problems mentioned earlier, but rather with the aim of
removing Harold and taking the crown.

In rather clichéd terms, in any offensive battle (from Harold's perspective),
both Harold and William would have to play to win; but in a defensive battle,
William had to win, while Harold could settle for a draw.

The arrival of Harold's men had not gone unnoticed, for they had been spot-
ted by William's scouts. This was, one imagines, something Harold would have
anticipated, though his subsequent behaviour might suggest otherwise. Given
that William would almost certainly have by now known of Harold's use of surprise in his victory at Stamford Bridge, in a guessing game he may have
'expected the unexpected' from Harold, namely an immediate offensive attack
during the night. His own base was probably some five or six miles or so down
the peninsula from Caldbec Hill (that is, a position somewhat to the north of
Hastings rather than in Hastings itself), and no doubt his scouts would have
alerted him to the fact that Harold's men had stopped there at Caldbec and
were preparing to sleep.[162] One wonders whether William in turn contemplated a night attack, which would surely reverse the element of surprise in his
favour, but he did not do so, perhaps because it would have been dangerous for
his cavalry.

Nevertheless, he kept his troops on battle alert all night, and also retained an
element of surprise, for at daybreak on the 14th (around 6.45 a.m.) they set off
towards Caldbec, catching Harold rather unawares around 8.30–9 a.m., with the
commencement of battle following half an hour or so later.[163] Fortunately
Harold's sentries gave him enough advance warning for him to deploy some of
his troops on Senlac Ridge, though according to the sources he was not able to
do exactly what he wanted.[164] He did nevertheless manage to establish a shield
wall, of between three and twelve men deep,[165] across the 800 yards or so of the
ridge to where it fell away either side into ground that was wooded and marshy,
being especially marshy, though less steep, in front of Harold's right flank.[166] (It
is possible that Harold may also have been able to make some sort of basic but
ultimately ineffective field defence, in the form of a trench and/or palisade, but
I shall return to this later in my questions about Harold's actions.) Harold – and
possibly also, at least initially, his brothers Gyrth and Leofwine – was in the centre of the wall by his personal standard (a fighting man) and that of Wessex (a
dragon), surrounded by his housecarls. Other housecarls were deployed, but

Figure 3.8 Marshy ground at Battle on the western side of the battle site, where English casualties were particularly numerous.

probably thinly, to the flanks either side, the idea being that their battle-experience and training would boost the efficiency of the fyrdmen there.

While it is clear that Harold went to Hastings without all his army, there is furthermore a curious comment in the *Anglo-Saxon Chronicle* about his fighting alongside 'those men who would follow him',[167] clearly implying that there were those who did not wish to fight alongside him. This seems to be more than just a few last-minute deserters frightened once they actually saw the size of the enemy, and may perhaps refer to a larger scale defection occasioned by the sight of William's papal banner, a symbol of the fact that the Norman had God on his side. (Similarly, some men may have learnt of the papal support and chosen not to accompany Harold.) This view is possibly supported by a comment a few lines later in the same *Anglo-Saxon Chronicle* entry, that 'the French had possession of the place of carnage, as to them God granted for the people's sins'[168] – though of course it might just be the chronicler's personal interpretation of the reason for the English defeat, in an age when disasters were frequently seen as God's punishment for sinfulness. Worcester states that 'very few of a constant heart remained with him'.[169] This is susceptible of various interpretations, and may refer to defections through perceived imminent defeat, but this is unlikely given the nature of the battle, which as we shall see was only decided very late, up till which point the English defence had seemed sound.

No one knows for sure what exact exchange of messages there had been, but it is surely self-evident that William would have taken any opportunity to let Harold's men know that they were defying the pope – and hence God Himself – by taking arms against him, and that those who did would be excommunicated even if they were not killed in battle. Indeed, one source explicitly mentions this threat of excommunication and its disturbing effect on the English, whose spirits were then rallied again by a rousing speech from Gyrth.[170] The papacy was not always respected, but had re-established considerable authority in recent years, and, given the religiosity of the age, it may well have been a significant negative factor in the mindset of Harold's men – just as it had no doubt been a positive one in aiding William's recruitment of combatants, and their commitment.

It is worth mentioning here that David Howarth[171] feels that Harold did not know of this papal support till he was told this, to his great shock, in London in early October by an envoy, either of William's or his own (returning from William's base). Howarth believes Harold tried to keep the news to himself to prevent disheartening his men, and that this was instrumental in his abrupt departure for Hastings, in that he hoped to see off William before the news leaked out – which would also very likely mean he intended to fight an offensive battle. He also feels that William was secretive and had kept the card of papal support close to his chest to play at the last moment, moreover telling only Harold. However, it seems to me that Harold's men would anyway sooner or later see William's papal banner, and as mentioned above, William, who would seem to have been a reasonably astute tactician, would surely have taken all possible steps to spread the news of papal support, rather than just keeping it to shock Harold personally. Pitched battles were always risky affairs, and William must have felt it better to spread the news to discourage as many men as possible from joining Harold, rather than risk Harold somehow managing to keep it secret and muster enough men to prevail. No one knows for sure when exactly the papal support (symbolised by the banner) was given, though as stated earlier it was probably before late April. But whenever it might have been given, it seems unlikely Harold would not know of it, given the widespread use of spies and the apparent fact that William was using papal support as an aid to his recruiting.

While I find it difficult to accept all of Howarth's arguments, it is possible that some of Harold's men might not have known about it – or felt it was just a rumour – till they actually saw the papal banner, and this may, as suggested above, account for some defections. But at the same time we have to wonder why, if papal support was so crucial, so many English were to fight on after 1066, by which stage it would presumably have been completely out in the open, and moreover following a defeat for Harold that might well be taken as divine support for William.

Having mentioned Howarth and his view that papal support was a decisive factor, I should also mention that Ian Walker feels, by contrast, that there was no pre-Conquest papal support, let alone in the visible form of a banner, and that the whole story is a post-Conquest distortion of what may simply have been a pragmatic later sanction of the *fait accompli* of William's conquest.[172] Walker seems to imply that the not always reliable Poitiers was central in all this distortion,[173] but we should note that the papal blessing itself is also mentioned by Wace (admittedly not always reliable, and possibly based on Poitiers) and William of Malmesbury, and Orderic, who also names the envoy to Rome as Gilbert, Archdeacon of Lisieux.[174] Moreover, what appears to be the papal banner also features in the *Bayeux Tapestry*.[175] Again admittedly, these are all post-Conquest and largely Norman sources, and Walker does raise some important thought-provoking points about the relationship between the papacy and the Normans on the one hand (which may have been less positive than often believed) and the English on the other (which may have been more positive than often believed), but I personally am inclined to agree with the majority of scholars that in this case Poitiers and Wace are truthful. Both William's main biographers, David Douglas and David Bates, accept this. Bates, for example, writes regarding papal support that attempts to dismiss its credibility have 'never been entirely convincing'.[176]

Anyway, papal support or not, William's forces comprised Bretons on his left (i.e. Harold's right), Franco-Flemish on his right, and Normans in the centre. Archers were in the front, infantry next, and cavalry at the rear. The archers, probably with short bows limited to a range of some 150 yards,[177] opened hostilities, firing up the hill to Senlac Ridge, but were apparently ineffective at that stage. The infantrymen followed next, but were decisively repelled by Harold's shield wall. A cavalry charge followed against the English right (westerly) flank, where the ground was a shallower 1 in 33 gradient, and caused some damage but apparently not serious. In fact, the Bretons on that westerly flank got into difficulty – seemingly genuine rather than feigned[178] – and fell back, exposing some of the Norman forces in the centre.

The retreat of the Bretons was to lead to a crucial point, for they were chased by quite a few Englishmen from the right flank, probably untrained fyrdmen,[179] who thereby broke the formation of the shield wall, seemingly contrary to Harold's orders. William also appears to have been dislodged from his horse at this point. If, in this 'window of opportunity', the shield wall as a whole had advanced in controlled and proper formation it may possibly – but only possibly – have resulted in a speedy English victory. There is indeed some suggestion that at least part of the advance of that right flank was orderly, possibly around some housecarls there who may have decided to accompany the fyrdmen against their better judgement. However, there was also a lot of disorderly advancing. William saw this and, snatching another

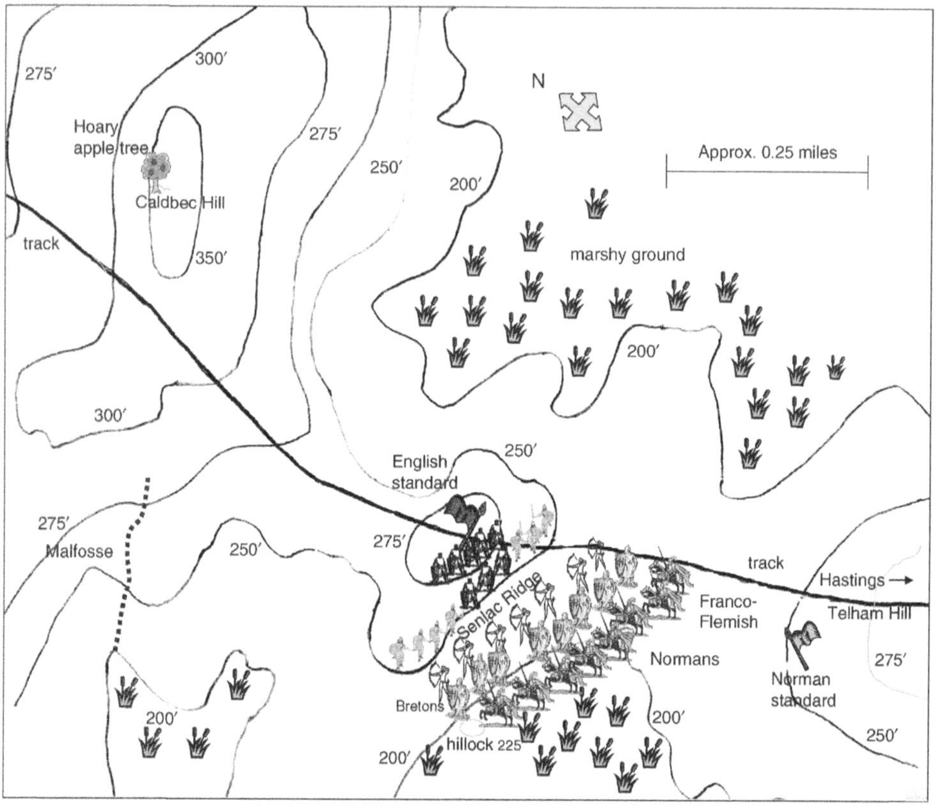

Figure 3.9 The assumed dispositions at the Battle of Hastings.

horse, lifted his helmet to show he was still alive. He successfully urged the fleeing Bretons – and others for there appears to have been a wider panic spreading through his men – to turn on their disorganised pursuers. As the fleeing Bretons themselves were disorganised this was a remarkable feat, again testament to his forcefulness. The advancing English were soon cut off from their comrades by William's knights and, despite a valiant last-stand on a hillock, were slaughtered.

Despite this setback the English shield wall re-formed and still remained formidable. There followed a long period of several hours in which there was much confusion, in which the Normans may have tried a number of ruses including localised feigned flights (perhaps having seen the effectiveness of the earlier and probably unplanned retreat),[180] but with limited success, though one or two retreats – feigned or otherwise – do seem to have drawn out some of the English and led to further casualties. Poitiers describes it as an unusual type of combat, one side trying various modes of attack while their opposition stood as if they were rooted to the ground.[181] So, following the early disaster when the retreating Bretons were pursued, apart from occasional minor breaches of formation the shield wall generally remained firm, which was perhaps also an indication of the basic defensive intent of the English.

Sunset that day was around 6 p.m., and as the afternoon wore on William must have been growing increasingly desperate. If the battle continued till dark it would mean he would almost certainly have lost, for his cavalry could not have operated with surety in darkness and by the morrow Harold's forces would inevitably be strengthened by reinforcements, who had apparently already been trickling in during the day. (Though we are not sure how many may have trickled out by way of defection, or when.)

With great determination William, as he fell back and regrouped his forces, now planned a last concerted attack – though really this was his only option other than ignominious surrender or risky retreat to his ships, and may have had an element of desperation too. This time he may well have intended to concentrate on Harold himself,[182] for the loss of a leader could turn a battle even if otherwise a different outcome might have been expected. He appears to have directed his archers to use a high-angled plunging trajectory, over the heads of his own knights and infantry, and coming down on to the heads of the shield-bearers.[183] This would not produce high casualties, as the arrows would have lost much of their strength, but it could distract the housecarls as they would have to lift their shields to guard against the falling arrows, and perhaps William's knights and infantrymen could exploit this. He is said to have asked four of his knights – seemingly Eustace of Boulogne, Hugh de Montfort, Walter Giffard, and Hugh of Ponthieu (the son of the man who had imprisoned Harold in 1064)[184] – to concentrate on Harold. That he may indeed have also made a similar request to his archers is further suggested in the closing scenes of the *Bayeux Tapestry* which show the shields of the men around Harold with numerous arrows in them.

Even if William did deliberately ask his archers to focus on Harold, or the shield wall around him, it could be said that he literally 'struck lucky' in that one of the arrows did indeed strike Harold in the eye. It did not kill him outright, much of its force having been spent, but sent him to his knees, and shortly afterwards the four knights, exploiting a particularly weak spot on the English flank, drove in and finished him in comprehensive fashion.[185] The first knight (though not necessarily in the order listed above) struck Harold with a lance that went through his shield and into his chest, the second with a virtually simultaneous sword slash that opened his stomach, and the third with an axe blow that took off his head from behind as he slumped. The fourth knight is reputed to have

Figure 3.10 The death of Harold as depicted in the Bayeux Tapestry. Most scholars believe both the figure with the arrow in the eye and the figure having his leg hewn off represent Harold. (By special permission of the City of Bayeux.)

then cut off Harold's leg (as indeed suggested by the *Bayeux Tapestry*) and carried it aloft, but this may possibly be a euphemism for genitals.[186] The bodies of his brothers Gyrth and Leofwine were apparently alongside Harold's, though it is not clear exactly when and how they died.[187] Some sources[188] say Gyrth was killed early, possibly during the chasing of the Bretons, in which case it may be that his body was brought to Harold. The same may have applied to Leofwine.

The battle – 'the most decisive battle in English history', according to not a few historians[189] – was now effectively over. Harold's remaining housecarls fought to the death, but once the shield wall was breached they were doomed against William's mounted knights – not entirely helpless, and they inflicted further casualties on horse and rider alike, but presently, in the gathering dusk, they were finished.

The remaining English, overwhelmingly fyrdmen with even less chance against the mounted knights than the housecarls had had, now fled into the gloom. There was at least one small moment of relative joy for them at this point, when many of the pursuing knights fell in the darkness into an ancient overgrown ditch full of holes and ridges – seemingly the remains of an ancient fortification, and to which they may have been deliberately lured – and were either killed by the fall or by nearby English. This ditch was later named by the Normans as Malfosse or Evil Ditch. Other fyrdmen were cut down, though some luckier ones would have been able to grab horses used by some of Harold's mounted troops and left tethered at Caldbec.

Despite his victory William was apparently in no mood to be generous, and made no attempt to bury the English dead. Far from it, some accounts have his

Figure 3.11 Holy Trinity Church at Bosham in Sussex, a favourite of Harold Godwineson's, and the site of his departure to the continent in 1064. He is said by some to have been buried beneath its chancel.

men looting the corpses.[190] He did order Harold's decapitated and mutilated body to be located, but in the end this may have been done by Edith, Harold's common-law wife.[191] She seems to have been waiting nearby, along with Harold's mother Gytha. Later that night Gytha is said to have asked William to release Harold's body for proper burial, even offering him the equivalent weight in gold.[192] He is said by some sources to have refused, and to have ordered instead that the body should be buried in an unmarked grave on the shore.[193] Another source says that the body was given to two canons from Waltham Abbey (which Harold had refounded in 1060), who had accompanied Harold's army expressly for the unhoped-for task of bringing Harold's body back should he be killed, and that William agreed to this.[194] Yet another source has William giving the body to Harold's mother Gytha 'unransomed' for removal to Waltham.[195] Still other accounts say he was buried (or reburied) at Bosham Church,[196] and, inevitably, that he was not actually killed at all and saw out his life peacefully as a hermit. While there is much confusion about his remains, what is indisputable is that William founded Battle Abbey upon the very spot where Harold fell.

3.6   After Hastings

In the remaining months of 1066 William was to extend his grip on England, though not without resistance. Directly after the battle he waited some time at Hastings, apparently expecting the surviving nobles to come to him and swear fealty to him as king, though it is possible that he was waiting to see if the expected English reinforcements were planning further battle with him. When neither of these scenarios happened he set off on a rampage through Kent, easily taking Dover and Canterbury. Some opposition was formed around Edgar Aetheling, largely in London, and largely driven by the archbishops Stigand and Ealdred, theoretically but ineffectively supported by Edwin and Morcar, who most probably were not at Hastings.[197] It might have been expected that Harold's sister ex-Queen Edith, given her fondness for her 'foster son' Edgar, might have been involved in the support of Edgar, but this does not appear to be the case, though details are not the clearest. Nor did she seem to show any noteworthy grief over the loss of Harold or her other brothers. Certainly she made her peace quickly with William, who treated her well, and she generally lived a life of comfort till her death in December 1075. The relationship between her and Edgar during these years is unclear.

Edgar was designated King Elect in late October by the remnants of the *witan* – but curiously he was not immediately crowned, suggesting support for him was still provisional. His supporters did have one small victory over William as the latter headed for London in that they held the Thames bridges and forced him to cross at Wallingford, but soon this resistance crumbled and Edgar submitted to William, who was crowned William I on Christmas Day at Westminster Abbey, probably by Ealdred. He was to remain king till his death in 1087, when the crown passed to his son William II (Rufus, r. 1087–1100).

Normally one might expect that victory in one battle would not necessarily mean victory overall, but in this case a number of factors meant that Hastings was exceptionally decisive – indeed, it is described by R. Allen Brown as one of the most decisive battles in Western history.[198] One of these factors was that not only Harold, but also his brothers Gyrth and Leofwine had been killed, so there was no one else left among the Godwinesons to assume the mantle of military leadership and carry on the fight against William. Tostig too had been killed. Had he somehow survived Stamford Bridge and gone back into exile, support for his return as a military leader – and remotely possibly even as king – would have been questionable but might have been stronger than support for William (except perhaps in the North).

Another factor was that the three battles that year – Fulford Gate, Stamford Bridge, and Hastings, all occurring remarkably within little more than three weeks – had sorely depleted England's military leaders and fighting men alike. Among those left alive and in England, the earls Edwin and Morcar were still young and relatively inexperienced as military leaders – despite their earlier rout of Tostig. Certainly their support for Edgar Aetheling was not exactly decisive. They may even have naively been hoping William would somehow give approval for an independent northern kingdom. Their sister Queen Alditha, who had moved north to safety while Harold was fighting William, gave birth to Harold's son, also named Harold, shortly after Hastings, probably in late November or more likely December, and this may also have affected her brothers' support for Edgar. They were later, in 1068 and again two years later, to attempt rebellion against William in the name of their young nephew Harold, but were unsuccessful. Their opposition to William resulted in the death of Edwin in 1070 or 1071, while attempting to raise a Welsh rebellion, while at more or less the same time Morcar participated in the Fenland campaign with Hereward (the Wake), and was captured. He died – or was killed – in prison, seemingly in 1071.[199]

As mentioned earlier, their young nephew Harold was taken with his mother to Norway, under the protection of Hardraada's spared son King Olaf Haraldsson. He seems to have been raised as a Norwegian, and is recorded as fighting in a Norwegian force involved in a local skirmish in Anglesey in 1098, but after that disappears from history.

Swein of Denmark was also to attack in 1069, in theory in response to pleas for Danish help from rebellious English leaders though in practice more likely in support of his own claim to the throne rather than young Harold's, but he too was unsuccessful – though interestingly, as seen in Part 2, William seems to have bought him off, rather than fight him off. Even earlier, in immediate post-Hastings 1066, he may indeed have been powerful enough to attack William – and by all accounts had already done so indirectly in 1066 in that he had sent troops to support his cousin Harold at Hastings – but he may not have wished to take William on directly at that stage, especially after the apparent loss of some of his men at Hastings. These and a number of other rebellions in the north resulted in William's notorious punitive Harrying of the North in 1070 – a scorched earth policy whose consequences were to remain for decades. We also saw in Part 2 the intended large-scale invasion of England under Swein's son Cnut in 1085, which, much to William's apparent relief, never got underway. Thereafter there was no further Viking threat of any significance. Strickland remarks that William was fortunate in that he was never forced to confront the Vikings, either in 1066 or on those subsequent occasions.[200]

Unfortunately King Harold appears to have left no designated successor or any contingency plans, despite the possibility that England could be left leaderless. He may have assumed that his eldest 'common law' son Godwine, who was probably around 20 at the time, would carry on the fight, and in fact Godwine did try to do so, along with his brothers Edmund and Magnus, but it seems that there had been no obvious grooming of him either for battle leadership or kingship. Very little is known of Godwine prior to 1066, and of course Harold was only king for a short time, and had moreover formally married Alditha whose offspring would normally – if appropriate – be expected to take precedence over those of Edith. However, given the perils facing the kingdom and the obvious possibility of Harold's death, one would have imagined that, in addition to any expectations placed on Harold's own brothers, similar plans might have been made for Godwine. This is especially the case when taking age into account, for Harold would have had to live another 15 years or so for any reasonable expectation that any son of Alditha's, rather than Godwine, would succeed him. It could be argued that immediately after Hastings, as the eldest and sufficiently old enough son of the immediate past monarch, Godwine had more right than Edgar to be king. It is puzzling why there does not seem to have been more support for him. One is tempted to speculate about possible reservations about his personality, or even reservations about the Godwinesons in general, perhaps in conjunction with a feeling that Edgar was the rightful king after all.

The subsequent key figure in Godwine's cause – and indeed a symbolic rallying point for resistance against William – was Harold's aging mother Countess Gytha, who despite being well into her sixties joined with her grandsons Godwine, Edmund, and Magnus to put up spirited resistance in Exeter. Presently they were pursued by William and in 1068 fled – at the cost of some of the family's treasure – to seek refuge with King Diarmait in Dublin, who had also hosted Harold himself during the Godwine family's exile in 1051/2. From here over the next couple of years these three sons of Harold launched several attacks on England, striking in the southwest, but met with little success or even support. Whether this lack of support was a reflection of lack of sympathy, as suggested above, and/or fear of harsh reprisal by William, is not clear. It seems probable Magnus was killed in one of these attacks, though there is a possibility that he became a hermit in Suffolk.[201]

Indeed, as a sort of part-epilogue to this narrative it may be of interest to follow briefly the subsequent lives of Harold's children.[202] The lives of his adversary William's children are of course well documented and need no delineation here.

In 1070 or thereabouts Countess Gytha went, along with her daughter (Harold's sister) Gunnhild, to seek refuge in Flanders with Baldwin VI (Baldwin V having died in 1067), despite Flanders being an ally of Normandy, and apparently both saw out their days there (Gunnhild becoming a nun). Godwine and Edmund, along with their sister Gytha, may have gone with them and then moved on later to Swein in Denmark, or they may have gone directly to him. In any event they ended up in the early 1070s with Swein. The brothers disappear from history after his death in 1076, nor is there any mention of any children they might have had.

But Harold's daughter Gytha did not fade from history, and indeed is very probably, from the perspective of subsequent lineage, the single most important of Harold's children. Through Swein, around 1075 she was sent to marry one of his allies, the young Vladimir Monomakh, Russian Prince of Smolensk (later Grand Prince of Kiev). The following year they had a son Msistislav – the first of a dozen children. Interestingly, his unofficial name was Harold. This 'Russian Harold' succeeded his father as Grand Prince of Kiev in 1125 (Gytha herself having died in 1107). He had a daughter Ingibiorg, who was to marry the Dane Cnut Lavard and bear him a son who became King Valdemar I of Denmark (i.e. Gytha's great-grandson), from whom Elizabeth the present-day queen of England is descended. Thus the blood of Harold Godwineson still flows, through an admittedly meandering route, in the current English monarchy.

Two others of Harold's children can be mentioned. His daughter Gunnhild stayed in England and, like her namesake aunt, also became a nun. However, in 1093 she was abducted by Alan the Red, Earl of Richmond, and after his death shortly afterwards seems to have sought to marry his brother, and certainly had a relationship with him, earning the disapproval of the church authorities. Subsequent details are unclear.

Even less is known about Harold's youngest son, Ulf (Wulf).[203] Probably an adolescent in 1066, he was imprisoned by the Normans – though how and when he fell into their hands is unclear – but, unlike his unfortunate uncle Wulfnoth (Harold's hostaged brother), who was to stay in prison till his death in 1094, he was released on William's death in 1087. He was even knighted by William's eldest son Robert Curthose, who succeeded William as Duke of Normandy (but who was excluded from the throne of England, this going instead to William's second son William Rufus and later to another son, Henry I). Nothing is known, however, of what became of Ulf thereafter, though some believe he may have gone to Scotland.

So, as a result of the Conquest, Anglo-Saxon/Anglo-Danish England effectively became Anglo-Norman in many regards, and in that sense it might be said that the loss at Hastings had epochal consequences. Among other things, most of the English nobility was shortly replaced by Norman nobility and Norman customs and values inevitably came to be seen as models – at least in theory. The mid nineteenth century historian Lord Macaulay, notorious for his many overstatements, went so far as to say that 'during the century and a half which followed the Conquest, there is, to speak strictly, no English history'.[204] But that period most definitely witnessed an Anglo-Saxon contribution. The Normans necessarily still relied heavily on the English in terms of day-to-day administration of what was a considerably sophisticated existing infrastructure, throughout England at least – as the famous Norman-initiated *Domesday Book* of 1086 ironically reveals – and indeed an infrastructure that in some cases, such as local landowning patterns, is still evident today.[205] Moreover, unlike the case with the Anglo-Saxon Advent and the Viking settlements, in the Norman case there were not many settlers, particularly among the lower classes. Of course the use of French spread in certain mostly aristocratic quarters, and many French words entered the English language, but use of the French language itself by the English general public was limited. Nor does one see too many Norman place-names. And the Normans just somehow did not seem 'at home' and were certainly not particularly welcome. As seen for example in the legend of Robin Hood, noted for fighting the 'Norman dogs' – personified by the cruel and evil Sheriff of Nottingham, ensconced in one of the many Norman castles that came to dot the landscape – not a few Anglo-Saxons continued for many years, indeed generations, to treat the Normans as enemy. The stubbornness of this view is perhaps one testament to the sense of unity and Englishness that had come to prevail in late Anglo-Saxon England, an England that James Campbell refers to as an early example of a 'nation state' with a 'national consciousness'.[206]

Again with some irony, the sense of nationhood amongst the English is further revealed by Anglo-Norman historians writing within a century or so after the Conquest. For example, writing some 60 years after Hastings, William of Malmesbury reveals his apparent leaning towards his English side when he laments:

> England is become the residence of foreigners, and the property of strangers: at the present time, there is no Englishman either earl, bishop, or abbot; strangers all, they prey upon the riches and vitals of England; nor is there any hope of a termination to this misery.[207]

It was not the first occupation of England, for as we have seen, the Romans had been occupiers for almost 400 years, and the Anglo-Saxons themselves, from the perspective of the native Britons, had soon replaced the Romans as occupiers. Presently the Anglo-Saxons in turn were to suffer, in varying degrees, at least partial occupancy of their new land by the Vikings. And despite the impact of the Normans and a legacy they would leave in both tangible and intangible forms, such as architectural styles and a system of feudalism, before too long they themselves would somewhat puzzlingly disappear from history as a force in their own right, being replaced in England by the Angevin line.[208] Indeed, as is often the case with an occupying people, especially when relatively few in number, despite their power-holding it can be argued that the Normans became 'indigenised', and ended up being Anglicised as much as, if not more than, they Normanised the Anglo-Saxons.[209]

Though the Anglo-Saxon element has remained remarkably strong during the centuries, to the point that the majority of Caucasian English people today still seem to identify themselves with considerable pride as Anglo-Saxons (when in fact most are apparently genetically 'Celtic', though they may not realise it), it is nonetheless a reality that after the Conquest things would never be quite the same again for the Anglo-Saxons, or the Anglo-Danish. Though ironically the Normans ('Northmen') were themselves originally of Viking stock, they represented a southern, Franco-Latin world, and their conquest of England resulted in the transfer of a very rich asset from the Scandinavian world to that Franco-Latin world. Put simply, England moved south.

3.7   Why did things happen the way they did?

The questions here are almost all based around Harold's actions, though the final question is of a broader nature. This focus on Harold is because, in my opinion, he is the main player in the determination of outcomes in this pivotal moment of history, even more so than William. This is particularly the case when it comes to the matter of folly. Perversely, I will proceed through regression and go backwards chronologically (more or less) in assessing some of Harold's actions.

(1) *Why was England left leaderless after Hastings?*

Harold seemingly failed to envisage – or worse, didn't care – that he could lose not only his own life but also those of his brothers Gyrth and Leofwine. This is despite Gyrth apparently advising him that he should not risk his own life for exactly this reason of the country needing a leader.[210] Harold is supposed to have replied very forcefully that it would be seen as shameful if he did not lead the field, and one can perhaps see his reasoning, for it could be argued that if Harold himself did not 'front up' against William it could be seen as a lack of belief in the legitimacy of his own right to the throne. Moreover it was common in those days – though not an absolute requirement – for kings and dukes actually to lead their forces, and, given the circumstances of their rivalry, William would have thought it odd if Harold did not. Not only might he have thought it a sign of Harold's lack of belief in his right to the throne, as mentioned above, he may even have thought Harold a coward. On the other hand, so what if William did have such thoughts, if they were only going to be carried to his waiting grave? However, the possible effect of Harold's absence on the morale of his men and the public perception of him may have been more important. Also, Harold might have felt with some justification that he was the senior man in the English force in terms of experience as well as rank.

So, we can probably conclude that it was not an error on Harold's part to risk his own life, but why did he allow both his brothers to fight with him – or even insist upon it, as some interpretations have it[211] – and thereby risk their lives too? They would have been useful contributors, but their value would have been greater with at least one of them being left out of the battle. That all three took part is surely foolishness, but not just on Harold's part: Gyrth and Leofwine should also have realised this, and, having seen that Harold was determined to take part in the battle, they should have recommended the withdrawal of one or both of them and carried this out regardless of any attempt by Harold to force them to be present.

At the very least, once the tide of battle was seen to be turning against them, one of them should have withdrawn (if able to). In fact, not just Gyrth and/or Leofwine, but even Harold himself could possibly have withdrawn (possibly even after he had been struck, if assisted away). Frank Barlow too wonders why Harold fought to the death, since it was no disgrace for a defeated commander to escape in order to raise another army and fight again.[212] In fact, it was a frequent occurrence regardless of time or place: Caesar, for example, did this on several occasions on the continent, and in more recent times so too did Cnut after fleeing from Lindsey in 1014.

The fact that Harold also failed to make any obvious contingency plans for such a defeat, especially centred on either his eldest son Godwine or on Edgar Aetheling, would also seem short-sighted. One can perhaps imagine that not a few leaders would similarly fail to make such contingency plans, perhaps seeing this as negative and inauspicious thinking, though they too would be guilty of the same foolishness. By contrast, William did make such plans before leaving Normandy. Charles Oman, a venerable scholar and strong supporter of Harold, has argued that

> During his nine months' reign Harold had shown himself a most resourceful, active and capable ruler, and it seems hard to find him guilty of inadequacy because of the tactics of one fight. It might even be said that the chance arrow from on high which slew him turned a still possible victory into a defeat.[213]

I would agree with Oman regarding the arrow and the role of chance, for even if William was targeting Harold there was still an element of chance in it actually striking home, and I would agree to a large extent (though with qualifications) with the basic generalisation about Harold the man, but I cannot agree with a verdict of 'not guilty' regarding the 'one fight'. I do feel his tactics during the fight were inadequate, but the main point made in response to this question is that Harold should not have let defeat in this 'one fight' be so decisive. That is, in a fight such as at Hastings it is not merely the on-field tactics that have to be considered, but the context of the fight as well, including the possible consequences of defeat. In fact, it can be argued that in some cases 'contextual tactics' are even more important than field tactics. The age-old wisdom to the effect that you can lose the battle but win the war should have been uppermost in Harold's mind, and he should have made adequate preparation for such a scenario.

(2) *Why did Harold lose the actual battle? (I refer here largely to the fighting and tactics, and treat as a separate question [3] the matter of the immediate lead-up to it, though they are obviously related in some regards.)*

Harold had only to draw, unlike William, who had to win. Thus the pressure was on William to make the play and take all the risks. William relied significantly on cavalry, as Harold would have known and should have responded to accordingly. Even though Harold may not personally have been too familiar with anti-cavalry tactics, he should have been thinking about it since January, and should also have sought specialist advice, or even put together a 'think tank'. (He may well have, but it is not evident.) While it was likely that William would attack at an early stage, possibly as soon as he could upon seeing the English forces, Harold should still have made better defensive plans, including the preparation of anti-cavalry devices, even in large part simply on the basis of common sense. This is especially so in view of the fact that he knew the terrain and seems to have been able to occupy the position he wanted from the outset, Senlac Ridge, though not perhaps with the exact deployment he wanted.

The ridge was already naturally defended to a significant extent by the uphill slope the enemy would have to climb. However, it would have been obvious that it could have been made even more effective by the digging of a trench, which is a recognised defence against cavalry and would also obviously have hindered infantry too. Moreover it was by no means uncommon in English warfare of the day for trenches to be dug (and/or ramparts erected) to reinforce defensive hilltop positions, even if mounted attackers were not involved and the defence was merely against infantry.[214] Knowing he was going to wage a defensive battle, Harold should have made sure his men were properly equipped with shovels (as William's were for the construction of their motte-and-bailey fortifications upon arrival). Given he had enough men at least for a line of at least three (and probably many more) men deep all along the ridge, digging a trench just ahead of the ridge (and piling soil behind them) would not have been a particularly demanding or time-consuming task. Similarly, in addition to a trench, and particularly directly in front of any trench, he should have dug numerous 'pots' (small holes from which we get the term 'pot-hole'). These too, especially if they are concealed by grass, are a recognised effective defence against cavalry. Even the Vikings, not normally associated with anti-cavalry tactics, were able to make such 'pot and trench' defences in some of their engagements on the continent.[215] Harold should have given far more thought to anti-cavalry defences, especially as he would have known that the Normans planned to make significant use of cavalry (which his spies in Normandy would have conveyed to him at an early stage).

These tasks should have been seen as vital and been undertaken the moment Harold arrived, even if his men had to work through the night – in fact, especially during the night, for the Normans would not have been able to use their cavalry during the darkness, and the location of any pots could be better concealed from watching eyes. He may perhaps have been intending to dig trenches and/or pots the following morning, but did not have time to do so – or at least to do so fully – because the Normans almost literally 'caught them napping'.

A palisade (ideally of sharpened stakes) to enhance the efficacy of a trench would obviously take longer, but would not have been impossible if appropriate material and tools had been brought along in carts (and the woods were not far away anyway). A much easier if less effective form of trench-enhancement would be an earthen rampart, using the soil dug out from the trenches. This too was not uncommon in English warfare of the day. Depending on circumstances, a palisade could also have been erected independently of a trench and still be quite effective, as happened, for example, some centuries later in English campaigns in France during the Hundred Years War.

So, did Harold actually dig a trench, or at least show an intention to? And if he did dig a trench, did he fortify it by a palisade or rampart? And/or did he construct palisades anywhere else?

While a number of sources refer to ditches, these may have been natural. Alternatively, even if man-made, they could have been dug centuries earlier. It seems that the Malfosse to the northwest of the battlefield may have been an earlier fortification (as opposed to a natural feature), possibly Roman and part of the 'Saxon Shore' forts, and William himself built his base near Hastings on earlier fortifications.[216] Thus the same might therefore be said of any earthworks in the area.

There would seem to be only one source that does actually make explicit reference to Harold having a trench dug, and that is Wace. He writes: 'Harold looked at the place [the ridge] and had it enclosed by a good ditch; he left three entry points on three sides, giving orders that they should be guarded.'[217]

So, if Wace is to be believed – and it is odd that no other source mentions this – it would seem that Harold did dig a trench, and that it was deemed a 'good' one if ultimately ineffective. There is no obvious reference, however, to it being enhanced by a palisade or rampart.

The matter of a palisade is actually somewhat contentious. Some scholars (notably Freeman, discussed below) have referred to a linguistically difficult and ambiguous passage in Wace and claim that this indicates the construction of a palisade.[218] The latest and seemingly most reliable translation of this passage gives:

> The English foot soldiers carried axes and pikes, which were very sharp; they had made shields for themselves out of shutters and other pieces of wood. They had them raised before them like hurdles, joined closely together; from them they had made a barrier in front of themselves. They left no gap

through which any Norman, intent on discomfiting them, could get amongst them. They surrounded themselves with shields and small planks, thinking they could defend themselves that way. If they had held firm, they would not have been beaten that day.[219]

Though this barrier – which was presumably on the inside of any trench – would seem to have been reasonably effective, it is clearly not a proper barricade of stakes, but a collection of bits and pieces, presumably brought along by men who did not possess proper shields and had to resort to taking the wooden shutters from the windows of their houses.[220] (It was not uncommon for mere fyrdmen, as opposed to professional soldiers, to be ill-equipped and go into battle with little or no armour or other protection, and with only crude weapons. One notes for example that the missiles hurled by the English in the initial stages of the battle included crude and seemingly makeshift objects such as stones lashed to pieces of wood.[221]) Other sources refer to a shield wall, though it is not clear whether it is this same barrier referred to above, or a regular shield wall of proper shields used as a standard defensive ploy by housecarls, or, most likely perhaps, a combination of both, with the housecarls in the line forming proper shield walls and the fyrdmen elsewhere along the line forming a more makeshift one. The *Bayeux Tapestry* depicts a shield wall,[222] but it is composed of proper shields. Thus it is quite hard to know what exactly to make of Wace's description, though we can safely conclude that it does not constitute evidence of a proper palisade.

Based on Wace, the influential nineteenth century scholar Edward Freeman, strongly supportive of Harold, concluded that he had constructed a palisade immediately in front of his shield wall: 'He occupied the hill; he surrounded it on all its accessible sides by a threefold palisade, with a triple gate of entrance, and defended it to the south by an artificial ditch.'[223] With all respect to this venerable scholar, Freeman appears to have confused and/or conflated ditches and palisades, which are not the same thing, and appears to be mistaken in the reference to a palisade. (In fact he was subsequently criticised for a mistaken interpretation.)

Among present-day scholars M. K. Lawson feels that there is a possibility of fortification by both trench and palisade, though his positioning may not coincide with that of Freeman. He identifies a scarp running midway across the slope to the present Battle Abbey,[224] and also focuses in particular on a hillock surrounded by marshy ground some way away from the ridge (the hillock widely associated with a valiant last stand by those English who pursued the retreating Bretons and were then cut off and killed by Norman cavalry). He feels that not only was it possible that the English line extended to this hillock from the outset, but that it was 'likely' that a nearby watery ditch was fortified by stakes.[225] His claim centres on a scene from the *Bayeux Tapestry*[226] showing

Figure 3.12 This scene from the Bayeux Tapestry surely shows reeds (at bottom right) and not a palisade. Note the definite plant, and also note the angle of inclination of the pointed items alongside it. The general flow of the action in the Tapestry has the Normans advancing from the left, which means that the 'spikes' are pointing the wrong way to be a defence against them. (By special permission of the City of Bayeux.)

horses stumbling in front of a stream-like body of water at the base of a hillock. A number of sharply tapered teeth-like triangular shapes emerge from this water (or its far edge), which he interprets as stakes. I personally do not share this view, for I see them quite simply as reeds. My view is partly based on the fact that immediately alongside the triangles is a very obvious and unmistakable drooping plant. In fairness to Lawson he too admits that it is possible that they are indeed just plants.[227] And of course horses could easily stumble at what seems to be a watery ditch hidden among long reeds, but it might be a purely natural feature (or an earlier ditch).

This possibility of ditches being natural or ancient as opposed to being made by Harold's men also applies to a comment in Henry of Huntingdon's *History of the English* about many Normans falling into a 'large ditch cunningly hidden' (*foueam magnam dolose protectam*),[228] to which Lawson also refers. This too could be a natural or ancient feature, but – as indicated by the term *dolose* ('cunningly'), which strongly suggests human agency[229] – one enhanced in its concealment by human hand. It does not categorically indicate a trench wholly of contemporary human construction, although this once again might be a possibility. (Given that Huntingdon locates this trench as being in the path of a retreat, it may well be one and the same trench discussed immediately above with regard to 'stakes vs. reeds'.)

Clearly, the battlefield did contain some ditches and depressions, but it is questionable as to the extent of human input – or more exactly, input from Harold's men. It seems from Wace that the English did manage (probably hastily) to make some sort of fortification of their position by means of a trench (or possibly trenches), and a cobbled-together hurdle of various bits of wood (in addition to the regular shield wall around the professional soldiers). However, it is curious that no mention of a categorically man-made trench or palisade occurs in other sources. Nor is there any reference to the English bringing along tools or material for fortifications. And the *Bayeux Tapestry*, while indicating ditches, does not indicate any construction of them, and neither does it show any obvious palisade. (Yet, as mentioned earlier, it does show the Normans bringing shovels and constructing their motte-and-bailey defences upon landing.) If there were such a palisade, omission to mention it is surprising, for logically, one would expect the Normans, in any reference to the battle in literary or visual form, to exaggerate rather than downplay English resistance in order to amplify the greatness of the Norman victory. The English writers, for their part, might do likewise to make a point that the English tried their best.

Harold may have intended to make better fortifications, including perhaps a palisade, but did not have time to do so – we have already seen that he was caught unawares and was unable to deploy his men as he wished[230] – or else he may not have intended any such thing. Either way, I think he messed up. He should have made sure that he could complete, quickly and efficiently, adequate fortifications for optimising a defensive engagement from what was already a strong location.

Jim Bradbury is of the view that it is highly unlikely Harold set up any kind of palisade or defence.[231] This may be a little overstated if Wace is correct about the trench, but it reflects a widespread view among scholars, and, with the qualifications outlined above, I am inclined to share the basic negative sentiment in that I believe any fortifications Harold might have made were simply not good enough. I will now move on to what I see as other factors in Harold's defeat in the battle.

Though this might admittedly be expecting a lot of an eleventh century military leader, especially one with only limited experience of cavalry, Harold could also have taken more specialised anti-cavalry defensive equipment with him to Hastings, such as caltrops. These are fist-sized iron clusters of four spikes, constructed in such a way that they always have one spike sticking upright. That is, they could simply be scattered over a piece of ground, taking very little time. They were used in particular at Bannockburn two and a half centuries later, but had in fact been a recognised anti-cavalry device since Roman times.[232] If he had had several thousand made ready and waiting to scatter on whatever site William sought battle on, whenever and wherever he came, they would have significantly hampered, or even possibly prevented, any effective cavalry action, and thereby denied William a significant part of his military resources. These caltrops could have been carted to Senlac. Even if he himself or anyone he

Figure 3.13 A caltrop, a recognised defence against cavalry since at least Roman times. Caltrops always maintain an upward spike regardless of how they are scattered.

might have consulted did not know about caltrops, surely someone could have come up with the same basic principle.

Since Harold had at least a week's notice of where the battle was likely to take place (for William's behaviour suggested he was keeping his forces in the area near to his landing site and expecting Harold to come to him), and would have known that his own English forces would very likely be occupying high ground, he should also have planned to make use of gravity to roll down boulders and logs, and should have arranged for a plentiful supply of these to be carted to Senlac. Even if these did not take out many men and horses, they would still have provided obstacles for the advancing forces, especially the cavalry. Stones do seem to have been rolled down by men on the separate hillock discussed above,[233] but not from the main ridge. So, summarising the above, one major reason for the loss of the actual battle was failure to take adequate defensive measures, especially against cavalry.

Another major reason for Harold's defeat, in my view and that of many others, is his lack of full and systematic use of ranged (missile) weapons, in particular the bow, despite the fact that it was an arrow that killed Hardraada and possibly also Tostig. Harold's men did use throwing-spears, which were effective at relatively short distance. However, he seems to have had almost no archers with him. As military technology specialist Matthew Strickland remarks, this was a 'crucial deficiency' and a 'fatal weakness', for having no archers meant that the Norman archers could not be kept at a distance.[234] This paucity of archers is suggested symbolically in the *Bayeux Tapestry* by the depiction of a single diminutive English archer being set in opposition to numerous larger Norman ones.[235]

Nowadays, as a result of later battles won by English archers, notably Agincourt, and probably also because of romanticised ideas about Robin Hood, it is easy to think that bows – especially the longbow – have been used traditionally by the English. In fact the longbow proper was not developed till at least a century after Hastings. Till that point, archers generally used smaller and less efficient types of bow, such as the self-bow, but nonetheless they were effective enough. By the time of Hastings crossbow technology had also been available in France since at least the tenth century, and was thus known and available to both sides if they wished to use it. Though there is no record of English usage, the Normans almost certainly did bring some crossbowmen to Hastings.[236] However, bows in general were used only sparingly by Anglo-Saxons. As an indication of this, excavations of Anglo-Saxon warrior graves (not at Hastings or at that time), in which they were buried with their weapons, reveal arrowheads in only 1 per cent ([*sic*]: one per cent) of the graves, though all contained weapons of some sort.[237] At Hastings the Normans, by contrast, had plentiful bows and made significant – indeed ultimately decisive – use of them. Harold's failure to make proper use of archers, however much he might have been following tradition,[238] was in my view a very serious error, one that he should have avoided by his awareness of the Norman use of them if nothing else. (And it is of course an irony that Norman arrows were particularly effective against Harold himself.) I agree entirely with Jim Bradbury's observation that archers would have been invaluable against the Normans at Hastings and that Harold should have used some even if it meant waiting.[239]

Some scholars criticise Harold for (apparently) not making a large-scale orderly advance, while maintaining shield wall formation, at the point in time at which the Bretons were retreating, William was unhorsed and feared dead, and incipient widespread panic was evident. I do not support this criticism. I repeat that Harold did not have to win; he only had to avoid losing. It is understandable that his men may have wanted to finish things quickly and avoid future losses in defence against some further attack, but it was wise to hold the line. Descending down a hill into a valley would expose his men to a potentially highly impactive counter-charge against them down from the opposite hill (Telham Hill). It would have been an unnecessary risk.

By the same token, it was foolish of those men on Harold's right who did break formation to chase after the retreating Bretons. I am aware of a view that Harold actually ordered this,[240] which I personally find hard to believe,[241] but if it is true, then Harold would be guilty of foolishness on this count too. Similarly, if it is true that during the afternoon there were a number of further localised breaks of the shield wall formation in pursuit of retreats by William's men, feigned or otherwise, then these breaks would be even more foolish, suggesting that Harold's men lacked both discipline and the ability to learn from earlier mistakes – but perhaps an unpleasant reality, if one accepts that the more experienced housecarls were thin on the ground by this stage.[242] Needless to say – for it should be common sense – while the idea of infantry pursuing infantry is fine, when cavalry are mixed in with the fleeing infantry, they can very easily wheel and take advantage of their greater speed to attack the pursuing infantry.

It is often said that the key moment in the battle, when Harold was killed, was attributable to luck,[243] and that the arrow that effectively took out Harold was a 'stray' one. As I mentioned earlier, it was arguably 'lucky' in the sense that it did indeed strike the single most important target, moreover with great effect, but I would at the same time ask where is the evidence that it actually was 'stray'? Was it perhaps not also in large part a result of an attempt by William to focus on Harold? After all, Harold was making his presence – moreover a static presence next to his standard – very obvious as a target.

Similarly, often attributed to luck is the fact that defeat came so late in the day, and that if the English had hung on for another half hour they would have avoided defeat and ultimately thereby won. True, it was all late in the day, but is a sports team that scores in the last minute, as a result of a concerted attack (albeit launched in an all-or-nothing mode), lucky? Is the team that conceded unlucky? We may often say so, out of relief or despair depending on which team we are supporting, but in all honesty I think few would genuinely believe it was just luck. On the contrary, one admires teams that fight to the very last.

A final factor to consider in the actual battle is, of course, the fact that Harold was caught unprepared. As mentioned earlier, Worcester refers to Harold not only having just half his men with him at Hastings, but to having drawn up less than a third of those that he did have with him when William appeared. Why? William appeared around 8.30, two hours after daybreak. His men should have been awake and in position earlier, with defensive fortifications completed. If they were so tired they effectively overslept – or alternatively arrived in the early hours after an exhausting all-night march – then that is an error of generalship on Harold's part, which leads into the next area of possible error, that of the lead-up to the battle.

(3) *Why did Harold engage so early?*

As suggested above, Harold's men seemed exhausted. Why did he march them so fast? What was the rush? Why did he neglect proper preparations such as mentioned above? Why did he leave men behind to follow in his wake? William had shown he was going nowhere, and was indeed seemingly inviting Harold to come to meet him in battle, so surely Harold could not have believed he would take William by surprise?

But he may perhaps have tried to do just that, as indeed the Norman sources believed.[244] It would not be a total surprise, such as he had inflicted on Hardraada – and that itself was not just due to Harold's speed of arrival, but also due to Hardraada's complacency and astonishing failure to post lookouts. However, he was perhaps thinking that he would arrive sooner than William expected. That might be true, but it would be at the cost of Harold's having to leave half of his potential forces behind and at the expense of fatigue among his men, and it would still not be an effective surprise. Harold may perhaps have been misled by Hardraada's foolishness in failing to post lookouts, but he should not have expected William to make the same mistake. He should have expected that William would indeed post lookouts, including some very far advanced, who would be able to advise him of the size and nature of Harold's force, and that William would not be taken by surprise, for he was in a constant state of alertness. (The fact that Harold's men would be marching through forest till very close to their destination is not relevant in terms of concealment, for the roads through the forest were few and easily monitored by William's scouts, possibly more so than had the countryside been open, and if anything it was the scouts who would derive more benefit in terms of concealment.)

Numbers are not known, but judging from the close nature of the engagement it would seem reasonable to assume that Harold had enough men to give a good chance of victory, especially since they would be – or should have been – deployed defensively not offensively. Nonetheless, it would surely have been wiser to maximise the advantage of time that he had, and wait till overwhelming numbers had arrived before he set off to Hastings – and at an easier pace. As military historian William Seymour observes, despite the ravaging of the area by William, Harold could and should have played a waiting game, whereas William could not afford to play such a game.[245]

By way of balance we should note that by contrast with the great majority of scholars who believe that Harold was hasty and should have waited for more men, Edward Freeman, the venerable nineteenth century scholar, condemns criticisms of Harold for not waiting, dismissing them as 'the criticisms of monks on the conduct of a consummate general'.[246] Freeman argues that Harold had a sufficient force and that any greater number of men would be an impediment at the position he had chosen:

> And for the post which he chose, and for the mode of warfare which he contemplated, overwhelming numbers were in no way desirable. A moderate force, if thoroughly compact and thoroughly trustworthy, would really do the work better.[247]

I personally find this an extraordinary and illogical argument quite impossible to accept. This was not meant to be some sort of elite-detachment lightning raid, nor a formless Boudica-style attack crudely based on swamping the enemy: it was – or should have been – a matter of solid defence, and surely the more the men, the more solid. While factors other than mere numbers obviously came into play, the result surely suggests more men might have saved the day. Of course they could not all have crowded into the same defensive position, but surely it would have been useful to keep extra men in reserve back at Caldbec Hill. Even if not called into combat, they would still have had a demoralising effect on William's men.

Moreover, Harold should also have anticipated that William would almost certainly attack as soon as he knew his (Harold's) forces had arrived (probably with the caveat of daylight permitting), so as to try to 'outsurprise' Harold; so why on earth play into his hands? Harold surely could not have been naive enough to believe that William, having learnt that his opponent had arrived, would wait quietly while more and more men came to join Harold at the apple tree.

In fact, he perhaps should not have been at the apple tree at all. As Charles Lemmon points out, it was a 'strategic blunder' to concentrate his forces within striking distance of the enemy, and he would have done much better to centre his men on the North Downs, giving him control of both the roads William would have to take if he advanced inland – and if William did not advance, then Harold could simply play a waiting game till he had overwhelming numerical superiority and then advance on William.[248]

As suggested earlier, Harold may have been wanting to prevent any further abuse of the residents of the area, and this is morally commendable, but with a kingdom at stake it is not necessarily strategically commendable. And after all, we are only talking of a further day or so, and William had already been there for a fortnight. It was clear that William was wanting Harold to come to battle as soon as possible, and was goading him by ravaging the nearby area. It was a trap, but as Jim Bradbury wonders, how long could this have continued if Harold had not 'accepted the bait'?[249] Frank Barlow says basically the same thing that William was pressing for a battle and that it was not necessary for Harold to 'fall into the trap'.[250]

In fact, as the allegedly more sensible Gyrth is also said to have advised,[251] far from trying to save the environs of Hastings from further harrying by William, Harold could have done the very opposite and added some harrying of his own to the area, thereby depriving William of provisions, with a view to starving him out or even forcing him back to Normandy.[252]

'Scorched earth' tactics had been employed in Britain for at least a thousand years, so this would have been nothing new but standard practice. According to Wace, Gyrth gave his brother Harold the following advice, directly leading on from his earlier mentioned offer to lead the English forces in place of Harold:

> While I am going there and doing battle with the Normans, go through this land [the inland environs of the Hastings Peninsula] setting fire to everything, destroying houses and towns, capturing booty and food, swine, sheep and cattle, so that the Normans cannot find anything to eat; in this way you can frighten them greatly, and the duke himself will leave since his food will run out.[253]

Such a policy might well have proven effective even without Gyrth or anyone else going into a major battle. As it was, Harold appears to have refused, and an unstarved William had only to face a limited and beatable number of men, who were moreover tired and ill-prepared. I am tempted to say he could probably not believe his 'luck', but it is only luck from his perspective in that he could not reasonably have expected Harold's advantages to be so wasted. And from Harold's perspective, it was not bad luck but extreme folly, because he could and should have avoided that situation. David Douglas refers to Harold's 'impetuosity' at Hastings,[254] and even the *Waltham Chronicle*, which one would expect to praise Harold (Harold having refounded Waltham Abbey and become its very generous patron), refers to his acting 'too boldly and too rashly to advance his cause', trusting more in his own personal strength than that of his men.[255] One does indeed wonder whether – as I personally believe – this was an unfortunate trait in Harold's behaviour and character (and this is one reason why I discuss personality later).

I have already discussed to some extent the possibility suggested by Howarth of Harold's wish to attack very quickly in order to keep William's papal support secret, or at least lessen the impact of it. Even if for argument's sake one accepts this, it still does not account for Harold's failing to wait just 24 hours more, till the local levies had arrived. If, as Howarth maintains, he was keeping the matter secret, would he not also have been able to keep it secret from the men from the levies? Surely he would still have gained more additions than defections by waiting. And in a worst-case scenario, if he did have massive defections, then he should surely have postponed plans for confronting William so soon and instead urgently set about sorting the matter out.

It is also possible that Harold feared William might soon receive reinforcements, and it is true some did arrive shortly after the battle.[256] But could not Harold's fleet have kept any new arrivals at bay? Even if not, ultimately Harold could expect more reinforcements than William could, so would any threat of Norman reinforcements have motivated him to wait not a single day more – a single day that would have added the local levies (or at least other men) to his force?

One also has to mention, unlikely as it seems, the explanation for Harold's haste as given in the *Brief History of the Most Noble William*. This has Harold hurrying to find William before the latter could flee from England. Harold is described as 'puffed up by madness' and thinking the Normans would not dare to fight him. But as the account goes on to say, somewhat more realistically, he was soon to discover that the Normans had not crossed to England merely to flee from it.[257]

Perhaps it might be better to say that Harold hoped they might flee, rather than expecting it – unless he was indeed overconfident to the point of idiocy and/or he was seriously misinformed about the strength and determination of William's men.

In any event, it would seem that whatever argument is put forward Harold does not come out with credit. It would seem a case of trying to understand his folly rather than trying to deny it. And in terms of explanation I feel – as do many scholars – that Harold, who on a number of other occasions had shown prudence, was overconfident following his defeat of Hardraada. I would add that an exacerbating factor in this overconfidence was perhaps a less-than-full appreciation that his victory had almost certainly been as much attributable to Hardraada's own folly (no armour, no scouts) as to Harold's generalship. And again, one can perhaps see the above as reflections of Harold's character. Freeman, arguably Harold's staunchest supporter, has remarked that

> We may fairly assume that whatever captains like William and Harold did was the right thing to do in the circumstances under which they found themselves. The consummate generalship of Harold is nowhere more conspicuously shown than in this memorable campaign.[258]

I am once again bewildered by Freeman's interpretation of events and his apparent unshakeable faith in the infallibility of military leaders. Modern scholars, of course, have the benefit of detailed knowledge of campaigns such as in World War I, in which generals did not necessarily always do the right thing. But there were also much earlier examples, such as Caesar's errors, and some obvious ones in the early nineteenth century that would have been familiar to Freeman. Though there were to some extent elements of fortune in the result, notably the arrow actually hitting Harold even though it was probably directed at him, and there may well have been faults in the behaviour of others, notably the pursuers of the fleeing Bretons, I still find it very difficult to accept that Harold showed 'consummate generalship'.

According to Henry of Huntingdon, William is said to have described the English as a 'people devoid of military knowledge'.[259] This may be a bit extreme, but based on Harold's military showing at Hastings, perhaps understandable, for they played right into William's hands, wasting their advantage and allowing him to dictate too many of the terms. At the same time, if William's comment has some validity, then it might perhaps be something of a mitigation of Harold's personal military failings if they can be put into a context of 'traditional' failings – something Gildas, no doubt, would have agreed with.

(4) *Why was William (and for that matter Hardraada) able to land unopposed?*

Ideally, it should never have come to a pitched battle at Hastings. William should have been opposed immediately upon landing, and not allowed to establish a beachhead. Ideally, his fleet should have been prevented from ever landing at all, or at the very least depleted before doing so.

Edward the Confessor had allowed the fleet to decline somewhat in scale and importance, but even so Harold should have deployed his vessels better. They did nothing to stop Hardraada and nothing to stop William, though it is true they were moving into place to prevent any escape from Hastings (though whether they were actually in place or not by the 14th is not fully clear). Harold could have upgraded his fleet, following William's lead and building extra ships if necessary, though not necessarily of course on the same scale.

One can also wonder why he does not appear to have attempted to blockade or seriously harry William's fleet at Dives or St Valery? (As mentioned earlier, there is an intriguing possibility that Harold did attempt some sort of attack at some point, but this is not clear, and even if it did happen it was evidently not greatly significant.) Through his spies he certainly knew the state of progress with William's fleet building, and probably also William's movements. Admittedly the bad weather was a factor (though the winds were favourable for a trip from England to Normandy), but Harold should have been able to make more use of the fact that over several months he had a nautical advantage over William. In Harold's defence, he may have wanted to keep his ships in English waters to ward off a possible attack from Hardraada, though there is no evidence for this. But he could have used at least some of his ships to cause trouble and disruption to William – who was effectively a sitting duck at Dives.

In fact, it might also be argued that Harold could have attempted a serious pre-emptive attack, not just to disrupt but to destroy. It is worth noting that Harold would have known that his paternal grandfather, the thegn Wulfnoth Cild, had done something very similar in 1009 in a dispute with the powerful magnate Beorhtric, when he had opportunistically burnt and destroyed Beorhtric's fleet of some 80 vessels while they were beached following a storm. (Though admittedly this had had the unfortunate effect of seriously weakening English naval strength against Viking attacks.)

Given the fact that Britain is an island it would seem reasonable to assume that, notwithstanding the Viking heritage of the Normans, the British – or more narrowly the English – would have the edge in nautical experience and seamanship. In fact, in Harold's fleet there would very likely have been a significant number of English of more recent Viking descent, given the recent Viking presence in England. Surely, even after the fleet was sent back to London, he could have kept a number of fast and mobile vessels – Viking-style boats, perhaps – patrolling the Channel to harry any possible later crossing by William (ideally by identifying and focusing on William's vessel). If it is true that William's own vessel, the *Mora*, was separated from his main fleet, and thus extremely vulnerable, then this represents a lost golden opportunity.[260]

In the end, as mentioned above, the English fleet contributed nothing. Frank McLynn remarks on surprisingly poor seamanship and 'singularly inept naval dispositions',[261] and while I do not necessarily agree with him on the particulars,

I do agree with the criticism. However, I also feel that Harold may have been let down by his captains, for in the matter of naval strategy one could not reasonably expect Harold to have better knowledge than the specialist seamen.

Regarding land forces, the *fyrd* should not have been stood down when it was. Never mind the nicety of limitation of service, for this was indeed a mere 'legal' nicety. Why would men insist on going home if it meant they exposed the country to invasion and might possibly soon not have a home left to go to? Yes, they were short of provisions, but surely there should have been arrangements in place to acquire emergency provisions, such as from Swein in Denmark or Diarmait in Ireland. And yes, the crops needed harvesting, but there were women, children, and the elderly who could surely do this. In pre-mechanised agricultural economies it has typically been women who do most of the work in the fields. Were the menfolk really so desperately needed back on the farm? And even if they were, not all the men in England were on *fyrd* duty. Surely, given the extreme perils facing England, some arrangement could have been made to spread out the *fyrd* burden and similarly distribute a male labour force, The nationwide *fyrd* system seems to have been quite efficient, so there was very probably a usable infrastructure already in place that could be appropriately modified.

We should bear in mind that by 8 September it was known that William was serious and had a large fleet poised to invade, and it was very probably also known that William had been hampered by consistent bad weather and kept at Dives. (And possibly moreover, by around the 16th, when Harold probably first heard about Hardraada's landing, and though admittedly after the *fyrd* had been stood down, it may also have been known that William had suffered a setback on his attempted departure from Dives.) Knowing that hereafter the weather would typically get progressively worse to the point that by October an invasion fleet would almost certainly be unable to make a safe crossing, one can only conclude that Harold assumed that William would not attack that year. He gambled with the weather and lost. He also underestimated his opponent, and among other things seemed to overlook the point that William himself, having assembled his fleet and invested huge amounts of money into it and into provisions (which were also running short but not yet exhausted), would be very keen not to waste even the slimmest of opportunities to go that year, rather than risk having his supporters disperse if they had to wait till the following year.

Having disbanded the *fyrd* in the south, even when he had to march north to face Hardraada, Harold should not have left the south coast so vulnerable. It is true that he himself had initially (before Hardraada's arrival) intended to stay in the south, and that he also left a limited number of troops at Dover and Romney and elsewhere, but he still left gaps, such as at Pevensey and Hastings. William very probably was made aware of this at some point, but even if he wasn't, Harold must bear some responsibility for allowing him such an easy landing. One appreciates that Harold had limited resources, but leaving such gaps in the coastal defences would seem very risky. Given the increasingly bad weather, he should have realised that William would not be planning any lengthy sea voyage, meaning that he could concentrate his defences – both land and sea – on a relatively small number of likely 'at risk' coastal areas.

As mentioned earlier, there should, in my view, have been a coastwatch around all the shores of the kingdom, but with a particular concentration in the 'at risk' areas, and armed men at intervals sufficiently close for them to be able to respond to signals of sightings – even via basic beacons, though a more sophisticated system such as the Roman one[262] would have been preferable – and move speedily to a given landing site. Of course they would be small forces, but they could buy valuable time and also make sure the news was spread fast.

Harold's entire coastwatch – which in fairness to him he inherited – seems to have been inadequate, and should have been upgraded, especially in view of the threats he should have been guarding against. That regional military leaders and subsequently Harold himself were seemingly not alerted to Hardraada's ships at a much earlier stage, for example, suggests it was in a poor state. In a time of such perils from so many quarters, it seems it was simply not good enough.

(5) *Could Harold have prevented Fulford Gate and Stamford Bridge?*

This is a question that with hindsight can be answered in the affirmative, but at the time of Tostig's exile in late 1065 it may not have been apparent that the consequences of that exile would be so serious. Harold would not have expected Edward to die so very shortly afterwards. Nobles had been exiled before and returned, often after just a year or so. Indeed the whole Godwine family, including Tostig himself, were proof of that. The same was true of Earl Leofric, the late Earl of Mercia and father of Edwin and Morcar. And Tostig's and Harold's eldest brother Swein, a particularly fiery character, had been individually exiled twice (in addition to his subsequent exile as a member of the Godwine clan) and managed to return twice – though admittedly his returns were further cause of friction.

Harold was a bit too ready, perhaps, to accede to the requests of the Northumbrians, who seemed to be particularly vengeful towards Tostig in demanding his removal from the entire kingdom and not merely his earldom. Harold could have treated him a little more gently and positively, perhaps advising him as an elder brother that it would be in his best interests to remove himself from the country for a while (for it would be no exaggeration to add that his very life would be in danger were he to stay), and reassuring him that he would try to bring about a return in a couple of years, possibly even getting Edward to rearrange the boundaries of the earldoms – even taking some from Harold's own Wessex, perhaps – to create another down south that Tostig could more safely occupy. (Such boundary-shifting and redesignation had been done before.) After Edward's death, which at the time of the showdown was not predictable, he could have reaffirmed such a promise with more authority, even if he qualified it with a 'good behaviour' condition.

At a personal level it seems Harold and Tostig did not enjoy the best of relationships, and Harold may genuinely have wanted to get rid of his brother – in the extremities of whose behaviour he possibly saw something of Swein, whom he had hated and whose second return from exile he had indeed opposed, though his father's support prevailed in the end.

However, personal matters should have been overridden by political ones. Certainly after he became king, Harold should have made some overtures to Tostig, for he could not afford to upset such a potentially dangerous enemy. And of course he should have kept himself better informed of Tostig's actions. One has to say that the 'Tostig affair' was not particularly well handled by Harold, and was to prove disastrous for both of them.

Once Tostig's alliance with Hardraada was in place, and certainly once their ships had arrived, it would have been very unlikely that an armed engagement could have been prevented, but one does note again that Harold should have been informed earlier of the invaders' arrival and as a result responded even earlier than he did. We have seen that he appears to have been on board ship off the south coast for some days after the invaders first landed, and thereby apparently out of contact. This is undeniably unfortunate timing, but some means of signalling could surely have been put in place, especially since Harold – as mentioned above – should have been keeping a 'weather eye' on Tostig and his movements.

In fact, on the evidence we have, the whole matter of Harold's use of communications and monitoring and intelligence-gathering seems deficient. As one possible example of an overlooked source, he could surely have used his friendly cousin Swein to keep him informed of developments, whether or not he knew Tostig had visited Swein. In fact, one does wonder what exactly Swein told Harold about Tostig's visit, or indeed whether he told him anything at all. He probably did advise him, because it was after Tostig's visit that he sent the earlier-mentioned volunteers to Harold. And if he did, he would probably also have advised him that Tostig was heading north to visit Hardraada, for he would easily have been able to track Tostig's movements as he left Denmark for Norway. However, there is no record of any such communication.

(6) *Could Harold have prevented William from considering an invasion in the first place?*

This is a difficult question to answer because of the mystery surrounding William's claimed designation by Edward, and who exactly might have been aware of any such designation or of William's claims of one. William seems to have believed in his designation fervently, but there is no firm documentary evidence so far discovered to support his belief.

It is also unclear as to whether Harold was expecting to be designated himself on Edward's deathbed. It raises the question of what Harold would have done if he himself had not been designated. Would he have supported Edward's designation of another, even if it were William? Or would he have supported Edgar? Some scholars feel that Harold was angling for the crown from around 1057,[263] and that may be true, but I personally feel he would have referred the matter to the *witan*. Even if Edward had designated William, it is highly unlikely that the *witan* would have endorsed it. (For one thing, even before the conquest, Normans in England do not appear to have been looked upon with much affection.) However, had there not been such peril facing the kingdom, they may have endorsed a designation of Edgar, probably with Harold as regent.

A glib short answer would be that yes, Harold could have prevented William's invasion by ceding the crown to him voluntarily, but the result would still have been Norman domination of England – though presumably on a relatively cordial and more sharing basis, and with no bloodshed. But why should Harold cede the crown? We do not know the full details of the events of 1051 and it is possible that Harold knew something that we do not, but that has a major bearing on the question. However, as far as we know now, Harold was designated by Edward as his successor and that in itself should have been the end of the matter. The final designation, especially if it was endorsed by the *witan*, should have superseded and rendered academic any claims by anyone else to have been designated. Thus this would make William – not Harold – the ambitious upstart. Harold could have been more pro-active by broadcasting this far and wide, including to the pope – regardless of whether or not William had approached the pope to seek endorsement.

Donald Matthew has written that 'Edward the Confessor nominated Duke William as his heir and it was only the resistance put up by the Godwineson family that turned William's proposed peaceful accession into a conquest'.[264] I find this a remarkable dismissal of Harold's own claim, and I would point out that it might equally be argued *au contraire* that it was an aggressively ambitious William who turned Harold's accession into a bloodbath – though admittedly others too made it a less than peaceful accession. And what of William's treatment of Edgar and his blood claim, which was surely stronger than William's alleged nomination from Edward?

It seems very likely true that Harold had taken an oath in Normandy in 1064 to uphold William's claim, but it was equally very likely obtained under duress and was therefore able to be broken. Indeed, Ian Walker raises the possibility that Harold might have been absolved of any oathbreaking by his friend Bishop

Wulfstan.[265] One can, however, criticise Harold for his naivety in making that trip at all (unless he was ordered to make it by Edward, though this seems unlikely), even though he certainly would not have expected the treatment he received. One can also criticise him over a couple of specific incidents during his time with William that he could and should have handled better, even though at the time he probably would not have expected his actions to become so controversial so soon.

First, even if for argument's sake Harold had no idea until his visit that William had been – or believed he had been – designated by Edward, or even if this was before William raised it, he should still have realised the difficulty he would be in with multiple fealties and could have politely refused to be knighted by William, on the grounds that his fealty was to Edward. In fact, this was actually the true case, and it is rather odd that he accepted arms from William – though he no doubt wished to avoid upsetting him, and it is also true that in practice multiple fealties were not unknown. Such a refusal would indeed no doubt have angered William, but he would have been unable to do anything about it. (Though this could not have been predicted at the time, when Harold later took the crown in January 1066 he could have argued that he was simply obeying his liege lord Edward by accepting Edward's designation of Harold himself.) Alternatively, he could perhaps have made vague arguments to the effect that an earl could not receive a lesser rank of knight. Some way or other he should have avoided being knighted and thereby incurring some degree of fealty to William.

Second, he could perhaps have played a little smarter when asked to swear on the sacred relics, though in all fairness it may have been sprung on him leaving little time to think (and he may possibly not have been told about the relics – which were perhaps hidden – till afterwards), and we have to bear in mind too that the freedom of the hostage Hakon almost certainly depended on his answer. But he could legitimately and politely have asked William in turn to show good faith by swearing on the same relics that he would honour Edward's final wishes, and then hope that he (Harold) could change Edward's mind before Edward died. (In 1064 Edward was around 60 and despite occasional illnesses did not seem on the point of imminent death, but by the standards of the day it would still be unlikely he would survive for too many more years.) He could also at least have asked William to swear to release both hostages, not just one, or even have asked William himself to provide hostages.

Having said that, the reality is that we were not there and we do not know just how much pressure Harold was under. He may well have feared for his life, as some sources have already been seen to confirm. Open murder of Edward's chief earl by his host William would have been diplomatically serious, but on the other hand fatal 'accidents' or 'illnesses' or 'sudden strokes' happened frequently in the eleventh century, even to earls – and heirs apparent, as in Edward the Exile's case. But by the same token, after his return to England Harold could have arranged an 'accident' or similar for William if he considered him such a danger. Assassination was by no means uncommon. (It could be argued, still by the same token, that William could have arranged Harold's assassination in England in 1066, but he almost certainly wanted a military presence there too to enforce his claim to the throne.)

To return to the troublesome matter of papal support, we have already seen that Howarth feels it was of vital importance but unknown to Harold till very late, while Walker feels it never happened. But staying with the majority view that it did indeed happen, it could be argued that in the first place Harold should have been aware of it, including the petition to Rome led by Archdeacon Gilbert of Lisieux (according to Orderic). No defence case was presented to Rome by Harold.[266] Of course, if Pope Alexander II was benignly disposed towards the Normans he may not have been inclined to inform Harold of the case against him, but Harold should surely have been using intelligence agents to keep him informed of developments around William. If he did not know, then it was seemingly a failure of his intelligence network. If he did know, then failure to make a response would seem a serious error, for a case made to Rome would surely have delayed and possibly (though unlikely) even have nullified support for William. Freeman is of the view that Harold may have avoided presenting a case to the papacy because this would oblige him to accept a papal decision, which may have gone against him.[267] However, making no case at all did not look good – though if Walker is right, and there was no papal support for William, then obviously this criticism should be ignored.

One might also say that, when Harold took the crown in January 1066, prompting William to send messages of protest, Harold could perhaps have responded more constructively to those messages, even if he had no intention to relinquish the crown. Among other things he could have suggested a peaceful meeting with William to discuss it, and perhaps something like putting it to a public vote (at least something broader than merely acclaim by the *witan*) as to who was the choice for monarch by the English themselves. This would almost certainly have been unacceptable to William, but it would have made Harold look a lot better to any third-party observers – other than perhaps Pope Alexander, though even Alexander might have found it more difficult to give unqualified support to William if Harold had been so open – and would possibly also have weakened support for William.

Harold's options, then, were limited, whereas William's passionate belief in his right to rule England seemed without limit. Unless he gave in to William, or had him murdered, or perhaps made a crippling pre-emptive attack on him, or appealed successfully to the pope, Harold would have found it next to impossible to dissuade William from attempting an invasion.

In summary, we can list Harold's questionable actions as follows:

(1) *Failure to make provision for defeat*
   - should not have put so many potential leaders at risk in the first place;
   - should have withdrawn himself, or ordered appropriate others to withdraw, once the battle seemed lost;
   - lack of contingency plans to safeguard the kingdom.

(2) *Failure in battle itself*
   - inadequate field defences against cavalry;
   - inadequate archers;
   - allowed ill-discipline among some fyrdmen;
   - entered field with exhausted men;
   - inadequate deployment;
   - premature engagement (see 3 below).

(3) *Rushing to do battle*
   - failed to wait till overwhelming numerical superiority achieved;
   - jeopardised condition of men;
   - fell into William's trap, effectively allowing William to dictate terms;
   - should have followed a containment policy, perhaps including a scorched earth policy to starve William of provisions;
   - should have given more thought to base/assembly point;
   - apparently overconfident, letting emotion dominate reason.

(4) *Allowing William's unopposed landing*
   - coastal defences inadequate;
   - signalling/communication systems inadequate;
   - ineffective use of fleet (both for harrying and defending);
   - should not have stood down the *fyrd*;
   - questionable use of intelligence/information;
   - ineffective or non-existent pre-emptive measures.

(5) *Allowing Fulford Gate and Stamford Bridge to happen*
   - could have handled Tostig better;
   - should have realised threat posed by Tostig;
   - should have monitored Tostig's movements;
   - (as with 4) ineffective use of intelligence/information;
   - (as with 4) ineffective or non-existent pre-emptive measures.

(6) *Allowing William to consider an invasion*
   - could have handled the oath-taking incident better, and the incurring of fealty to William through being knighted;

- could have handled William's initial protests (in January) better;
- should have monitored William better and at least responded to his approach to the pope;
- should have broadcast the legitimacy of his own claim;
- should have tried more diplomatic measures;
- if diplomacy failed, should have tried to assassinate William or to attack William's fleet while a sitting duck at Dives.

It may be that some of the above actions (or failures to act) are linked to a greater or lesser degree to Harold's personality, though personality is always a contentious area as it is so hard to demonstrate, and I do not want to overemphasise it despite its importance. In any event, for what it is worth I offer below some observations on the personalities of Harold and William, based in large part on the observations made by their modern biographers. But first, let us consider a final question, one not based on Harold.

(7) Was Harold the only person in the affairs of 1066 who may have been foolish?

The answer in my view is 'definitely not'. For a start, Harold's nemesis William, while normally seeming an astute general, was surely foolish in planning the venture at all. Frank Barlow has described the outcome of William's expedition to England in 1066 as characterised by 'almost miraculous success',[268] and most definitely it was something close to a miracle, for the odds were strongly against William. Notwithstanding the Roman respect for a lucky general, taking a massive gamble is not a good way to conduct a campaign. It would seem very much the case that William was driven on by passion, more specifically self-righteous indignation, and that too is not a good basis on which to conduct a military campaign, for it invites irrational behaviour. He was extremely fortunate to have had his adversary make so many wrong moves, and of course the timely attack by Hardraada also helped him greatly – as did, ultimately, the weather. He could easily have lost, and gone down in history as foolish. Though this is not intended to lessen his undoubted strengths, or to claim that I have encyclopaedic knowledge of history, I personally think he is one of the luckiest major figures in world history – a luck that extends back to his early childhood, when he became Duke of Normandy at the age of seven and almost miraculously survived sundry attempts on his life. But I stray from 1066.

Harold's other major 'foreign' adversary, Harald Hardraada, while admirably cautious in leaving a significant body of men to guard his ships (a good amphibious warfare tactic), nevertheless undid all his caution by foolishly failing to post lookouts, and not insisting that his men wear their armour. He was leader of a force in hostile territory, and should not have let his guard down. Of course, learning of Harold and his men being in the south, he badly underestimated

Harold's speed in moving north, which may, to some extent, be understandable but not excusable. To be caught by surprise, certainly in circumstances like that, is a serious disgrace for a general. More realistically, he should have been wary anyway, of more localised opposition. Unfortunately we do not know why Stamford Bridge was chosen as the site for the hostage handover, and this may have some relevance, but as it stands one has to say that it was too far from his ships and almost invited attack, either on his main body or the ships.

By way of mitigation he may have been lulled into a false sense of security by Tostig, who must also share some of the blame, and in addition bear blame for apparently having a false perception of his own support base. Tostig too appears foolish, but perhaps more in the sense of a rather immature rashness. His own cause would surely have been far better advanced had he not been so seemingly impatient and extreme.

Harold's other brothers Gyrth and Leofwine must also have question marks against their behaviour, for at least one of them should have stayed away from Hastings to cover a 'worst case' scenario of English defeat and Harold's death. They very probably must also share some of the criticisms levelled at Harold regarding the actual engagement at Hastings, such as hastiness, lack of proper defensive fortifications, location of base, and so on. In particular, if the view that either Gyrth or Leofwine ordered the pursuit of the fleeing Bretons is correct, their culpability would become considerably greater.

Some of the men who fought for Harold, though they may have given their lives, may also have let him down. However, this may be a case of inefficiency rather than folly. The possibly imaginative story of the defender of the bridge at Stamford Bridge does not suggest anything like efficiency, but rather bumbling inefficiency, though the English did eventually prevail. The apparent breaches of the shield wall at Hastings, particularly in the case of the fleeing Bretons, were decidedly unhelpful – though one has to bear in mind the possibility that the breach was done under orders. And then there is the question of the seemingly 'invisible' fleet. Just how much was its ineffectiveness due to Harold, and how much due to the admirals and captains? Harold may in theory have had overall command of the fleet, but he could not possibly have had the particularised knowledge that the seamen did, and would surely have been guided by their advice and suggestions. As mentioned earlier, I personally think he was badly let down in this matter.

Finally, we might consider Edward. He does not appear to have been a particularly decisive person, and he could have saved much trouble (which I believe he must have anticipated) by being more decisive and explicit about the designation. He was not totally incapacitated after he first fell ill, and would have had time and ability to make (or sign) a written designation in front of impartial witnesses (which his advisers should have insisted on). Surely, even if he expected to pull through his illness, he would have had sense enough to realise that at the age of 60 or so he would not be long for this world, and regardless of health should have made his intentions far clearer and in an indisputable way. It is in fact surprising that he had not done this already, other than through seemingly vague and inconsistent and questionable verbal utterances. There is, of course, a possibility that he did make it all clear, and stated his intentions indisputably in writing, but that the document was 'mislaid'. But for once I am not going to be cynical, for there is no evidence to suppose that he did write anything.

3.8   Some observations on the personalities of the two main protagonists

Having examined some of the actions of the two main protagonists, Harold and William, it may now be appropriate to consider their characters and – as best as we can – flesh them out as human beings, not merely names in a history text. This is not the main aim of Part 3, for to do so properly would require detailed examination of their entire careers, but I do believe it useful to make some comments, principally using the observations of their well informed main biographers.

I do indeed believe that personality – in the fullest sense of the sum total of the behavioural and mental characteristics that make up an individual – plays a significant part in the shaping of history, and that it also relates to the issue of folly and fortune. But this question of personality is a tricky one. On the one hand it is obvious that it must have an importance in response to or generation of events. Consider for example the difference between the timid and the bold, the irresolute and the determined, the pragmatic and the principled, the cruel and the benign, the wise and the foolish, and so on. Such character traits also surely have a bearing, *inter alia*, on the ability of history's protagonists to 'make their own luck', and especially so in an age when government and leadership were so personal. One might even say that an examination of historical events is missing a key dimension if it ignores personality. But on the other hand, we are not all psychoanalysts, and we can easily make sweeping assumptions that we inadvertently apply *a priori*. And of course, contexts and values will be different from what we ourselves are familiar with.

Anyway, with the above caveats, I start by supporting my above contention with a quotation from David Douglas, one of the two main biographers of William:

> William displayed the ineluctable connection between personality and power, and demonstrated how, in the shaping of events, decision and fortitude may be of more importance than material resources.[269]

Douglas goes on to make the following observations of William, which I list in no particular order:

> undoubtedly repellent . . . exceptional in his wanton disregard of human suffering . . . brutal . . . bestially cruel . . . his avarice was repulsive . . . his rapacity was infamous . . . strong and pitiless . . . constantly active . . . vigorous leadership . . . inherent authority . . . a man to fear . . . pious . . . abstemious . . . [sexually] continent . . . on occasion even affable and generous [qualified by Douglas as a 'surprising trait in his character'].[270]

The other main biographer of William, David Bates, similarly remarks on the importance of William's personality:

> It is to a very high degree doubtful whether so great a feat as the Norman Conquest of England could have been accomplished without this remarkable man's extraordinarily strong personality.[271]

He paints a not dissimilar picture to Douglas's:

> an extremely effective ruler, who was not an especially appealing man . . . an outstanding soldier, a very capable general and a warrior who led by example. He possessed great fortitude and acted with an unbending insistence on his own authority . . . ruthlessness and shameless manipulation of facts . . . his methods of government were brutal . . . he was rigid, puritanical, and intolerant . . . his most noticeable faults were cruelty and avarice . . . he was religious . . . he had the ability to think on a large strategic scale . . . [he] had that mixture of intelligence, will-power and charisma which could persuade others to follow him on hazardous enterprises . . . a brutal and highly successful opportunist.[272]

Physically, William was fortunate enough to have an imposing physique and considerable strength, plus a commanding voice. His skeletal remains reveal he was 5 feet 10 inches – tall by the standards of the day – and powerfully built, though his muscle in later life turned to fat. His hair appears to have been red, again making him stand out physically. He also had great stamina, a 'capacity to endure great physical hardship',[273] and generally enjoyed good health.

It should be pointed out that he appears to have remained devoted and faithful to his wife Matilda (daughter of Baldwin V of Flanders), whom he married probably in 1051 and who bore him a dozen or so children. There is a popular story, possibly apocryphal, that she was initially reluctant to marry a man of illegitimate birth but was presently attracted to him by his physical abuse of her and changed her mind.[274] Anyway, her death in 1083 devastated him, and he was a broken man till his own death four years later. Their marriage is also remarkable for the fact that he was tall (as mentioned, 5 feet 10 inches) and very burly and she extremely short (4 feet 2 inches), and they must have formed, as Douglas observes, 'a remarkable couple'.[275]

Both Douglas and Bates quite properly place William in the context of his day, and point out that William was in many regards just a vivid example of norms of the day for rulers, such as in harsh enforcement of his will, and support for the church.

It should also be borne in mind that William's early years must have had a formative impact on his approach to life. He was born with the stigma of illegitimacy as the son of Robert I, Duke of Normandy, and a lowly tanner's daughter Herleve, and from the age of seven, upon his father's early death in 1035, he was to experience a number of attempts on his life and be constantly vigilant against threat. He also participated at a youthful age in a number of military campaigns, and was only in his early twenties when he committed his notorious atrocities at Alençon, horribly mutilating 32 men in revenge for being taunted about his illegitimacy.

Though this book has been concerned with just a part of William's life, and we have seen nothing, for example, of his relationship with Matilda, we can nevertheless conclude that nothing has surfaced that may contradict any of the descriptions by Douglas and Bates. William has been seen to possess a very forceful personality; to be a man of determination, indomitability, willpower, authority, and self-belief; and one who lets nothing stand in his way. Regardless of whether or not he had papal support, it was quite a remarkable achievement to persuade men to follow him in his venture, men who were initially understandably reluctant. It is even more remarkable when one considers that he himself did not have the strongest claim, for both Harold as the later designee and Edgar through descent had stronger claims. At the same time he has shown considerable intelligence, particularly in the sense of 'street smarts' in matters military. He would not seem to be characterised by finer feelings or much consideration for others, and indeed not a man to be crossed. He very much seems born to be a man of destiny, one who shapes history by sheer brute force. Indeed, in Spencerian and Hobbesian terms, he amply proved his fitness to survive in an age of brutality, and instead of 'William the Lucky Bastard' might well merit rather the epithet 'William the Total Bastard'. One can feel some sympathy for Harold, who had to confront him.

Harold was almost certainly born around 1022 and was therefore some six years older than William. He is less fully described than William, and is evidently of a less pronounced personality. Like William he was born into a very powerful family, that of Earl Godwine of Wessex, but unlike William, legitimately, and similarly unlike William his childhood was relatively stable, largely thanks to the survival skills of his father.

John of Worcester describes Harold as pious, humble, and affable to all good men, detesting malefactors.[276] The *Waltham Chronicle*, which admittedly might show some degree of bias towards its benefactor, describes him as a fine soldier, tall, strong, handsome, wise, militarily skilled, and extremely generous to the church.[277] Even Orderic Vitalis, who often spoke very badly of Harold, conceded that he was brave and valiant, strong and handsome, pleasant in speech, and a good friend to his own followers.[278]

In terms of appearance, Harold does seem to have been taller than average, possibly around 5 feet 11 inches and thus even taller than William,[279] but with a trimmer and more athletic build. He does genuinely seem to have been very strong (as witnessed by his rescue of two Norman soldiers in the quicksands of Brittany) and to have had great stamina. He was indeed by all accounts considerably handsome, had long golden hair, and wore a moustache in the fashion of warriors. In terms of health, he may not have been as robust as William. Among other things he seems to have suffered a serious illness in his twenties which entailed fever and temporary partial paralysis and which from time to time came back to plague him in later life, and it is worth noting that he was said to have been quite ill in late September of 1066.[280] This may have affected his behaviour in a way not clear to us nowadays.

Harold's present-day principal biographer is Ian Walker. In general Walker accentuates the positive in Harold – particularly understandable in the face of the unjustified condemnation Harold received from William's propaganda writers such as Poitiers. Walker points out something of a duality in Harold's character: on the one hand he was a warrior, and on the other hand a man of peace. He refers to a blending of these attributes leading to qualities such as wisdom, courage, patience, temperance, prudence, diplomacy, and, when the occasion called for it, ruthlessness – though other observers may form other views about this duality and blending, myself included. He further observes that Harold was also reasonably but not fervently religious, and a good family man, staying with his common-law wife Edith from his 'marriage' around 1044 till early in 1066, when he married Alditha of Mercia in a formal politically driven marriage.[281]

Other modern scholars have added that Harold was relatively open (at least relative to his brother Tostig), fair-minded, polite, easy-going, dependable, affable, cheerful, generally even-tempered, and possessed of a sense of humour.[282] Frank McLynn is one who acknowledges Harold's basic shrewdness, but he too sees a duality in his character (also perceived by Harold's contemporaries), among other things observing Harold was said by some to be too slow whereas others said he was too impetuous, including failing to think things through.[283]

Walker defends Harold against scholars who accuse him of recklessness in what many if not most see as a premature engagement of the Normans.[284] In this book I clearly take a different view. Rather, I extend the duality in Harold's character to an occasional and seemingly unpredictable shift from patience to hastiness, from prudence to a lack of caution, and from wisdom to folly, and I trust I have illustrated my reasons for thinking this. He does not necessarily deserve to be characterised in all aspects as the *fatuus rex* ('foolish king'), as described in the *Song of the Battle of Hastings*,[285] but in my view he was guilty of a number of serious follies.

Though I think a critical assessment of Harold is necessary for a full under-standing of the events of that year, it does trouble my conscience somewhat to cast him in such a negative light, for to me, at a personal level, and despite the view of some scholars that he had a devious and possibly even murderous eye on the throne, he generally seems to have been a 'decent bloke', 'human' and quite likeable – certainly relative to William. He may well have been a very good king had he lived long enough.

But to my mind William was undoubtedly the more effective military com-mander of the two, and I agree with those such as David Douglas who feel that he 'out-generalled' Harold.[286] Though Harold was himself a strong and deter-mined man, William nevertheless seemed stronger. Essentially, he was tougher, and he was smarter (when it mattered), and he is testimony to the harsh real-ity that being feared can be more effective than being liked. Harold, by con-trast, is perhaps testimony to the same harsh reality that the nice guys don't always come out on top.

3.9   Conclusion

We have seen the extraordinary tide – or more exactly maelstrom – of the events of 1066 and related earlier events. Our understanding of these events is all too frequently marred by a frustrating lack of reliable detailed information, exacerbated by vague and/or often conflicting primary sources. It is very hard to assess material from such sources, characterised as they are by frequent error and/or deliberate propagandist distortion, and scholars are almost inevitably doomed to accusations of selectivity as they endeavour to sort wheat from chaff. There can be few such major moments in early history that have been subject to such varied interpretation, but at the same time it is probably the case that is indeed because it is such a major moment that it has been written about so much and led to so many interpretations – to which this present book is obviously adding its own humble contribution.

In this part of the book I have tried to focus on what I personally see as key issues, and among these I have focused in particular on the actions of Harold Godwineson. My conclusion is that he made a number of errors of judgement that proved costly, the most serious of these being his early engagement of William at Hastings, which I feel was unnecessary, poorly planned, and poorly prepared. I feel the battle itself, largely as a consequence, was poorly fought tactically, however valiant the English combatants may have been. Moreover, the unnecessary involvement of so many English leading figures at Hastings, for which involvement Harold bears some responsibility, was to leave the kingdom vulnerable and hence soon conquered.

As a sort of 'post-match comment' I have added some thoughts on personality, for, much as I recognise the dangers of trying to assess the personalities of historical figures, in this case I see personality as potentially very important in the protagonists' powers of judgement. Sadly, though Harold seems to have been a respected and likeable fellow, he would appear to have lacked the solidity and generalship of his much less likeable adversary William – though at the same time one should not overestimate William's generalship, for really he should have lost at Hastings, and it was not necessarily superb generalship on his part that brought him an unlikely victory.

Though I have also argued that 'luck' is often in actuality a potentially predictable consequence of actions, it was ill luck for Harold that Hardraada attacked when he did, for it is far more likely that William would have been defeated if Harold could have met him with a fuller and fresher army – though I do not use that as an excuse-all, for as stated above I still believe Harold should have won anyway. Perhaps Harold's greatest and genuine misfortune is that William should happen to have existed at the same point in time and place. A less determined foe than William may well not have capitalised on Harold's shortcomings, and in that sense, it might be argued that the most important determinants in the events of 1066 were not just related to Harold's poor judgement but also to the forceful personality of William – and, of course, the role of Fortune should not be overlooked. John Gillingham, in a brief biography of William, ends by remarking that 'few kings can have enjoyed so much luck as William the Bastard, but few took such full advantage of their good fortune'.[287] I think that is a very fair comment, but I would also ascribe to William a certain element of foolishness, that makes his luck all the greater.

We have seen that William did have good luck on his side, in a classic illustration that one person's misfortune can be another's good fortune. Certainly, he was fortunate in that Harold was guilty of errors of judgement that perhaps (pleasantly) surprised William, even though we are told William was exploiting his knowledge of Harold's character. And of course he was also very fortunate in the matter of the 'distraction' of Harald Hardraada's attempted invasion. (It is remotely possible – if unlikely – that to some extent he factored this into his own agenda, but this might be overestimating William's generalship and the state of communications in those days.) If he had not been so lucky, he may well have ended up being recorded as one of history's greatest fools in his attempt to take England the way he did.

As we saw, Frank Barlow has described the outcome of William's expedition to England in 1066 as characterised by 'almost miraculous success'. Was it a 'miracle' – perhaps, some might argue, even divinely inspired, if William really did have God and the pope on his side? Or did he make his own luck? Or, after all, was it just the falling of the Dice of Fortune?

Conclusion

So Just How Foolish or Fortunate Have We Been?

Early Britain, and more particularly what is now England, seems to have been quite susceptible to invasion. Even before the Vikings and the Normans appeared on the scene, Gildas had made this same observation. But just why was Britain/England so popular, and why did it 'get beaten' so often?

In the case of the Romans it seems to have been targeted largely for political reasons, basically to boost the standing of ambitious individuals, notably Caesar and Claudius. In some regards, there are similarities with Britain's own later empire-building: the land was there, it had reasonable resources, it didn't have a particularly 'civilised' populace, they seemed beatable, so why not add it to the empire and get some kudos for doing so? Adding Britain to the empire would in fact bring more than normal kudos, thanks to the fearsome Ocean that had to be faced first, for all Romans knew that the Ocean indicated the edge of the world. To add worldly lands to the empire was meritorious enough, but to conquer land beyond the edge of the world was truly intrepid and not dissimilar to modern humans' ventures into space. The symbolic and political value of the conquest of other worlds is enormous.

The man who led the early assaults, Caesar, was probably not fully intending occupation. However, since he is the only real commentator on himself and his intentions as regards Britain, it is hard to say. Whatever his intent, he made foolish mistakes, and could easily have been the first major Roman figure to end his life in Britain. For his first assault, in 55 BC, his choice of landing place was poor, his vessels were inappropriate for the attempt, he failed to safeguard them, he was uninformed about the tide, he split his forces too readily, and he didn't have cavalry (though this was not necessarily his fault). He was lucky to survive – though of course that meant he had the backing of the gods, so at least in the public eye, but not necessarily the eyes of the more astute observers, it was a success.

Why was he not promptly repelled? Largely because, it would seem, the Britons could not act with any real unity and decisiveness. They missed a number of very

244

good opportunities, such as when the Romans were struggling to land, and when the seventh legion was isolated while cutting grain, and particularly after Caesar's ships had been damaged by Mother Nature and one of her storms. As a 'national' defence, the Britons 'messed up', despite Nature/Fortune pointing the way for them. If they had been a real 'nation' in the sense of being a unified entity, then they would rightly be deemed very foolish and incompetent. But, they were not a nation, and they were not sufficiently unified. I will not follow Roman commentators here with regard to making generalisations about Celtic fickleness in battle, but one must at least conclude that militarily it was not a good performance by the 'Celtic' Britons. Moreover, the Britons were aware of the Romans' fear of the Ocean, and should – even in those days – have waged a type of psychological warfare aimed at capitalising on already low morale in the Roman troops, especially in the very early stages.

Caesar's second assault the following year, despite its greater scale, had certain remarkable similarities to the first, in that once again his choice of landing place was poor (the same site in fact), his ships were once again damaged by a storm, and once again he acted in a militarily questionable way, this time in marching exhausted men through hostile unknown territory during the night. He may well have had a local guide, and a defector/captive or two, but just how trustworthy they might have been is another matter. If the Britons had been properly assembled and alert, he could have suffered a disastrous defeat and the loss of his own life. Even afterwards, if the Britons had persisted with guerilla tactics the outcome could have been different. At least this time round the Britons did try a relatively concerted attack on the ships, under four major leaders, but this was too late and too ineffective. It should have been made before the ships were repaired and defences put in place. But once again, it was a lack of unity that was the telling blow for the Britons – a lack of unity that was something else the Roman commentators remarked upon, and that Caesar no doubt used to his advantage.

Claudius's campaign almost a century later in AD 43 was far harder to stop, being better organised, and with larger numbers, though again if there had been better unity – say under Caratacus – there might have been a chance to repel the invaders in the years immediately after their arrival. Cartimandua's betrayal of Caratacus was a key factor, I feel, though it appears, from the limited evidence we have, that Caratacus can be accused of folly in allowing himself to fall into the hands of such a well known Roman sympathiser. For Britannia overall, it was the same old story of 'divide and conquer', with the dividing being well advanced even without Roman intervention.

It was Roman foolishness that triggered major moments of British resistance, the first being a revolt in 47 over the requirement that all tribes should relinquish their arms, even client kingdoms, and of course the second was the revolt in 60 following the abuse of Boudica and her daughters (and many of the Iceni nobles). The latter revolt, more particularly in its final confrontation with the Romans, is surely one of the most disastrously wasted opportunities in the history of any country. We can never be sure about exactly what happened, and we are not even fully sure where the final confrontation took place. Nor can we be sure about numbers, though evidently by all accounts Boudica's forces (excluding non-combatants) massively outnumbered the Romans. They must certainly have been a very large force, for they did destroy three significant towns. On the evidence we have to go off, Boudica's tactics were disastrously foolish for the situation, though in some mitigation it can be said those tactics were a product of the time and culture. Paulinus was probably expecting those tactics and was not surprised, but, like Caesar, let us just say that he was fortunate the Britons were so predictably foolish, for otherwise he and his men could and should have been annihilated. This in turn would almost certainly have resulted in the permanent Roman abandonment of plans to occupy Britain, as had effectively been the case with Germany.

As I mentioned several times in the text, I do not personally think Boudica should shoulder all the blame for this, for she must surely have had experienced battle-leaders alongside her and advising her (and she may even have been largely a figure-head). However, in a sense this makes the defeat even worse, for it means it was collective folly, not just individual folly. If Boudica was the sole leader, one could perhaps deflect the blame from her as an individual to her inexperience in battle (for the sackings of the three towns cannot really be deemed battles, and it is hardly likely she took part in any battle in 47). But if this was the case, and she was the sole leader, it would be equally disastrous folly for experienced battle-leaders to leave command to such an inexperienced leader. Whatever way we look at it, we cannot escape folly, and in this case, because of the consequences in entrenching Roman occupation, we might even call it 'epochal folly'. Nor would it seem excusable by any obvious element of ill fortune. Indeed, it can be argued that Boudica's fortune was greater than Paulinus's, in that he and his force were far away at the time of the outbreak of the revolt and she could perhaps have capitalised on his absence better. Once again one suspects that lack of unity may have been a major factor in the final outcome, this time a lack of unity among battle-leaders, resulting by default in totally inadequate tactics.

In Part 2 we looked at the supposed folly of Vortigern in the post-Roman mid fifth century, the man who invited the Anglo-Saxons to lend a helping hand against the raiding Picts and couldn't get rid of his guests. In fact, he is even said in some popular quarters to have angered his guests so much by not treating them properly that they took over the place. I have made it clear in the text that in my own view this is facile and unfair scapegoating. Yes, it was a dangerous move in the sense that the Anglo-Saxons had themselves been doing a fair bit of raiding of Britain over the previous century or so and were potential enemies, but not only was Vortigern's decision merely the continuation of a long-established practice of employing one group of barbarians against another, it was a decision made in conjunction with a council. Moreover, the idea that the Anglo-Saxons only turned nasty after some sort of default by Vortigern regarding compensation seems very naive. He may well have angered them and provided a particular irritant, but it would be a massive overreaction on their part to take over his kingdom for it. One also has to consider the motives of the Anglo-Saxons, who seem to have seen Britain as a wealthy and fertile place that was attractive relative to their homelands, and we should not forget their above-mentioned earlier raids. In my view, they would have come anyway. Their motives were not like those of the Romans and they were not seeking to acquire British territory for the sake of political prestige or the expansion of an empire. It seems to have been a more personally driven type of territorial acquisitiveness.

I see no great degree of folly in Vortigern's behaviour, or any epochal consequences of which he is a major cause, and I certainly do not place him in the same league as Boudica in that regard. I believe the main reasons for the subsequent Anglo-Saxon Advent were acquisitive desire on the part of the Anglo-Saxons and lack of unity once again on the part of the Britons. In effect, as I have also said of the Vikings, they came and raided and then settled because they wanted to and they could. This was obviously at the expense of the Britons, but we have seen that there is considerable difference of opinion as to the scale and nature of this. However, personally, from the Britons' perspective I cannot see the Saxon Advent as a 'good thing' (to use a favourite term of Sellar and Yeatman).

To a large extent the Vikings seem to have done unto the Anglo-Saxons that which the Anglo-Saxons had done unto the Britons, and one may feel there is a certain 'natural justice' in this. The Viking 'Advent' started with raids and then turned to territorial acquisition and settlement. And here too there were cases of employment of Vikings to guard against other Vikings, such as in Aethelred's employment of Thorkell (though admittedly this particular example was at a late stage). Once again, in broad terms we have a story of the newcomers' motives being acquisitive and a lack of unity (at least for much of the time) in the targeted area(s) that was unhelpful in the thwarting of this acquisitiveness. Once again, the newcomers did what they did because they wanted to and they could.

But still in broad terms, one difference is that the Anglo-Saxons were not dispossessed of their land and power (and language) by the Vikings to the extent that the Britons had been by the Anglo-Saxons. Rather, they shared such things with the newcomers, again generally on more egalitarian terms than seems to have been the case with any Britons who remained in Anglo-Saxon territory. For a while the country was essentially split, with Scandinavians to the north and east and Anglo-Saxons to the south and west (but not generally into Wales), though by the middle of the tenth century it could be said to have been a reasonably united 'nation', under the dominance of Wessex. Alfred the Great, though perhaps rather excessively lauded by some, had nonetheless played a significant part in this dominance of Wessex that contributed to the unification of England.

By contrast, poor old Aethelred (also of Wessex) has come in for great criticism. He has been widely condemned, particularly in popular quarters, for his frequent and large payments to the Vikings to buy them off and even then failing to stop them taking over the throne. I do not personally see him as a great or wise king by any means, for amongst other things he was foolish enough to order the extermination of Danes, causing a predictable backlash, and he was deficient in controlling his magnates, but I have nonetheless defended him on a number of counts. Above all, though he may have been a bit too 'ready' with his payments – somewhat ironic in the light of his popular if incorrect perception as 'unready' – he can only be blamed in the matter of degree, for he was most definitely not the first to start such a practice. It had been in place for well over a century, in other countries as well as England, and had been resorted to on more than one occasion by Alfred, as well as other kings. And technically, he himself did not lose the kingdom (unless one bases this claim on the very brief reign of Swein Forkbeard). Rather, it was lost under his son Edmund – though I do not intend in this to imply any shortcoming on the part of Edmund, for by that stage the Viking presence was very strong, obliging Edmund to split the kingdom with Cnut, who then became sole monarch after Edmund's conveniently prompt death.

It could be argued that Aethelred has some culpability for allowing such a strong Viking presence to come about, but at the same time it was an extremely powerful and determined 'new wave' of Vikings, often prepared to ignore any affiliation they might have had with the earlier Vikings, who had by this stage settled in quite well to their new country.

Rather than foolishness, Aethelred seems to me to have been a weak king who was dogged by ill fortune. His reign got off to an unfortunate start following suspicions that he was involved in the murder of his elder half-brother, he was still young when he succeeded to the throne, and within a few years the new wave of Viking attacks had started – perhaps in part through opportunism. And then things went from bad to worse. However, for the most part, I see him too as the victim of another simplistic scapegoating, though arguably perhaps a little more deserving of it than Vortigern.

During Aethelred's reign we saw valiant defence at Maldon by the aged Byrhtnoth, who has also been accused by some of foolishness, though not to the extent of Aethelred. While a modern strategist may well have adopted a different approach from that of Byrhtnoth and not allowed the Vikings to cross the causeway, I do defend him against accusations of foolishness.

And then we come to Part 3, and the Norman Conquest. I have pilloried Harold, and highlighted what I see as numerous failings on his part, which in some cases seem to be sheer foolishness. They relate to his behaviour before 1066, to his behaviour earlier in 1066, to his behaviour immediately leading up to Hastings, and his behaviour at Hastings, and they include accusations of foolishness by both commission and omission. There are so many questionable points that I will not repeat them here, but rather refer the reader back to the listings towards the end of Part 3 (section 3.7).

But he too is in part the victim of ill fortune, especially in the timing of Hardraada's invasion, and in broader terms, having to face an opponent of the determination – and luck – of William. I say that William was lucky for a number of reasons, one of which is that his opponent Harold made so many mistakes, but that apart, he was certainly a recipient of good fortune. He was fortunate to be alive at all in 1066, given the sundry attempts to assassinate him during his childhood, and he was remarkably fortunate in the way things turned out for him that year. Essentially, his whole invasion was so risky it is questionable whether even an inveterate gambler would have contemplated it. The odds against its success were enormous – we saw the renowned Barlow refer to that success as 'almost miraculous' – and it is a testimony to his strength of personality (and no doubt the papal blessing, and possibly also other means we are not aware of) in persuading any men to follow him at all, for they were initially not at all enthusiastic. Playing on his illegitimacy, he has been termed 'William the Lucky Bastard', and there would be few who would disagree – except perhaps those who would prefer 'Total Bastard'.

This good fortune masks the foolishness of his invasion, which was seemingly driven on by a passionate sense of righteous indignation rather than rationality, and in defiance of more legitimate claimants to the throne of England – for Harold as the later designee, and Edgar by descent, both had more legitimate claims than William, while Harold's cousin Swein Estrithsson of Denmark also seems to have had a stronger claim through both designation and reasonably direct blood links with Cnut. William could easily – and by any objective forecasting should – have been soundly beaten at Hastings, and gone down in history as a deluded fool. History itself would have followed an alternate path, and of course the recording of it would have had a different bias to it as well.

Unfortunately for Harold, particularly through the fact that he lost his life there (and that was perhaps somewhat unluckily, though I have part-argued against that), Hastings was an event of epochal proportions. Thus the mistakes he made, which others in his position may also have made, and which would probably have been completely glossed over had he won (and it was after all still a close affair), have taken on the status of 'epochal folly'.

In this he joins Boudica. I believe that in terms of folly, these two figures, Harold and Boudica, have been major factors – but obviously not sole factors – in epochal changes in early British history. But there are differences between them. Harold's case can be mitigated to some extent by an undoubted element of misfortune, whereas Boudica's cannot. And whereas Harold seems to have been a popular and respected person, his image as a 'decent fellow' continuing to the present, Boudica does not quite present the same positive image. She may well be seen as heroic in her spirited resistance to the Romans, which undoubtedly drew others to her, and of course she is an enduring symbol of female strength, but – as Antonia Fraser was seen to observe – she has curiously remained somehow dissociated from atrocity. If she did participate in or condone the hypocritical slaughter of 'collaborator' Britons and the gruesome torture of Roman female elites, an argument might be made that she deserves to be condemned as a vicious villain – or do we say more exactly, a product of vicious and villainous times? But in both cases we have to qualify conclusions with the observation that we are to a significant extent dependent on sources that are often contradictory and not necessarily reliable on points of detail, especially in the case of the very scantily recorded Boudica.

Highlighting these two figures for a sort of 'wooden spoon of the millennium' does nevertheless trouble me at a personal level, for I have considerable sympathy towards them as people seemingly locked into a particular destiny. While Boudica remains a distant and relatively obscure figure, it is possible to learn quite a lot about Harold – perhaps even more than one's next-door neighbour, for example. I have been interested in 1066 over many years, and, though I may be deluding myself, I feel I have gotten to know Harold quite well, and I see him as a basically decent man whom one could readily befriend. It is a tragedy that he sealed his own fate through shortcomings that in other circumstances – that is, victory at Hastings – may not even have been noticed.

It is clear that a number of other figures who feature in early British history have also demonstrated folly, with greater or lesser consequences depending on the circumstances – and in this, of course, I am mindful of Chaos Theory and the Butterfly Effect. One that springs readily to mind is Harald Hardraada, whose foolishness at Stamford Bridge cost him not only his life, it effectively signalled the end of Viking aggression in England and indeed, in the view of many, the end of the Viking Age. Clearly, his folly too was epochal, though its consequences were not felt – or more exactly realised – in Britain directly as much as in the case of Boudica and Harold.

As something of an aside it is interesting to speculate what might have happened if Hardraada had not lost to Harold. Similarly, following (one line of) causality upstream, we could speculate as to what might have happened if Tostig had not encouraged (or at the very least supported) Hardraada; and if Tostig had not been upset by his brother Harold's refusal to help him; and if Harold had not been placed in such a predicament; and if the apparent main cause of that predicament, the revolt in Northumbria, had not happened; and if the apparent main cause of that revolt, Tostig's behaviour, had been different; and if Tostig had not been born at all, etc. etc. History is full of 'what ifs', but in not a few cases I personally believe we can legitimately say 'what if so-and-so had not been so silly?'

I will not, however, dwell further on other individual figures associated with folly and will round off with what I might call a 'persistent shared folly', and that is the persistent failure of the early British (including 'Celts', Anglo-Saxons, and Vikings) to make effective use of ranged (missile) weapons, especially the bow and arrow. Given the legend of Robin Hood and the effectiveness of British archers at Agincourt and elsewhere in later years, this is surprising. It is also puzzling. As I have said in the text, especially in Q 3 of section 2.8 but also elsewhere, (Western) bows prior to the development of the longbow proper were not wonderful, but were functionally efficient. When one examines battles in early British history, one can see just how much the British disadvantaged themselves by their failure to use the bow. On the face of it, notwithstanding any mitigating socio-cultural factors, such as regarding the social status of archers, I would still deem this a profound military folly.

As another 'persistent shared folly', given that external attacks on Britain would necessarily be amphibious in their early stages, I believe the British seriously neglected to target vessels, which is a recognised counter-measure against amphibious attacks even subsequent to landings. This was a particularly serious omission in the case of Caesar's incursions, but extends throughout the period covered in this book.

In principle we can also extend this criticism to other conveyances, this time on land, and of course this mostly means horses. Hastings is a powerful lesson of the consequences of not taking simple but effective measures to nullify (the Norman) cavalry by taking out their horses.

Having said all the above, I am no expert on folly – though I can be very good at demonstrating it on occasion – and others might strongly disagree with my conclusions. Nonetheless, I hope that through this book I have at least stimulated a greater interest in the role of human behaviour in the unfolding of history. There have been quite a number of historical studies that have pursued positive human attributes such as heroism, and perhaps this book can be seen as helping to provide a balance to such studies, for, after all, and even though we might not like to dwell on it too much, to err is very definitely human.

Appendix 1

The Question of Arthur

It might seem ironic that one of Britain's best-known 'historical' figures is associated with a period of which so little is known, that of the fifth and sixth centuries, but it can be argued that it is precisely because so little is known that Arthur has loomed so large. It is precisely the dearth of hard fact that allows so much scope for imagination and the creation of myth and legend. And it is also quite logical that a British hero-figure should loom large and shining out of a gloomy backdrop of defeat and destruction for so many Britons.[1]

This leads us on to the difficult question of textual reliability. As mentioned in the Introduction and elsewhere, there is always an element of subjectivity in any writing, even if it is genuinely intended as a sincere and objective record. At one end of the spectrum, which we might call 'mild' or 'honest', subjectivity can still be seen in such matters as the decision to write the item in the first place (even if ordered to do so, for that would still reflect someone else's subjectivity) and what terminology to use, how much space to devote to it, and so on. At the other end of the scale, which we might call 'extreme' or 'dishonest', there is downright propaganda, such as deliberate falsification, bias, 'labelling', and so on. Put another way, writing is an act and has a purpose, and that purpose will reflect the time and place of the act. It might just be a private scribbled diary entry that shows your mood at that point in time and space, but in the case of 'published' literature it is very often political and/or cultural, tailored to achieve a given impact towards a desired end. (Nowadays, cynics will observe that commercial aims may be felt to dominate.) In times and places of restricted literacy, storytelling takes over the role and is obviously even more open to manipulation.

As a number of scholars have pointed out, in the case of figures such as Arthur, who have such limited provable historicity (i.e. an actual historical existence) yet loom so much larger than life, we have to be particularly careful to appreciate the political context.[2] It may well be that there was no real Arthur at all, and that he was a fictional creation of various politically motivated writers.

Perhaps because of the dominant Anglo-Saxon presence in England, the story of Arthur did not really become well known (at least outside Wales) till it was popularised by Geoffrey of Monmouth – believed to be a Breton whose family had moved from Brittany to Wales – in his fanciful *History of the Kings of Britain* (*Historia Regum Britanniae*) of 1136. It would seem likely that the recent Norman conquest had stimulated an interest in British history, especially given the link between the Normans and the Bretons (who fought at Hastings alongside William, himself possibly part-Breton through his mother) and the fact that neither group was Anglo-Saxon and may have found it timely and useful to promote a non-Saxon hero.

But this is not to claim categorically – unlike some scholars[3] – that Arthur was nothing but a creation. Certainly there is much that is fanciful in the Arthurian legends, but that does not mean there is not at core an element of actuality. It is always much harder (if not impossible) to prove the non-existence of something, and indeed, as mentioned in Part 1, archaeologists have a saying that 'absence of evidence is not evidence of absence'.[4] Personally I do believe on balance – though admittedly not with immovable conviction – that there probably was an actual figure called Arthur, who was an effective warrior. However, proving that with absolute certainty is something that no one has yet been able to achieve, despite innumerable books claiming to do so,[5] and I am certainly not going to attempt anything like that in this brief discussion of him. Doubts have been expressed about Arthur's historicity for centuries, even during the popularity of the legend in the Middle Ages. This is acknowledged, for example, by the printer William Caxton, though himself a believer in Arthur, in his *Preface* to his 1485 edition of Thomas Malory's 1469 romance *Le Morte D'Arthur* (*The Death of Arthur*):

> Divers men hold opinion that there was no such Arthur, and that all such books as be made of him be but feigned and fables, by cause that some chronicles make of him no mention nor remember him no thing, nor of his knights.[6]

Many of the elements of the Arthurian legends are clearly post-Galfridian (post-Geoffrey, Latin name Galfridus Monemutensis) and some from the continent. Chrétien de Troyes, writing in the late twelfth century, can be credited with a number of them. For example, he was the first to introduce Lancelot, and his romance with Guinevere; and he was also the first to introduce Camelot, and the Holy Grail.[7] He was partly inspired by Wace's modified translation in 1155 of Geoffrey's work as *Roman de Brut* (*The Story of Brutus*), Wace for his own part introducing the idea of the Round Table in this work. Geoffrey was the first to introduce Merlin, and Avalon, and Excalibur (as Caliburn). It is sometimes said that Geoffrey also introduced Guinevere as Arthur's wife, but there are in fact references in seemingly earlier Welsh legends (see below) to Arthur's wife being Gwenhwyfar.[8]

Pre-Galfridian mentions of Arthur are fewer, and very much so in the case of contemporary or near-contemporary sources. Arthur is first mentioned in the *Gododdin* (*Y Gododdin*), allegedly first written around 600 and attributed to the poet Aneirin, though the manuscripts available are from the thirteenth century. This tells of the Gododdin (Votadini) warriors of present-day south-east Scotland in a battle against the Angles believed to have taken place in the mid sixth century at what is now Catterick, and makes a reference to Arthur not as a warrior present at the battle but as a kind of measure of valiance – or more particularly, of ability to slay the enemy ('feed the crows'), for it refers to a warrior called Gorddur who could 'bring black crows down' in defending his town – 'though he was not Arthur'.[9] That is, Arthur is seen as a great warrior few – even the foe-slaying Gorddur – could hope to emulate.

Arthur appears in a number of ancient Welsh legends, notably 'Culhwch and Olwen' and others included in the *Mabinogion* collection,[10] but these were seemingly written down in the tenth and eleventh centuries and one cannot be precise about their date or origin. The Arthur in these Welsh legends, which at times are very clearly fanciful, does not come across as a particularly exemplary figure, which in my view does tend to suggest some degree of actuality at core, though not a few scholars treat the collection as myth. It is worth noting that just a few years before Geoffrey, William of Malmesbury, a respected historian and clearly a believer in a real Arthur and indeed an admirer, wrote in his *Chronicle of the Kings of England* (*Gesta Regum Anglorum*) of 1125, that Arthur deserved better treatment than the nonsense in the legends:

> It is of this Arthur that the Britons tell so many fables, even to the present day; a man worthy to be celebrated, not by idle fictions, but by authentic history. He long upheld the sinking state, and roused the broken spirit of his countrymen to war.[11]

Question marks regarding date of writing also apply to two very brief references to Arthur in the *Annals of Wales* (*Annales Cambriae*), 516 (Battle of Badon) and 537 (death in battle with Medraut/Mordred),[12] for the annals in the form which we have them today were not written down till the mid tenth century, even though they are based on material of which some is believed to have been written much earlier. This again raises problems as to when exactly the Arthur-related entries were made. Moreover, some scholars would argue that the two dates are 15–20 years too late.[13]

The British cleric Gildas, our best contemporary or near-contemporary source and accepted by most scholars as living in the early-mid sixth century, does not mention Arthur – at least by name[14] – and this omission in itself seems rather odd if Arthur was an actual person of heroic status who was alive in Gildas's own lifetime, especially as Gildas does mention the Battle of Badon. Just a sentence or two before the reference to the battle, Gildas refers to Ambrosius Aurelianus leading an armed uprising by the Britons, and this has led some scholars to believe that Gildas may have intended to indicate Ambrosius as the victor at Badon.[15] One explanation given for Gildas's silence regarding Arthur is a reference in the *Life of Gildas* (c. 1130–50), by Caradoc of Llangarfan, to an elder brother of Gildas, named Hueil, being killed by Arthur.[16] Though Caradoc says Gildas was courteous to Arthur and forgave him, if the story is true – and we should note in this regard that Gildas and the fiery Hueil are referred to as princely brothers in 'Culhwch and Olwen', and there is a reference as well to a feud between Arthur and Hueil[17] – Gildas may have preferred to omit Arthur because of painful associations or indeed enmity towards him. Another oft-heard explanation is that Arthur was so well known there was no need to mention him by name.

Neither Bede nor the *Anglo-Saxon Chronicle* mention Arthur either, an omission often explained by the argument that the Anglo-Saxons would not want to acknowledge a hero of British resistance. That could be true, but a counter-argument could also be made that by recognising a British hero the Anglo-Saxon achievement would become all the more meritorious. One also has the feeling that Bede, a priest-scholar relatively well respected by present-day historians, would have made some mention of Arthur if he knew about him. Does this mean Arthur did not exist, or was it indeed simply that Bede knew nothing of him – as Barber and Pykitt suggest[18] – or that he omitted him for some other reason? Unfortunately, we will probably never find out.

One major, if controversial, source for Arthur is the British cleric 'Nennius', writing in the early ninth century – or more accurately, an author who was in a much later version named as Nennius. We should note from the outset that some scholars, such as Nick Higham,[19] feel strongly that this text attributed to Nennius is a heavily politicised work intended *inter alia* to rouse British nationalism – in almost certainly deliberate contrast to the Anglo-Saxon Bede's portrayal of the British as deserving of invasion by a superior people (i.e. God's chosen Anglo-Saxons), and similarly to counter-balance Gildas's negative portrayal of Britons as weak and sinful and punished by God through the heathen Anglo-Saxons. That is, these various views, all supposedly representing God's will, can be seen as contested providential history.

And of course, for 'Nennius' to achieve his aim it was necessary to find a symbolically suitable hero-figure, even perhaps if that hero had to be created. Section 56 (50 in some manuscripts) of his *History of the Britons* contains a list of 12 battles Arthur is supposed to have fought, all successfully, the last being Badon.[20] They have been the subject of much debate as to their location, for the names used are susceptible of various spellings and interpretations, and in some cases their historicity has been questioned,[21] but there would at least seem to be broad agreement that they are spread around the country, ranging from the far southwest to the far north. Badon is the most accepted of these battles in terms of historicity, its location said by many to be near Bath, though Oliver Padel prefers Badbury Rings near Wimbourne Minster in Dorset.[22]

There are two further points to note about 'Nennius' in the same section. The first is that he names Arthur as *dux bellorum* – 'battle leader', not king – and the second is that Arthur is described as fighting 'alongside the kings of Britain': *Tunc Arthur pugnabat contra illos in illis deibus cum regibus Brittonum, sed ipse dux erat bellorum.* This second point can be taken simply as following on from the first point, namely that Arthur was not actually king (at least at that stage), or it can be taken to mean that he was king but also *dux bellorum* and that he commanded the other kings of Britain when they fought alongside him, or it can be taken to mean that Arthur was not British. This last interpretation has led to various theories that he was Pictish (though Picts are now known to be early-arriving Celts), or perhaps a foreign mercenary.

In fact, theories about Arthur's identity are legion, closely followed by theories about his base, Camelot – and of course theories about all the other elements associated with him. I will not dwell in detail on these matters, but merely indicate below a range of 'theorised identities' and make a comment on Camelot. Regarding the other elements, I would simply observe that while some are obviously fanciful, others seem to have a stronger claim to core authenticity. Casting a sword into a lake, for example, was an actual practice among British warriors.[23] And Merlin, as another example, could well be based on a real person, though whether or not such a person was in reality linked to Arthur (assuming for argument's sake Arthur too was real) is another matter.[24]

Regarding Camelot, suggested sites (in no particular order) have included Tintagel in Cornwall, South Cadbury/Cadbury Castle in Somerset, Winchester in Hampshire, Colchester in Essex, the vicinity of Caerleon in Newport, Wroxeter (Viroconium) in Shropshire, and Roxburgh near Kelso in Scotland.[25] My own view is that Arthur (if he existed) was clearly very mobile, and so from a military perspective it would make sense for him to have multiple bases, deep enough within British territory to be reasonably secure in his absence. In fact, it would be remiss of him not to. In having multiple bases, he would be following Roman practice. It might well be true that a specific Camelot did exist and that it might have been his main base, but focusing too much on that risks overlooking the military likelihood that he frequently moved around British territory, with his elite cavalry at least, between bases even when not intending to engage in battle. Thus some or all of the above sites might be valid to some extent – though I personally cannot envisage Colchester, despite its old name of Camulodunum being close to and possibly inspirational of the name 'Camelot'. If for argument's sake one had to identify a main base for Arthur, again from

Figure A.1 The steep defensive banks and ditches of the Iron Age hill fort at South Cadbury, Somerset, felt by many scholars to have been a base for King Arthur.

Figure A.2 Tintagel, long believed to have been a special place for King Arthur. 'Merlin's Cave' is visible at the bottom right. You have to be physically quite fit to tackle the steep climbs.

a military perspective it would make logistical sense for it to be in the centre of British territory, i.e. Wales and not the southwest or the far north. However, choice of main base may have been affected by wherever his 'home territory' was. In any event, I repeat that I most favour the idea of multiple bases.[26]

Regarding Arthur's identity (and again in no particular order), theories have included Riothamus (a fifth century warrior who campaigned in Brittany), Athrwys ap Meurig (a king from Gwent, though usually associated with the seventh century), Owain Ddantgwyn ('Owain White Teeth', a fifth century king from Rhos or Powys or arguably Gwynedd), Ambrosius Aurelianus (a fifth century Romano-British military leader: see Part 2), and Lucius Artorius Castus, apparently a late fifth century descendant and namesake of the Roman commander responsible for bringing the Sarmatian forces to Hadrian's Wall in the late second century.[27] Of course, there is a view that Arthur was simply himself in his own right – that is, he was Arthur, that this was his name and identity, and there is no need to seek some alias. And, conversely, there is a view that Arthur was nobody except a fictitious figure.

It would seem clear that Arthur has acquired many accretions, some from actual historical figures, some from myth, and that he has become a composite even though he may at core be real. It is possible that one day the issue will be resolved for good, but more likely such a day will never eventuate. He remains, in the public consciousness at least, a light looming large in the so-called Dark Ages, and perhaps we would not really welcome the extinguishing of that light, either by exposure as complete myth, or by reduction to mundane actuality. Literary research on the one hand, and studies into bicamerality of the brain on the other, have shown that humans seem to have a need in their lives for both *logos* and *mythos*. *Logos* represents 'fact'-based rationality and reasoning and belongs within the world as humans have constructed it, whereas *mythos* represents a more emotional need for imaginative identification with the natural and indeed supernatural world – an escape, as it were, from grey reality to the bright colours of the dreamworld. Whether Arthur is fact or myth, he is important to us one way or another.

Appendix 2

Timeline of Major Events in Early British History

55 BC	Julius Caesar's first expedition
54 BC	Julius Caesar's second expedition
AD 43	Claudius's invasion
47	Partial revolt against Romans
51	Cartimandua betrays Caratacus
60	Boudica's revolt
c. 83	Agricola defeats Calgacus at Mons Graupius
c. 122	Hadrian's Wall commenced to guard against Pictish raids
c. 142	Antonine Wall commenced
306	Constantine I becomes emperor and presently promotes Christianity, some Britons convert, especially among upper class
360s	Particularly intense Pictish raids
Late fourth century	Anglo-Saxon raids commence (possibly earlier)
383	British-based Maximus becomes emperor, takes many men overseas
407	British-based Constantine III becomes emperor, takes more men overseas
410	Rome sacked, formal end of Roman presence in Britain
Early fifth century	Intensification of raids by Anglo-Saxons and especially Picts
Mid fifth century	Vortigern employs Anglo-Saxons as defenders, start of 'Saxon Advent'
Late fifth century	Anglo-Saxons arrive in number, with aggressive/expansive intent, many Britons displaced from southeast
c. 500	Britons defeat Anglo-Saxons at Badon Hill, bringing period of peace

Mid sixth century	Anglo-Saxon expansion recommences, Britons pushed to 'outer' areas, with Anglo-Saxon territory forming core of 'Aenglaland'
c. 600	Anglo-Saxon overlord Aethelberht becomes Christian, inspires others, establishes first archbishopric of Canterbury
Seventh century	Spread of Christianity among Anglo-Saxons; entrenchment of Anglo-Saxon dominance; firming up of kingdoms, but much strife between them despite informal unity under overlords
Eighth century	Mercia the dominant kingdom under Aethelbald and then Offa, with Aethelred of Northumbria also a very powerful figure in last quarter
789	First Viking assault, at Portland, though relatively minor
793	First major Viking raid, on Lindisfarne
Early ninth century	Vikings concentrate on Ireland and continent rather than England; Wessex becomes dominant kingdom under Egbert and Aethelwulf
Mid ninth century	Viking raids on England recommence
865	Viking Great Army arrives, sustained raids and land acquisition
871	Alfred becomes king of Wessex; Viking reinforcements arrive
878	Wessex left as only kingdom to resist Vikings, Alfred defeats Guthrum, presses Christianity upon him
886	Alfred takes London, country split with 'Danelaw' in east and north
Late ninth century	Wessex and Mercia ally against continued Viking aggression
Early tenth century	Aethelflaed of Mercia and Edward of Wessex push Vikings back and substantially reclaim Danelaw
937	Athelstan consolidates Wessex/English dominance at Brunanburh with victory over combined force of Vikings and Scots
Mid tenth century	England effectively a united nation and in relative peace, especially under Edgar the 'Peaceable'
980	Viking attacks resume in 'Second Wave', during reign of the then child-king Aethelred the 'Unready'
991	Vikings defeat Byrhtnoth at Maldon, payments to Vikings restart
1002	Aethelred orders extermination of Danes in England
1003	Swein Forkbeard leads major Viking attack

1009	English fleet substantially damaged by (the Englishman) Wulfnoth, Thorkell leads another major Viking attack
1012	Thorkell enters Aethelred's employ
1013	Swein re-attacks England, and is acknowledged by many as king, Aethelred flees to Normandy
1014	Swein dies, leaving son Cnut in charge of England; Aethelred returns (on condition of better behaviour) and forces Cnut to leave
1015	Cnut returns with invasive intent
1016	Aethelred dies, son Edmund 'Ironside' succeeds, fights against Cnut, loses at Assandun, agrees to divide kingdom, dies just weeks later, leaving Cnut as sole king
1035	Cnut dies, his son Harold 'Harefoot' succeeds
1036	Aethelred's son Alfred tries to claim throne, but is brutally murdered, allegedly by Earl Godwine
1040	Harefoot dies, brother Harthacnut succeeds
1042	Harthacnut dies, Aethelred's son Edward the 'Confessor' (Harthacnut's half-brother) invited to assume throne
1051	Childless Edward allegedly promises throne to William of Normandy, Earl Godwine and his sons go into exile
1052	Godwine and his family successfully return
1053	Godwine dies; son Harold becomes Earl of Wessex and most powerful magnate
1064	Harold makes mysterious visit to continent, ends up swearing allegiance to William regarding claim to throne
1065	Harold's brother Tostig, Earl of Northumbria, forced into exile by revolt, civil war narrowly avoided, Harold declines to help him
1066 (Jan)	Edward dies, Harold takes crown, apparently designated by dying Edward; William protests in vain, starts planning invasion
1066 (May)	Tostig harries south and east coast; Harold calls out *fyrd* and fleet
1066 (Sept)	Harold stands down *fyrd* and fleet (8th); William's assembled fleet apparently sets out for England from Dives (12th), but is driven by storms to St Valery, and kept there by adverse winds; Tostig and Norwegian ally Hardraada land in northeast (c. 16th) and defeat earls Edwin and Morcar at Fulford (20th); Harold hurries north, gathering men *en route*, catches them by surprise, defeats and kills them at Stamford Bridge (25th); just days afterwards William lands at Pevensey/Hastings (28th)

1066 (Oct)	Harold hears of William's arrival and hurries back south, waits a few days in London (c. 6th–c. 11th) to gather troops, then sets off to Hastings, arriving late 13th/early 14th; William advances on Harold, battle follows, Harold killed and English defeated (14th), William moves out from Hastings towards London, taking towns *en route*
1066 (late Oct)	Edgar declared King-Elect, but soon submits
1066 (Dec)	William crowned King William I of England (Christmas Day)
1068	Harold's mother and some of his sons put up resistance at Exeter but flee to Ireland, from where they make unsuccessful attempts to regain England over the next few years before going to Denmark
1069–70	Swein of Denmark (Harold's cousin) attacks in northeast but returns to Denmark, seemingly bought off by William
1070	William severely harries the north as punishment for resistance
c. 1071	Edwin and Morcar perish after attempted resistance
1085	Major Danish invasion of England planned by Swein's son Cnut, but aborted
1087	William dies and is succeeded in England by his son William Rufus

Appendix 3

Chronology of Kings and Overlords of England from the Anglo-Saxon Advent to the Norman Conquest

Please note that I have included some early regional kings who were arguably the major power-holders in the country at the time, even though they were not formally termed *bretwaldas* (overlords). In some cases reigns overlapped. From Athelstan on, I have put regional associations in brackets, since they were widely and more formally recognised as national kings (though some scholars would argue it should be from Alfred, or Edward the Elder, or Edgar).

Vortigern of the Britons	mid fifth century?
Ambrosius of the Britons	mid-late fifth century?
Arthur of the Britons?	late fifth–early sixth century?
Aelle of Sussex	488–c. 514?
Cerdic of Wessex?	early-mid sixth century
Ceawlin of Sussex	560–91
Aethelberht of Kent	591–c. 616
Raedwald of East Anglia	616–27
Edwin of Deira	617–33
Oswald of Bernicia	633–41
Oswy of Northumbria	641–58
Wulfhere of Mercia	658–75
Ecgfrith of Northumbria	670–85
Caedwalla of Wessex	685–8
Ine of Wessex	688–726
Aethelbald of Mercia	716–57
Offa of Mercia	757–96
Aethelred of Northumbria	774–c. 779 (first reign)
Aelfwald of Northumbria	c. 779–90
Aethelred of Northumbria	790–c. 796 (second reign)
Ecgfrith of Mercia	796 (141 days)
Coenwulf of Mercia	796–821

Egbert of Wessex	802–39
Aethelwulf of Wessex	839–58
Aethelbald of Wessex	856–60
Aethelberht of Wessex	860–5
Aethelred I of Wessex	865–71
Alfred of Wessex and the 'English'	871–99
Edward the Elder of Wessex	899–924
Athelstan (Wessex)	924–39
Edmund I (Wessex)	939–46
Eadred (Wessex)	946–55
Eadwig (Wessex)	955–9
Edgar the Peaceable (Wessex)	959–75
Edward the Martyr (Wessex)	975–8
Aethelred II Unraed (Wessex)	978–1016
Swein Forkbeard (Denmark)	1013–14 (25 Dec.–3 Feb.)
Edmund II Ironside (Wessex)	1016 (23 Apr.–30 Nov.)
Cnut (Denmark)	1016–35
Harold I Harefoot (Denmark)	1035–40
Harthacnut (Denmark)	1040–2
Edward the Confessor (Wessex)	1042–66
Harold II Godwineson (Wessex)	1066 (6 Jan.–14 Oct.)
Edgar the King Elect (Wessex)	1066 (late Oct.–25 Dec.)
William I Conqueror (Normandy)	1066–87

Notes

Introduction

1. See Tuchman (1984), esp. pp. 5, 25, 33.
2. Durschmied (1999), p. xv.
3. William of Malmesbury, *History of English Kings*, Clarendon edition, I, 3, pp. 18–19.

1 The Roman Eagle Lands

1. Suetonius, *Lives*, 'Claudius', Section 3, Gavorse edition p. 209. Moreover, according to Suetonius (also p. 209), his grandmother too 'treated him with the utmost contempt'.
2. See *Vindolanda Tablets Online*, http://vindolanda.csad.ox.ac.uk/.
3. Webster and Dudley (1973), p. 3. The great majority of Greek and Roman geographers fixed the limits of the habitable world at the Ocean's edge, meaning that in their opinion Britain – moreover an inhabited Britain – simply shouldn't have existed and was viewed with considerable trepidation.
4. Suetonius, *Lives*, 'Julius Caesar', 47, Gavorse edition p. 28.
5. Julius Caesar, *Gallic War*, Book IV, Section 20: 'Caesar resolved to proceed into Britain because he discovered that in almost all the wars with the Gauls succours had been furnished to our enemy from that country'.
6. Caesar, *Gallic War*, V, 12: 'The interior portion of Britain is inhabited by those ... born in the island itself; the maritime portion by those who had passed over from the country of the Belgae [Belgium] for the purpose of plunder and making war ... and having waged war, continued there and began to cultivate the lands'. Some of the more recent arrivals may perhaps have been fleeing from the Romans in Gaul.
7. Caesar, *Gallic War*, IV, 21.
8. Caesar, *Gallic War*, IV, 23.
9. John Wacher points out (Wacher 1979, p. 2) that although the shingle beach as it appears now would seem a poor place for a landing, for which Caesar has been criticised by some, given the changing nature of coastlines it may well have been a more suitable sandy beach at the time. Sheppard Frere (Frere 1987, p. 19) nonetheless feels that any open beach was not good, certainly in terms of shelter, and finds it surprising that neither Volusenus nor Caesar appears to have found what must have been relatively sheltered and better anchorage around the mouth of the Stour, another seven miles or so to the north (as seemingly used later in the Claudian invasion). However, T. Rice Holmes (Rice Holmes 1907, pp. 310–11) believes Volusenus was deliberately seeking an open beach with level access to the interior in order to avoid ceding high ground to the enemy. As a more generalised comment, Peter Salway (Salway 1993, p. 21) remarks that lack of information about the coastal conditions proved almost 'fatal'. My own view is similar to Frere's.
10. Caesar, *Gallic War*, IV, 24.
11. Salway (1993), p. 22.
12. Ellis (1978), p. 89, remarks that this was through Caesar's ignorance of such matters.

13. The *catapulta* (plural *catapultae*) was a machine that could hurl a heavy javelin as far as 1000 yards. See Ellis (1978), pp. 89–90.

14. Caesar, *Gallic War*, IV, 25. The origin of the eagle as the well known standard of Rome is not fully clear, but by the first century BC it had emerged as the favourite of five creatures used as standards: the eagle, wolf, minotaur, horse, and boar. Gavorse (1931), p. 35, n. 1, comments that 'the principal standard was a silver eagle with outspread wings and clutching a golden thunderbolt in its claw. . . . In camp it stood in a little shrine'.

15. See for example Suetonius, *Lives*, 65–70, Gavorse edition pp. 36–9. Suetonius refers, *inter alia*, to Caesar's use of the friendly term 'comrades' when addressing his men (67), or sometimes 'citizens' (70), how he had earned the devotion of his men (68), how they never mutinied during the ten years of the Gallic War (69), and how a lot of his men followed him voluntarily even after discharge (70).

16. Caesar, *Gallic War*, IV, 28.

17. Rice Holmes (1907), p. 320: 'Caesar's officers and, it would seem, Caesar himself were ignorant of the connexion between tide and moon'. Caesar himself (*Gallic War*, IV, 29) states that 'the circumstance was unknown to our men'.

18. Caesar, *Gallic War*, IV, 29.

19. He did at some point send a vessel back to the continent with a request for provisions to be sent, but details are unclear. It seems highly unlikely that the requested provisions arrived.

20. Caesar, *Gallic War*, IV, 33. Caesar gives quite a detailed account of chariot fighting in this section and was clearly very impressed by the efficacy and skill of their drivers. Contrary to popular belief, the chariots do not appear to have had scythes on the axles, which would surely have been as dangerous to one's own men as to the enemy in the mêlée of battle. However, that is not to deny the possibility that under certain circumstances some chariots may have had them fitted, despite the apparent danger, and there are indeed several near-contemporary references to them, though not in accounts by actual campaigners. For example, the first century AD poet Lucan, in lines 483–5 of his epic poem *Pharsalia*, refers to their having been in use in earlier days on the continent, by the Belgae, and moreover seemingly in battle. Lucan's contemporary Pomponius Mela, in his *De Chorographia* III, 6, 52, refers specifically to Britons also using them in battle: see Ireland (1986), p. 34. A third contemporary, Silius Italicus, also refers (in his *Punica*) to scythed chariots in Thule (Britain). Ireland (p. 34) dismisses the British use of scythes as 'fallacious', but accepts their use in Persia. Antonia Fraser (1999), p. 3, writing of Boudica, emphatically asserts that Boudica's chariot did not have scythes, but, while she may well be right, she offers no evidence for such a strong view. See also Knightly (1982), p. 12, for a more accommodating view.

21. Caesar, *Gallic War*, IV, 32, and Dio, *Histories*, XXXIX, Loeb Classical Library Edition vol. III, p. 385.

22. Rice Holmes (1907), p. 324.

23. Caesar, *Gallic War*, IV, 34.

24. Caesar, *Gallic War*, IV, 34.

25. Commius had thereby seemingly shown his allegiance lay with Caesar, though in practice he seems to have had a foot in both camps and is one of history's more elusive characters.

26. Webster (1993), p. 35.

27. Frere (1987), pp. 20–1.

28. Rice Holmes (1907), p. 323.

29. Rice Holmes, (1907), p. 316.
30. Ellis (1978), p. 84.
31. Peddie (1987), pp. 4, 9.
32. Dio, *Histories*, XXXIX, Loeb Edition vol. III, p. 387.
33. Suetonius, *Lives*, 'Julius Caesar', 58, Gavorse edition p. 34.
34. Salway (1993), p. 18.
35. Caesar, *Gallic War*, IV, 26 (and accompanying annotation). See also, for example, Suetonius, *Lives*, 'Julius Caesar', 25, Gavorse edition p. 16.
36. With the exception of the Seventh, the legions are not named. However, Caesar would almost certainly have taken the Tenth, both because it was his favourite legion and also, like the Seventh, it had experienced Britain the previous year. We also know from the name of a particular commander that the Fourteenth was almost certainly present. The other two legions, however, remain unclear.
37. Dio, *Histories*, XL, Loeb Edition vol. III, p. 409.
38. Caesar, *Gallic War*, V, 8. Caesar refers to being carried off course and having to rely on the oarsmen to make the same landing site he had used the summer before and thought 'the best landing-place'.
39. Caesar, *Gallic War*, V, 9: 'He [Caesar] discovered from the prisoners in what part the forces of the enemy had lodged themselves'.
40. Caesar states (*Gallic War*, V, 20) that Cassivellaunus had killed Mandubratius's father, who had been king of the Trinovantes.
41. Ellis (1978), p. 103.
42. Caesar, *Gallic War*, V, 9.
43. Caesar, *Gallic War*, V, 10.
44. Rice Holmes (1907), pp. 338–9.
45. Caesar, *Gallic War*, V, 11. The ten-day labour of the soldiers is generally taken to apply to the building of the fortification, though it may have included reference to their working on the ship repairs as well.
46. Caesar, *Gallic War*, V, 11.
47. Caesar, *Gallic War*, V, 16.
48. Caesar, *Gallic War*, V, 16.
49. Caesar, *Gallic War*, V, 17.
50. Caesar, *Gallic War*, V, 18.
51. Caesar, *Gallic War*, V, 18–19. It is remotely possible that one of the reasons for the Britons' flight was the terrifying sight of an elephant, which Caesar may have brought with him or had sent for from Gaul. The Greek Polyaenus, writing c. 163, refers in his *Stratagems* (Strategica, VIII, 23, 5) to the use of an elephant in Caesar's campaign in Britain, specifically at the crossing of a great river and causing Cassivellaunus and his chariots to flee in panic. However, the reference is usually treated as a confusion with Claudius's campaign of AD 43, when elephants definitely were present. This matter is discussed further in Section 1.6.
52. Rice Holmes (1907), p. 346, entertains the same thought.
53. Caesar, *Gallic War*, V, 19.
54. It is also possible, though less likely, that Caesar had an advance force swim across some way away from the battlefield and then attack the Britons at the ford from the flank, though one imagines that the Britons would have tracked any such flanking and that Caesar would have realised the risk of having that advance flanking force isolated and picked off.
55. Caesar, *Gallic War*, V, 20.

56. Caesar, *Gallic War*, V, 21.
57. Ellis (1978), p. 134. Caesar himself seems to have returned briefly to his ships around this time, but exact timing and other details are unclear. He did not participate in their defence.
58. Caesar, *Gallic War*, V, 22.
59. Caesar, *Gallic War*, V, 22.
60. Caesar, *Gallic War*, V, 23: 'When he had received the hostages he led back the army to the sea.'
61. Ellis (1978), p. 135.
62. Salway (1984), p. 37.
63. Caesar, *Gallic War*, V, 23.
64. The best-known example is probably the slaughter in 52 BC of virtually the entire population of 40,000 men, women, and children of the town of Avaricum (present-day Bourges) following his successful breach of its defences after a month-long siege. Caesar apparently sanctioned this slaughter – which earned him considerable criticism back in Rome, and from not a few present-day historians – partly to relieve his men's feelings of frustration over the length of the siege and other military setbacks, and partly to set an example of the price of resistance.
65. Suetonius, *Lives*, 'Julius Caesar', 25, Gavorse edition, p. 16.
66. The Wordsworth edition, 'Julius Caesar', Section 25, has the similarly strong term 'utterly conquered'.
67. Webster (1993), pp. 35–6.
68. Webster (1993), p. 35.
69. Tacitus, *Agricola*, 13. His comments relate to Caesar's overall campaign against the Britons, not just the first expedition.
70. Salway (1984), p. 38.
71. Tacitus, *Agricola*, 12.
72. Creighton (2006), p. 16.
73. Caesar, *Gallic War*, VII, 76.
74. Cunliffe (2003), p. 84.
75. See, for example, Pryor (2005), pp. 8–9.
76. Sykes (2006), pp. 279–284. See also Pryor (2005), Chapter 1.
77. Sykes (2006), p. 282, argues that there is no fundamental genetic difference between Pict and Celt. The Picts have long been the least understood people of Britain. Hugh Kearney (1995), p. 37, for example, feels that Pictish culture is a major unsolved issue and that it is still obscure. Steel (1985), p. 25, is of the view that they are indeed early-arriving Celts but that we know little about them, adding that Fife (between the Firth and the Tay), where there is a strong Pict presence, is still thought of as an almost independent territory. Certain other scholars, such as Redknap (1996), pp. 754, 769, believe the Picts to be a mixture of Britons and earlier non-Celtic peoples and thus only part-Celtic.
78. Caesar, *Gallic War*, I, 1.
79. Green (1996b), p. 6, remarks on the ethnic flexibilities within the Celtic grouping.
80. See, for example, Diodorus, *Library of History*, V, 26, regarding drunkenness, and the following quotation from Strabo regarding readiness to fight.
81. Strabo, *Geography*, 4.4.2.
82. Strabo, *Geography*, 4.4.5.
83. Polybius, *Histories*, III, 70, and see also 78: 'the fickleness of the Celts'.
84. Diodorus, *Library of History*, V, 21. Diodorus is believed to have drawn heavily on the now largely lost writings of the fourth century BC Greek explorer Pytheas (born in

Marseilles), who explored the Atlantic coast of Europe around 320 BC, and appears to have circumnavigated the isles of Britain. His comments might therefore apply to Britons some centuries before Caesar. Caesar himself was familiar with Pytheas.

85. See, for example, Cunliffe (2003), pp. 85–6.
86. Caesar, *Gallic War*, V, 12: 'The number of the people is countless and their buildings exceedingly numerous'.
87. See Wild (1985), p. 32, for 5 million; Frere (1987), p. 6, for 1 million; and Pryor (2005), p. 50, for 1.5–2.5 million.
88. Frere (1987), p. 4.
89. Ellis (1978), p. 26. See also Pryor (2005), p. 50, regarding cleared forests and farming settlements.
90. Millett (1985), p. 37.
91. *Times* release, my source *The Press* (Christchurch), 4 August 2006. The excavations were in 2003 at Clonycavan, Ireland, and the bodies dated as 2300 years old, with gel made from pine resin and plant oil that came only from southwestern France or Spain.
92. There appears to be some diversity of opinion on this issue. Ellis (1978), p. 27, for example, an expert on Celts, refers to a Celtic aversion to slavery, yet there is evidence of it happening on a reasonably significant scale, and some scholars refer to inter-tribal raids to obtain slaves – see, for example, Salway (1993), p. 29. Contrasting slavery in Britain with that of Rome, Kearney (1995), p. 29, remarks that slavery existed in the tribal societies of the pre-Roman period [in Britain] but that it was not a central institution. In Ireland, however, slavery seems to have been deeply institutionalised. Timothy Champion (1996), pp. 90–1, writes of Ireland that there were slaves who seem to have been regarded as chattels with no legal rights, and that slavery was indeed of considerable economic importance, with an early value system using female slaves as units.
93. Ellis (1978), pp. 27–8.
94. Caesar, *Gallic War*, V, 14.
95. Ellis (1978), p. 44.
96. For example, *Caesar: Invasion of Britain*, by Welch, W., and Duffield, C., Elementary Classics Series, Macmillan, 1919.
97. Ellis (1978), p. 41.
98. Strabo, *Geography*, 4.4.6.
99. See for example Aldhouse-Green (2006), pp. 102–3.
100. In discussion of military equipment I largely follow Cunliffe (1997), pp. 93–104.
101. Cunliffe (1997), p. 94. I would add that the same was also true of Anglo-Saxons later. This is puzzling given the efficacy of ranged weapons, especially in guerilla warfare, and especially since a bowman could carry far more missiles than could carriers of spears and javelins.
102. Polybius (*Histories*, III, 114), for example, refers to Celts fighting naked alongside unarmoured but clothed Spaniards: 'the Gauls naked and the Spaniards in short tunics'.
103. Cunliffe (1997), p. 99. See also Webster (1993), p. 28, who feels rather that the Celts disliked being encumbered by armour, and relied on the magic of their woad.
104. Knightly (1982), pp. 11–12. There are some obvious exceptions to this.
105. Cunliffe (1997), p. 103.
106. *Vindolanda Tablets*, Tablet 164, Inventory Number 85.032.a.
107. Wacher (1979), p. 44.

108. There is some difference of opinion as to whether Druidism was spread throughout the entire 'Celtic' world or confined to a few countries, notably Britain and Gaul. The noted authority Peter Ellis is of the former view. See Ellis (1995), p. 46.

109. This is virtually universal in animism, and is seen, for example, in proto-Shinto in Japan at around the same time, and in New Zealand Maori beliefs even today.

110. Wait, (1996), p. 495, confirms that the Celts practised human sacrifice.

111. Caesar, *Gallic War*, VI, 16.

112. Strabo, *Geography*, 4.4.5.

113. Caesar, *Gallic War*, VI, 14: 'They wish to inculcate this as one of their leading tenets, that souls do not become extinct, but pass after death from one body to another, and they think that men by this tenet are in a great degree excited to valour, the fear of death being disregarded'.

114. Ellis (1995), p. 121.

115. Strabo, *Geography*, 4.4.5. Polybius, *Histories*, III, 67, also refers to the Celts' practice of decapitation.

116. Caesar, *Gallic War*, VI, 13.

117. Caesar, *Gallic War*, VI, 13.

118. Caesar, *Gallic War*, VI, 13: 'They assemble at a fixed period of the year in a consecrated place in the territories of the Carnutes, which is reckoned the central region of the whole of Gaul'.

119. Wacher (1979), pp. 45–6.

120. Salway (1993), p. 37.

121. Salway (1993), p. 38.

122. Salway (1993), pp. 38–9.

123. See, for example, Webster and Dudley (1973), p. 26.

124. Webster (1996), p. 629, observes that many tribes looked to Rome to protect them from their British oppressors.

125. Such persons were referred to as *obsides*, which is often translated as 'hostages'. Webster (1996), p. 628, remarks that the policy was developed by Augustus and was a requirement not a choice, and adds that the children were in effect hostages. See also Creighton (2006), p. 16.

126. Salway (1993), p. 30.

127. Caesar, *Gallic War*, VII, 75, 76, and 79.

128. Dio, *Histories*, Book XL, Loeb Edition vol. III, p. 471.

129. See Suetonius, *Lives*, 'Caligula', 44, Gavorse edition, p. 193, for 'King of the Britons'. However, it is also translatable as 'a British king', as in the Wordsworth edition, 'Caligula', Section 44.

130. Suetonius, *Lives*, 'Caligula', 44, Gavorse edition p. 193. Creighton (2006), p. 27, draws attention to the fact that Adminius's plight was the result of an internal dispute, not external aggression, and that this should be noted as a possible indicator that British tribes were not necessarily always fighting each other.

131. Suetonius, *Lives*, 'Caligula', 46, Gavorse edition p. 194.

132. For example, Grant (1985), p. 26.

133. Webster and Dudley (1973), p. 4.

134. See for example Suetonius, *Lives*, 'Claudius', 2, Gavorse edition pp. 208–9: 'The vigor of both his mind and his body was dulled, and even when he reached the proper age he was not thought capable of any public or private business'. His physical health did apparently improve in later years (30, p. 230). That he was an object of ridicule is also clear from Suetonius: among other abuses, 'they used also to put slippers on his hands as he lay snoring, so that when he was suddenly aroused he might rub his face with them' (8, p. 212).

135. Dio, *Histories*, LX, Loeb Edition vol. VII, p. 367.
136. Suetonius, *Lives*, 'Claudius', 10, Gavorse edition p. 213.
137. Dio, *Histories*, LX, Loeb Edition vol. VII, p. 415.
138. Orosius, *Seven Books of History*, VII, 6.
139. Dio, *Histories*, LX, Loeb Edition vol. VII, p. 415.
140. Salway (1993), p. 60.
141. Dio, *Histories*, LX, Loeb Edition vol. VII, p. 417.
142. For example, Peddie (1987), pp. 60–1, favours the former and Salway (1993), p. 62, the latter.
143. See for example Cunliffe (2002), and more particularly Manley (2002). On the other hand, such a view is by no means universally accepted. For example, writing in 2006, Miranda Aldhouse-Green remarks that 'Richborough appears to have been the principal landing base' (p. 40).
144. Dio, *Histories*, LX, Loeb Edition vol. VII, p. 417.
145. Unless stated otherwise, the following account draws on Dio, *Histories*, LX, Loeb Edition vol. VII, pp. 417–25.
146. Dio, *Histories*, LX, Loeb Edition vol. VII, p. 417.
147. Peddie (1987), p. 68.
148. Dio, *Histories*, LX, Loeb Edition vol. VII, p. 417.
149. Peddie (1987), p. 51.
150. Dio, *Histories*, LX, Loeb Edition vol. VII, p. 417.
151. Dio, *Histories*, LX, Loeb Edition vol. VII, p. 417. The closeness to the Ocean would seem very much to support the view that Richborough was the main landing site, as also the proximity of the Thames and Medway. Moreover, there would seem to be no really suitable 'first river' in the case of a Fishbourne landing.
152. Peddie (1987), p. 51. By now it would be very late indeed in the season, probably well into September.
153. Polyaenus, *Stratagems*, VIII, 23, 5, in Krentz and Wheeler (1994), vol. I, pp. 759–61. An excerpt is also to be found in Ireland (1986), p. 36, who explicitly treats the matter as a confusion with Claudius's campaign.
154. Aldhouse-Green (2006), p. 42.
155. Manley (2002), p. 61, feels it would have been no more than ten, and adds that he feels these would have been ready and waiting for him on the north bank of the Thames. He further adds (his note 9 on p. 151) that elephants can maintain a pace of over 3 mph over long distances.
156. Dio, *Histories*, LX, Loeb Edition vol. VII, p. 421.
157. Usually taken to indicate, at least as a first phase, land southeast of a diagonal line between the Exe and the Humber. The Brigantes' territory (technically a client kingdom) lay north of this, and was probably seen as a buffer zone against the hostile tribes of the far north, rather than a firm part of the Roman province.
158. Salway (1993), p. 64.
159. Suetonius, *Lives*, 'Claudius', 17, Gavorse edition p. 219.
160. Tacitus, *Annals*, XII, 36.
161. The battle is described by Tacitus, *Annals*, XII, 33–5. Caratacus had chosen a strong hilltop position defended by a river, and reinforced by ramparts, but was eventually defeated by the Roman testudo. Caer Caradog, near Knighton, is seen by some as a possible site.
162. Tacitus, *Annals*, XII, 36.
163. Peddie (1987), p. 170, shares this view.
164. Ireland (1986), p. 55.
165. Tacitus, *Annals*, XII, 36.

166. Tacitus, *Annals*, XII, 37.
167. Dio, *Histories*, LXI, Loeb Edition vol. VIII, p. 23.
168. Tacitus, *Histories*, III, 45.
169. Tacitus, *Annals*, XII, 40.
170. Tacitus, *Histories*, III, 45.
171. Tacitus, *Histories*, III, 45.
172. Webster (1996), p. 632, is of the view that only a section of the Iceni revolted.
173. In fact, the reference Tacitus makes to Boudica being of royal descent (Tacitus, *Annals*, XIV, 35) tends to suggest she married into the Iceni. However, if so, the tribe – or possibly sub-tribe – of her birth is not clear. Her name means 'Victory' (similar to the modern Victoria), but it is not known whether it is her birth-name or a later adopted name.
174. This is also the view of T. W. Potter: see Potter (2004), pp. 785–6. By contrast, Webster (1993) feels that Prasutagus was probably made king in AD 43 (p. 54) and retained his kingdom through the revolt of AD 47 since – as mentioned in the notes above – in Webster's view only a part of the Iceni revolted, and Prasutagus was presumably deemed not to have been involved (pp. 59–60). Fry (1978), p. 60, also believes that Prasutagus was indeed king at this stage, but that he probably did not take part in the fighting. Miranda Aldhouse-Green (2006), p. 22, and Paul Sealey (2004), p. 5, note that at the time of Claudius's invasion, and seemingly a little beyond that, the Icenian king (from AD 25) was Antedios. There also seems to have been another Iceni ruler named Esuprastus at around the same time, certainly from around AD 54 (see Sealey 2004, p. 10), and so it is possible that the Iceni were a tribal confederation (Aldhouse-Green 2006, p. 72), with Prasutagus perhaps an over-king (or sub-king?).
175. Fry (1978), pp. 58–9.
176. Tacitus, *Annals*, XII, 31.
177. Salway (1993), p. 74.
178. Tacitus, *Agricola*, 13.
179. The exact date is not absolutely clear, and some feel it may have been AD 61. The majority of scholars, however, opt for AD 60. See Frere (1987), p. 79, n. 37; and Salway (1993), p. 81.
180. See for example Suetonius, *Lives*, 'Claudius', 43, Gavorse edition p. 236; and see also Grant (1985), p. 33.
181. Suetonius, *Lives*, 'Nero', 18, Gavorse edition p. 251: 'So far from being actuated by any wish or hope of increasing or extending the empire, he even thought of withdrawing the army from Britain and changed his purpose only because he was ashamed to seem to belittle the glory of his [adoptive] father [Claudius]'. However, reasons for his initial idea of withdrawing are not given.
182. Robinson (2003), p. 27.
183. Tacitus, *Annals*, XIV, 31.
184. Dio, *Histories*, LXII, Loeb Edition vol. VIII, p. 83.
185. For Seneca, Dio, *Histories*, LXII, Loeb Edition vol. VIII, p. 83; for currency equivalence, Robinson (2003), p. 28; and Collingridge (2006), p. 191. Dio's Greek is ambiguous at this point: it is possible that Seneca gave his money to the Britons along with other earlier investors, but it is also possible that he might have supplied the sum at the Britons' request, that is, at a later stage, possibly in order for the Britons to pay back the sums given by earlier investors. In any event, he called in his loan quickly and seemingly to the Britons' surprise and dismay. See also Knightly (1982), pp. 34–5.

186. Salway (1993), p. 78; Liversidge (1973), p. 11.
187. Salway (1993), p. 78.
188. Tacitus, *Agricola*, 15.
189. Aldhouse-Green (2006), p. 68.
190. For example, Schama (2003), p. 33, remarks that Boudica herself had 'offered to share her realm with Nero'. He is far from alone in assuming she had regnant authority. Moreover, as discussed below, Boudica's husband, who did have such authority, left her in no legal position to offer anything.
191. Webster (1993), p. 87. See also Aldhouse-Green (2006), pp. 87, 178.
192. Tacitus, *Annals*, XIV, 31.
193. Aldhouse-Green (2006), p. 180, feels we can 'probably assume they were pubescent virgins'.
194. Webster (1993), pp. 87–8.
195. Aldhouse-Green (2006), pp. 87–8. Collingridge (2006), p. 189, makes a similar suggestion but does not elaborate.
196. Aldhouse-Green (2006), p. 88.
197. Tacitus, *Annals*, XIV, 31. Some translations state that they were actually 'made slaves', but subsequent translations favour 'treated like', which seems more likely. Curiously, especially given his apparent penchant for drama, Dio makes no such mention of the flogging and raping.
198. Aldhouse-Green (2006), p. 178.
199. Fraser (1999), p. 63, takes a similar view.
200. Aldhouse-Green (2006), p. 179.
201. Collingridge (2006), pp. 198–9.
202. Dio, *Histories*, LXII, Loeb Edition vol. VIII, pp. 83–5.
203. For a similar view see Collingridge (2006), p. 201, citing a conversation with the archaeologist Philip Crummy.
204. Again, Crummy shares this view: see Collingridge (2006), p. 201.
205. Dio, *Histories*, LXII, Loeb Edition vol. VIII, p. 93.
206. Collingridge (2006), p. 223, also estimates at most ten miles a day, as opposed to Roman soldiers making 25 miles a day, and that from Norfolk it would have taken around a week for her army to arrive at Camulodunum.
207. Dio, *Histories*, LXII, Loeb Edition vol. VIII, p. 85, refers to her 'army numbering some 120,000', but it is not clear whether he is referring to combatants only (though this would be unlikely). In any event, Dio is often felt to exaggerate.
208. Dio, *Histories*, LXII, Loeb Edition vol. VIII, pp. 85–9.
209. Dio, *Histories*, LXII, Loeb Edition vol. VIII, p. 91.
210. Dio, *Histories*, LXII, Loeb Edition vol. VIII, p. 85.
211. Dio, *Histories*, LXII, Loeb Edition vol. VIII, p. 85.
212. Dio, *Histories*, LXII, Loeb Edition vol. VIII, p. 83.
213. Tacitus, *Annals*, XIV, 29, suggests that his main reason for this expedition was to outdo a rival successful commander elsewhere in the Empire.
214. For example, Aldhouse-Green (2006), pp. 159–60.
215. It would seem that once the events triggering the revolt took place momentum developed quite fast, but it is possible – though in my view unlikely – that Boudica was aware of Paulinus's incursion into Wales and was able to delay her revolt to some extent till she could be sure he was 'safely' far away. Fraser (1999), p. 69, shares my scepticism regarding coordination.
216. Frere (1987), p. 70. See also Fry (1978), p. 4, who refers to Anglesey being a granary for Wales.

217. Imported grain – of a type not grown in Britain – was found in the burnt ruins of Londinium from that same year. See Collingridge (2006), pp. 236–7.
218. Tacitus, *Annals*, XIV, 30.
219. Tacitus, *Annals*, XIV, 30.
220. The boats would almost certainly have been made at shipyards in the estuary of the River Dee, near Chester. See Fry (1978), p. 4.
221. Tacitus, *Annals*, XIV, 30.
222. Tacitus, *Agricola*, 15: 'At last Heaven itself was taking pity on Britain: it was keeping the Roman general at a distance and his army in the seclusion of another island'.
223. Tacitus, *Annals*, XIV, 32.
224. Dio, *Histories*, LXII, Loeb Edition vol. VIII, p. 99; Tacitus, *Annals*, XIV, 32.
225. Tacitus, *Annals*, XIV, 32.
226. Tacitus, *Annals*, XIV, 32.
227. For example, the bronze head of a statue of Claudius, believed to be taken from Camulodunum, was found in the early twentieth century in the bed of the river Alde near Saxmundham in Suffolk. Even if not from Camulodunum itself, the fact it was crudely hacked off indicates deliberate rough destruction.
228. Tacitus, *Annals*, XIV, 32.
229. For example, Robinson (2003), p. 33; and Collingridge (2006), pp. 212–13.
230. Tacitus, *Annals*, XIV, 33. One should note his qualification 'it appears'. Robinson (2003), p. 38, also doubts this figure, and Collingridge (2006, p. 244) and Frere too (1987, p. 253) feel it is exaggerated. Dio, *Histories*, LXII, Loeb Edition vol. VIII, p. 83, gives an even higher figure of 80,000 overall total for those who 'perished', but curiously (and on several occasions) mentions only that 'two cities were sacked' and not three sites. He may have dismissed Londinium as technically not a city, or he may have dismissed Verulamium as British rather than Roman. Unfortunately he does not name any site in his account. However, it is apparent from his reference to betrayal that one of them was Camulodunum. The second, interestingly, he describes as 'abandoned'. See Dio, *Histories*, LXII, Loeb Edition vol. VIII, p. 99.
231. Tacitus, *Annals*, XIV, 33: Regarding assumption of comprehensive slaughter, see also, for example, Bennett (1984), p.11 and Frere (1987), p. 253, who appear explicitly to use Tacitus's figure of 70,000 to 'back-estimate' the sum population of the three sites – in fact, allowing for some exaggeration by Tacitus, they estimate a sum population somewhat fewer than 70,000. Both suggest Camulodunum had around 15,000, Londinium 30,000, and Verulamium 15,000 at the time of the revolt, giving a total of 60,000.
232. Collingridge (2006), p. 222.
233. Collingridge (2006), p. 223.
234. Collingridge (2006), pp. 221–2. However, with regard to the temple she is nonetheless of the view that all those inside, including women and children, were slaughtered (p. 213). See also Webster (1993), p. 116, for confirmation of a dearth of human remains, mentioning a mere one mangled skeleton.
235. See, for example, Aldhouse-Green (2006), p. 61.
236. Fraser (1999), p. 85.
237. Collingridge (2006), p. 224.
238. For example, Aldhouse-Green (2006), pp. 185–7.
239. Hunt (2003), pp. 89–92. Though I do not share all of Hunt's interpretations, he also raises (e.g. p. 81) the interesting possibility that Boudica herself may not have been present at the attack on Camulodunum, and that this was carried out not by Iceni but by local Trinovantes.

240. Tacitus, *Annals*, XIV, 32.
241. Tacitus, *Annals*, XIV, 33.
242. Tacitus, *Annals*, XIV, 33, states that 'with wonderful resolution, he marched amidst a hostile population to Londinium'. By contrast, Dio, *Histories*, LXII, Loeb Edition vol. VIII, p. 95, states that he 'set sail thither from Mona'. It is possible that Paulinus travelled by boat from Mona to Chester, but unlikely he made the entire trip to Londinium by boat (unless he acquired local cavalry or infantry).
243. Tacitus, *Annals*, XIV, 33.
244. Tacitus (*Annals*, XIV, 33) goes on to refer to the slaughter of those left behind, but I question this. A number of ancient decapitated skulls – apparently of young males – have been discovered over the years in the Walbrook, a former stream that emptied into the Thames. However, they have been largely discounted as having any relationship to Boudica's sacking of the town. Reasons include the fact that young males would have been amongst the ablest and could have fled with little difficulty, and, more cogently, none of the skulls had jawbones, suggesting that the flesh had decomposed well before they were thrown into the Walbrook. Such a time frame would be hard to reconcile with Boudica's campaign or any subsequent 'clean-up' (which would have been of random corpses). Moreover, all finds have occurred in a small area of the upper reaches of the Walbrook, around Liverpool Street Station, which is not consistent with random slaughter. Rather, it suggests some formal execution, possibly sacrificial. See Robinson (2003), p. 39, for a sceptical view of these as victims of Boudica, but see also Wood (1987), p. 29, and especially Knightly (1982), p. 47, for an opposed view.
245. See for example Robinson (2003), p. 38, for both; and Collingridge (2006), p. 224, for the latter.
246. Dio, *Histories*, LXII, Loeb Edition vol. VIII, p. 95. As mentioned earlier, on several occasions Dio refers to just two cities being sacked, and nowhere gives a name.
247. Fraser (1999), p. 88.
248. Fraser (1999), p.89. Fraser feels the dislocation between these associations is attributable to Boudica's female gender, leading to a focus on her in the legends as a victim of violence and not as a perpetrator.
249. Tacitus, *Annals*, XIV, 33. This somewhat contradicts his comment in *Agricola*, 16, where he refers to Boudica's army attacking garrisons *en route* to Camulodunum: 'After pursuing the soldiers scattered among the Roman forts and capturing the garrisons, they invaded the colony [the *colonia* of Camulodunum] itself.' Perhaps the passage of time here is significant and Tacitus intends that as time went by Boudica's army became increasingly distracted by plunder.
250. Tacitus, *Annals*, XIV, 37.
251. Excavations at South Cadbury suggest some unrest around this time. See Frere (1987), p. 80, n. 38.
252. Dio, *Histories*, LXII, Loeb Edition vol. VIII, p. 97.
253. Webster (1993), p. 96, comments that the inhabitants of Verulamium would have had ample time to flee.
254. Webster (1993), p. 124. See also p. 96.
255. Webster (1993), p. 96.
256. Webster (1993), p. 96.
257. Webster (1993), p. 116.
258. Tacitus, *Annals*, XIV, 34. Hunt (2003), pp. 101–4, suggests it might have been as many as 26,000 in total, possibly including men sent by the loyally pro-Roman southern king Cogidubnus, though there is no compelling evidence for this. By contrast, Webster (1993), p. 99, feels it would have been no more than 13,000.

259. See Webster (1993), p. 97, who strongly favours Mancetter. There is a popular story that the battle took place in North London and that Boudica is buried beneath platforms 9 and 10 at King's Cross Station, but this would seem to represent a 'backwards' step by her forces (though in later years it may have inspired J. K. Rowling). See also Hunt (2003), pp. 104–5, who raises the possibility of a site even further south, in the Leatherhead/Boxhill area.

260. Tacitus, *Annals*, XIV, 34. Given that Tacitus's future father-in-law, Agricola, was amongst Paulinus's men (though it is not absolutely certain that he was present in this particular engagement), like most scholars I follow Tacitus in the account of the battle. Dio's account (Dio, *Histories*, LXII, Loeb Edition vol. VIII, pp. 97–103) differs significantly, and seems highly improbable and unreliably imaginative.

261. Webster (1993), p. 97.

262. Tacitus, *Annals*, XIV, 34.

263. See also Webster (1993), p. 99.

264. Webster (1993), p. 24.

265. Webster (1993), p. 99, refers, perhaps slightly imaginatively, to the Britons being 'in a state of wild disorder', and being a 'large unruly mob in a state of high exultation, confident of a great victory'.

266. Webster (1993), p. 25.

267. Fraser (1999), p. 106.

268. Tacitus, *Annals*, XIV, 35.

269. Tacitus, *Agricola*, 5, tells us that 'his apprenticeship to war was in Britain, where he commended himself to Suetonius Paulinus', but as mentioned earlier it is not absolutely clear that he was actually in Paulinus's force that faced Boudica in her final battle. Hanson (1987), pp. 34–5, feels that had that been the case Tacitus would probably have made more of it. Nevertheless, even if not there in person, Agricola would no doubt have discussed it with soldiers who were in the battle, and passed their views on to Tacitus. Webster (1993), p. 17, also feels that Paulinus's speech is probably authentic, thanks to Agricola. This would still be a relatively rare proximity to events for a historian at that time.

270. Tacitus, *Annals*, XIV, 36.

271. Webster (1993), p. 100, makes a similar observation.

272. See also Aldhouse-Green (2006), p. 199, who remarks that recent experimental archaeology, together with consultation with equestrian experts, indicate that 'chariots used in battle would have been no match for well drilled and experienced cavalry'.

273. Tacitus, *Annals*, XIV, 37.

274. Tacitus, *Annals*, XIV, 37. Helpfully, Tacitus specifically distinguishes between dead and wounded (see following note).

275. The term 'casualties' is nowadays sometimes used rather vaguely, usually (correctly) including both wounded and dead, but sometimes confusingly referring to fatalities alone. In modern warfare there are typically two or three times as many wounded as dead, but in earlier times the proportion of dead would have been significantly higher, since more wounds would have proven fatal and victors would be much more inclined to finish off any incapacitated enemy unusable as slaves.

276. Tacitus, *Annals*, XIV, 37; Dio, *Histories*, LXII, Loeb Edition vol. VIII, p. 105.

277. Fraser (1999), pp. 99–100.

278. Tacitus, *Annals*, XIV, 37.

279. Salway (1993), p. 85.

280. Elsewhere (*Histories*, II, 37), and in a later context, Tacitus refers to Paulinus's 'distinguished service' and how he had 'won fame and reputation in his distinguished British campaigns'.

281. See, for example, Webster (1993), p.15.

282. Fry (1978), p. 11.

283. Fry (1978), p. 10.

284. Orosius, *Seven Books of History*, VII, 7. See also my Note 230.

285. Gildas, *Ruin of Britain*, Section 5.

286. Gildas, *Ruin of Britain*, 6. Gildas often used animal metaphors: 'lioness' was not flattering.

287. Bede, *Ecclesiastical History*, I, 3, p. 14.

288. Henry of Huntingdon, *History of the English*, I, 20, pp. 40–3.

289. See Collingridge (2006), Chapter 17, for a fuller treatment.

290. Tacitus, *Agricola*, 37. See 29–38 for an account of the battle and its prelude. See also Hanson 87, pp. 127–39.

291. For example, Tacitus, *Agricola*, 21, writes of his father-in-law's pursuit of this policy of Romanisation: 'He exhorted individuals and assisted communities to erect temples, market places, houses . . . [and] began to train the sons of the chieftains in a liberal education. . . . As a result the nation which used to reject the Latin language began to aspire to rhetoric: further, the wearing of our dress became a distinction, and the toga came into fashion'.

292. Zosimus, *New History*, I, 66.

293. See Sawyer (1998), p. 262, and see also Breeze (1985), p. 30.

294. Salway (1984), p. 340.

295. Salway (2000), pp. 53–4 and Salway (1984), p. 343.

296. Salway (1984), pp. 342–3.

297. Salway (1984), p. 344, remarks that being a Christian was like being a Party member in some modern states.

298. For example, Liversidge (1973), p. 462, observes that even after Christianity had become the official religion, the old pagan gods were far from forgotten and indeed experienced periodic revivals.

299. Zosimus, *New History*, IV, 35.

300. Ammianus, *Later Roman Empire*, XX, 1. The Scots ('Scotti') had originally gone into Scotland from Ireland.

301. Zosimus, *New History*, III, 5.

302. Jones (1996), p. 204.

303. Zosimus, *New History*, VI, 10, 2. Since this advice to Britain comes rather awkwardly in the middle of Zosimus's discussion of northern Italy and Liguria, it has been suggested by some scholars that 'Britain' – 'Brettania' – might be a miscopying of 'Brettia', a variant of 'Bruttium', a reference to Calabria in Southern Italy. See Esmonde-Cleary (1989), pp. 137–8. However, most scholars seem to accept that 'Brettania' is correct.

304. Jones (1996), p. 249, n. 19 (who incidentally does not accept the 'Bruttium' interpretation), feels that Honorius sent the letters to Britain *before* the expulsion of Constantine's officials, and that it was not just Constantine's officials who were expelled, but all Roman officials.

305. Zosimus, *New History*, VI, 5, 2–3.

306. Nennius, *History of the Britons*, 28. See also Jones (1996), pp. 249–50.

307. 'Amphibious warfare' is often misunderstood as the use of 'all-terrain' vehicles that can operate on both land and water. Correctly speaking, such vehicles are

'amphibian', not 'amphibious', and clearly these are modern developments. (The horse has always been to a degree an amphibian carrier, but only over very short stretches of water and with limited carrying capacity.)
308. Hunt (2003), p. 125.

2 The Coming of the Pagans

1. The Angles came mostly from the southern part of the Danish Peninsula and became particularly associated with East Anglia, Mercia, Northumbria, and (with the East Saxons) Essex; the Saxon homelands were to their west, in the North Sea coastal plain of north Germany down to around the Weser and later beyond, and in England they are particularly associated with Essex, Sussex, and Wessex; the Jutes originally came from Jutland (though they may have moved to Frisia), and are associated with Kent and the Isle of Wight.
2. For example, Campbell (1982b), p. 34, points out that in East Anglia the settlers of the fifth century seem to have been Angles, with some Saxons, but that in the sixth century the rulers there appear to have been Swedish.
3. John (1996), pp. 5–6.
4. The term 'Sub-Roman' refers to a perceived degeneration in the quality of pottery relative to the preceding Roman Period. As such it is an evaluative term similar to the 'Dark Ages', which is a reference to a perceived lack of sophisticated culture. In recent times such evaluative terminology has tended to be avoided. Confusingly, some scholars seem to interpret 'Sub-Roman' as applying only to the first few decades of the fifth century: see Pryor (2005), p. 3.
5. There were a handful of sixth century British bards, such as Taliesin and Aneirin, but their works were generally transmitted orally and not written down till several centuries later, making it hard to identify what exactly was their own work and what was later accretion.
6. Higham (2002), p. 59, dismisses the popular idea that Gildas was of royal birth. See Higham (1994), Chapter 4, for discussion of his being based in the Wiltshire-Somerset region.
7. Higham (1994), Chapters 5 and 6. In my view a very persuasive rebuttal of this early date is made by David Howlett in a review of Higham's 1994 work. Among other arguments Howlett points out that there is a letter of c. 600 from Columban of Bangor in Bobbio to Gregory the Great in Rome remarking on the correspondence that had taken place between Gildas and a fellow Briton named Vinniau, who is recorded as having died in December 549. Though not impossible, it seems unlikely that someone dying in 549 would have been corresponding with someone writing around 480. See Howlett (1996), p. 73.
8. This is based on a reference in the tenth century *Annals of Wales* (Annales Cambriae) to the date of the Battle of Badon, which Gildas referred to as happening in the same year as his birth, as being 516, combined with a possible interpretation of an ambiguous passage in his *Ruin* to the effect that the work was written 44 years after his birth – i.e. 560. See Appendix 1 on Arthur for further discussion, and note also that the *Annals* record Gildas's death as occurring in 570.
9. Gildas, *Ruin of Britain*, 15 and 18.
10. The name 'Nennius' is first given in a later version of the work, and most scholars now prefer to treat the author as anonymous, or as 'Pseudo-Nennius'. It is possible that it is the same person as a known Welsh writer from around the same time,

Ninnius, but about whom very little is known. For convenience I retain the name 'Nennius' in this book, but within apostrophes.

11. Sawyer (1998), p. 50.
12. For example, see Higham (2002), p. 98.
13. Consular, AD, Passionist, and World Age. See Sims (1998), Part 1 (website). Also, years could begin anywhere from September to March, a difficulty lying behind many of the 'corrected' dates in sources such as some modern versions of the *Anglo-Saxon Chronicle*.
14. Campbell (1982b), p. 29.
15. For example, Snyder (1997) (website).
16. Fisher (1973), p. 1.
17. Blair (2000) p. 11.
18. Hollister (1992), p. 19, remarks that it was Rome's most enduring legacy.
19. See for example Yorke (1995), pp. 149–53.
20. Gildas, *Ruin of Britain*, 20, refers to an appeal to 'Aetius, now consul for the third time', which must be at the earliest 446, and at the latest 454, when Aetius entered his fourth term, dying that same year.
21. Campbell (1982b), p. 30; Campbell (1985), p. 59; and Blair (2000), pp. 3–4.
22. See for example Campbell (1982b), p. 30; Campbell (1985), p. 59; Blair (2000), pp. 3–4; and Fisher (1973), p. 23. Bede, *Ecclesiastical History*, I, 15, p. 27, also mentions depopulation of certain Germanic homelands, as does the *Anglo-Saxon Chronicle*, Ms A and E, entries for 449.
23. Gildas, *Ruin of Britain*, 19.
24. See Gildas, *Ruin of Britain*, 23, for the three boats. Hengist and Horsa were said to be descended from the gods and may have been mythical. However, it is widely felt that Hengist at least was probably real.
25. Bede, *Ecclesiastical History*, I, 15, pp. 27–8.
26. Many scholars have pointed out that Vortigern not only seems to have spanned a long (but not impossible) period, but also to have had a dual existence, with, for example, two sets of dates, two wives, two bases – one in the southeast and one in Wales – and even two differing deaths. Sims (1998) examines this duality in considerable detail. See also Thornton (2004), p. 599, and Phillips and Keatman (1992), Chapter 10.
27. Gildas, *Ruin of Britain*, 25, writes of Ambrosius that he was modest, virtually the only Roman left alive in Britain, and that his recently slain parents had been 'adorned with the purple', i.e. ennobled.
28. See for example Holmes (1996), pp. 67–8, and Laing and Laing (1979), p. 30.
29. Gildas, *Ruin of Britain*, 25, remarks of the fleeing Britons that some were forced reluctantly to go overseas. Some Britons had in fact already moved to Brittany during the fourth century.
30. Padel (2004), p. 530, prefers Badbury Rings near Wimborne Minster in Dorset, as does Thomas (1986), p. 46 (who also offers as a possibility Liddington Castle near Swindon).
31. Fisher (1973), p. 31, gives as an example some Angles from Britain relocating to Thuringia in the 530s.
32. This is mentioned in 'Nennius', *History of Britons*, 62. It is often assumed that a large contingent of the Votadini (also known as the Gododdin, which is also the name of their kingdom) from present-day southeast Scotland, under a leader Cunedda, and possibly at the command of an over-king (such as Vortigern), assisted greatly in this matter, that the expulsion of the Irish was mainly attributable to them, and that the Votadini maintained a powerful Welsh presence thereafter, in particular in the ruling house of Gwynedd. This is particularly frequently assumed by Arthurian scholars,

many of whom see a link between the Votadini, Wales, and Arthur, and in some cases Arthur is specifically seen as a descendant of Cunedda. Similarly specialists in Welsh history have often assumed this Votadini migration to be fact (e.g. see Dodd 1979, pp. 15–16). The Gododdin specialist Kenneth Jackson, writing in 1969, accepts the basic authenticity of the story, but with a caution about 'obscurities' and possible 'eponymous inventions' (Jackson 1969, p. 28, and see also pp. 74–5). Another later Gododdin specialist, John Koch, and others such as Nora Chadwick and David Dumville, see it as an origin legend rather than proven fact. Koch, (1997), p. xcvi, cautions that nowadays we should treat the migration more sceptically than was the case a generation ago.

33. Campbell (2000), p. 31, refers to the term 'heptarchy' as being misleading, and that the reality was more complex.

34. It can also be interpreted as 'broad ruler'. Both terms seem interchangeable, appearing in various manuscripts of the *Anglo-Saxon Chronicle*, wherein the term(s) was (/were) first applied in the ninth century to Egbert of Wessex. It was then applied retrospectively to the seven rulers stated by Bede to have had *'imperium'* over much of Britain. See for example Campbell (1997) or Keynes (1999a) for a brief but helpful discussion of some of the difficulties with this term. Both treat it as an informal designation.

35. According to Bede, *Ecclesiastical History*, II, 1, pp. 70–1, Gregory was motivated, prior to becoming pope, by seeing two fair-haired children for sale as slaves in a Roman market. Learning they were heathen Angles from Deira – presumably captured by Picts – he resolved to bring Christianity to their people. He is reputed to have made the well known observation of the boy-slaves that they were 'not Angles but angels' (*non Angli, sed Angeli*), but this may well be a fanciful 'poetic' attribution along with other word-plays associated with Gregory.

36. For an account of this, see Bede, *Ecclesiastical History*, I, 25–6, pp. 39–41, and see also I, 32, pp. 58–60, for Pope Gregory's 'glorification' of Aethelberht.

37. Starkey (2004). As a practice the widespread displacement (or straight-out slaughter) of defeated males of a given people is certainly not unknown in world history from early times on. The whole question of DNA 'proof' is unfortunately somewhat muddied in this case, along with that of the later Scandinavian arrivals (including Scandinavian-derived Normans), since it is hard to distinguish genetically between Germanic and Scandinavian (see Sykes 2006, p. 283). Thus precise figures would seem to be speculative.

38. Sykes (2006), p. 286 for males and p. 281 for females.

39. See Laing and Laing (1979), p. 32.

40. Gildas, *Ruin of Britain*, 24.

41. See for example Higham (2002), p. 46.

42. See for example Schama (2000), Part One.

43. Pryor (2005), p. 22. See also Chapter 6.

44. Holmes (1996), p. 84.

45. Gildas, *Ruin of Britain*, 25. It should also be noted that the old English word 'wealh', which gave rise to 'Wales'/'Welsh', originally meant 'foreigners' but came to mean 'slaves' and was used of the Britons in general: see Blair (2000), p. 10. It is understandable that many of that nation prefer the term 'Cymry', meaning 'citizens'.

46. Blair (2000), p. 10; Kearney (1995), p. 42.

47. 'British Survival' is the recognised term relating to the question of what happened to the Britons, especially in Anglo-Saxon territory. Hugh Kearney (1995), p. 40, is one who shares this view regarding localised extermination.

48. See also Sawyer (1998), pp. 51–6 for discussion of commonalities: he cites hierarchy, graded compensation, the importance of family and lords, elected kingship, the preeminence of the ideals of courage and generosity, and the principle of reciprocity.
49. Estimates for the number of Anglo-Saxons in the early stages vary hugely from hundreds to many tens of thousands, though it is clear that numbers increased significantly with the passing of time, as is also evidenced by depopulation in some Anglo-Saxon homelands. Estimates for the British population at the time of the Advent are less varied, typically ranging from half a million to two million.
50. We should note in passing that the dominance of 'English' strongly suggests a linguistic unity among the Germanic arrivals.
51. See for example Yazaki (1964).
52. For example, Korean resistance to the imposition of Japanese following Japan's annexation of Korea in 1910, or Maori resistance to the imposition of English in New Zealand.
53. Laing and Laing (1979), p. 35, refer to a growing Germanic taste in late Roman Britain.
54. *History of the Britons* 66.
55. *Ecclesiastical History* I, 15, p. 26.
56. Alcuin, *Letter to Ethelred*, p. 842.
57. Schama (2000), Part One. In the book version (in the 2003 edition, p. 43), the term 'blunders' is replaced by the slightly softer 'misjudgements', but the thrust is the same.
58. Holmes (1996), p. 63.
59. Thomas (1986), p. 43.
60. Gildas, *Ruin of Britain*, 23.
61. Gildas, *Ruin of Britain*, 21.
62. Hollister (1992), p. 26.
63. For example, Fisher (1973), pp. 14–15, refers to archaeological evidence of an Anglian settlement, near present-day Caistor-by-Norwich, dating to before the end of the fourth century, and states that this has been interpreted as a federate (*foederati*) type of settlement. The Anglo-Saxon village at West Stow in Suffolk also firmly dates an Anglo-Saxon presence there at c. 420, interestingly of a familial nature. This may perhaps have been former *foederati* staying on, with families, after the Romans left.
64. See for example Reid (2001), pp. 157–77; Moffat (1999), pp. 84–7, 96, 172–3.
65. Gildas, *Ruin of Britain*, 22 and 23. Note also that while it is widely believed that Gildas does not specifically name the 'proud tyrant', and that this name was supplied later by Bede, some manuscript versions of Gildas, as the one used here, do name him as Gurthrigern/Vortigern. In any event, even if the naming is a later entry, it is almost universally accepted that Gildas intended Vortigern.
66. *Chronicle of Aethelweard*, c. 985, Book 1, Chapter 3, refers to all the British nobles 'yielding to Vortigern's counsel' (Campbell's translation: 'assenting' in Giles's translation) in the matter of bringing in help from Germany. The source for this does not appear to be Bede, or Alcuin, or the *Anglo-Saxon Chronicle*. (This same *Chronicle of Aethelweard*, incidentally, provides further support for a date of c. 450 for the Advent, stating that Hengist and Horsa arrived 'more than 334 years' before the first Viking raid in 789, though in this case possibly influenced by the dating in Bede or the *Anglo-Saxon Chronicle*: see Book 3, Chapter 1.)
67. A position also taken by, among others, David White, 2000 (website).
68. See also Higham (2002), pp. 128–36, for a detailed discussion of how and why Vortigern was scapegoated in the *History of the Britons*.
69. The following list of vices is taken from the *History of the Britons*, passim sections 31–9, esp. 31, 37, 39 and 43–8.

70. St Germanus of Auxerre did travel to Britain, once in 429 and again at some point in the 440s. His main concern, however, was Pelagianism among the British elite. This was the teaching of the British born Pelagius who argued that the idea of inheritance of original sin was invalid, and that individuals had free choice and did not need God's guidance. Obviously this had undesirable theological and political ramifications for the church. On his 429 visit Germanus is said to have converted a number of Britons and then led them to a victory in battle over a combined Pict-Saxon force by simply shouting 'Allelujah!'. (See Bede, *Ecclesiastical History*, I, 20.) There is no reason to doubt that he did have discussions with Vortigern on one or more occasions.
71. Higham (2002), pp. 166–9. The inscription itself is given on p. 166.
72. Kearney (1995), p. 39.
73. Kearney (1995), p. 41. See also Campbell (2000), p. 27, regarding the relative weakness of the Anglo-Saxon family (especially in the later stages of the period).
74. See Campbell (2000), pp. 26–8, for further discussion of Anglo-Saxon individualism.
75. Campbell (2000), p. 27.
76. A thegn typically held at least 5 hides, a hide – at least initially – being the amount of land deemed to be needed for one family. The hide was surprisingly large by present-day standards, ranging from 40 to 120 acres. An 'upwardly mobile' ceorl could become a thegn if he managed to acquire 5 hides. 'Hidage' was primarily used for assessment, such as for taxation or provision of men for levies. A common 'hidage' assessment for a village was between 5 and 20 hides. A 'hundred' was made up of a 100 hides, which among other things was the basis for 'hundred courts', namely district courts.
77. Crossley-Holland (1975), p. 136.
78. For example, *Laws of Ethelbert, King of Kent* (c. 602), Clause 11, mentions slaves of the third class; while *Laws of Ine, King of Wessex* (c. 690), Clause 54.2, differentiates between Englishmen and Welshmen. By the end of the tenth century, under Aethelred, the difference between a slave and a freeman, as reflected in *wergeld*, was 25-fold (as also in the Viking part of England): see *Ethelred's Treaty with the Viking Army*, 994, (also known as *II Aethelred*), Clauses 5 and 5.1, p. 438.
79. *Laws of Ine, King of Wessex*, Clauses 7, 7.1, and 7.2. Note also that a child as young as 10 years of age could be held liable for theft.
80. Yorke (1995), pp. 261–2.
81. Page (1970), p. 63.
82. *Beowulf* (Crossley-Holland trans. p. 102). Vengeance features on numerous occasions in the poem.
83. For example, see *Beowulf* (Crossley-Holland trans. p. 85), in which King Hrothgar tells Beowulf that he settled his father's feud by payment.
84. For example, it could be dangerous to go wandering in a wood away from your home area, at least without a strong voice, a horn, or a wealthy redeemer. Clause 20 of the *Laws of Ine, King of Wessex*, states that if a foreigner or indeed anyone who is not a local goes through a wood other than by following the track, and does not make clear his presence by shouting or blowing a horn, he is to be assumed a thief, and either killed or redeemed.
85. For example, *Beowulf* (Crossley-Holland trans. p. 146), refers to 'single-handed' vengeance.
86. Fletcher (2002), pp. 8–10.
87. For example, *Laws of Ethelbert, King of Kent*, Clause 23 refers to kinsmen having to pay half the *wergeld* if a person guilty of killing leaves the land.
88. (King) *Edmund's Code Concerning the Blood-Feud*, of c. 940, Clause 1.1 states that if a killer's kindred abandon him, then they are deemed exempt from the feud, provided they do not give him food or protection afterwards.

89. Fletcher (2002), p. 10.
90. Crossley-Holland (1999), Introduction, p. x. Fate, like vengeance, features numerous times in *Beowulf*, including reference to it as 'every man's master' (p. 137).
91. Crossley-Holland (1999), Introduction, p. x.
92. One is also mindful of unflattering Roman descriptions of Celtic battle attitudes outlined in Part 1.
93. *Laws of Ine, King of Wessex*, Clauses 5 and 5.1.
94. The idea of sanctuary in a church was also very enduring. For example, in the early 1060s Tostig, Earl of Northumbria, though in many regards a deeply religious man, was thought of very badly by the people of his earldom for allegedly employing men prepared to ignore it in the pursuit of his enemies (see Fletcher 2002, p. 155), and this would almost certainly have been a significant (though not the sole) factor in their dissatisfaction with him and his consequent expulsion and exile in 1065, which in turn played its part in the events of the following year (see Part 3).
95. As mentioned earlier, see Campbell (1997).
96. Blair (2000), p. 17.
97. Bede, *Ecclesiastical History*, II, 15, p. 98.
98. Hollister (1992), p. 53.
99. *Anglo-Saxon Chronicle*, Ms A, E, and F, entries for 792, corrected to 794. Ms A, for example, states in a very matter-of-fact way that 'Offa, king of the Mercians, ordered King [of East Anglia] Aethelberht's head to be struck off.'
100. Charlemagne, *Letter to Offa, King of Mercia*, p. 848. Charlemagne calls Offa his 'dearest brother', and later in the letter refers to the various episcopal sees of 'your kingdom and of Aethelred's'.
101. Campbell (2000), p. 6.
102. Alcuin, *Letter to the Mercian Ealdorman Osbert*, p. 855.
103. Alcuin, *Letter to Offa, King of Mercia*, p. 846.
104. Malmesbury, *Chronicle of the Kings of England*, Bohn edition, I, 4, p. 77.
105. Malmesbury, *Chronicle of the Kings of England*, Bohn edition, I, 4, p. 78.
106. *Anglo-Saxon Chronicle*, Ms A, E, F, entries for 787, corrected to 789. The location is given in the *Annals of St Neots*, entry for 789 (Dumville and Lapidge 1985, p. 39). See the following chapter for further discussion.
107. *Anglo-Saxon Chronicle*, Ms E, F, entries for 793: this quotation from Thorpe edition.
108. Seaman (1982), p. 19.
109. F. Donald Logan, for example, remarks that the expansion of the Vikings is still a 'puzzling historical phenomenon': see Logan (2003), p. 24. He himself sees population growth as a significant factor.
110. These are discussed in Brondsted (1965), pp. 23–7, and Hadley (2006), pp. 16–20. Regarding overpopulation, we should note (Brondsted p. 24) that primogeniture meant that later sons generally had to leave home and seek their fortune elsewhere. Sawyer (1997b), p. 3, remarks that while the idea of overpopulation has often been put forward as the main cause, this could only be applied with any validity to western Norway, and even then only partly. Sawyer's own view is that few left Scandinavia out of necessity, but rather out of a desire to seek wealth. His view is shared by Hadley, who also stresses the importance of economic factors, particularly the importance of trade (p. 17) and political instability in Scandinavia (pp. 18–19).
111. Barbara Crawford (2003), p. 42, takes a similar view. She recognises economic and political factors in Scandinavia, as well as technological improvements with Viking vessels and also a possible pagan response to encroaching Christianisation, but then adds that, in more general terms, we should also recognise that piracy is invariably

profitable when the circumstances are conducive and a suitable victim is 'waiting to be exploited'.

112. James (2003), p. 57.
113. See Sawyer (1971), and see also Hadley (2006), p. 4 and p. 92.
114. See Hadley (2006), pp. 130–2.
115. See also Hadley (2006), pp. 83–4.
116. For example, Roesdahl (1991), Logan (2003), and Oxenstierna (1966).
117. Keynes (1997), p. 49.
118. Keynes (1997), p. 49.
119. James (2003), p. 57. The tenth century Bloodaxe (as discussed later) was several times king of York; his contemporary Skullsplitter was earl of Orkney.
120. Logan (2003), p. 35, and see also Hadley (2006), p. 16.
121. Hadley (2006), p. 16.
122. Roesdahl (1991), p. 3.
123. Roesdahl (1991), pp. 3–4. See the *Vinland Sagas* for details of the Viking expeditions to Vinland (North America). As a point of interest, I would add that the claim that the Vikings were the first 'Europeans' in America is recently being questioned by scholars who believe this distinction should go to the Solutreans (Solutrians) from what is now east-central France, during the Ice Age some 17,000 years ago.
124. Roesdahl (1991), p. 4.
125. Logan (2003), p. 36.
126. *Anglo-Saxon Chronicle*, entry for 787 corrected to 789, quotation from Thorpe edition, vol. II, pp. 47–8; Old English insertions from vol. I, p. 97. Logan (2003), pp. 38–9, believes that despite the mention of Hordaland there is doubt as to whether these men in 789 were actually Norwegian, and believes it more probable that they were in fact Danes. (He does accept that the attacks on Lindisfarne in 793 and Jarrow in 794 were by Norwegians.)
127. *Chronicle of Aethelweard*, Book 3, Chapter 1.
128. Some texts, including some versions of the *Anglo-Saxon Chronicle*, give 8 January, but this is based on a transcription error ('Ian' for 'Iun'). See *Anglo-Saxon Chronicle*, Swanton edition p. 17, Footnote 15.
129. Alcuin, *Letter to Higbald, Bishop of Lindisfarne*, p. 845.
130. Alcuin, *Letter to Ethelred, King of Northumbria*, p. 842.
131. Alcuin, *Letter to Ethelred, King of Northumbria*, pp. 843–4.
132. Symeon, *Tract on the Church of Durham*, II, 5, pp. 88–9, and again IV, 2, pp. 226–7.
133. Alcuin, *Letter to Ethelred, King of Northumbria*, p. 843.
134. Alcuin, *Letter to Ethelred, King of Northumbria*, p. 842.
135. Roesdahl (1991), p. 223, is firmly of the 'easy loot' view, and dismisses any ideological motive such as antipathy towards Christianity. By contrast Keynes (1997), p. 50, queries whether there really was a focus on churches, and on pp. 59–62 points out that there were probably other factors than the Vikings in the decline in the quality of religious life in England at the time, such as 'negligence and complacency'.
136. Oxenstierna (1966), p. 20.
137. Oxenstierna (1966), p. 52. Unfortunately, despite stressing the 'written sources' in his reference to cattle, Oxenstierna does not specifically cite any (other than a general bibliography), and I myself have been unable to locate any source referring to cattle in the Lindisfarne attack. This is not to deny that any cattle – which were often kept by monasteries – were indeed seized by raiders, but whether they were the primary targets is another matter, moreover a highly debatable one.

138. Oxenstierna (1966), pp. 52–3. Malmesbury, I, 3, Bohn edition p. 69, makes the same point.
139. *Anglo-Saxon Chronicle*, Ms A and E, entries for 835 corrected to 838, Swanton edition, pp. 62–3.
140. Logan (2003), pp. 112–14, and Roesdahl (1991), pp. 195–6.
141. Technically he succeeded Offa's unfortunate son Ecgfrith, murdered after a mere 141 days. Since Coenwulf was only a very distant relative, one may imagine his involvement in Ecgfrith's demise.
142. Ingwaer is believed to be the basis for the later legend of Ivar the Boneless. He was particularly active in establishing Viking settlements in Ireland and Scotland.
143. *Anglo-Saxon Chronicle*, Ms A and E, entries for 871, Swanton edition pp. 72–3.
144. Keynes and Lapidge (1983), p. 16.
145. See Sturdy (1995), p. 113, and see also Asser's *Life of King Alfred*, paragraph 43, Keynes and Lapidge edition p. 81, and their Note 79 against the above entry; Blair (2000), p. 40; and the *Anglo-Saxon Chronicle*, Ms A and E, entries for 871, Swanton edition pp. 72–3.
146. See Roesdahl (1991), p. 199.
147. Roesdahl (1991), p. 196 for Frisia and p. 198 for Paris.
148. The attribution of authorship to Asser has been challenged for more than 150 years, in recent years particularly by Alfred Smyth, based for example on the fact that the *Life* does not continue beyond 893 (or effectively, in terms of chronology, 887) although Asser lived till 909 and thus had the opportunity to update his work subsequent to Alfred's death in 899, and that it is reasonable to assume that the writing of a true contemporary of Alfred, especially one who was in Alfred's circle, would have been less coincident with the entries in the *Anglo-Saxon Chronicle*. Smyth argues that the work was in fact written c. 1000 by the monk-scholar Byrhtferth of Ramsey Abbey in Huntingdonshire, at the request of Oswald of Worcester (later St Oswald), to revive Christianity. That is, Byrhtferth assumed the role of Asser in order to produce a hagiography of a perfect Christian king in Alfred. See Smyth (2002) and Smyth (1995), esp. Part 2.
149. Asser's *Life of Alfred*, paragraph 43, Keynes and Lapidge edition, p. 74.
150. *Anglo-Saxon Chronicle*, Ms E and A, entries for 876, Swanton edition, pp. 74–5. Again, we read simply that the king [of Wessex] 'made peace' with the Vikings, but Crawford (2003), p. 57, remarks that 'made peace' means 'handed over silver'.
151. For detailed discussion of the story and its provenance, see Keynes and Lapidge (1983), Appendix 1, pp. 197–202. See also Smyth (1995), Chapter XIII, esp. pp. 325–9.
152. Asser's *Life of Alfred*, paragraph 56 (Keynes and Lapidge edition pp. 84–5). The stronghold may have been Chippenham, a known Viking base at that time.
153. Crawford (2003), p. 58, refers to the relatively ready acceptance of Christianity by the Vikings in their various overseas settlements in Christian lands as a key element in their adjustment to life there. To my mind this would seem to indicate that the Vikings had pragmatically accepted that they were not (at least at that point) powerful enough to impose their own religion on the people of their new lands. It might also suggest that Christianity had made significant inroads by this stage into their Scandinavian homelands. Harald Bluetooth was to declare Denmark a Christian country in the middle of the next century, Norway was to follow at the beginning of the eleventh century, and Sweden (though it was a relatively minor player in the Viking attacks on England) somewhat later during the course of the eleventh century – see Roesdahl (1991), p. 147. However, see below regarding actual depth of conversion.

154. See, for example, *Egil's Saga*, Chapter 50, Fell edition p. 74, Eddison edition p. 98.
155. See for example Logan (2003), p. 150–1.
156. Keynes (1997), p. 57, suggests that the division may have been made as early as 879/80, and that London, though not occupied by Alfred till 886, had in fact remained nominally English since the fall of Burhred in 874.
157. Keynes (1997), p. 63.
158. Whereas the great majority of female mitochondrial DNA in Britain is Celtic, the area of the former Danelaw shows a significant overlay of Germanic or Scandinavian DNA, strongly suggesting substantial immigration by females. As mentioned earlier, it is difficult to distinguish between Germanic and Scandinavian DNA, but in this case it seems very likely to be Scandinavian rather than Anglo-Saxon. See Sykes (2006), pp. 282–3, who also feels it is Scandinavian.
159. For further Anglo-Saxon place-names see Knightly (1982), p. 98.
160. Bates (1995b).
161. Yorke (1995), p. 122.
162. Logan (2003), p. 150–1.
163. Paragraph 74 of Asser's *Life of Alfred*, (Keynes and Lapidge edition pp. 88–90, actually comprising four good-sized paragraphs), is dedicated to a discussion of these maladies. As a youngster he had chronic piles, which presently subsided, but just after feasting at his wedding in 868, at the age of 19, he was struck down by a 'sudden severe pain quite unknown to all physicians' (p. 88). The locus of the pain is unspecified, but it seemingly plagued him almost constantly, 'remorselessly day and night', and even in the rare moments when it ceased, he was still in fear of it (p. 90). Any digestive problem caused by the feasting would either have passed relatively quickly or killed him, but the extreme pain of some indigestive (or gallstone-based) colic may perhaps have triggered in him a psychosomatic condition. He seems to have driven himself very hard in whatever he did, and it may be an anxiety or stress-related problem, compounded by obsessiveness. It is unfortunate – and surprising – that Asser does not identify the locus of the pain.
164. Smyth (1995), p. 601.
165. This epithet appears to have been first used in the sixteenth century. See Keynes and Lapidge (1983), p. 44.
166. See Lund (1997), p. 172, who writes that the epithet was 'in acknowledgement of the empire he eventually established'. Logan (2003), p. 139, feels that Cnut was a greater monarch than Alfred.
167. Yorke (2003), p. 362. We should note also that Charlemagne was called 'the Great' within two centuries after his death, whereas in Alfred's case it was seven centuries.
168. Brooke (1967), p. 116.
169. Woodruff (1974), p. 181. See also p. 183.
170. Higham (2001), p. 1.
171. Keynes and Lapidge (1983), p. 16.
172. The *Will of King Alfred* stipulates that his brother's son Aethelwold should receive estates at Godalming, Guildford, and Steyning (Keynes and Lapidge 1983, pp. 173–8, at p. 177). These mere three estates are the equal smallest endowment of all the beneficiaries listed. By contrast eight estates were given to Aethelwold's brother Aethelhelm – a relatively mysterious figure about whom little is known, and who may or may not be Ealdorman Aethelhelm of Wiltshire, but who in any case did not pursue any claim to the throne.
173. Keynes and Lapidge (1983), p. 173.

174. *Anglo-Saxon Chronicle*, Ms D (and C), entry for 901 corrected to 899 [900 in some versions]. This quotation is taken from Thorpe edition p. 75.
175. Campbell J. (2001), p. 21. See also *Anglo-Saxon Chronicle*, Ms A, entry for 904, corrected to 903 [and almost certainly beginning in September 902], Swanton edition p. 92; and for 'king of the Danes' see the *Annals of St Neots*, entry for 903 (Dumville and Lapidge (1985), p. 104).
176. Campbell J. (2001), p. 21.
177. Campbell J. (2001), p. 22. See also Campbell J. (2003), p. 4.
178. Aethelred was in poor health during the last years of his life and Aethelflaed had effectively been the ruling monarch of Mercia for some time before 911.
179. William of Malmesbury, *Chronicle of the Kings of England*, Bohn edition, II, 5, pp. 123–4.
180. *Anglo-Saxon Chronicle*, Ms C, entry for 918, Thorpe edition p. 81.
181. Yorke (1997).
182. There is some apparent confusion here over the dating of Ms A, which gives the entry as 922 (corrected in Swanton to 921), so I follow Whitelock (1979), p. 216, in treating it as an extension of the entry for 918. Quotation from Thorpe edition, p. 81.
183. Stafford (1989), p. 33.
184. Bailey (2001), p. 117.
185. The *Anglo-Saxon Chronicle* gives the entry as 919, (e.g. Swanton edition p. 105). It is similarly dated as 919 in the *Mercian Register*, a fragment sometimes considered part of the *Anglo-Saxon Chronicle*, and with very similar wording (text in Whitelock 1979, p. 217). Again, many scholars, and I myself, feel that this could and should be read as a continuation of the previous year, namely 918. It would make more sense for Edward to remove Aelfwyn sooner rather than later. Quotation is Thorpe edition, p. 81.
186. Bailey (2001), p. 117.
187. Bailey (2001), pp. 122–5.
188. See also Keynes (1997), p. 70, for an indication that a rift still existed in the mid tenth century.
189. Technically, Athelstan, Edward's eldest son, was given Mercia while his younger half-brother Aelfweard was given Wessex. However, Aelfweard died after just 16 days, possibly murdered. Wessex may then have been given temporarily to another younger half-brother, Edwin, since Athelstan did not become king of Wessex till over a year later. Edwin was presently drowned, in 933, according to some sources on the orders of his brother Athelstan: see Swanton (1996), p. 107, n. 11.
190. For example, Dumville (1992), p. 142.
191. Dumville (1992), p. 171.
192. See *Egil's Saga*, Chapter 50 (esp. Fell edition), for the Viking mercenaries in Athelstan's employ. Clearly, Norwegian fought Norwegian.
193. *Anglo-Saxon Chronicle*, entry for 937, Thorpe edition pp. 86–8.
194. Bates (1995a), p. 290.
195. For example, Higham (1997), p. 4, is of the view that he received a poor press for making his own appointments and for standing up against those who had acquired too much influence. Malmesbury (Bohn edition II, 7, pp. 143–4), by contrast, refers to Eadwig's 'despising the advice of his councillors', and adds that he was a 'wanton youth' who indulged in 'illicit intercourse', seemingly even in public.
196. See Seaman (1982), pp. 46–9, for comment on the prevalence of disease and the limitations of medical treatment, which meant that few Anglo-Saxons could expect either a very long life or a particularly healthy one.

197. Lavelle (2002), p. 27, for example, states unequivocally and without further quali-fication that Eadwig died of 'natural causes', though he cites only the sources referred to below in this text, which in my view do not rule out poison or similar foul means. He may be correct in his inference, but I reserve my right to be cynical.
198. *Life of St Dunstan*, p. 902.
199. *King Edgar's Establishment of Monasteries*, p. 920.
200. Campbell (2000), p. xxi, pp. 10–11, and p. 36.
201. For example, by Patrick Wormald. See Wormald 83, and also discussion of his views in Campbell (2000), pp. 44–5.
202. According to Osbern of Canterbury, writing in the 1080s, the virgin was from Wilton Abbey. See Keynes (1980), p. 163.
203. After his mother Aelfthryth married Edgar in 964 she had a first son Edmund (who presently died in 971). Thus it is very improbable that Aethelred was born before at the earliest 966, and many scholars prefer a slightly later date of around 968.
204. Keynes (1991), p. 82.
205. Keynes (1980), pp 164–5.
206. William of Malmesbury, Bohn edition II, 9 (pp. 163–4), gives a gruesome and pos-sibly imaginative description of the deed and treats Aelfthryth as the instigator, get-ting her servant to stab Edward while she distracted him. Not a few present-day scholars are of the view that Aelfthryth was very probably involved in the murder: see for example Higham (1997), p. 14. Symeon, *Tract of the Church of Durham*, II, 20, pp. 142–3, also explicitly blames Aethelred's mother for the murder. However, Keynes (1980), pp. 166–74, is of the view that she was probably not guilty, and that it was more likely to have been zealous thegns personally opposed to Edward, act-ing in their own interests in the belief that they would fare better under Aethelred. (A view repeated in Keynes 2004, p. 410.) A particularly important point he makes (1980, pp. 174–5) is that, had the murder been planned at high level, we could have expected Aethelred's formal coronation to take place very quickly, yet in fact it was over a year later. (On the other hand, it was almost a year till Edward's body was discovered, for it had apparently been hastily buried in the garden of a nearby house.) A further point made by Keynes is that there was no upheaval in the com-position of the king's council and other high positions.
207. Higham (1997), p. 17. See also the *Anglo-Saxon Chronicle*, Ms E, entry for 979 cor-rected to 978 (Thorpe edition p. 100), which states pointedly: 'Him his earthly kins-men would not avenge, but his Heavenly Father has amply avenged him.' We should also bear in mind that the ethics of the blood feud were still strong. Keynes (1980), p. 173, points out that Aethelred may not have known the culprits since he was so young, but it can be counter-argued that those adults acting as his advisers could have made investigations. I personally agree with Higham that the apparent failure of Aelfthryth to make any such investigations into the death of her step-son suggests some complicity on her part – or at least an acceptance after the fact that it was to her advantage.
208. *King Ethelred's Code of 1008* (also known as *V Aethelred*), Clause 16, Whitelock (1979), p. 444.
209. Williams (2003), p. 14.
210. Williams (2003), pp. 14, 17. By contrast, Keynes (1980), p. 171, argues that no indi-cation of contrition is evident.
211. Keynes (1980), p. 173.
212. In his *Chronicle of the Kings of England*, Bohn edition II, 10, pp. 165–6, Malmesbury states of Aethelred that 'The career of his life is said to have been cruel in the

beginning, wretched in the middle, and disgraceful at the end.' However, in the immediately following lines Malmesbury is inconsistent, blaming Aethelred for complicity in Edward's murder but then describing his grief when he heard of his brother's death: 'In the murder [of his kinsman] to which he gave his concurrence, he was cruel', but then also, a few lines further on in the same passage, repeating a story in circulation at the time, he refers to Aethelred's despair when he heard talk that his brother had been murdered, lapsing into such a fit of tears that his mother beat him senseless with a candle and gave him a life-long fear of candles as a result. Still in the same passage, Malmesbury also tells of Aethelred's life being inauspicious from the outset, symbolised by his alleged defecating in the font at his christening, prompting Archbishop Dunstan, a supporter of Edward, to say of Aethelred that he would be 'a sorry fellow' when he grew up.

213. Keynes (1980), pp. 163, 169.
214. Sellar and Yeatman (1960 edition), Chapter 8, p. 20.
215. From around 965 the regular supply of Islamic silver into Russia and thence Scandinavia dried up, though the reasons for this are not the clearest. This is seen by many scholars as the impetus for renewed attacks on Britain, which Roesdahl (1991, p. 233) describes as one of the Vikings' best sources of income. See also Roesdahl (1991), pp. 250, 285 regarding Islamic silver, and see too Crawford (2003), p. 67.
216. Sawyer (1997b), p. 17.
217. Sawyer (1997b), p. 17.
218. *Anglo-Saxon Chronicle*, Ms A, entry for 993, corrected to 991.
219. See Keynes (1991), pp. 89–90.
220. Gordon (1968), pp. 16–17, remarks that Byrhtnoth became Ealdorman of Essex in 956, and that his approximate age at the time of his encounter with the Vikings was a formidable 65 years old.
221. *Anglo-Saxon Chronicle*, Ms A, entry for 993, corrected to 991, gives 93.
222. *The Battle of Maldon*, line 39 (pp. 18–19).
223. *The Battle of Maldon*, lines 42–61 (pp. 18–21).
224. *The Battle of Maldon*, lines 84–90 (pp. 20–1).
225. *The Battle of Maldon*, lines 246–54 (pp. 28–9).
226. *The Battle of Maldon*, line 189 (pp. 26–7).
227. *The Battle of Maldon*, lines 237–43 (pp. 28–9).
228. For example, James (2003), p. 66, refers to it as a 'tactical misjudgement', but recognises the heroism.
229. *Anglo-Saxon Chronicle*, Ms E and F, entries for 991, both specify 10,000 pounds payment and that the decision to pay was Sigeric's. See also Malmesbury, Bohn edition, II, 10, p. 167.
230. *Ethelred's Treaty with the Viking Army* (also known as *II Aethelred*), Clause 1, pp. 437–38. For many years some scholars felt it possible that this treaty, and the concomitant payment of 22,000 pounds, was made in 991. However, Donald Scragg (1991b), p. xiii, confirms it is now accepted as 994. For supporting details see Keynes (1991), pp. 103–4.
231. *Ethelred's Treaty with the Viking Army*, Clause 7.2, p. 439.
232. Malmesbury, Bohn edition, II, 10, p. 167.
233. Malmesbury, Bohn edition, II, 10, p. 167. He adds further that when Aethelred learnt of this perfidy, he had Aelfric's son (Aelfgar) blinded while Aelfric himself appears to have avoided serious punishment even despite subsequent desertions. If it is true that the blinding was as a result of his father's act and not some misdeed of the son, then this would be a disturbing illustration of Anglo-Saxon law enforcement, and/or

Aethelred's personality. Campbell (2000), p. 174, believes this to be the first such punishment in British history, and remarks that it occurred in an exceptionally violent period – often politically violent – that was to continue through the first quarter of the eleventh century However, we should note that the principle of punishing the innocent family of a miscreant, sometimes even more than the miscreant, is not uncommon in world history. See also *Anglo-Saxon Chronicle*, Ms E, entries for 992 and 993, regarding Aelfric's desertion and his son's subsequent blinding.

234. *Anglo-Saxon Chronicle*, Ms E, entry for 999, Thorpe edition p. 109.
235. Williams (2003), pp. 50–1.
236. Keynes (1980), p. 202.
237. Williams (2003), p. 55, refers to the possibility of a degree of panic in the king's circle.
238. MacDonald (1997) states that Aethelred was probably provoked by Pallig, who had received many gifts from Aethelred and pledged loyalty to him. Pallig, who may perhaps have been King Swein's brother-in-law, broke his pledge and joined a raiding party. For details of Pallig and his breach of pledge, see *Anglo-Saxon Chronicle*, Ms A, entry for 1001, and see also Keynes (1980), pp. 204–5.
239. Henry of Huntingdon, *History of the English*, VI, 2, pp. 340–1, states that with Emma's arrival King Aethelred's pride increased, and links this to his decision to have the Danes exterminated.
240. *Anglo-Saxon Chronicle*, Ms E, entry for 1002, Thorpe edition p. 111. There is some division of opinion about whether this means the massacre was to be set for that given day, or whether it means that the order was given on that day, though the former is most favoured. Henry of Huntingdon, *History of the English*, VI, 2, pp. 340–1, recalls that in his childhood he had heard old men talk of the king sending secret letters to all the cities, following which the English killed or injured 'all the unsuspecting Danes on the same day and hour'. It is technically possible that the young Henry (c. 1088–c. 1157), in the late 1090s or thereabouts, could indeed have spoken to very old men who had heard stories from their parents or grandparents. Unfortunately the full extent of the attacks on the Danes is not clear, making it difficult to judge, but one would have to say that the carrying out of such a large-scale plan at a given time would be administratively and logistically challenging, with a very high risk of the 'secret' being divulged, which in turn could have possible adverse consequences for the planners and their agents. Nonetheless, this appears to be what happened.
241. See for example Keynes (2004), p. 413.
242. Aethelred, *Renewal for the Monastery of St Frideswide*, p. 591.
243. Seaman (1982), p. 24 views it as an impolitic act that lost Aethelred the support of many Scandinavians who had hitherto been loyal to him.
244. Henry of Huntingdon, *History of the English*, VI, 2, pp. 340–1.
245. Williams (2003), pp. 53–4.
246. *Anglo-Saxon Chronicle*, Ms E, entry for 1003, Thorpe edition pp. 111–12.
247. For example, Higham (1997), p. 27, and Lavelle (2002), p. 104.
248. *Anglo-Saxon Chronicle*, Ms E, entry for 992; and Malmesbury, Bohn edition, II, 10, p. 167.
249. Lavelle (2002), p. 104.
250. Lavelle (2002), p. 104.
251. John of Worcester, *Chronicle*, entry for 1007, pp. 460–1.
252. Keynes (2004), p. 415.
253. Barlow (2003), p. 26, gives 300 but does not indicate his source. Lavelle (2002), pp. 116, 119, assumes 200, following Richard Abels' calculation of the potential

sum contribution of the various naval districts. Keynes (1997), p. 79, working from the same calculation base, gives 150–250.

254. *Anglo-Saxon Chronicle*, Ms E, entry for 1009, Thorpe edition p. 115.
255. *Anglo-Saxon Chronicle*, Ms E, entry for 1009, Thorpe edition p. 114.
256. *Anglo-Saxon Chronicle*, Ms E, entry for 1009, Thorpe edition p. 115.
257. *Anglo-Saxon Chronicle*, Ms E, entry for 1010, Thorpe edition p. 116.
258. *Anglo-Saxon Chronicle*, Ms E and Ms C, entry for 1011, Thorpe edition pp. 116–17.
259. Williams (2003), pp. 105–6.
260. Williams (2003), p. 108.
261. For example Williams (2003), p. 110, Lavelle (2002), p. 93, or John (1996), p. 147, following the contemporary German chronicler Thietmar.
262. Roesdahl (1991), p. 254.
263. There is some confusion over whether Aethelred had another wife before Aelfgifu. See Williams (2003), pp. 24–5. It should also be noted that Aelfgifu (Aelfgyfu) was a very common female name. Queen Emma, when married to Aethelred, was also known by an Anglo-Saxon rendition of her name as Aelfgifu; and Cnut, who was later to marry Emma, also had a first wife named Aelfgifu (of Northampton).
264. *Anglo-Saxon Chronicle*, Ms E, entry for 1013 (Swanton edition p. 144, Thorpe edition p. 119) appears somewhat self-contradictory, stating that 'the *whole* nation had him as full king (*full cyng ofer eall Englaland*)', but immediately going on to say that *afterwards* the townspeople of London submitted to him (my italics). The *Eulogy for Queen Emma*, written about 30 years later, Book I, 5, pp. 14–15, states that he was 'enthroned over the whole country (*rex tota Anglorum patria est intronizatus*)'. Alistair Campbell, editor and translator of the *Eulogy*, feels that the term *intronizatus* does not necessarily imply a formal coronation, but rather is equivalent to the *Anglo-Saxon Chronicle*'s term 'full king' (*full cyng*), which term was used regularly to imply 'kingly power without perfect constitutional standing' (Introduction to *Eulogy*, p. liii). In other words, Swein was a *de facto* king, not a *de jure* king. Present-day historians seem more or less equally divided on the issue, judging from a quick check of several dozen books I have immediately to hand, both specialised and generalised. For example, among more generalised reference books, the 1995 *History Today Companion to British History*, the 2002 *Macmillan Encyclopedia*, and the 1987 *Collier's Encyclopedia* refer to him only as King of Denmark. By contrast, the 1997 *Oxford Companion to British History*, the 1985 *Cambridge Historical Encyclopedia of Great Britain and Ireland*, and Christopher Brooke's 1963 work *The Saxon and Norman Kings* (which also includes Viking kings) refer to him as both King of Denmark and King of England.
265. *Anglo-Saxon Chronicle*, Ms E., entry for 1014, Thorpe edition p. 120.
266. *Anglo-Saxon Chronicle*, Ms E., entry for 1014, Thorpe edition p. 120.
267. *Anglo-Saxon Chronicle*, Ms C and D, entry for 1014. Ms E omits ears. (Swanton edition p. 145.)
268. Lavelle (2002), p. 131. At the risk of digression, I would wholeheartedly endorse Lavelle's sentiment of pathos, and give a reminder that we should never forget the human cost in the unfolding of history. 'Glorious' battles that illuminate historical documents entail in actuality much suffering and slaughter, much grief and misery, even among the victors let alone the defeated. And it is often the young and innocent who suffer. In this particular case we should not overlook the fact that Cnut was only around 19 at the time, and thus still a young man himself, though he was obviously far from 'innocent'.
269. Like the Anglo-Saxons, the Vikings too had a slave society. See for example Roesdahl (1991), pp. 53–6.

270. Wulfstan, *Sermon of the Wolf*, passim.
271. Wulfstan, *Sermon of the Wolf*, pp. 933–4.
272. Keynes (1997), pp. 79–81, elaborates upon the English recourse to prayer, treating it as one of six significant English 'defensive strategies' employed against the Vikings at various times under Aethelred (the others being payment, use of mercenaries, trying on occasion to befriend their foes, the marriage of Aethelred to the Norman Emma, and a programme of development of military strength such as in ship-building). I myself would add a seventh, namely actually fighting, and – based on the St Brice's Day Massacre – a possible eighth, namely selective extermination.
273. One notes that his positive by-name 'Ironside', symbolising toughness, stands in stark contrast to his father's negative by-name.
274. Williams (2003), p. 133.
275. Williams (2003), p. 134.
276. *Anglo-Saxon Chronicle*, Ms E, entry for 1015, Thorpe edition p. 121.
277. *Eulogy for Queen Emma*, II, 3, pp. 18–19. See also Williams (2003), p. 136, who discounts this account.
278. *Anglo-Saxon Chronicle*, Ms E and F, entries for 1016, Swanton edition p. 147.
279. *Anglo-Saxon Chronicle*, Ms C, entry for 1016 (and see also footnotes), Swanton edition p. 148.
280. Williams (2003), pp. 149–50.
281. Brooke (1967), p. 131.
282. Miller (1999), p. 214.
283. Keynes (2004), p. 409.
284. Keynes (2004), p. 415.
285. Keynes (1997), pp. 81–2.
286. *Anglo-Saxon Chronicle*, Ms D, E, and F, entries for 1016, Thorpe edition p. 123.
287. In contrast to Aelfric and Eadric, Ulfcytel is widely seen as one of Aethelred's best appointments, though he was never to attain the status of ealdorman and thus had relatively limited authority. He had put up sterling resistance to the Vikings over the previous decade, and some historians feel that had he been in a more powerful position during that decade the outcome for England may have been different.
288. Henry of Huntingdon, *History of the English*, VI, 13, pp. 360–1, has the two protagonists fight a duel, with Edmund getting the upper hand and Cnut, 'in fear for himself', suggesting the split. William of Malmesbury, *Chronicle of the Kings of England*, II, 10, p. 195, has Edmund asking for single combat but Cnut rejecting it because 'he [Cnut] was apprehensive of trusting his diminutive person against so bulky an antagonist'. Both accounts are considered apocryphal.
289. John of Worcester, *Chronicle*, entry for 1016, pp. 492–3, states this, but must be treated with caution since there are clear errors elsewhere in his account of the meeting of Cnut and Edmund.
290. Trow (2005), pp. 70–1, remarks that there is an 'infuriating silence' among the sources concerning Ironside's death. Trow believes that either it was the result of infection of a wound, or that Cnut had him murdered, probably by poison. By contrast, Lawson (1993), p. 20, remarks that it is possible Edmund died from an illness or wound incurred around late October and does not include murder as a possibility. Higham (1997), pp. 67–8, similarly assumes it was a wound. Henry of Huntingdon, *History of the English*, VI, 14, pp. 360–1, and William of Malmesbury, *Chronicle of the Kings of England*, II, 10, Bohn edition p. 195, both (though with variations, Malmesbury explicitly saying it is only rumour) have him murdered in the lavatory by assassins acting for Eadric Streona, but this is given little credence.

(On the other hand, murder while the victim is performing toilet functions is by no means uncommon in world history, for obvious reasons.) Some Scandinavian sources also have Eadric as the murderer, such as the *Saga of St Olaf* (C 21 [some versions C 24], p. 179).

291. *Eulogy for Queen Emma*, II, 14, pp. 30–1.
292. Trow (2005), p. 101, and see also pp. 100–4 for names.
293. Emma's date of birth is unclear. Stafford (1997), p. 211, gives between the early 980s and c. 990.
294. Roesdahl (1991), pp. 256–7.
295. Lawson (1993), p. 214, and see also p. 215.
296. Symeon, *Tract on the Church of Durham*, III, 7, pp. 166–7, greatly praises Cnut's piety.
297. Henry of Huntingdon, *History of the English*, VI, 17 pp. 366–9.
298. See Pollock (2002), main text p. 2, and supplement p. 2.
299. Lawson (1993), p. 113, suggests he had reasonable advance warning that he was dying, which would indicate an illness. Trow (2005), p. 208, while remarking on the unknown nature of Cnut's cause of death, suggests as a possibility, based on Scandinavian sources, that it may have been jaundice.
300. See the *Anglo-Saxon Chronicle*, Ms E, entry for 1070. Lund (1997), p. 178, states clearly that 'William agreed to pay them tribute'. See also Lawson (1993), p. 212, who adds that Swein would have realised that despite the effective pay off, he was dealing with a very different man than Aethelred.
301. Roesdahl (1991), pp. 258–9, whom I principally follow in recounting this episode.
302. Roesdahl (1991), p. 296.
303. Roesdahl (1991), pp. 245–6. She puts the figure at some 600 words, but I am of the view that it is significantly larger than that.
304. Roesdahl (1991), p. 192. In particular she refers to the notorious 'blood eagle', in which the victim's back (some say chest) is cut open, the ribs separated from the backbone and bent outwards, and the lungs pulled out to form the vague shape of an eagle, exposing the heart, as being in fact a concoction from the twelfth century.
305. Roesdahl (1991), p. 145.
306. See Lavelle (2002), p. 64 for potential carrying capacity, and p. 67 for his view that 2,000–3,000 men would seem a likely estimate for the actual force.
307. Roesdahl (1991), p. 143.
308. Strickland (1997), p. 355.
309. *The Battle of Maldon*, lines 269–72 (pp. 28–9).
310. *The Battle of Maldon*, lines 70–1 (pp. 20–1).
311. My view on both counts is shared by Nicholas Brooks, who writes (Brooks 1991, p. 12) that the bow was apparently regarded as capable of wounding but not as effective in killing. He adds in more general terms that in those days the bow was seen as a weapon of the 'unfree or semi-free', not of the noble or proper warrior. Matthew Strickland (1997), p. 355, also makes the same point that archers belonged to the poor class.
312. For more information regarding the role of the sword, including its personification and symbolic value, see for example Burton (1987), pp. xv–xvi.
313. This clearly does not apply to all warrior societies. For example, in early Japan, despite the Japanese sword eventually being seen as arguably the world's most effective, and despite the supposed ideal of one-on-one combat, warrior-nobles often preferred bows and were praised for bowmanship. There were, however, strict restrictions in Japan on the possession of weapons by commoners, especially after

the introduction of firearms in the sixteenth century. The preference for use of the bow by the Mongols and native Americans should similarly not be overlooked.

314. The role of the sniper is another important but seemingly under-recognised matter, clearly relating to projectile weapons – in modern times with a range of a mile or more. This applies not just in military engagements, but in political assassinations and so forth. And should we view them as professionals or even heroes, or as sneaks using 'dirty' tactics?

315. Barlow (2003), p. 25.

316. See for example Keynes (1980), pp. 189–90.

317. Brooke (1967), p. 132, also makes this latter point, as does Keynes (1980), p. 203.

318. Keynes (1980), p. 203.

319. MacDonald (1997).

320. Keynes (1980), p. 205.

321. Lavelle (2002), p. 37.

322. Keynes (1980) p. xviii.

323. Barlow (2003), p. 26.

324. Hollister (1992), p. 87.

325. The mid nineteenth century historian Lord Macaulay, though not the most respected of authorities on early Britain, makes the same point: see Macaulay 1848/1967, vol. 1, p. 8.

3   The Improbable Norman Conquest

1. *Life of King Edward*, p. 76.

2. 'I commend this woman [Edith] and all the kingdom to your protection.' *Life of King Edward*, p. 79.

3. *Anglo-Saxon Chronicle*, Ms E, p. 197. Norman sources, such as Orderic Vitalis (*Ecclesiastical History*, pp. 136–9) and William of Poitiers (*Deeds of William*, pp. 100–1), unsurprisingly claim that he seized the crown. Orderic adds that it was, moreover, without acclaim. William of Malmesbury (*Chronicle of the Kings of England*, II, 13, Bohn edition p. 255) also feels Harold seized the crown through ambition and disputes the claim that he was granted it by Edward. Henry of Huntingdon (*History of the English*, VI, 27, pp. 384–5) goes even further and says that Harold 'usurped the crown'. The *Brief History of Most Noble William*, pp. 29a–29b, refers to his 'seizing the crown' but 'with the consent of the citizens of London and with many others supporting his madness'. William's biographer David Douglas (1964), p. 182, remarks with some degree of compromise that 'the indecent haste of these proceedings indicates that the earl's seizure of the throne was premeditated, and that he feared opposition. It is very probable, however, that the Confessor on his deathbed, either of his own free will or under persuasion, had nominated the earl as his successor.' The Norman source Wace's *Story of Rollo*, lines 5725–840, also accepts that Edward, under pressure from the English magnates at his bedside, nominated Harold, though he would have much preferred William. Lines 5823–4 state explicitly *Issi a fait Heraut son eir quant Guillaume ne pout aveir* ('In this way he made Harold his heir since he could not have William'). Similarly L. C. B. Seaman (1982), p. 58, remarks, 'What may also have governed Edward's ultimate designation of Harold was the near certainty that William's claim would be opposed in England but that Harold's would not.'

4. See for example Walker (1997), p. 137; Douglas (1964), p. 182; and McLynn (1999), p. 177. It should however be noted that John of Worcester, who was favourably

disposed towards Harold, was the only near-contemporary source to state this. See the *Chronicle of John of Worcester*, pp. 600–1. See also Lawson (2003), pp. 62–3.

5. The grounds were that he had been appointed before the death of his predecessor, Robert of Jumièges, an appointment moreover, in which Harold's father Earl Godwine, had been instrumental some years earlier (discussed later in the text).

6. Bates (2004), p. 98. Hollister (1992), p. 93, remarks there was 'no clear, unambiguous principle' at the time regarding royal succession.

7. See Barlow (2003), pp. 21, 25.

8. Williams (1999a), p. 228, dates the marriage as c. 1023 (and similarly Harold's birth as c. 1026 as opposed to the more widely accepted c. 1022), but her sources are unclear.

9. Stafford (1989), p. 97.

10. Stafford (1997), p. 83.

11. Malmesbury, *Chronicle of the Kings of England*, II, 13, Bohn edition p. 253; Worcester, *Chronicle*, pp. 574–7.

12. Worcester, *Chronicle*, pp. 582–3.

13. Douglas (1964), p. 192, implies that Harold himself may have been implicated, and that Harold had designs on the crown from this point. Higham (1997), p. 171, refers to such suspicions about Harold's involvement, but dismisses them, claiming his death was natural and that Harold was supportive of Edward the Exile. Ronay (2000), pp. 136–42, in a specialist study of Edward the Exile, strongly believes that Edward was indeed murdered, and that it was very likely by Harold or possibly his supporters, though he does also point out that if William of Normandy had been promised the crown by this stage (to be discussed presently), then William too (through his agents in Britain) was a possible suspect. Unfortunately, there is no compelling proof to date that Edward's death was not due to a heart attack or something similar (though he was only in his early forties), nor as to the perpetrator should it have been murder. Personally, the cynic in me yet again notes a 'convenient' death.

14. Stafford (1997), p. 272 feels he was probably old enough to rule alone.

15. See Stafford (1997) pp. 76, 89, 269, 272 for comment on Edith's role as ward and 'mother' to the so-called 'royal heirs'. The other heir was ironically called Harold, and was the son of the late Earl Ralph of Hereford who himself was the son of Edward's sister Goda (Godgifu) by her first husband, Count Dreux of the Vexin. That is, young Harold was, like Edgar, a grandnephew of Edward the Confessor. In another parallel to Edgar's case, Harold's father Ralph had also died in 1057. Harold was a few years younger than Edgar, and was commonly seen as a 'reserve' heir.

16. For example, William of Poitiers in the *Deeds of William*, pp. 114–15, refers to the distance between Edith and Harold, even stating that she 'fought him', and that she disliked him to such an extent that she much preferred William to be king than her brother. This seems to extend beyond mere Norman propagandist vilification of Harold and elevation of William. Nor, in stark contrast to their mother Gytha, is there any record of her being distressed by Harold's death (or for that matter, the deaths at Hastings of her other brothers Gyrth and Leofwine). Similarly there is no evidence that she tried to help Harold's children after his death.

17. See for example Higham (1997), p. 165, who states that Edith's 'partiality' for her brother Tostig is beyond doubt.

18. *Life of King Edward*, pp. 74–6. See also William of Malmesbury's *Chronicle of the Kings of England*, II, 13, Bohn edition p. 252, for the vision and prophecy of doom.

19. He was canonised in 1161. Saints were generally placed in one of two categories, martyr or confessor.

20. Notably Poitiers, *Deeds of William*, pp. 18–21.

21. Barlow (1970), p. 51, argues that Edward's fondness for Normandy has been exaggerated, as too any fondness he might have had for William.

22. Poitiers, *Deeds of William*, pp. 120–1. Those named are Archbishop Stigand, Earl Godwine, Earl Leofric, and Earl Siward.

23. *Anglo-Saxon Chronicle*, Ms D, entry for 1052 corrected to 1051, Swanton edition p. 176, and Worcester, *Chronicle*, pp. 562–3.

24. However, Brown (1984), p. 50, favours the Norman view that the recognition of William was formal.

25. At that time, Godwine himself was Earl of Wessex and the principal earl in the kingdom, his eldest son Swein was Earl of Hereford, his second son Harold was Earl of East Anglia, and his eldest daughter Edith was of course Edward's politically arranged wife. The firebrand Swein – declared a *nithing*, an outlawed 'nobody' whom anyone could legally kill – was a particular irritant, having by that stage already been exiled twice by Edward (for abducting and raping a nun and for murdering his cousin Beorn respectively), and twice Godwine had pressured Edward into reinstating him.

26. Cnut had died in late 1035 and had been assuming that his son by Emma, Harthacnut, would succeed him as king of both Denmark and England. However, Harthacnut was kept very busy in Denmark and the English crown was taken up by his half-brother Harold Harefoot, Cnut's son by his first wife Aelfgifu of Northampton. Godwine was originally a supporter of Harthacnut but ended up having to accept Harefoot. The following year Edward's elder brother Alfred (both being born of Emma but in her first marriage, to Aethelred Unraed) attempted to return from Normandy, where they had both been in exile, to push his claim for the throne over Harefoot. The details are not clear, but, apparently acting on Harefoot's orders, Godwine had arrested Alfred. Subsequently, while in custody, Alfred was blinded so violently that he was killed. Godwine maintained that it was Harefoot's men who had done this dreadful act, and that he had not ordered it. However, despite swearing oaths to this effect, he was still viewed with some suspicion by Edward and many others till the end of his life (in 1053). Interestingly, even the anonymous author of the *Life of Harold* (*Vita Haroldi*), though kindly disposed towards Godwine's son Harold, clearly indicates his belief that Godwine was not only guilty of this particular deed but was in general a 'deceitful' and 'villainous' man. See *Life of Harold*, pp. 3–4. Henry of Huntingdon, *History of the English*, VI, 20, pp. 372–3, also deems Godwine guilty.

27. Barlow (2003), p. 56, shares this view, but with a different metaphor, that the basic cause was Edward's desire 'to get the Godwines off his back'.

28. *Anglo-Saxon Chronicle*, Ms E, entry for 1048 corrected to 1051, Swanton edition p. 172–3, uses the term 'one-sided account'.

29. *Anglo-Saxon Chronicle*, Ms E, entry for 1048 corrected to 1051, Swanton edition p. 172. Ms D, entry for 1052 corrected to 1051, Swanton edition pp. 173, 175, does not refer to the armour but indicates that Eustace's men were the instigators.

30. *Anglo-Saxon Chronicle*, Ms D, entry for 1052 corrected to 1051, Swanton edition p. 175. John of Worcester, *Chronicle*, pp. 558–9, follows D.

31. However, Walker (1997), pp. 30–1, who favours the Ms E version, does see the distinct possibility of Edward being behind it.

32. The *Life of King Edward*, p. 19, says of Jumièges that he provoked and opposed the earl as much as he could and, explicitly, that 'he often attacked Godwine with schemes'.

33. *Anglo-Saxon Chronicle*, Ms E, entry for 1048 corrected to 1051, Swanton edition pp. 174–5, refers merely to accusations made by the Normans, but the *Life of King Edward*, pp. 19–20, is more specific, stating that Jumièges told Edward that Godwine

was guilty of arranging Alfred's death, of stealing church land, and of 'guilefully scheming to attack him [Edward]'. See also Barlow (2003), p. 56.

34. *Anglo-Saxon Chronicle*, Ms E, entry for 1048 corrected to 1051, Swanton edition pp. 175–6.

35. *Life of King Edward*, p. 21.

36. Edward confiscated Emma's estates shortly after his coronation in 1043, though he was later persuaded to relent. Barlow (1970), p. 38, remarks that his punishment of his mother so soon after being crowned testifies to the long grudge he had against her for her neglect of him.

37. Williams (1999b), p. 161, states controversially that Edward did offer the crown to William, but her sources are unclear.

38. Worcester, *Chronicle*, pp. 574–7; see also *Anglo-Saxon Chronicle*, Ms C and D, entries for 1054, Swanton edition pp. 184–5.

39. Malmesbury, *Chronicle of the Kings of England*, II, 13, Bohn edition p. 253: 'The king, in consequence of the death of his relation, losing his first hope of support, gave the succession of England to William earl of Normandy.'

40. Barlow (1970), p. 72 and pp. 133–4.

41. Their return was probably also facilitated by the convenient death of the troublesome Swein shortly beforehand – yet another timely death. He died near Constantinople, apparently of fever, while returning from a pilgrimage of penance to Jerusalem.

42. Eadmer, *History of Recent Events in England*, p. 6, states that the hostages were sent to Duke William after the return of the Godwine/sons, i.e. in 1052 not 1051. See also Walker (1997), p. 50, and pp. 37–49, who draws the same conclusion independent of Eadmer. By contrast, Freeman (1869), vol. 3, pp. 220–1 and pp. 671–7, does not believe any hostages at all ended up in William's hands prior to 1064 at the earliest, though most scholars disagree.

43. As an aside, which may say something about Malmesbury himself, or Harold, or the standards of the day, one notes with interest William of Malmesbury's comment (*History of English Kings*, II, 228, pp. 418–19), that if he had to, Harold would gladly pay a ransom to Duke William, but not to an 'effeminate like Guy'. (The Bohn edition, II, 13, p. 254, refers rather to 'the contemptible Guy'.)

44. For example, Eadmer, *History of Recent Events in England*, p. 7.

45. Malmesbury states (*Chronicle of the Kings of England*, II, 13, Bohn edition p. 255) that this oath-taking was done 'of his own accord' by Harold 'still more to ingratiate himself' with William. By contrast, the *Song of the Battle of Hastings* has Harold stating that he 'foolishly' (*folement*, line 6818) took an oath to secure his own release and not of his own free will, for he was in a difficult situation, in which William very much had the upper hand, and feared he might not be able to return to England unless he did what William wanted (lines 6820–8). Eadmer, *History of Recent Events in England*, pp. 7–8, gives a very similar explanation to the *Song*.

46. *Life of Harold*, pp. 20–1.

47. See Douglas (1964), p. 188, who writes that since the Battle of Civitate (1053) and the Synod of Melfi (1059) the papacy had become ever more dependent on an alliance with the Normans, a situation which the Normans used to their advantage, including by 'posing as champions in a holy war'. See also McLynn (1999), p. 183, who writes that the pope was at this stage the 'creature of the Normans' and would do what the Normans wanted him to.

48. Malmesbury, *Chronicle of the Kings of England*, II, 13, Bohn edition p. 254. Interestingly, though the story itself seems hard to accept, Malmesbury's tone suggests that sea

fishing was not an uncommon pastime. Freeman (1869), vol. 3, p. 221, also believes Harold was on a 'pleasure-trip', accompanied by Hakon and Wulfnoth.

49. According to a later Norwegian account, Snorri Sturluson's *Heimskringla*, specifically the volume *King Harald [Hardraada]'s Saga*, LXXVI, p. 219. See also Howard (2005), p. 51.
50. For example, William of Poitiers, *Deeds of William*, pp. 120–1.
51. See Douglas (1964), pp. 393–5.
52. Eadmer, *History of Recent Events in England*, p. 6.
53. *Bayeux Tapestry*, plates 1 (pre-departure) and 31 (post-return) in Stenton (1957). Eadmer, *History of Recent Events in England*, p. 8, puts words into Edward's mouth for the latter: 'Did I not tell you that I knew William and that your going might bring untold calamity upon this kingdom?' Bates (2004), p. 96, similarly interprets the scene following Harold's return from Normandy as 'appearing to represent an admonishing King Edward telling a humbled and flustered Harold "I told you so"'.
54. This same apparent confidence reflects one reason why it is hard to believe that the purpose of Harold's trip was to confirm Edward's alleged promise of the crown to William. Regardless of whether or not Harold had any personal ambition towards the throne at this point, it was at this very time that he was in his strongest position to date, and would surely not have acquiesced – even in the unlikely event that it came from the king – in anything that might strengthen the position of a foreign 'warrior-leader'.
55. Wace, *Story of Rollo*, lines 5925–32; William of Jumièges, *Deeds of the Norman Dukes*, pp. 160–1.
56. Brown (1984), p. 50, however, makes much of William's 'kin-right' and describes it as vital to the conquest. Given that his kinship was very distant and not as close as Edgar's, I find this puzzling.
57. Schama (2003), p. 84, for example, is very strongly of the view that papal support was the key to William's ability to muster men and resources.
58. Edward became king in June 1042 upon the death of his half-brother Harthacnut, but was not crowned till April 1043. Also confusingly, he returned from exile in Normandy to England in 1041, seemingly involved in an informal co-sharing of the crown, at the invitation of Harthacnut. Thus, depending on sources and focus, there may appear to be some inconsistency in references to Edward's return and succession.
59. See Barlow (1970), p. 58, regarding the promise to Swein, which actually seemed relatively explicit.
60. Howard (2005), p. 52.
61. For example, in 1048 he had declined to send naval support to Swein despite the latter's pressing request. See Worcester, *Chronicle* pp. 544–5, and *Anglo-Saxon Chronicle* (D), entry 1049 [1048], though both say that Edward's refusal was on behalf of the people, who opposed this military assistance. Earl Godwine, by contrast, was strongly in support of sending assistance (some 50 ships).
62. See McLynn (1999), pp. 188, 215, regarding Swein's dispatch of men to Harold.
63. See for example *King Harald's Saga*, XCIX, p. 239. See also DeVries (1999), pp. 23–4. He is described by the Icelander Snorri Sturluson as 'five ells' tall, an Icelandic ell being 18 inches (it is 45 inches in England), giving a height of 90 inches or 7 feet 6 inches. This is almost certainly an exaggeration, or a misinterpretation (a Danish ell for example being somewhat shorter), but nonetheless shows how exceptionally tall he must have been. Schama (2003), p. 86, gives a precise figure of 6 feet 4 inches, but how he arrived at this is not clear.
64. *King Harald's Saga*, III, p. 162.

65. Worcester, *Chronicle*, pp. 598–9, refers not only to murders attributed directly to Tostig, but to the murder of the Northumbrian thegn Gospatric on the orders of Queen Edith, on account of her brother Tostig. See also Stafford (1997), pp. 270–4.

66. Worcester, *Chronicle*, pp. 596–9; *Anglo-Saxon Chronicle*, 1065, Ms C, Swanton edition pp. 190, 192, Ms D, pp. 191, 193; Huntingdon, *History of the English*, VI, 26, pp. 382–5; *Life of King Edward*, pp. 50–3. See also Fletcher (2002), pp. 149–62, and Stafford (1989), pp. 95–9, for more details on Tostig and the rebellion.

67. Worcester, *Chronicle*, pp. 598–9; *Anglo-Saxon Chronicle*, Ms D, 1065.

68. *Life of King Edward*, p. 53, states that the troops actually deserted him, and that this was the cause of his subsequent terminal illness. The cause of Edward's death shortly afterwards is unclear, but his condition may perhaps genuinely have been exacerbated by stress over this 'slap in the royal face', as indeed by the whole business of the rebellion and Tostig's plight.

69. *Life of King Edward*, p. 53. Schama (2003), p. 80, goes so far as to say that Harold 'sold his brother down the river', and accuses Harold of 'evicting' Tostig from Northumbria. This seems a rather extreme interpretation. Schama goes on to remark that the feud between the brothers has often been under-estimated, and that 'the family feud killed off Anglo-Saxon England'. It was certainly one factor, but one among several.

70. Henry of Huntingdon, in his *History of the English*, VI, 25, pp. 382–3, refers to Tostig's jealousy towards Harold and a remarkable incident in 1063 in which Tostig and Harold quarrelled at Windsor, following which Tostig went in a rage to Hereford, where Harold was to entertain King Edward with a banquet, and proceeded to kill and dismember Harold's servants, putting their body parts into the drink that was to be served. Huntingdon was not kindly disposed towards the Godwinesons, but even allowing for exaggeration, this would seem to indicate how Tostig was viewed as unstable and dangerous, especially when crossed. See also Lawson (2003), p. 71.

71. Worcester, *Chronicle*, pp. 598–9.

72. Williams (1999a), p. 228, refers to Harold 'persuading' Edward to ratify Morcar as the new earl, but her source for this is unclear.

73. Wace, *Story of Rollo*, lines 5925–32; William of Jumièges, *Deeds of the Norman Dukes*, pp. 160–1.

74. The *Life of Harold*, p. 21, points out that it was lawful for Harold to break an oath extracted from him in this way.

75. *Anglo-Saxon Chronicle*, Ms C and D, entries for 1066, Swanton edition pp. 194–5; *Life of Harold*, pp. 108–9.

76. Fletcher (2002), p. 165.

77. These were, in order of seniority, Godwine, Edmund, Magnus, Gunnhild, Gytha and Ulf. (Actually she had borne seven, but one died in infancy, name and gender unknown.)

78. *Anglo-Saxon Chronicle*, Ms C and D, entries for 1066, Swanton edition pp. 194–5.

79. Unsurprisingly, the victorious Normans chose to interpret it as an omen of doom for Harold and a felicitous one for William. Poitiers, apostrophically addressing the dead Harold in *Deeds of William* (pp. 140–5), writes that 'the comet foretold your doom', then goes on to mention 'the felicity that the same star portended' for William.

80. *Anglo-Saxon Chronicle*, Ms C and D, entries for 1066, Swanton edition pp. 194–5; Worcester, *Chronicle*, pp. 600–1.

81. *Anglo-Saxon Chronicle*, Ms C and D, entries for 1066, both suggest this initial misidentification quite strongly. D, for example (Thorpe edition, p. 165), states (immediately after commenting on Tostig's arrival): 'He [Harold] gathered so great a naval force, and also a land force, as no king here in the land had before gathered; because it had for

truth been said to him that Count William from Normandy, King Eadward's kinsman, would come hither and subdue this land, all as it afterwards came to pass.'

82. *Anglo-Saxon Chronicle*, Ms C, entry for 1066, Swanton edition p. 196.
83. For example, *King Harald's Saga*, LXXVIII, p. 221, states that Tostig went from Flanders to Denmark (via Frisia).
84. *King Harald's Saga*, LXXVIII and LXXIX, p. 222.
85. See a brief mention in Orderic's contribution to the *Deeds of the Norman Dukes* (vol. II, pp. 162–3), in which he refers to the duke 'sending' Tostig to England, from which he was repelled by Harold's fleet. He also mentions this, and elaborates further, in his *Ecclesiastical History*, pp. 140–3. (I will return to the use of the word 'sent' later in the notes.)
86. *King Harald's Saga*, LXXIX, p. 223.
87. DeVries (1999), p. 236.
88. *King Harald's Saga*, LXXIX, p. 223.
89. See Douglas (1964), p. 190.
90. Orderic, *Ecclesiastical History*, pp. 141–3.
91. Such a view is probably based on a reference in the *Anglo-Saxon Chronicle*, D and E manuscripts, entries for 1066, stating that Tostig, having sailed north to Scotland after his raiding, met Hardraada and that 'Tostig submitted to him and became his man' (Thorpe edition p. 166). If Tostig's submission is seen as having happened only at that point, it does understandably make it seem as though it might be a chance meeting and that Tostig had opportunistically thrown in his lot with Hardraada, but it is far more likely, in my interpretation, that it is merely a reference to Tostig being designated second-in-command of their joint force (which he is known to have been) rather than leader. Other evidence, notably reference to *Anglo-Saxon Chronicle* Ms C (see below) and to Scandinavian sources, clearly support a case that there had been some prior arrangement.
92. *Anglo-Saxon Chronicle*, Ms C, entry for 1066, Thorpe edition p. 167.
93. *King Harald's Saga*, LXXIX, pp. 222–3. See also DeVries (1999), pp. 236–8, for discussion.
94. See Fletcher (2002), p. 157 and pp. 169–70, for details of Copsig the man.
95. See DeVries (1999), pp. 239–40, for discussion.
96. DeVries (1999), pp. 247–8, also considers the idea of a planned diversionary attack a strong possibility. It is also worth noting that, irrespective of how much William may or may not have known about any plans involving Hardraada, he may well have endorsed Tostig's harrying of the south coast, seeing it as a useful means of testing Harold's defences and keeping him guessing. This would accord with Orderic's statement that the duke actually *sent* Tostig to England (*Deeds of the Norman Dukes*, pp. 162–3, my italics). McLynn (1999), p. 187, supports the view that William encouraged Tostig in this matter, but for unclear reasons he dates Tostig's visit to William as January, concluding that Tostig sailed to the Isle of Wight from Flanders not Normandy. Though unlikely, it is possible that Tostig may in fact have made two separate visits to Normandy.
97. Gillingham (1996), p. 108, confirms the 'normal practice' of using spies and the value placed on reconnaissance and reminds us that spies were necessarily more numerous than the records show, since by their nature they would only come to light if caught. He also observes (p. 109) that William frequently profited by good advance information.
98. Poitiers, *Deeds of William*, pp. 106–7.

99. It is possible, however, that only one *fyrd* was called out (if so, the southern), and their period of duty was extended to four months. The fleet had been stationed off the Isle of Wight but was sent back to London.

100. *Anglo-Saxon Chronicle*, Ms C, entry for 1066, Swanton edition p. 196.

101. It seems from Wace, *Story of Rollo*, lines 6293–328, that it was quite early on, in that it appears to have arrived before the appearance of Halleys Comet on 24 April. It also predated William's shipbuilding (lines 6329–42), which he set about in earnest after receiving it. It is interesting, but probably fruitless, to speculate whether Tostig, if he did indeed visit William in April, was aware of the papal support. And if he was, did he inform Hardraada?

102. For a detailed discussion of this see Gillmoor (1996).

103. Again, for a detailed discussion of this see Gillmoor (1996).

104. Seymour (1979), p. 13, estimates the number of housecarls at around 3000, while some scholars think the numbers would have been lower: see for example Dodds (1996), p. 15.

105. For example, Bradbury (1998), p. 139, writes: 'It is almost certain that William would have come to England earlier had the weather allowed it, so he had fortune . . . on his side.' Walker (1997), p. 166, is another who feels the timing was not planned. Grainge and Grainge (1996), p. 141, also state, 'we do not believe that he would have deliberately delayed sailing until he knew they [the *fyrd*] had disbanded. We believe that he would have sailed as soon as the wind blew fair.' By contrast, McLynn (1999), p. 194, along with others, feels it was planned, and that the explanation of contrary winds is 'unconvincing'. This is but one example of many areas of vastly different interpretations of the events of that year.

106. Poitiers, *Deeds of William*, p. 109.

107. For example, Douglas (1964), p. 193, writes that William 'moved his own fleet from Dives to the mouth of the Somme in order to take advantage of the shorter sea-crossing'. However, not only do contemporary sources such as Poitiers indicate otherwise (as discussed in the text above), St Valery represented a hazardous lee shore and experts on those coastal waters feel it was simply too risky. Christine and Gerald Grainge, expert sailors as well as scholars, remark (Grainge and Grainge 1996, p. 136): 'We cannot see William risking his fleet in the dangerous St Valery area.' They further state (p. 141): 'Interpreted in the light of the prevailing meteorological conditions and with a proper understanding of nautical and navigational issues, the contemporary records suggest that the invasion fleet sailed from Dives in the middle of September in marginal conditions, with the intention of reaching England, but was forced to run downwind to the Somme estuary.'

108. *Anglo-Saxon Chronicle*, Ms E, entry for 1066, Swanton edition p. 197.

109. *Deeds of the Norman Dukes*, vol. II, pp. 162–3.

110. There is an intriguing reference in the *Domesday Book* for Essex (Chapter 6, Holdings of St Peter's, subsection 9, the Hundred of Ongar) to an Ailric (Alric), formerly landowner of Kelvedon (Hatch), who 'went away to a naval battle against King William', which does suggest some engagement did take place against William – presumably quite large if it is referred to as a 'battle' – but there is precious little other evidence. See also Lawson (2003), pp. 35–6.

111. Poitiers, *Deeds of William*, pp. 112–13.

112. The exact date of 8 September is given by DeVries (1999), p. 251, though the source is not clear. However, chronologically, the 8th would indeed seem just about right. And of course, it coincided with the date of the standing-down of the *fyrd*.

113. The *Anglo-Saxon Chronicle*, Ms C, entry for 1066, Thorpe edition p. 167, states that Harold was informed that the invaders 'had landed near York'.
114. *Anglo-Saxon Chronicle*, Ms C, entry for 1066, Thorpe edition p. 167.
115. Schama (2003), p. 86, gives the precise date of 19 September, though how he arrived at this is not clear. To me, it seems too late.
116. *Anglo-Saxon Chronicle*, Ms C, entry for 1066, Thorpe edition p. 167.
117. Huntingdon, *History of the English*, VI, 27, pp. 386–7.
118. This does seem remarkable, but there is no evidence to the contrary and scholars, equally surprised as I myself am, accept that there simply were no scouts. See for example DeVries (1999), p. 268, who terms it 'astounding', and Bradbury (1998), p. 132.
119. *Anglo-Saxon Chronicle*, Ms C. entry for 1066, Thorpe edition p. 168.
120. Seymour (1979), p. 15.
121. *King Harald's Saga*, LXXXVII, p. 228, states that from each company two men went for every one that was left behind.
122. *King Harald's Saga*, LXXXVII, p. 228, states that it was 'uncommonly fine weather with hot sunshine', causing the troops to leave their armour behind.
123. Seymour (1979), p. 17.
124. *King Harald's Saga*, XCII, p. 232.
125. Butler (1966), p. 191. Freeman (1869), vol. 3, p. 373, by contrast, refers to Tostig's head being 'cloven to the chin' by an axe.
126. Hollister (1992), pp. 97–8.
127. Points also noted, with similar admiration for Harold and his men, by the military historian William Seymour (1979), p. 16.
128. Seymour (1979), p. 13.
129. For example, *Anglo-Saxon Chronicle*, Ms C, entry for 1066, Swanton edition p. 198; Malmesbury's *Chronicle of the Kings of England*, II, 13, Bohn edition p. 256; and Huntingdon's *History of the English*, VI, 27, pp. 386–9.
130. In those days the bridge was possibly some 400 yards upstream from the present bridge, and the banks almost certainly steeper: see Seymour (1979), pp. 9, 17.
131. See for example Huntingdon, *History of the English*, VI, 27, pp. 386–7. Huntingdon refers to a remarkable – and questionable – three hours.
132. *Anglo-Saxon Chronicle*, Ms C, entry for 1066, Swanton edition p. 198, and Huntingdon, *History of the English*, VI, 27, pp. 386–7.
133. Malmesbury, *Chronicle of the Kings of England*, II, 13, Bohn edition p. 256.
134. Malmesbury, *Chronicle of the Kings of England*, II, 13, Bohn edition p. 256.
135. *Anglo-Saxon Chronicle*, Ms C, entry for 1066, Thorpe edition p. 168. The relevant passage is a twelfth century addition, seemingly by a non-English scribe (see Note 5 on p. 198 of the Swanton edition).
136. *King Harald's Saga*, XCII, p. 231.
137. Oman (1921), p. 640, n. 1, is of this view: 'The tale looks like that of Hastings transferred to Yorkshire.' Freeman, (1869), vol. 3, pp. 366–7, also completely dismisses the use of cavalry at Stamford Bridge, as does Matthew Strickland (1997), p. 360.
138. *King Harald's Saga*, LXXXVII, p. 228.
139. *King Harald's Saga*, XCI, pp. 229–30.
140. *Anglo-Saxon Chronicle*, Ms D, entry for 1066, Swanton edition p. 199.
141. There is a view that William actually intended to land at the Isle of Wight, but this would imply serious navigational problems in ending up at Pevensey (clearly the wind would not have been a factor, but there was some fog), and more importantly

that he would have chosen to land on an island. This seems most unlikely from a strategic perspective. Brown (1996), p. 201, along with most scholars, similarly feels William deliberately chose the Pevensey-Hastings area.

142. *Song of the Battle of Hastings*, pp. 10–11.

143. See for example the *Bayeux Tapestry*, plates 50 and 51 in Stenton (1957).

144. Wace, *Story of Rollo*, lines 6593–8, and *Chronicle of Battle Abbey*, pp. 34–5. However, they differ in that the former refers to them being deliberately holed, the latter to them being burnt. William was obviously a very determined man, and no doubt prepared to fight to the death, but I personally do not believe he would have gone this far, or that his men would have allowed him to. Neither, it would seem, does William's biographer David Bates: see Note 148 below.

145. See McLynn (1999), p. 210, regarding the troop withdrawal.

146. Poitiers, *Deeds of William*, pp. 116–17.

147. Bradbury (1998), p. 163, agrees that a quick battle was the best option for William. See also Gillingham (1996), p. 111, for a similar view.

148. Bates (2004), p. 105, makes the same points that William's strategy of keeping his army near to the point of disembarkation gave him the advantage of keeping his lines of communication short and 'permitting a retreat to his ships', whereas advancing inland would have risked being cut off and becoming vulnerable to a war of attrition. This comment of Bates lends further support to the idea that William did not destroy his ships.

149. For example, Bates (2004), p. 105; Brown (1984), p. 63; Bradbury (1998), pp. 159, 162; and William of Poitiers, *Deeds of William*, pp. 124–5, all agree that these were William's tactics. It was probably simply good fortune for William that the location where he landed was Harold's own territory, but nonetheless it is interesting to speculate whether William, when crossing to England, was consciously factoring this into his plans, and similarly whether Harold would have been so quick to respond if it were someone else's territory – judging from Stamford Bridge, he probably would have been.

150. Douglas (1964), p. 371. It is worth noting that one of the scenes in the *Bayeux Tapestry*, relating to William's ravaging of the local area, shows a mother and child fleeing from a burning house. This is the first known deliberately focused depiction in European art of the suffering of any such civilian victims in any campaign – obviously showing that they had been ignored till this point, rather than that there had been none.

151. Seymour (1979), p. 25, for example, is of the view that William knew of Harold's impetuous nature, and that it would be very difficult for Harold to wait while part of his kingdom was being attacked. Brown (1984), p. 63, is of a similar view, feeling William probably exploited Harold's pride and impetuosity.

152. Lieutenant-Colonel Charles Lemmon (1966a), p. 95, is of a similar view regarding the situation.

153. This is a point also strongly emphasised in Lawson (2003), especially Chapters 2 and 3.

154. See Gillingham (1996).

155. See Worcester, *Chronicle*, pp. 604–5. DeVries (1999) also gives 22 October.

156. However, Worcester, *Chronicle*, pp. 604–5, states that they were.

157. See Orderic's *Deeds of the Norman Dukes*, pp. 166–9, and William of Malmesbury's *Chronicle of the Kings of England*, III, Bohn edition p. 275.

158. McLynn (1999), p. 215. In any event, it is clear that Harold left before certain men had arrived – see for example *Anglo-Saxon Chronicle*, Ms E, Thorpe edition p. 169: 'And

Harold came from the north and fought against him [William] before his army had all come.'

159. If the *Song of the Battle of Hastings* (pp. 14–15) is accurate, William was provocatively insulted by Harold in this message, for Harold, who was William's senior by only around six years, stated he was prepared to forgive William's actions to date in the Hastings area in view of William's 'age and callowness'. The 38-year-old William is said to have replied furiously that he was no longer a boy.

160. Lemmon (1966a), p. 107, feels it is possible given Harold's character. So too does Seymour (1979), pp. 27–8, though he feels that Harold would perhaps be trying to do both, namely blunt William's forces first by inviting him to attack, and then go on the offensive. See also Howarth (1978), p. 160, and discussion of Howarth's views later in this text.

161. Alençon in 1051, where (according to the sources) he skinned alive and/or chopped off the hands and feet of 32 men, is one well known example, but is by no means unique. He was also notoriously to blind a victim in front of the city walls of Exeter, a site of resistance, in 1068.

162. The idea that the English spent the night in revelry, as suggested in some sources (e.g. Malmesbury, Bohn edition, III, p. 276), would seem bizarre under the circumstances.

163. Jumièges (*Deeds of the Norman Dukes*, pp. 168–9), Worcester (*Chronicle*, pp. 604–5), and Orderic (*Ecclesiastical History*, pp. 172–3), all give 'the third hour' (of the day), and most scholars feel it unlikely that battle would have commenced before 9.30. See for example Seymour (1979), p. 30.

164. *Anglo-Saxon Chronicle*, Ms D, 1066, Thorpe edition p. 167, states 'William came upon him unawares, ere his people were in battle order.' Worcester, *Chronicle*, pp. 604–5, refers to Harold not only having just half his men with him, but also to the fact that those he did have were less than a third deployed when William attacked that morning.

165. Boxer (1999), p. 19.

166. Lawson (2003), pp. 150–1, and p. 206, feels it possible that the English line extended down into the valley to Harold's right at one point, and may even have extended to occupancy of a hillock somewhat detached from the ridge. By contrast Seymour (1979), p. 32, feels this might have been occupied by the Bretons.

167. *Anglo-Saxon Chronicle*, Ms D, 1066, Thorpe edition p. 167.

168. *Anglo-Saxon Chronicle*, Ms D, 1066, Thorpe edition p. 167.

169. Worcester, *Chronicle*, pp. 604–5.

170. Wace, *Story of Rollo*, lines 7211–24 regarding excommunication, and lines 7225–94 for Gyrth's speech.

171. Howarth (1978), pp. 161–5.

172. Walker (1997), pp. 148–9.

173. Poitiers, *Deeds of William*, pp. 104–5.

174. Wace, *Story of Rollo*, lines 6293–328, and 7575–8; Malmesbury, *Chronicle of the Kings of England*, III, Bohn edition p. 273; Orderic, *Ecclesiastical History*, pp. 142–3.

175. See for example plate 51 in Stenton (1957). Charles Gibbs-Smith, writing the commentary on the plates, explicitly refers to it as the papal banner (p. 172 in Stenton 1957).

176. Bates (2004), p. 101.

177. Seymour (1979), p. 22. Dodds (1996), p. 14, is one of a number of scholars who believe there would probably also have been some crossbows which were in use by the Normans at that time.

178. However, the *Brief History of the Most Noble William*, VII, pp. 32–32a, states that a feigned retreat took place at the beginning of the fight and does not refer to a real retreat. Henry of Huntingdon (*History of the English*, VI, 30, pp. 392–3), writes in very similar vein, as does William of Malmesbury *(Chronicle of the Kings of England*, III, Bohn edition p. 277).

179. Seymour (1979), p. 33, feels this is probably the case, but also leaves open the possibility that a sub-commander such as Gyrth or Leofwine might have ordered the pursuit. Dodds (1996), pp. 18–19, is more inclined to a probable deliberate counter-attack by Gyrth and/or Leofwine.

180. Some scholars feel that feigned retreats were too difficult to implement, but many disagree. For example, Dodds (1996), p. 19, accepts feigned retreats as a distinct possibility and points out that they were common in those days in warfare on the continent. Indeed, as we have seen, the tactic may have been used by Harold himself at Stamford Bridge. By contrast Seymour (1979), p. 37, feels they were probably real retreats, quickly responded to by William with reserve cavalry.

181. Poitiers, *Deeds of William*, pp. 132–3.

182. This is also suggested by Freeman (1869), vol. 3, p. 497. See also below in the text.

183. See for example Henry of Huntingdon, *History of the English*, VI, 30, pp. 394–5. Some scholars have suggested that this tactic is a later interpretation of the *Bayeux Tapestry*'s depiction of some of the archers shooting high, but there is no reason to doubt it, especially given its established efficacy in those days as a tactic for countering shield walls.

184. The identity of these knights varies according to interpretation of a difficult unpunctuated passage in the *Song of the Battle of Hastings*. An alternative interpretation is William himself, Eustace of Boulogne, Hugh of Ponthieu (nephew of Guy of Amiens, the putative author of the *Song*), and Giffard/Gilfard (possibly Robert not Walter).

185. There has been much debate over the exact manner of Harold's death, not least because the *Bayeux Tapestry* (plates 71 and 72 in Stenton 1957) covers two figures under the single rubric *Hic Harold Rex interfectus est* ('Here King Harold is killed'), one with an arrow in the eye (or face), the other being slashed in the thigh by the sword of a mounted knight. Many scholars have assumed the first figure is Harold (directly under *Harold*) but many have also claimed it is the second figure (directly under *interfectus est*), and not unnaturally there is also a third school claiming both figures are Harold, and that the repetition merely indicates chronological progression. This last interpretation seems (in my view) the best fit in terms of common sense and other probable information about the battle, such as the non-fatal nature of the arrows intended to fall on English heads, etc. In recent years the third school has indeed been greatly strengthened by the discovery that close examination of the second figure shows unfinished stitch marks next to the head of the second figure, suggesting the weaver was going to depict the arrow for this figure too but abandoned the idea for some reason (possibly the nearby axe being too close). See Bradbury (1998), p. 207. Some scholars, notably David Bernstein, accept that both figures are meant to be Harold but that the first one, with the arrow in the eye, is an invention of the *Tapestry*'s designer to indicate divine punishment for perjury, for which blinding was a recognised punishment. There is also confusion about the timing of Harold's death. The *Deeds of the Norman Dukes*, pp. 168–9, has Harold killed very early on, while Wace has him injured in the eye early (lines 8161–8) but not actually killed till the later stages (lines 8829–34), but most scholars accept that

he was struck in the eye late in the battle, probably shortly after sunset, and was dead soon afterwards.

186. Castration of a corpse was not uncommon in medieval times – the case of Simon de Montfort in 1265 being particularly well known – but it was nonetheless considered unchivalrous. Malmesbury, *Chronicle of the Kings of England*, III, Bohn edition p. 278, has William being disgusted by the mutilation of Harold's corpse and punishing the knight responsible by stripping him of his knighthood, but this may be an embellishment.

187. For example, Poitiers, *Deeds of William*, pp. 140–1. Wace, *Story of Rollo*, lines 8819–28 (for Gyrth), and Henry of Huntingdon, *History of the English*, VI, 30, pp. 394–5 (for both Gyrth and Leofwine), state that one or both of the brothers were actually struck down alongside Harold.

188. Notably the *Song of the Battle of Hastings*, pp. 28–9, but also the *Bayeux Tapestry* (plates 64 and 65 in Stenton 1957).

189. For example, Hollister (1992), p. 98.

190. For example Orderic, in *Deeds of the Norman Dukes*, pp. 170–1.

191. *Waltham Chronicle*, pp. 54–5.

192. For example Poitiers, *Deeds of William*, pp. 140–1; and *Song of the Battle of Hastings*, pp. 34–5.

193. *Song of the Battle of Hastings*, pp. 34–5, and Poitiers' *Deeds of William*, pp. 140–1. Poitiers adds that William jested that Harold could thereby guard the shore, and further that the burial was entrusted to one William Malet. Orderic, *Ecclesiastical History*, pp. 178–9, follows Poitiers. Seymour (1979), p. 38, points out that since William had staked much of his claim on Harold's alleged perjured oath, he would be undermining his own cause if he allowed Harold's burial – at least at that time – in hallowed ground.

194. *Waltham Chronicle*, pp. 50–5. The names of the canons are given as Osgod and Aethelric. The same source states (pp. 46–7) that Harold had called in at the church to pray on his way to Hastings.

195. William of Malmesbury, *Chronicle of the Kings of England*, III, Bohn edition pp. 280–1.

196. See for example Pollock (2002).

197. However, Worcester, *Chronicle*, pp. 604–5, states that they were present, but 'slipped away' from the battle with their men.

198. Brown (1996), p. 200.

199. Henry of Huntingdon, *History of the English*, VI, 33, pp. 396–7, gives 1071 for Edwin's death and states that he was killed by his own men (though he does not elaborate), and also states that Morcar was killed the same year by William's men.

200. Strickland (1997), p. 381.

201. See Barlow (2003), p. 169.

202. In this I largely follow Walker (1997), pp. 183–98, and Barlow (2003), pp. 156–71.

203. There are greatly differing opinions about Ulf. Some (e.g. Barlow 2003, p. 128) feel he may have been a twin to Harold, born in 1066 to Aÿditha. Others (e.g. Walker 1997, p. 197) reject this and believe him to be a further son to Edith, probably born around 1050. I personally favour the latter view, largely for the reason that if Ulf was a twin to Harold, why was he not taken to Norway along with his supposed brother and his supposed mother Aÿditha?

204. Macaulay (1848/1967), vol. 1, p. 10.

205. See for example Campbell (2000), pp. xi–xxvii, esp. p. xi (continuing land patterns and value of *Domesday Book*) and p. xxv (English administrators).

206. Campbell (2000), p. xxi, and pp. 10–11.

207. Malmesbury, *Chronicle of the Kings of England*, II, 13, Bohn edition p. 253.
208. See for example Davis (1976). He writes (p. 9), and not just in connection with the Normans in England, that the most puzzling feature of the Normans is the way they disappeared.
209. Davis (1976), p. 122, makes the same point.
210. For example, Malmesbury, *Chronicle of the Kings of England*, III, Bohn edition p. 275, 'quotes' Gyrth as telling Harold: 'I think it ill-advised for you . . . to contend with him [William]. You will act wisely if, yourself withdrawing from this pressing emergency, you allow us [Gyrth and Leofwine] to try the issue of a battle, . . . we who are free from all obligation [to William].' Gyrth goes on to point out that if Harold fights he risks being killed, whereas if he allows his brothers to fight on his behalf, even if they are killed, he will be able to rally the English and avenge the dead. Malmesbury condemns Harold's 'rashness' in not heeding this advice. See also Orderic, *Deeds of the Norman Dukes*, pp. 166–9, who gives a similar account.
211. See McLynn (1999), pp. 215, 228. McLynn also condemns Harold strongly on this point. Schama (2003), p. 91, also refers to Harold's 'foolish' insistence that Gyrth and Leofwine fight alongside him.
212. Barlow (2003), p. 152.
213. Oman, (1921), p. 650.
214. Barlow (2003), p. 5.
215. See for example Strickland (1997), p. 379.
216. See for example the *Song of the Battle of Hastings*, pp. 10–11, which states that William repaired the remains of earlier fortifications. Roman ruins are still to be seen in the general area.
217. Wace, *Story of Rollo*, lines 6969–72: *Heraut a le leu esgardé, closre le fait de boen fossé; de treis parz laissa tris entrees, qui a garder sunt commandees.* The translation is by Glyn Burgess (2004, p. 169). See also 7847–8 and 8079–96 for further references.
218. Wace, *Story of Rollo*, lines 7791–804: *Geldons engleis haches portent e gisarmes qui bien trenchoent; fair orent devant els escuz de fenestres e d'altres fuz, devant els les orent levez, comme cleies joinz e serrez, fait en orent devant closture; n'i laisserent nule jointure par onc Normant entrels venist qui desconfire les volsist. D'escuz e d'ais s'avironerent, issi deffendre se quiderent; e s'il se fussent bien tenu ja ne fussent le jor vencu.*
219. Burgess (2004), p. 178. My thanks are due also to Margaret Burrell, Professor of French and medieval specialist at the University of Canterbury, who independently arrived at essentially the same translation.
220. Some earlier scholars, such as Charles Oman (1921), p. 643, n. 2, have treated the word *fenestres* (now *fenêtres* meaning 'windows') as a mistake. He deems it 'impossible', seemingly overlooking the 'wooden shutters' interpretation.
221. See for example Poitiers, *Deeds of William*, pp. 128–9.
222. For example, plate 63 in Stenton (1957).
223. Freeman (1869), vol. 3, p. 445. See his illustration of the battleground, inserted between pp. 442–3, for his positioning of this palisade and trench.
224. Lawson (2003), Illustration no. 70, between pp. 224–5.
225. Lawson (2003), pp. 206–7, and see also pp. 204, 151.
226. Lawson (2003), Illustration nos 45, 46, between pp. 160–1 (plates 66 and 67 in Stenton 1957).
227. Lawson (2003), p. 151, n. 65.
228. Huntingdon, *History of the English*, VI, 30, pp. 392–3.
229. I am indebted to Graham Zanker, Professor of Classics at the University of Canterbury, for confirming this.

230. Worcester, *Chronicle*, pp. 604–5.
231. See Bradbury (1998), p. 179, for further discussion.
232. A collection of Roman caltrops can be viewed at Wroxeter Roman City Museum.
233. For example, Malmesbury's *Chronicle of the Kings of England*, III, Bohn edition p. 277.
234. Strickland (1997), p. 355.
235. Plate 63 in Stenton (1957). Lawson (2003), pp. 81, 206, feels that it is dangerous to assume that this single figure suggests few archers, and that in fact the figure 'hints at lines of skirmishing missile troops' (p. 206), but I myself follow the majority of scholars in concluding that Harold had few archers. Certainly, any such archers do not feature in the written records. If Harold had indeed had a reasonable number of archers, then the Norman knights – and for that matter infantry – would surely not have been able to approach so closely to the English shield wall.
236. See for example Strickland (1997), pp. 355, 358–9. As Strickland points out, the use of the crossbow in open battle is limited since it takes much longer to load than a normal bow, and so it became more associated with sieges, but in a case such as Hastings where one side was virtually static, and moreover densely packed, it became very effective against that static 'semi-besieged' force.
237. See DeVries (1999), pp. 218–19.
238. Oman (1921), p. 648, feels that 'a couple of thousand bowmen might have saved Harold', but is not critical of Harold for their absence, attributing this rather to traditional custom.
239. Bradbury (1998), p. 168.
240. For example McLynn (1999), p. 221.
241. Wace, *Story of Rollo*, lines 7811–18, states that Harold did indeed emphasise to his men the importance of holding their positions.
242. It would be even more foolish if, as the Norwegian chroniclers described and as we saw earlier, Harold had indeed used feigned cavalry retreats himself as a tactic at Stamford Bridge just a few weeks earlier but failed to recognise them at Hastings. It is possible, in my view, that he was aware and warned his men accordingly, but was nonetheless let down by them in the heat of battle.
243. For example Lawson (2003), p. 242.
244. For example, Poitiers, *Deeds of William*, pp. 124–5; Jumièges, *Deeds of the Norman Dukes*, pp. 168–9. Hollister (1992), p. 98, also suggests this as a possible factor, along with possible overconfidence, but still concludes that Harold's haste was a 'serious error', moreover with no real reason for it.
245. Seymour (1979), p. 25.
246. Freeman (1869), vol. 3, p. 438.
247. Freeman (1869), vol. 3, p. 440.
248. Lemmon (1966a), p. 98. Barlow (1999), p. 67, also feels Harold's position was too close, and indeed believes that this – and not rashness – was in fact the major cause of his failure.
249. Bradbury (1998), p. 159.
250. Barlow (2003), pp. 152–3.
251. Wace, *Story of Rollo*, lines 6925–38. It should also be noted that the Norman sources not infrequently show Gyrth in a more positive light than Harold, possibly to deprecate Harold (as they clearly do elsewhere) but also possibly because that might have been their genuine perception.
252. Freeman (1869), vol. 3, p. 435, makes a similar point, despite his overall praise of Harold.

253. Wace, *Story of Rollo*, lines 6925–38. Even if these words are put into Gyrth's mouth by Wace, it still comes across as a sort of near-contemporary critical commentary as to what Harold should have done.

254. Douglas (1964), p. 196.

255. *Waltham Chronicle*, pp. 48–9.

256. *Anglo-Saxon Chronicle*, Ms D, 1066, Swanton edition p. 200. The *Waltham Chronicle*, pp. 46–7, also states that Harold believed he would be attacking a weak and unprepared force before reinforcements from Normandy could arrive, but adds (pp. 48–9) that he acted 'too rashly' and ended up facing an army 'four times as large as his'. (By contrast, the *Song of the Battle of Hastings* (pp. 20–1, 26–7) states William told his men not to fear the English despite the latter's greater numbers.)

257. *Brief History of Most Noble William*, pp. 30a–30b.

258. Freeman (1869), vol. 3, pp. 438–9.

259. Huntingdon, *History of the English*, VI, 29, pp. 392–3.

260. In a related comment Dodds (1996), p. 10, remarks on William's good fortune in that the fleet had recently been sent back to London. I agree, but go further and feel that William was also lucky that there do not appear to have been any roving vessels deliberately left behind.

261. McLynn (1999), p. 210.

262. This consisted of a number of planks set in see-saw fashion across the fulcrum of a cross-beam, with beacons at the forward end of the planks. By raising and lowering planks in a given pattern a reasonably complex semaphore system was possible, more visible than flags and of course able to be used at night as well.

263. For example, Douglas (1964), p. 172 and Wood (1987), p. 212.

264. Matthew (2003), p. 97.

265. Walker (1997), p. 99.

266. Malmesbury, *Chronicle of the Kings of England*, III, Bohn edition p. 273: 'Harold omitted to do this, either because he was proud by nature, or else distrusted his [own] cause, or because he feared that his messengers would be obstructed by William and his partisans, who beset every port.'

267. Freeman (1869), vol. 3, p. 318.

268. Barlow (1999), p. 63.

269. Douglas (1964), p. 374.

270. Douglas (1964), pp. 371–6, passim.

271. Bates (2004), p. 16.

272. Bates (2004), pp. 15–16, passim.

273. Douglas (1964), p. 368.

274. See for example the Wikipedia entry for 'Matilda of Flanders', http://en.wikipedia.org/wiki/Matilda_of_Flanders.

275. Douglas (1964), p. 370.

276. Worcester, *Chronicle*, pp. 600–1.

277. *Waltham Chronicle*, pp. 26–7.

278. Orderic, *Ecclesiastical History*, pp. 170–1. On the negative side, on the same page he refers to Harold's 'tyranny', having earlier referred (pp. 138–9) to Harold's 'nefariousness', 'evil', and his being guilty of 'crimes too horrible to relate'.

279. McLynn (1999), p. 135.

280. See *Life of Harold*, pp. 5–7, 21.

281. Walker (1997), pp. 120–35 passim. Note especially the remark about the 'essential dual nature of Harold's character' on p. 121.

282. See for example McLynn (1999), pp. 135–6.
283. McLynn (1999), p. 136.
284. Walker (1997), pp. 169–72.
285. *Song of the Battle of Hastings*, pp. 12–13.
286. See also Lawson (2003), p. 241, who, despite a generally positive portrayal of Harold, concludes that William was probably a better commander than Harold.
287. Gillingham (1975), p. 30.

Appendix 1

1. Kearney (1995), p. 43, makes the same point.
2. See especially Higham (2002), who discusses in detail the context and perceived political purpose of all major references to Arthur throughout history.
3. For example Higham (1994) (even more strongly than in Higham 2002), p. 211, states clearly that 'Arthur himself did not exist'.
4. See, for example, Aldhouse-Green (2006), p. 61.
5. I do not claim to have read every book on Arthur. My interest is merely moderate. For very useful overviews of the question of Arthur's historicity as opposed to historicisation, see, for example, Higham (2002) or (1994), or Green (2000) (website), though ardent fans of Arthur should be warned that these authors' conclusions might not necessarily make happy reading.
6. Caxton (1485), p. 2.
7. For the first naming of Lancelot, in de Troyes' first poem-story 'Erec and Enide' (Eric et Enide), see de Troyes (1991), p. 58; the first idea of romance between Lancelot and Guinevere is in his third story 'The Knight of the Cart' (Le Chevalier de la Charrette), which also, in its opening sentence, makes the first reference to Camelot, for which see ibid., p. 207; and for the Holy Grail see his final story 'The Story of the Grail' (Le Conte du Graal [Perceval]).
8. See for example the story 'Culhwch and Olwen' in the *Mabinogion*, specifically p. 84.
9. Aneirin, *Gododdin*, lines 1241–2, in Koch (1997), entry B2.38, p. 23. Some scholars have suggested this entry might be a later interpolation from the ninth or tenth century, but, based on detailed textual analysis, Koch sees no reason to support such a view and moreover appears to favour an actual historical existence for Arthur: see his notes, ibid., pp. 147–8. However, see also Higham (2002), pp. 180–5, for a rather more guarded view regarding the entry's reliability as a sixth/seventh century item. Higham believes it likely that it is derived from Nennius's *Historia Brittonium* of 829–30.
10. See the *Mabinogion* (pp. 80–115 for 'Culhwch and Olwen').
11. Malmesbury, *Chronicle of the Kings of England*, I, 1, Bohn edition p. 11.
12. *Annales Cambriae 447–954*, text at http://www.fordham.edu/halsall/source/annalescambriae.html.
13. One reason for this view is Gildas, the sixth (some believe fifth) century monk, and I will go into the matter in some detail with the additional aim of illustrating the difficulty in being precise in this period and hence difficulty in aspects of the study of Arthur. In his *Ruin of England*, widely accepted as probably being written c. 540–5 – though Higham (1994) argues controversially for a much earlier date of around 480, and others have argued for c. 520 (see Kerlouegan 2004, p. 223) – he refers to the passing of 44 years in relation to the Battle of Badon. He clearly states that this battle took place in the year of his birth. Unfortunately, not only is his date of birth unknown, the rest of his Latin in this passage is also ambiguous and can be

interpreted either as 'forty-four years ago from the time of his writing' or 'forty-four years after the coming of the Anglo-Saxons'. The latter is the interpretation followed in the Giles translation (Gildas 26). The Latin is: *Usque ad annum obsessionis Badonici montis, novissimaeque ferme de furciferis non minimae stragis, quique quadragesimus quartus, ut novi, orditur annus mense iam uno emenso, qui et meae nativitatis est.* Phillips and Keatman (1992), pp. 60–2, analyse the Latin in detail and similarly conclude that the second interpretation is the more likely. The first interpretation would give a date of around 496–501, following the popular dating of *Ruin* as c. 540–5. The second interpretation is further complicated by uncertainty over the date of the Anglo-Saxon Advent. Bede, who follows this second interpretation (*Ecclesiastical History*, I, 16, p. 29), gives the Advent as 449–55 (ibid., I, 15, p.26), which would give a date of 493–9 for the battle. (Higham 1994, controversially, dates the battle much earlier at c. 430.) In either case – unless one took a date of c. 472 for the Advent, which few scholars would accept – it would seem the dates in the *Annals* are too late.

14. He does (*Ruin of England*, 32) make a brief and somewhat obscure reference to a bear, which is sometimes taken to refer to Arthur, for in Brythonic the name 'Arthur' can be interpreted as 'Bear-Man', and it was not uncommon for persons to be metonymically likened to certain animals. Phillips and Keatman (1992) offer a variant explanation of the name 'Arthur', namely the Brythonic 'arth' for 'bear' and 'ur' as an abbreviation of the Latin 'ursus', pointing out that in a (post-)Romano-British context the combination of Brythonic and Latin in names was not uncommon either. Thus, not unlike 'Vortigern', there is a possibility that 'Arthursus/Arthur' could have been used (at least initially) as a title rather than a specific given name. Barber and Pykitt (1997), p. 38, also point out that 'Arthwyr', meaning 'Bear Exalted', was used as a title for leaders in times of crisis, a reference to a Celtic bear deity. We should also note that Gildas often used animal metaphors.

15. For example, Padel (1994), p. 16. See also *Ruin of England*, Sections 25 and 26.

16. Caradoc, *Life of Gildas*, 5–6.

17. *Mabinogion*, p. 85 for the brothers (Hueil is described as 'never submitting to a lord's hand') and p. 87 for the feud. Higham (2002), p. 59, dismisses the idea that Gildas was of royal birth.

18. Barber and Pykitt (1997), p. 285.

19. See Higham (2002), e.g. pp. 58, 98–9, 123.

20. The first was at the mouth of the River Gleni/Glein; the second, third, fourth, and fifth at the River Dubglas in the region of Linuis/Linnius/Linnuis; the sixth at the River Bassas; the seventh in a wood called Cat Coit Celidon; the eighth near Gurnion/Guinnion Castle; the ninth at the City of the Legion/Cair Lion; the tenth at the River Trat Treuroit/Tribuit; the eleventh on the mountain Breguoin/Cat Bregion/Agnet; the twelfth at Mount Badon. In this listing, in addition to the translation of 'Nennius' by Giles (where it is Section 50), I refer also to Wade-Evans' translation of this important section (in this case Section 56): see References.

21. See, for example, Wood (1987), p. 55, in which he refers to a known practice of ascription, to heroes such as Arthur, of victories in battles in which they were not even present; and he believes this is the case with a number of these battles.

22. Padel (2004), p. 530.

23. See, for example, Pryor (2005), pp. 17–18.

24. For example, see Moffat (1999), pp. 120–2, who argues convincingly that Merlin was a real figure, Myrddin, but that he lived some 60 years later than Arthur.

25. The following are just a few illustrative examples. Tintagel, a long-time favourite since its identification by Geoffrey of Monmouth, had its cause enhanced in 1998 by

the discovery of a plaque referring to an 'Artognou', which can be rendered as 'Arthnou'. This is not, however, definite proof of Arthur. For details of the find see Castleden (2003), p. 64 and pp. 225–6. South Cadbury as Camelot was mentioned by the antiquarian John Leland in the sixteenth century and has had support, at least initially, from Leslie Alcock (e.g. Alcock 1972), as well as Geoffrey Ashe. Winchester was favoured by Thomas Malory in his *Le Morte D'Arthur* of 1469. Colchester was favoured by John Morris (Morris 1993). De Troyes, in the first mention of 'Camelot' in the first sentence of 'The Knight of the Cart', writes that Arthur, on a certain Ascension Day, was 'in the region near Caerleon and held his court at Camelot'. This is usually taken to be Caerleon in Newport/Gwent and Barber and Pykitt (1997) identify a site just north of the nearby town of Caerwent as a strong contender for Camelot. Viroconium is favoured by Phillips and Keatman (1992), while Roxburgh is favoured by Moffat (1999).

26. Castleden (2003), pp. 175–7, also suggests a moving base, but appears to limit it to the southwest. I myself favour a moving base on a larger scale.

27. For example, Riothamus is favoured by Geoffrey Ashe (e.g. Ashe 1985); Barber and Pykitt (1997) very strongly favour Athrwys ap Meurig and believe that his common placement in the seventh century is incorrect and should be in the sixth century; Phillips and Keatman (1992) favour Owain Ddantgwyn; Lawrence James (2003), pp. 34–5, favours Ambrosius; the later Artorius is proposed by Turner (1993), while Higham (2002), though sceptical of Arthur's actual existence, feels that 'Nennius' may well have taken the name Arthur from the earlier Artorius.

References

Primary

Aethelberht, c. 602, *Laws of Ethelbert, King of Kent*, in Whitelock 1979, q.v., item 32, pp. 391–4.

Aethelred, 994, *Ethelred's Treaty with the Viking Army* (also known as *II Aethelred*), in Whitelock 1979, q.v., item 42, pp. 437–9.

Aethelred, 1004, *Renewal for the Monastery of St Frideswide*, in Whitelock 1979, q.v., item 127, pp. 590–3.

Aethelred, 1008, *King Ethelred's Code of 1008* (also known as *V Ethelred*), in Whitelock 1979, q.v., item 44, pp. 442–6.

Aethelweard, c. 985, *Chronicle of Aethelweard*, ed./trans. Campbell, A., Thomas Nelson, London, 1962; also in Giles, J., ed./trans., *Six Old English Chronicles*, pp. 1–40, Bohn, London, 1848.

Agricola – see Tacitus.

Alcuin, between 787–96, *Letter of Alcuin to Offa, King of Mercia*, in Whitelock 1979, q.v., item 195, pp. 846–7.

Alcuin, 793, *Letter of Alcuin to Ethelred, King of Northumbria*, in Whitelock 1979, q.v., item 193, pp. 842–4.

Alcuin, 793, *Letter of Alcuin to Higbald, Bishop of Lindisfarne, and his Monks*, in Whitelock 1979, q.v., item 194, pp. 844–6.

Alcuin, 797, *Letter of Alcuin to the Mercian Ealdorman Osbert*, in Whitelock 1979, q.v., item 202, pp. 854–6.

Alfred, c. 880, *Will of King Alfred*, in Keynes and Lapidge 1983, q.v., pp. 173–8.

Ammianus Marcellinus, c. 392, *The Later Roman Empire*, Books 14–31, trans. Hamilton, W., Penguin, Harmondsworth, 1986.

Aneirin, c. 600, *Gododdin, Y Gododdin*, trans. and introduction by Koch, J. (ed.), 1997, q.v.

Anglo-Saxon Chronicle, ed./trans. Thorpe, B., 2 vols (vol. I original texts, vol. II translation), Longman, London, 1861.

Anglo-Saxon Chronicle, ed./trans. Swanton, M., Dent/Orion, London, 1996.

Anglo-Saxon Chronicle 600 B.C. to A.D. 1042, in Whitelock 1979, q.v., item 1, pp. 145–261.

Annales Cambriae – see *Annals of Wales*.

Annals – see Tacitus.

Annals of St Neots, probably early twelfth century – in Dumville and Lapidge 1985, q.v., pp. 1–107 (Latin text).

Annals of Wales, mid-late tenth century, *Annales Cambriae* 447–954, trans. Giles, J., text available at http://www.fordham.edu/halsall/source/annalescambriae.html.

Asser, 893, *Life of King Alfred*, in Keynes and Lapidge 1983, q.v., pp. 66–110 (annotations pp. 223–75).

Battle of Maldon, end tenth century, trans. Scragg, D., in Scragg 1991, q.v., pp. 18–31.

Bayeux Tapestry, probably late eleventh century, plates in Stenton et al., 1957, q.v.

Bede, 731, *Ecclesiastical History of the English People, Historia Ecclesiastica Gentis Anglorum*, trans. Colgrave, B., ed. McClure, J. and Collins, R., Oxford University Press, Oxford and New York, 1994.

Beowulf, eighth century, trans. Crossley-Holland, K., in Crossley-Holland 1999, q.v., pp. 74–154.

Brevis Relatio – see *Brief History*.

Brief History of the Most Noble William, Count of the Normans, c. 1110, *Brevis Relatio de Guillelmo Nobilissimo Comite Normannorum*, original and translation in Van Houts 1999, q.v., Section VII.

Caesar, Julius, 51 BC, *The Gallic War, De Bello Gallico*, trans. McDevitte, W. and Bohn, W., in *Caesar's Commentaries on the Gallic and Civil Wars*, George Bell, London, 1908.

Caradoc of Llangarfan, c. 1130–50, *The Life of Gildas*, text available at http://www.fordham.edu/ halsall/basis/1150-Caradoc-Life of Gildas.html.

Carmen de Hastingae Proelio – see *Song of the Battle of Hastings*.

Caxton, W., 1485, *Preface* to Malory 1469/85, q.v.

Charlemagne, 796, *Letter of Charles the Great to Offa, King of Mercia*, in Whitelock 1979, q.v., item 197, pp. 848–9.

Chronicle of Aethelweard – see Aethelweard.

Chronicle of Battle Abbey, c. 1180, ed./trans. Searle, E., 1980, Clarendon Press, Oxford.

Chronicle of John of Worcester – see John of Worcester.

De Bello Gallico – see Caesar.

De Chorographia – see Pomponius Mela.

De Excidio – see Gildas.

De Troyes, Chrétien, late twelfth century, *Arthurian Romances* (five stories), trans. and introduction by Kibler, W. (with one translation by Carroll, C.), Penguin, London, 1991.

De Vita Caesarum – see Suetonius.

Dio, Cassius, early third century, *Histories*, 9 vols, trans. Cary, E., Loeb Classical Library, Heinemann, London, 1914.

Diodorus Siculus, first century BC, *Library of History, Bibliotheca Historica*, 12 vols, trans. Oldfather, C., Loeb Classical Library, Heinemann, London, 1952.

Domesday Book: 32: Essex, general editor Morris, J., *Essex* ed. Rumble, A., Phillimore, Chichester, 1983.

Eadmer, c. 1123, *History of Recent Events in England, Historia Novorum in Anglia*, trans. Bosanquet, G., Cresset Press, London, 1964.

Edgar, c. 980, *King Edgar's Establishment of Monasteries*, in Whitelock 1979, q.v., item 238, pp. 920–3.

Edmund, c. 940, *Edmund's Code Concerning the Blood-Feud*, c. 940, in Whitelock 1979, q.v., item 38, pp. 427–9.

Edmund's Code Concerning the Blood-Feud – see Edmund.

Egil's Saga, thirteenth century, ed./trans. Eddison, E., Cambridge University Press, London, 1930; and also ed./trans. Fell, C., J. M. Dent, London/University of Toronto Press, Toronto, 1975.

Eirik's Saga – see *Vinland Sagas*.

Encomium Emmae Reginae – see *Eulogy for Queen Emma*.

Ethelred – see Aethelred.

Eulogy for Queen Emma, c. 1040, *Encomium Emmae Reginae*, ed./trans. Campbell, A., Camden Third Series vol. 72, for the Royal Historical Society, London, 1949.

Gallic Chronicles, fifth and sixth centuries, text available for entries 452 and 511 at http://www.britannia.com/history/bb441.html.

Geoffrey of Monmouth, c. 1136, *History of the Kings of Britain, Historia Regum Britanniae*, trans. Thorpe, L., Penguin, Harmondsworth, 1966.

Gesta Guillelmi – see William of Poitiers.

Gesta Normannorum Ducum – see William of Jumièges and Orderic Vitalis.

Gesta Regum Anglorum – see William of Malmesbury.

Gildas, c. 545, *Concerning the Ruin and Conquest of Britain, De Excidio et Conquestu Britanniae*, in Giles, J., ed./trans., *Six Old English Chronicles*, pp. 294–380, Bohn, London, 1848: also at www.fordham.edu/halsall/basis/gildas-full.html.

Gododdin – see Aneirin.

Graenlendinga Saga – see *Vinland Sagas*.

Guy of Amiens – see *Song of the Battle of Hastings*.

Heimskringla – see Sturluson.

Henry of Huntingdon, c. 1129, *History of the English People, Historia Anglorum*, ed./trans. Greenway, D., Clarendon Press, Oxford, 1996.

Historia Adversus Paganos – see Orosius.

Historia Anglorum – see Henry of Huntingdon.

Historia Brittonum – see 'Nennius'.

Historia Ecclesiastica – see Orderic.

Historia Ecclesiastica Gentis Anglorum – see Bede.

Historia Novorum – see Eadmer.

Historia Regum – see Geoffrey of Monmouth.

Histories – see Polybius or Tacitus.

Huntingdon – see Henry of Huntingdon.

Ine, c. 690, *Laws of Ine, King of Wessex*, in Whitelock 1979, q.v., item 29, pp. 391–407.

John of Worcester, c. 1140, *Chronicle of John of Worcester*, vol. II, ed. Darlington, R. and McGurk, P., trans. Bray, J. and McGurk, P., Clarendon Press, Oxford, 1995.

Jumièges – see William of Jumièges

King Edgar's Establishment of Monasteries – see Edgar.

King Ethelred's Code – see Aethelred.

King Harald's Saga – see Sturluson.

Laws of Ethelbert, King of Kent – see Aethelbert.

Laws of Ine, King of Wessex – see Ine.

Life of Gildas – see Caradoc.

Life of Harold, c. 1200, *Vita Haroldi*, ed./trans. Swanton, M., in *Three Lives of the Last Englishmen*, Garland Publishing, New York and London, 1984.

Life of King Edward, c. 1100, *Vita Edwardi Regis*, ed./trans. Barlow, F., Nelson, London, 1962.

Life of St Dunstan, early eleventh century, in Whitelock 1979, q.v., item 234, pp. 897–903.

Lucan, c. AD 65, *Pharsalia*, 'The Civil War', Book I, in the Online Medieval and Classical Library, maintained by Tennant, R., text available at http://omacl.org/Pharsalia/book1.html.

Mabinogion, original tales possibly twelfth century, trans. Jones, G. and Jones, T., J. M. Dent, London, 1995.

Malmesbury – see William of Malmesbury.

Malory, T., 1469/85, *The Death of Arthur, Le Morte D'Arthur*, ed. Rhys, J., 2 vols, Dent, London/Dutton, New York, 1908.

Mercian Register, 903–24, in Whitelock 1979, q.v., pp. 208–18.

'Nennius', c. 829, *History of the Britons, Historia Brittonum*, sections 1–66, in Giles, J., ed./trans., *Six Old English Chronicles*, pp. 381–416, Bohn, London, 1848; also at http://www.yale.edu/lawweb/avalon/medieval/nenius.htm [*sic*] [nenius]. See also Wade-Evans, A., ed./trans., *Nennius's 'History of the Britons'*, Society for Promoting Christian Knowledge, London, 1938, and http://www.fordham.edu/halsall/source/nennius.html.

Orderic Vitalis, c. 1142, *Ecclesiastical History, Historia Ecclesiastica*, vol. II, ed./trans. Chibnall, M., Clarendon Press, Oxford, 1969.

Orderic Vitalis, early twelfth century, *Gesta Normannorum* – see under William of Jumièges.

Orosius, 418, *Seven Books of History against the Pagans, Historia Adversus Paganos,* trans. Deferrari, R., The Catholic University of America Press, Washington, 1964.

Pharsalia – see Lucan.

Poitiers – see William of Poitiers.

Polyaenus, c. 163, *Strategica* (*Stratagems*), in Krentz and Wheeler 1994, q.v., pp. 1–849.

Polybius, late second century BC, *Histories, Historiae,* 6 vols, trans. Paton, W., Loeb Classical Library, Heinemann, London, 1922.

Pomponius Mela, c. AD 43, *De Chorographia,* in Ireland 1986, q.v., p. 34.

Punica – see Silius Italicus.

Roman de Rou – see Wace.

Saga of St Olaf, c. 1230, extract in Ashdown 1930, q.v., pp. 176–83.

Silius Italicus, first century AD, *Punica,* excerpt in Knightly 1982, q.v., p. 12.

Song of the Battle of Hastings, possibly by Guy of Amiens, possibly 1067, *Carmen de Hastingae Proelio,* ed./trans. Barlow, F., Clarendon Press, Oxford, 1999.

Strabo, first century BC and AD, *Geography, Geographica,* 8 vols, trans. Jones, H., Loeb Classical Library, Heinemann, London, 1923.

Strategica – see Polyaenus.

Sturluson, Snorri, c. 1225, *King Harald the Stern's Saga,* in *Heimskringla: The Norse Kings' Sagas,* trans. Laing, S., ed. Beveridge, J., Dent, London/Dutton, New York, 1930.

Suetonius, 121, *Lives of the Twelve Caesars, De Vita Caesarum,* translator unspecified, edited with notes and introduction by Gavorse, J., Modern Library/Random House, New York, 1931.

Suetonius, 121, *Lives of the Twelve Caesars, De Vita Caesarum,* translator unspecified, Wordsworth Editions, Ware, 1997.

Symeon of Durham, c. 1110, *Tract on the Origins and Progress of this the Church of Durham, Libellus de Exordio atque Procursu Istius, Hoc Est Dunhelmensis, Ecclesie,* ed./trans. Rollason, D., Clarendon Press, Oxford, 2000.

Tacitus, 98, *Agricola, De Vita et Moribus Iulii Agricolae,* trans. Hutton, M., in *Tacitus: 'Dialogus', 'Agricola', 'Germania',* Loeb Classical Library, Heinemann, London, 1914.

Tacitus, c. 109, *Histories, Historiae,* vol. I, trans. Moore, C., Loeb Classical Library, Heinemann, London/Harvard University Press, Cambridge MA, 1925.

Tacitus, c. 117, *Annals, Annales,* trans. Church, A. and Brodribb, W., Macmillan, London, 1906.

Vindolanda Tablets Online, http://vindolanda.csad.ox.ac.uk/.

Vinland Sagas, eleventh century, *Graenlendinga Saga and Eirik's Saga,* trans. with introduction by Magnusson, M., and Palsson, H., Penguin, Harmondsworth, 1965.

Vita Edwardi Regis – see *Life of King Edward.*

Vita Haroldi – see *Life of Harold.*

Wace, c. 1175, *Le Roman de Rou, The Story of Rollo,* French edition, ed. Holden, A., 1971, Picard, Paris; and English translation in Burgess, L., 2004, *The History of the Norman People: Wace's 'Roman de Rou',* Boydell Press, Woodbridge.

Waltham Chronicle, c. 1177, ed./trans. Watkiss, L. and Chibnall, M., Clarendon Press, Oxford, 1994.

Will of King Alfred – see Alfred.

William of Jumièges, Orderic Vitalis, and Robert of Torigni, late-eleventh – early twelfth centuries, *The Deeds of the Norman Dukes, Gesta Normannorum Ducum,* vol. II, ed./trans. Van Houts, E., Clarendon Press, Oxford, 1992–5.

William of Malmesbury, c. 1125, *Chronicle of the Kings of England, Gesta Regum Anglorum*, ed./trans. Giles, J., Bohn's Antiquarian Library, George Bell, London, 1876.

William of Malmesbury, c. 1125, *History of the English Kings, Gesta Regum Anglorum*, vol. 1, ed. Mynors, B., Thomson, R., and Winterbottom, M., Clarendon Press, Oxford, 1998.

William of Poitiers, c. 1077, *The Deeds of William, Gesta Guillelmi*, ed./trans. Davis, R. and Chibnall, M., Clarendon Press, Oxford, 1998.

Worcester – see John of Worcester.

Wulfstan, c. 1014, *Sermon of the Wolf to the English*, in Whitelock 1979, q.v., item 240, pp. 928–34.

Zosimus, early sixth century, *New History*, trans. Ridley, R., Australian Association for Byzantine Studies, Canberra, 1982.

Secondary

Alcock, L., 1972, *Was This Camelot? Excavations at Cadbury Castle 1966–70*, Stein & Day, New York.

Aldhouse-Green, M., 2006, *Boudica Britannia: Rebel, War-leader and Queen*, Pearson Longman, London.

Ashdown, M., 1930, *English and Norse Documents relating to the Reign of Ethelred the Unready*, Cambridge University Press, London.

Ashe, G., 1985, *The Discovery of King Arthur*, Guild Publishing, London.

Bailey, M., 2001, 'Aelfwynn, Second Lady of the Mercians', in Higham and Hill 2001, q.v., pp. 112–27.

Barber, C. and Pykitt, D., 1997, *Journey to Avalon: The Final Discovery*, Weiser Books, Newburyport.

Barlow, F., 1970, *Edward the Confessor*, Eyre & Spottiswoode, London.

Barlow, F., 1999, *The Feudal Kingdom of England 1042–1216*, Longman, London and New York.

Barlow, F., 2003, *The Godwins: The Rise and Fall of a Noble Dynasty*, Pearson/Longman, London.

Bates, D., 1995a, 'Eric Bloodaxe', in Gardiner and Wenborn 1995, q.v., p. 290.

Bates, D., 1995b, 'Alfred the Great', in Gardiner and Wenborn 1995, q.v., p. 18.

Bates, D., 2004, *William the Conqueror*, Tempus Publishing, Stroud.

Bennett, J., 1984, *Towns in Roman Britain*, Shire Archaeology, Aylesbury.

Blair, J., 2000, *The Anglo-Saxon Age: A Very Short Introduction*, Oxford University Press, Oxford.

Boxer, A., 1999, *The Battle of Hastings*, English Heritage, London.

Bradbury, J., 1998, *The Battle of Hastings*, Sutton Publishing, Thrupp.

Breeze, D., 1985, 'Warfare and International Relations: Britain and Rome', in Haigh 1985, q.v., pp. 24–31.

Bronsted, J., 1965 (orig. 1960), *The Vikings*, trans. K. Skov, Penguin, Harmondsworth.

Brooke, C., 1967, *The Saxon and Norman Kings*, Collins, London.

Brooks, N., 1991, 'Weapons and Armour', in Scragg 1991a, q.v., pp. 208–19.

Brown, R. Allen, 1984, *The Normans*, Guild Publishing, London.

Brown, R. Allen, 1996, 'The Battle of Hastings', in Morillo 1996, q.v., pp. 196–218.

Burgess, L., 2004, *The History of the Norman People: Wace's 'Roman de Rou'*, Boydell Press, Woodbridge.

Burton, R., 1987 (orig. 1884), *The Book of the Sword*, Dover, New York.

Butler, D., 1966, *1066: The Story of a Year*, Anthony Blond, London.

Campbell, A., 1949, 'Introduction' to *Eulogy for Queen Emma*, q.v., pp. xi–lxix.

Campbell, J. (ed.), 1982a, *The Anglo-Saxons*, Book Club Associates/Phaidon Press, London.

Campbell, J., 1982b, 'The Lost Centuries: 400–600', in Campbell 1982a, q.v., pp. 20–44.

Campbell, J., 1985, 'Government and Politics 409–1042: Saxons and Scandinavians', in Haigh 1985, q.v., pp. 59–65.

Campbell, J., 1997, 'Bretwalda', in Cannon 1997, q.v., p. 122.

Campbell, J., 2000, *The Anglo-Saxon State*, Hambledon & London, London and New York.

Campbell, J., 2001, 'What Is Not Known about the Reign of Edward the Elder', in Higham and Hill 2001, q.v., pp. 12–24.

Campbell, J., 2003, 'Placing King Alfred', in Reuter 2003, q.v., pp. 1–23.

Cannon, J. (ed.), 1997, *The Oxford Companion to British History*, Oxford University Press, Oxford.

Castleden, R., 2003, *King Arthur: The Truth Behind the Legend*, Routledge, London.

Champion, T., 1996, 'Power, Politics and Status', in Green 1996a, q.v., pp. 85–94.

Collingridge, V., 2006, *Boudica*, Ebury Press, London.

Crawford, B., 2003, 'The Vikings', in Davies 2003, q.v., pp. 41–71.

Creighton, J., 2006, *Britannia: The Creation of a Roman Province*, Routledge, London and New York.

Crossley-Holland, K., 1975, *Green Blades Rising: The Anglo-Saxons*, Andre Deutsch, London.

Crossley-Holland, K. (ed. and main trans.), 1999, *The Anglo-Saxon World: An Anthology*, Oxford University Press, Oxford and New York.

Cunliffe, B., 1997, *The Ancient Celts*, Oxford University Press, Oxford and New York.

Cunliffe, B., 2002, Foreword to Manley 2002, q.v., p. 7.

Cunliffe, B., 2003, *The Celts: A Very Short Introduction*, Oxford University Press, Oxford and New York.

Davies, W. (ed.), 2003, *From the Vikings to the Normans*, Oxford University Press, Oxford.

Davis R., 1976, *The Normans and Their Myth*, Thames & Hudson, London.

DeVries, K., 1999, *The Norwegian Invasion of England in 1066*, Boydell Press, Woodbridge.

Dodd, A., 1979, *A Short History of Wales: Welsh Life and Customs from Prehistoric Times to the Present Day*, Batsford, London.

Dodds, G., 1996, *Battles in Britain 1066–1746*, Arms and Armour Press, London.

Douglas, D., 1964, *William the Conqueror*, Eyre & Spottiswoode, London.

Douglas, D., 1966 – see Whitelock et al. 1966.

Dudley, D., 1973 – see Webster and Dudley 1973.

Dumville, D. and Lapidge, M. (eds), 1985, *The Annals of St Neots with Vita Prima Sancti Neoti*, D. S. Brewer Ltd, Cambridge.

Dumville, D., 1992, *Wessex and England from Alfred to Edgar*, Boydell Press, Woodbridge.

Durschmied, E., 1999, *The Hinge Factor: How Chance and Stupidity Have Changed History*, Coronet Books, London.

Ellis, P., 1978, *Caesar's Invasion of Britain*, Book Club Associates, London.

Ellis, P., 1995, *The Druids*, Constable, London.

Esmonde-Cleary, A., 1989, *The Ending of Roman Britain*, Batsford, London.

Fisher, D., 1973, *The Anglo-Saxon Age c. 400–1042*, Longman, London.

Fletcher, R., 2002, *Bloodfeud: Murder and Revenge in Anglo-Saxon England*, Penguin, Harmondsworth.

Fraser, A. (ed.), 1975, *The Lives of the Kings and Queens of England*, Book Club Associates, London.

Fraser, A., 1999, *The Warrior Queens: Boadicea's Chariot* (originally 1983 with title and sub-title reversed), Arrow Books, London.

Freeman, E., 1869, *The Norman Conquest*, 6 vols (esp. v. 3), Clarendon Press, Oxford.

Frere, S., 1987, *Britannia: A History of Roman Britain*, 3rd edition, Routledge & Kegan Paul, London.

Fry, P., 1978, *Boudicca*, Target/W. H. Allen, London.

Gardiner, J. and Wenborn, N. (eds), 1995, *The History Today Companion to British History*, Collins & Brown, London.

Gavorse, J., 1931, introduction and annotations to Suetonius, *Lives of the Twelve Caesars* (Modern Library edition), q.v. under 'Suetonius'.

Gibbon, E., 1776–1788, *The History of the Decline and Fall of the Roman Empire*, 6 vols, Strahan & Cadell, London.

Gibbs-Smith, C., 1957, 'Notes on the Plates', in Stenton et al. 1957, q.v., pp. 162–176.

Gillingham, J., 1975, 'William I', in Fraser 1975, q.v., pp. 26–30.

Gillingham, J., 1996, 'William the Bastard at War', in Morillo 1996, q.v., pp. 95–112.

Gillmoor, C., 1996, 'Naval Logistics in the Cross-Channel Operation, 1066', in Morillo 1996, q.v., pp. 113–28.

Gordon, E., 1968 (orig. 1937), *The Battle of Maldon*, Methuen Educational, London.

Grainge, C. and Grainge, G., 1996, 'The Pevensey Expedition: Brilliantly Executed Plan or Near Disaster?', in Morillo 1996, q.v., pp. 130–42.

Grant, M., 1985, *The Roman Emperors: A Biographical Guide to the Rulers of Imperial Rome, 31 BC–AD 476*, Weidenfeld and Nicolson, London.

Green, M. (ed.), 1996a, *The Celtic World*, Routledge, London and New York.

Green, M., 1996b, 'Introduction: Who Were the Celts?', in Green 1996a, q.v., pp. 3–7.

Green, T., 2000, 'The Historicity and Historicisation of Arthur', http://www.users.global net.co.uk/~tomgreen/arthur.htm.

Hadley, D., 2006, *The Vikings in England: Settlement, Society and Culture*, Manchester University Press, Manchester and New York.

Haigh, C. (ed.), 1985, *The Cambridge Historical Encyclopedia of Great Britain and Ireland*, Guild/Book Club Associates, London, for Cambridge University Press.

Hanson, W., 1987, *Agricola and the Conquest of the North*, Barnes and Noble, Totowa, New Jersey.

Higham, N., 1994, *The English Conquest: Gildas and Britain in the Fifth Century*, Manchester University Press, Manchester and New York.

Higham, N., 1997, *The Death of Anglo-Saxon England*, Sutton Publishing, Thrupp.

Higham, N., 2001, 'Edward the Elder's Reputation: An Introduction', in Higham and Hill 2001, q.v., pp. 1–11.

Higham, N., 2002, *King Arthur: Myth-Making and History*, Routledge, London, 2002.

Higham, N. and Hill, D. (eds), 2001, *Edward the Elder, 899–924*, Routledge, London and New York.

Hill, D., 2001 – see Higham and Hill 2001.

Hollister, C. W., 1992, *The Making of England: 55 BC to 1399*, D.C. Heath, Lexington and Toronto.

Holmes, M., 1996, *King Arthur: A Military History*, Blandford, London.

Howard, I., 2005, 'Harold II: A Throne-worthy King', in Owen-Crocker 2005, q.v., pp. 35–52.

Howarth, D., 1978, *1066: The Year of the Conquest*, Viking Press, New York.

Howlett, D., 1996, 'Review of Higham's "The English Conquest"', *Arthuriana* 6.3, pp. 72–4.

Hunt, R., 2003, *Queen Boudicca's Battle of Britain*, Spellmount Publishers, UK.

Ireland, S., 1986, *Roman Britain: A Sourcebook*, Croom Helm, London and Sydney.

Jackson, K., 1969, *The Gododdin: The Oldest Scottish Poem*, Edinburgh University Press, Edinburgh.

James, L., 2003, *Warrior Race: A History of the British at War*, St. Martin's Press, New York.

John, E., 1996, *Reassessing Anglo-Saxon England*, Manchester University Press, Manchester and New York.

Jones, M., 1996, *The End of Roman Britain*, Cornell University Press, Ithaca and London.

Kearney, H., 1995, *The British Isles: A History of Four Nations*, Canto/Cambridge University Press, Cambridge.

Kerlouegan, F., 2004, 'Gildas', in Matthew and Harrison 2004, q.v., v. 22, pp. 223–5.

Keynes, S., 1980, *The Diplomas of King Aethelred 'The Unready', 978–1016*, Cambridge University Press, Cambridge.

Keynes, S., 1991, 'The Historical Context of the Battle of Maldon', in Scragg 1991a, q.v., pp. 81–113.

Keynes, S., 1997, 'The Vikings in England, c. 790–1016', in Sawyer 1997a, q.v., pp. 48–82.

Keynes, S., 1999a, 'Bretwalda/Brytenwalda' in Lapidge et al. 1999, q.v., p. 74.

Keynes, S., 2004, 'Aethelred', in Matthew and Harrison 2004, q.v., v. 1, pp. 409–19.

Keynes, S. and Lapidge, M. (trans. and intro.), 1983, *Alfred the Great: Asser's Life of King Alfred and Other Contemporary Sources*, Penguin, Harmondsworth.

Knightly, C., 1982, *Folk Heroes of Britain*, Thames and Hudson, London.

Koch, J. (ed.), 1997, *The Gododdin of Aneirin: Text and Context from Dark-Age North Britain*, University of Wales Press, Cardiff.

Krentz, P. and Wheeler, E. (eds and translators), 1994, *Polyaenus: Stratagems of War*, 2 vols., Ares Publishers, Chicago.

Laing, L. and Laing, J., 1979, *Anglo-Saxon England*, Routledge & Kegan Paul, London and Henley.

Lapidge, M., 1983 – see Keynes and Lapidge 1983.

Lapidge, M., 1985 – see Dumville and Lapidge 1985.

Lapidge, M., Blair, J., Keynes, S. and Scragg, D. (eds), 1999, *The Blackwell Encyclopedia of Anglo-Saxon England*, Blackwell, Oxford.

Lavelle, R., 2002, *Aethelred II: King of the English 978–1016*, Tempus, Stroud.

Lawson, M., 1993, *Cnut: The Danes in England in the Early Eleventh Century*, Longman, London and New York.

Lawson, M., 2003, *The Battle of Hastings 1066*, Tempus, Stroud.

Lemmon, C., 1966a, 'The Campaign of 1066', in Whitelock et al. 1966, q.v., pp. 77–122.

Liversidge, J., 1973, *Britain in the Roman Empire*, Cardinal, London.

Logan, F., 2003, *The Vikings in History*, Routledge, London and New York.

Lund, N., 1997, 'The Danish Empire and the End of the Viking Age', in Sawyer 1997a, q.v., pp. 156–81.

Macaulay, T. (Lord), 1848, *A History of England to the Death of William III*, 4 vols, this edition 1967, Heron Books, London.

MacDonald, A., 1997, 'St Brice's Day Massacre', in Cannon 1997, q.v., p. 832.

Manley, J., 2002, *AD 43: The Roman Invasion of Britain: A Reassessment*, Tempus, Stroud.

Matthew, D., 2003, *Chronicles of the Middle Ages*, Angus Books, London.

Matthew, H. C. G. and Harrison, B. (eds), 2004, *The Oxford Dictionary of National Biography: From the Earliest Times to the Year 2000*, Oxford University Press, Oxford and New York, 60 vols.

McLynn, F., 1999, *1066: The Year of the Three Battles*, Pimlico, London.

Millett, M., 1985, 'Settlement and Society: From Tribe to Province', in Haigh 1985, q.v., pp. 37–44.

Miller, S., 1999, 'Aethelred the Unready', in Lapidge et al. 1999, q.v., pp. 14–15.

Moffat, A., 1999, *Arthur and the Lost Kingdoms*, Weidenfeld & Nicolson, London.

Morillo, S. (ed.), 1996, *The Battle of Hastings: Sources and Interpretations*, Boydell Press, Woodbridge.

Morris, J., 1993, *The Age of Arthur: A History of the British Isles from 350 to 650*, Weidenfeld & Nicolson, London.

Oman, C., 1921, *A History of England: England Before the Norman Conquest*, 5th edition, v. I, Methuen, London.

Owen-Crocker, G. (ed.), 2005, *King Harold II and the Bayeux Tapestry*, Boydell Press, Woodbridge.

Oxenstierna, E., 1966, *The Norsemen*, trans. and ed. by Hutter, C., Studio Vista, London.

Padel, O., 1994, 'The Nature of Arthur', *Cambrian Medieval Celtic Studies*, 27, 1–31.

Padel, O., 2004, 'Arthur', in Matthew and Harrison 2004, q.v., v. 2, pp. 529–43.

Page, R., 1970, *Life in Anglo-Saxon England*, Batsford, London, and Putnam's Sons, New York.

Peddie, J., 1987, *Invasion: The Roman Conquest of Britain*, St. Martin's Press, New York.

Phillips, G. and Keatman, M., 1992, *King Arthur: The True Story*, Century, London.

Pollock, J., 2002, *Harold Rex. Is King Harold II Buried in Bosham Church?*, Penny Royal Publications, Bosham.

Potter, T. W., 2004, 'Boudicca', in Matthew and Harrison 2004, q.v., v. 6, pp. 785–6.

Pryor, F., 2005, *Britain AD: A Quest for Arthur, England, and the Anglo-Saxons*, Harper Perennial, London and New York.

Redknap, M., 1996, 'Early Christianity and Its Monuments', in Green 1996a, q.v., pp. 737–78.

Reid, H., 2001, *Arthur the Dragon King: The Barbaric Roots of Britain's Greatest Legend*, Headline, London.

Reuter, T. (ed.), 2003, *Alfred the Great: Papers from the Eleventh-Centenary Conferences*, Ashgate, Aldershot.

Rice Holmes, T., 1907, *Ancient Britain and the Invasions of Julius Caesar*, Clarendon Press, Oxford.

Robinson, T., 2003, *In Search of British Heroes*, Channel Four Books, London.

Roesdahl, E., 1991, *The Vikings*, Guild Publishing, London and New York.

Ronay, G., 2000, *The Lost King of England: The East European Adventures of Edward the Exile*, Boydell Press, Woodbridge.

Salway, P., 1984, *Roman Britain*, Oxford University Press, Oxford.

Salway, P., 1993, *The Oxford Illustrated History of Roman Britain*, Oxford University Press, Oxford.

Salway, P., 2000, *Roman Britain: A Very Short Introduction*, Oxford University Press, Oxford.

Sawyer, P., 1971, *The Age of the Vikings*, Edward Arnold, London.

Sawyer, P. (ed.), 1997a, *The Oxford Illustrated History of the Vikings*, Oxford University Press, Oxford and New York.

Sawyer, P., 1997b, 'The Age of the Vikings and Before', in Sawyer 1997a, q.v., pp. 1–18.

Sawyer, P., 1998, *From Roman Britain to Norman England*, Routledge, London and New York.

Schama, S., 2000, *A History of Britain* (television series), Part One, directed and produced by Davidson, M., BBC, UK. See also below.

Schama, S., 2003, *A History of Britain 1: 3000 BC–AD 1603: At the Edge of the World?*, BBC Books, London.

Scragg, D. (ed.), 1991a, *The Battle of Maldon AD 991*, Basil Blackwell with the Manchester Centre for Anglo-Saxon Studies, Oxford and Cambridge MA.

Scragg, D. (ed.), 1991b, 'Introduction', in Scragg 1991a, q.v., pp. xii–xiv.

Sealey, P., 2004, *The Boudican Revolt against Rome*, Shire Archaeology, Buckinghamshire.

Seaman, L., 1982, *A New History of England 410–1975*, Macmillan, Basingstoke.

Sellar, W. and Yeatman, R., 1960, *1066 And All That*, Penguin, Harmondsworth (orig. 1930, Methuen).

Seymour, W., 1979, *Battles in Britain and Their Political Background 1066–1746*, 2 vols, Book Club Associates, London.

Sims, D., 1998, 'Troubles with Vortigerns', http://www.britannia.com/history/ebk/articles/troubles1.html. (and . . . troubles2 . . .).

Smyth, A., 1995, *King Alfred the Great*, Oxford University Press, Oxford.

Smyth, A., 2002, *The Medieval Life of King Alfred the Great: A Translation and Commentary on the Text Attributed to Asser*, PalgraveMacmillan, Basingstoke.

Snyder, C., 1997, 'Sub-Roman Britain: An Introduction', *ORB*, http://www.the-orb.net/encyclop/early/origins/rom_celt/romessay.html.

Stafford, P., 1989, *Conquest and Unification: A Political and Social History of England in the Tenth and Eleventh Centuries*, Edward Arnold/Hodder & Stoughton, London and New York.

Stafford, P., 1997, *Queen Emma & Queen Edith: Queenship and Women's Power in Eleventh-Century England*, Blackwell, Oxford.

Starkey, D., 2004, *Monarchy* (television series), 'Anglo-Saxon Kingship', directed and produced by Wilson, D., Channel 4, UK.

Steel, T., 1985, *Scotland's Story*, Fontana/Collins and Channel Four/Scottish Television, London.

Stenton, F., Bertrand, S., Digby, G. W., Gibbs-Smith, C. H., Mann, J., Nevinson, J. L., and Wormald, F., 1957, *The Bayeux Tapestry: A Comprehensive Survey*, Phaidon Press, London.

Strickland, M., 1997, 'Military Technology and Conquest: The Anomaly of Anglo-Saxon England', in *Anglo-Norman Studies XIX: Proceedings of the Battle Conference 1996*, Boydell Press, Woodbridge, pp. 352–82.

Sturdy, D., 1995, *Alfred the Great*, Constable, London.

Swanton, M. (trans.), 1984, *Three Lives of the Last Englishmen*, Garland Publishing, New York and London.

Swanton, M. (ed./trans.), 1996 – see *Anglo-Saxon Chronicle*.

Sykes, B, 2006, *Blood of the Isles: Exploring the Genetic Roots of Our Tribal History*, Bantam Press, London.

Thomas, C., 1986, *Celtic Britain*, Thames and Hudson, London.

Thornton, D., 2004, 'Vortigern', in Matthew and Harrison 2004, q.v., v. 56, pp. 598–9.

Tuchman, B., 1984, *The March of Folly: From Troy to Vietnam*, Michael Joseph, London.

Turner, P., 1993, *The Real King Arthur: A History of Post-Roman Britannia AD410–AD593*, 2 vols, SKS Publishing, Alaska.

Van Houts, E., 1999, *History and Family Traditions in England and the Continent, 1000–1200*, Ashgate Publishing, Aldershot.

Wacher, J., 1979, *The Coming of Rome*, Book Club Associates, London.

Wait, G., 1996, 'Burial and the Other World', in Green 1996a, q.v., pp. 489–511.

Walker, I., 1997, *Harold the Last Anglo-Saxon King*, Sutton Publishing, Thrupp.

Webster, G., 1993, *Boudica: The British Revolt against Rome, AD 60* (aka *Boudica: The Roman Conquest of Britain*), Batsford, London.

Webster, G., 1996, 'The Celtic Britons under Rome', in Green 1996a, q.v., pp. 623–35.

Webster, G. and Dudley, D., 1973, *The Roman Conquest of Britain*, Pan, London.

Wheeler, E., 1994 – see Krentz and Wheeler.

White, D., 2000, 'Why Vortigern?', *Vortigern Studies*, http://www.vortigernstudies.org.uk/artgue/ guestdavid1.htm.

Whitelock, D., 1979 (ed.), *English Historical Documents, vol. I, c. 500–1042*, 2nd edition, Eyre Methuen, London, and Oxford University Press, New York.

Whitelock, D., Douglas, D., Lemmon, C., and Barlow, F., 1966, *The Norman Conquest: Its Setting and Impact*, Eyre & Spottiswoode, London.

Wild, J., 1985, 'Economy: the Arrival of Money', in Haigh 1985, q.v., pp. 32–7.

Williams, A., 1999a, 'Harold', in Lapidge et al. 1999, q.v., pp. 228–9.

Williams, A., 1999b, 'Edward the Confessor', in Lapidge et al. 1999, q.v., pp. 161–2.

Williams, A., 2003, *Aethelred the Unready: The Ill-Counselled King*, Hambledon and London Publishers, London and New York.

Wood, M., 1987, *In Search of the Dark Ages*, BBC Books, London.

Woodruff, D., 1974, *The Life and Times of Alfred the Great*, Weidenfeld and Nicolson, London.

Wormald, P. et al. (eds), 1983, *Ideal and Reality in Frankish and Anglo-Saxon Society*, Blackwell, Oxford.

Wormald, P., 1983, 'Bede, the *Bretwaldas* and the *Gens Anglorum*', in Wormald 1983, q.v., pp. 99–129.

Yazaki, G., 1964, *Japan's Lexical Borrowing* (Nihon no Gairaigo), Iwanami, Tokyo.

Yorke, B., 1995, *Wessex in the Early Middle Ages*, Leicester University Press, London and New York.

Yorke, B., 1997, 'Aethelfleda, Lady of the Mercians', in Cannon 1997, q.v., p. 8.

Yorke, B., 2003, 'Alfredism: The Use and Abuse of King Alfred's Reputation in Later Centuries', in Reuter 2003, q.v., pp. 361–80.

Index

The manufacturer's authorised representative in the EU is Springer
Nature Customer Service Centre GmbH, Europaplatz 3, 69115 Heidelberg,
Germany. If you have any concerns regarding our products, please
contact ProductSafety@springernature.com

Printed and bound by CPI Group (UK) Ltd, Croydon, CR0 4YY
23/04/2026
02095595-0020